Transnational Cooperation among Labor Unions

Transnational Cooperation among Labor Unions

Edited by
Michael E. Gordon
and Lowell Turner

ILR Press
an imprint of
Cornell University Press
Ithaca and London

Cornell International Industrial and Labor Relations Report Number 36

Copyright © 2000 by Cornell University

First published 2000 by Cornell University Press
First printing, Cornell Paperbacks, 2000

Printed in the United States of America

Library of Congress Cataloging-in-Publication Data

Transnational cooperation among labor unions / edited by Michael E. Gordon and Lowell Turner.
   p.   cm.
Includes bibliographical references and index.
  ISBN 0-8014-3779-2 (cloth : alk. paper)—ISBN 0-8014-8706-4 (pbk. : alk. paper)
  1. Labor unions. 2. International labor activities. I. Gordon, Michael E.
II. Turner, Lowell. III. Title.
  HD 6476.T753 2000
  331.88—dc21

00-010251

Cornell University Press strives to use environmentally responsible suppliers and materials to the fullest extent possible in the publishing of its books. Such materials include vegetable-based, low-VOC inks and acid-free papers that are recycled, totally chlorine-free, or partly composed of nonwood fibers. Books that bear the logo of the FSC (Forest Stewardship Council) use paper taken from forests that have been inspected and certified as meeting the highest standards for environmental and social responsibility. For further information, visit our website at www.cornellpress.cornell.edu.

1 3 5 7 9 Cloth printing 10 8 6 4 2
1 3 5 7 9 Paperback printing 10 8 6 4 2

FSC FSC Trademark © 1996 Forest Stewardship Cou
SW-COC-098

In memory of my parents who gave me life, and to Sally, Jeff, and Rusty who made life worth living

M. E. Gordon

Contents

NUA

BK Titles

Preface

Michael E. Gordon

About five years ago I embarked on a writing assignment for *Workplace Topics*, a now-defunct journal of the AFL-CIO's Economic Research Department. At the time, the editorial staff believed that trade union campaigns involving cross-border, transnational collaboration were becoming more numerous and more necessary, given the nature of the global economy and the character of multinational corporations (MNCs). We decided to contact officials in various international trade union associations to find contributors to an issue of *Workplace Topics* devoted to transnational union cooperation. Consequently, when I packed my belongings to assume a visiting professorship at the Katholieke Universiteit Leuven, in Leuven, Belgium, in the spring of 1995, I also brought a notepad and a list of names and addresses of union officials in Brussels, Geneva, and Paris.

Affiliation with the journal gave me an entrée to interview key officials of a number of international trade union associations. These officials expressed substantial interest in the project and several volunteered to contribute. At this point, three things happened. First, *Workplace Topics* was discontinued. Second, it became apparent that the subject of transnational collaboration required a larger stage. Third, it also became apparent that preparing a work of greater scope required more than a cub reporter with credentials in industrial psychology. Given this realization, I approached Lowell Turner, who has considerable research and teaching experience in international industrial relations.

The book we have assembled resembles the journal that inspired the project. Both academics and union officials have contributed chapters. The instances of collaboration that they describe constitute, for the most part, a set of "best practice" examples: unions leveraging their strength in dealing with a local or sector problem by creating a coalition of sympathetic organizations and individuals from other countries. The lessons that emerge from these papers are intended to help trade unions achieve their goal of improving employment conditions for workers around the world.

Interorganizational Cooperation

The study of interorganizational relations is of relatively recent vintage in organization science. Initially, *intra*organizational phenomena (such as informal groups, the impact of formal organization structure on member behavior, and organizational processes such as communication, decision-making, and leadership) were the foci of organizational research (for example, Hall 1972). Before the mid-1970s, researchers (with a few notable exceptions) ignored the fact that organizations are embedded in an environment made up of other organizations, as well as in a complex of norms, values, and collectivities. Neglect of these issues was surprising given the fact that large and critical areas of organized activity demand the involvement of several organizations acting together. For example, the formation of institutional linkages has been demonstrated to increase the probability of survival among new organizations (Baum and Oliver 1991). Indeed, the potential for independent action by any single organization has become increasingly limited (Lustick 1980), as the intensely competitive global economy requires complex and lengthy chains of interdependent action. Strategic alliances emerged as the preferred mechanism for such coordination among organizations (Lorange and Roos 1992), and these are now a frequent topic of study in the field of strategic management.

Interest in interorganizational cooperation evolved as a special facet of interorganizational relations (Rogers and Whetten 1982) and has focused on collaboration among many types of organizations, particularly joint action among public agencies (Althaus and Yarwood 1993; Whetten and Leung 1979) and international business alliances and joint ventures (Park and Russo 1996). However, except for the occasional mention of trade union confederations in taxonomies of interorganizational cooperation, researchers in organizational behavior and strategic management have not discussed cooperative actions among unions.

Nonetheless, cooperation among labor organizations has been studied for many years by institutional economists and labor historians. These writers described the development of associational networks of labor organizations, beginning with the creation of city centrals, then national unions, and finally confederations of national and international unions (Commons 1946; Rayback 1971). Treatises dealing with interorganizational conflict between labor and management offered information about alliances between unions and sympathetic organizations during historically significant job actions such as the Homestead strike (Serrin 1993) and the Pullman strike (Lindsey 1942), to name just two famous conflicts. Finally, a number of writers (Craft and Extejt 1983) described trade union efforts during the 1970s to mobilize shareholders and directors in so-called corporate campaigns.

With organized labor increasingly under fire in today's global economy, unions have had to become more resourceful in order to maintain their existing representation rights and to extend their reach through organizing campaigns. It is apparent that union successes in these areas still begin with the determination and bravery of workers intent upon achieving a meaningful voice at the workplace. Regardless of their resolve, however, local union activists often confront powerful adversaries, including multinational corporations with their enormous financial resources and close ties to sympathetic government officials. Consequently, national and international labor organizations must join forces with local trade unions to champion their causes, to identify other organizations that will provide material and moral support, and to lobby government agencies. Many of the most successful of these campaigns have involved leaders of organizations who are far removed from the site of the workplace conflict. Indeed, the contributors to our volume describe how the involvement of organizations headquartered in countries that are far from the locale of the conflict have played an enormously important role in successful campaigns.

Unions' transnational collaboration is based, by and large, on action sets. Unlike more permanent networks of organizations, an action set "is a coalition of organizations that have formed a temporary alliance for a limited purpose" (Aldrich and Whetten 1981, 387). The activities of such interorganizational coalitions have been described previously in the realm of civil rights, lobbying, and other political action. These alliances appear and then are likely to dissolve after the action is over. However, experience with transnational cooperation has taught union organizations the importance of being able to reconfigure quickly to respond to particular types of emergencies. Indeed, some have considered establishing more permanent structures to mount collaborative campaigns, such as councils that represent workers employed by a single multinational.

Goals and Plan of the Book

Transnational collaboration has become more varied and more sophisticated; our goal is to contribute to the understanding of this important industrial relations phenomenon. Although news of the successes and failures of these campaigns has been abroad for quite a while, there has been no attempt to gather more substantial evidence about transnational cooperation or to analyze these actions more deeply. Clearly, a broader perspective would help labor organizations to represent the interests of workers in the global economy. Similarly, transnational cooperation is a phenomenon that ought to interest academics of a number of stripes. The future of work, interorganizational cooperation, and social movements are among the many important themes inherent in such collaboration that ought to resonate with researchers from a number of disciplines.

Our discussion of transnational cooperation is divided into three parts. The first sheds light on the current industrial relations situation in the world, which affects the necessity for, and the potential success of, transnational collaboration. Chapter 1 offers a broad examination of conditions confronting organized labor in today's global economy. After documenting the decline of trade union density in many parts of the world, Lowell Turner and I describe some of the factors contributing to this diminution in labor's strength, such as increased employer resistance to organized labor. We discuss forces that encourage transnational collaboration (e.g., dwindling ideological differences among unions following the cessation of the Cold War) as well as factors that discourage it (e.g., threats to local or national union autonomy).

Harvie Ramsay focuses on perhaps the most powerful institution in the present global economy, the multinational corporation (MNC). Chapter 2, "Know Thine Enemy," encourages unions to learn more about the strategic planning methods of multinationals as a way of anticipating and meeting corporate threats. Ramsay stresses the importance of information sharing among unions, and he reminds us of the corporate foibles and vulnerabilities that debunk the myth of the invincible multinational.

Because the legal norms of the larger social systems in which trade unions operate ultimately govern the actions available to labor organizations, Jean-Michel Servais identifies the constraints upon transnational cooperation imposed by labor laws. Chapter 3 points out that industrial relations systems are defined at the national level in spite of the increasing economic interdependence among nations, and this circumstance clearly constitutes an obstacle to cross-border cooperation. Further, the legal environments in some countries inhibit the growth of free trade unions and therefore represent an even greater constraint. Indeed, the most ambitious and consequential type of transnational collaboration is intended to promote the adoption of labor laws throughout the world that are compatible with the principles of free trade unionism.

Adoption and enforcement of such labor laws is critical in Export Processing Zones (EPZs), one of the most distinctive and widespread manifestations of the global economy. In Chapter 4, I describe the background and operation of EPZs, including many of the discomfiting allegations about abuses of human and worker rights in the zones. EPZ employers represent very difficult but important targets for union organizing, as described later in Chapters 9 and 12.

The remainder of the book is organized following expository conventions established in the literature of interorganizational relations (Alexander 1995) that separately examine structure (Part II) and practice (Part III). In general, interorganizational structures have become the tool of choice to represent a variety of special economic, social, and political interests in the global economy (Galaskiewicz 1985), and those that promote and sustain cooperation among trade unions are the focus of Part II. Three chapters focus on international associations of unions, namely the International Confederation of Free Trade Unions (ICFTU), the European Trade Union Confederation (ETUC), and the international trade secretariats (ITSs). Coalition formation around particular issues confronting a local or national union may be facilitated enormously by links with these international bodies. The ICFTU is the preeminent international trade union association. In Chapter 5 I describe the formation and structure of the ICFTU and focus on a few of its activities that promote awareness about common problems confronting unions and provide assistance to cross-border union and human rights campaigns.

Whereas the ICFTU claims to speak on behalf of all types of workers throughout the world, the international trade secretariats focus on specific sectors, such as the chemical industry or the food industry. John Windmuller discusses the structure of the ITSs and their relations with affiliated unions, the ICFTU, and the ETUC. Chapter 6 covers the role of the ITSs in providing information and research, supporting particular humanitarian causes and industrial disputes, and mobilizing support for the collective bargaining goals of their member unions. Windmuller also discusses the possibility of impending changes in these roles and the structure of the ITSs.

Of all of the international trade union associations, the ETUC has the closest ties to a regional political body, in this instance the European Commission. In Chapter 7, Andrew Martin and George Ross describe the formation of the ETUC and its efforts to develop a transnational industrial relations policy for the region in the face of incentives for unions to retain their national identities and operations. Martin and Ross trace the accretion of ETUC influence through its advocacy of a number of Commission initiatives (for example, European Monetary Union) that, in retrospect, may actually prove to be inimical to labor's interests and the concept of transnational unionism.

Part III is devoted to the practice of transnational collaboration: assisting local workers to organize a union, to win a first collective bargaining agreement, or to settle a contract dispute. Jim Wilson's discussion of one ITS, Media Entertainment International, in Chapter 8 provides intimate details of the kaleidoscopic transformations that marked the development of representational structures of unions in the fields of journalism, broadcasting, and the entertainment business. Cooperation was hindered for many years by political and professional differences among the national unions and the international bodies with which they were affiliated. Wilson offers insights into the difficulties that Cold War tensions produced in unifying the institutional voice of labor. With the collapse of the Soviet Union, many of the ideological problems became less relevant and a number of cooperative actions took place. Wilson describes some of these campaigns, noteworthy given the nature of union representation in the industry: small local unions many of whose members typically work on jobs of short duration.

Chapter 9 describes the collaboration that contributed to winning the first collective bargaining agreement in an Export Processing Zone in the Dominican Republic and to changing the climate of labor relations in that Caribbean country. David Jessup and I describe the successful efforts of the AFL-CIO, the International Ladies Garment Workers' Union, and the Bibong Workers Union to create a climate within the country and the Bibong Apparel Corporation that permitted the negotiation of a labor contract. The important role of trade agreements, namely the General System of Preferences, is highlighted.

Organizing is also a prominent theme in Chapter 10. Larry Cohen and Steve Early of the Communications Workers of America describe a variety of forms of cooperation among telecommunications workers. Two of the cases once again involved invoking the provisions of a trade law, in this instance the Labor Side Agreement of the North American Free Trade Agreement. Cohen and Early expose the limitations of these side agreements.

Chapter 11 contains the saga of a successful international corporate campaign mounted by the United Mine Workers of America (UMWA) and its allies against a powerful multinational, Hanson PLC. Kenneth Zinn discusses a multiplicity of tactics used by the UMWA to resist Hanson and its chairperson, Lord James Hanson, when the corporation supported its subsidiary's (Peabody Holding Company) attempts to win a strike called by the UMWA. The dispute involved American coal miners who won support among British miners, in financial markets in the United States and the

United Kingdom, among shareholders of Hanson PLC, and among influential members of the press and clergy in both countries.

In Chapter 12, Mark Anner derives principles of transnational collaboration from three campaigns in Guatemala and Haiti. After analyzing the inherent weaknesses of the unskilled workers in the garment sector in terms derived from labor economics and industrial relations, Anner turns to social movement theory to account for their efforts to win union representation through connections with American unions and non-governmental organizations. He concludes that both strong union activism at the plant and creative and sustained pressure on the MNC or its customers in the United States are necessary for successful collaboration.

Following and broadening Anner's analysis, and as a way of concluding this collection, Lowell Turner and I attempt to derive a set of principles of transnational union collaboration. Chapter 13 is based upon ideas presented in the preceding chapters. Eight precepts are identified that help to establish supportive atmospheres for cooperation and effective campaign tactics. These ideas are offered in the spirit of a first step toward testing the efficacy of transnational union cooperation and toward the development of union programs to respond to the crises that threaten union members and the broader workforce.

Acknowledgments

Because of the complexity of transnational union collaboration, it would be difficult for an outside observer to provide descriptions and cogent analyses of these prolonged, arduous, and involved campaigns. That is why Lowell and I are so grateful to all of our contributors who have studied and participated in international labor affairs. We are especially grateful to those authors who shared their experiences from the front lines of union internationalism. Their accounts are enlivened by intimate details of the battle and by the urgent sense that winning these campaigns is vital for the future of unions.

I would be remiss if I did not acknowledge a huge debt of gratitude to Professor Leo Lagrou. Leo was my host at Katholieke Universiteit Leuven and helped in innumerable ways to make my research for this book possible. Also, I am indebted to the Belgian American Educational Foundation for funding part of my research on the project.

MICHAEL E. GORDON

New Brunswick, New Jersey

Transnational Cooperation among Labor Unions

Part I

The Industrial Relations Environment for Transnational Cooperation

1

Going Global

MICHAEL E. GORDON AND LOWELL TURNER

> In spite of national peculiarities the labor movement has overleaped national
> boundaries. Economic conditions are swiftly becoming the same the world
> over. . . . As trade becomes international and the market a world market, the
> labor leaders in the several countries tend to draw together to exchange ideas,
> work out programs for common action, and protect the workers of each coun-
> try against the competition of other countries.
>
> Mary Beard, *A Short History of the American Labor Movement*

Mary Beard was one of the first scholars to recognize the economic trends
pushing toward intensified global commerce and growing transnational
collaboration among trade unions. Surprisingly, though, Beard was writing in 1920. Her comments indicate that unions have had to be responsive
to international influences on labor relations for a long time. As global
pressures in the form of trade and capital flows have intensified, nationally
based unions have increasingly turned to transnational collaboration. And
there are signs that such collaboration may even be contributing to a re-
surgence of national and international labor movements. Peter Waterman
writes, "I note a definite revival of interest in labor as an international
movement recently, not only among socialist labor specialists but even
within national and international trade unions" (1998, 350).

Despite widespread prophecies of trade union demise in an increasingly
global economy, the evidence presented here supports the notion that labor
in the global economy can survive and grow, if not everywhere well, and
that this is true in both national and international arenas. Unions have developed a range of formal and informal responses, national and transnational, some of them quite successful, to protect and promote the interests
of labor. Although as yet we have no data on the extent or broad effect of
transnational collaboration, close observers are convinced that such campaigns and contacts are increasing in number (Ramsay 1997; Turner 1996).
These coordinated responses involve the development of new networks

3

among workplace representatives at plants and offices as well as at union headquarters in different countries (Martinez Lucio and Weston 1995). In some cases, campaigns take place worldwide, with new union structures that target multinational corporations (MNCs). As one example, the International Federation of Chemical, Energy, Mine and General Workers' Unions has launched an "action network" to link unions and members who work in different countries for Rio Tinto, the largest minerals company in the world (ICEM Update 1998). All such campaigns are based in part on the notion that "a small amount of leverage can elicit major gains and help redirect the entire labor movement" (Shostak 1991, 1).

Although a global marketplace can offer much in the way of economic growth and prosperity, it also has dangerous downsides. As large firms begin to operate on an international basis, it becomes possible for them to compel their workforces in different countries to compete against each other. Unions lose bargaining power, and workers stand helpless as individuals before company initiatives aimed at downsizing, cost-cutting, wage reductions, dislocation, and the casualization of labor. In the United States, increasing global competition during the 1980s and 1990s has been associated with a declining labor movement and a growing economic and social polarization between the upper twenty percent of the population and everyone else.

These are problems for workers, unions, and communities that ultimately threaten democracy itself. What is the point of democratic elections and processes if governments can no longer regulate the economy within their own borders?

What power can counter the growing strength of MNCs and the forces of globalization? National governments have an important role to play, singly and together, as do international institutions of regulation such as the European Commission, the World Trade Organization, and the International Labor Organization (ILO). Equally important, we would suggest, is the countervailing power of modernized labor movements working actively at local, national, and transnational levels. Further, we suggest that in the current era, the renewal of national and local labor movements may in fact depend greatly on increased coordination with the labor movements of other countries. Transnational collaboration will be—and should be— an increasingly important feature of tomorrow's global economy.

Labor Movements in Decline

Unions have been declining in most parts of the world for roughly two decades (Galenson 1994), although labor organizations have also grown as a result of successful national liberation movements, as in South Africa. The magnitude of worldwide decline is highlighted in a recent study showing membership losses of 35.9 percent in central and eastern Europe, 19.4 percent in Oceania, 19.0 percent in Central America, and 15.6 percent in western Europe (ILO 1997, 2).

The situation today, at least in industrial societies, is a far cry from the "golden age" enjoyed by organized labor from roughly 1945 to 1970. In most countries, unions emerged from World War II with enhanced legitimacy and played important roles in the postwar settlements that laid the basis for the coming economic prosperity. As *Financial Times* employment editor Robert Taylor puts it: "It was during this period that trade unions in the industrialized countries reached organizational maturity as they became less social movements of protest against degradation and injustice of workplace life and more permanent and legitimate institutions in the 'age of the common man' allied to center-left democratic parties. . . . Trade unions helped to shape and reflect a collectivist view of the political economy" (1998, 25).

In the decades since 1970, however, the picture has changed. Membership has remained stable only in those countries where unions have been integrated as social partners into state administration (as in Belgium and Scandinavia) or firm decision making (as in Germany, with comprehensive collective bargaining and codetermination). More typically, stable postwar settlements have weakened or come apart, and unions have come under attack. Aided by more relaxed labor laws, European employers now find it easier to fire full-time workers and replace them with temporaries.[1] Even Germany's strong unions have experienced declining membership in the 1990s. Union decline has been attributed to growing employer opposition (clearly, the primary cause), inadequate laws and institutions, and inadequate union adaptation and response to the new circumstances.[2] As a thumbnail sketch, the following dynamics are broadly relevant: employers found that they could avoid or in some cases even successfully attack union representation; non-union or anti-union approaches by employers thus started escalating beginning in the 1970s; organized labor found that it was inadequately protected by existing laws and institutions; unions were unable to change their own ways rapidly enough to respond effectively to the new challenges. As a result, unions in many countries entered a prolonged period in which membership declined, along with political, economic, and social influence.

From the 1970s through the 1990s, matters went from bad to worse. In many democracies, undisguised repression of trade union rights was frequently replaced by a less easily or generally recognized form of management anti-unionism. In the United States, the changed pattern of repression has been no less pernicious than when the law of the jungle ruled union-management relations. Phyllis Payne quoted the late George Meany on this subject: "Today's labor relations consultants carry briefcases instead of brass knuckles and they leave no visible marks on their victims. But their job is the same—frustrate human hopes and nullify human rights" (1977, 22).

Particularly in smaller companies, U.S. employers rely heavily on union suppression strategies to resist organizing attempts (which they and their management consultants found they could do under existing law). Indeed, workers virtually had lost the right to organize by the 1990s. Based on case studies of one hundred union organizing drives, Hurd and Uehlein (1994, 1) concluded, "In the face of determined employer opposition, it is virtually impossible for workers to achieve meaningful collective bargaining protections through the NLRB [National Labor Relations Board] process."

Union substitution strategies that remove the incentive for unionization are also quite popular, especially in large firms that can afford the specialized employee relations staffs required to implement these sophisticated approaches (Kochan and Katz 1988). American employers have developed new techniques of human resource management that, although not originally aimed at eliminating or pre-empting union representation, nonetheless exert a powerful substitution effect. Non-union grievance systems, formal and informal worker participation in workplace decision making, and employee selection systems that weed out potential union sympathizers are components of overall union substitution strategy at firms such as IBM, MCI, and Sprint.

If the combination of the stick (aggressive anti-union tactics) and the carrot (human resource techniques) worked well to weaken unions in the United States, the stick alone was the primary tool worldwide. Outright physical attacks on independent trade unions are commonplace throughout the non-Western world. "Violence and intimidation remain the most serious violation of the right to organize in many countries" (ICFTU 1994a, 15). Two widely discussed incidents were the late General Abacha's four-year imprisonment of Nigerian union officials Frank Kokori and Milton Dabibi and former President Suharto's long-term detention of the president of the Indonesian trade union federation, Muchtar Pakahan.

Alongside outright terror are the sophisticated attacks on trade union rights in the industrial democracies, where labor movements traditionally have played an important role in economic and social life. The increasing influence of neoliberalism in these countries is manifest in trends toward individualism and away from collectivism, with consequent erosion in the rights of unions and enhancement of the freedoms of management (Strauss 1998). For example, while Conservative governments ruled the United Kingdom from 1979 to 1997, Parliament at regular intervals passed legislation that weakened unions. The 1993 Trade Union Reform and Employment Rights Act enabled employers to insist that workers sign individual employment contracts, even though a consequence might be the debilitation or termination of collective bargaining. And Britain appears to have provided a model of union-bashing for other Commonwealth countries. Legislation to foster the use of individual contracts has been introduced in Australia at the state and federal levels (Lansbury and Bamber 1998). Intent on attacking union power in both the social policy and bargaining domains, Conservative Australian representatives have eliminated previously sacrosanct union rights such as the right of access to workplaces and have tried to restrict the closed shop and dues check-off among public sector employees. The New Zealand Council of Trade Unions has filed a complaint with the ILO against its national government, alleging that the Employment Contracts Act of 1991 violates ILO Conventions 87 and 98. The Act dismantled the country's arbitration system, decentralized bargaining to the enterprise level, promoted employment relations on the basis of individual and collective contracts, made union membership entirely voluntary, prohibited union preferences, and required a union to produce individual authorizations from workers before it could serve as a bargaining agent (Kelly 1995).

Even the very modest Conventions and recommendations of the ILO, concerning basic issues such as child labor, prison labor, the freedom of association, and the right to bargain collectively, came into question in the 1980s and 1990s. During the Cold War, communist governments claimed that the principles did not apply in socialist economies. Today, employers and non-communist governments are complaining about the "intrusiveness" of the Conventions. Indeed, the government of Malaysia went so far as to question the applicability of ILO Conventions to developing countries per se, thereby calling into question the very universality of trade union rights.

Paradoxically, even in regions of the world marked by favorable socioeconomic and political changes that would appear to enhance the bargaining power and influence of organized labor, trade unions remain ineffectual and politically marginalized. Deyo (1997) reports that throughout East Asia (e.g., South Korea, Taiwan, Thailand, and Malaysia), liberalization of previously restrictive labor laws (or, at the very least, the absence of heightened political controls), increasing industrialization, and rising levels of literacy have afforded unions new opportunities for organizing and collective action. Nonetheless, East Asian trade unionism remains numerically weak, and densities have even declined in countries where industrial development and democratic reforms have been most significant (South Korea and Taiwan). Economic gains by workers in the region appear to be attributable to labor scarcities in critical skill areas rather than to bargaining successes of unions. The paradox of weakening trade unions in countries where democratic reforms continue (although haltingly in some cases) may be attributable to the fact that liberalization has emphasized deregulation rather than protection. Thus liberalization typically results in increased employer domination without a corresponding strengthening of organized labor.

And so it has gone. Unions around the world have found themselves under attack, openly or more quietly (as in new plant locations), by employers and governments in an increasingly global economy. No immediate relief is in sight. According to one expert on international labor cooperation, "all the evidence suggests that the challenge to labor from international capital, seeking to integrate business strategy ever more effectively, is greater at the end of the millennium than it has ever been" (Ramsay 1997, 518).

Globalization: A New World Economy

> The need of a constantly expanding market for its products chases the bourgeoisie over the whole surface of the globe. . . . In place of the old local and national seclusion and self-sufficiency, we have intercourse in every direction, universal inter-dependence of nations.
>
> Marx and Engels, *The Communist Manifesto*

"Globalization" has no accepted definition. We will not join the ongoing debates over whether globalization exists or how it should be defined.[3] Rather, we accept as obvious the fact that nations, firms, and workers find themselves increasingly subject to international economic forces that influence (indeed, may supercede) the national and local contexts that have shaped and continue to influence their options and decisions. In accord with the ILO, we believe that globalization in the 1980s and 1990s refers to "the worldwide wave of liberalization of trade, investment and capital flows and the consequent growing importance of these flows and of international competition in the world economy" (ILO, 1997, p.1).

Liberalization, of course, describes the increasing predominance of the market economy in world financial affairs. With the collapse of communism in the former Soviet Union and its satellites, the market economy reigns supreme, ideologically if not everywhere in practice. Barriers to freer markets and freer international trade are coming down throughout the world. Global economic liberalization exerts massive pressure for change, undermining established ways of doing things, including economic and labor market regulation. Established practices and institutions often prove painfully inadequate to serve the needs of workers in the new world economy. Jean-Michel Servais points out in Chapter 3 that labor law, for example, is traditionally written at the national level, whereas union-management relations are increasingly subject to transnational forces.

Developing Countries

Globalization is responsible for the emergence of developing countries as integral parts of the new world economy. By developing countries we mean nations whose primary products and most important exports traditionally were raw materials such as food and minerals. Although most foreign direct investment supports projects in Europe and the United States, the developing countries have been the recipients of an increasing proportion of these monies. "The average annual flows have increased more than three-fold since the early 1980s for the world as a whole, while for developing countries it had increased fivefold by 1993" (ILO, 1997, 2). Most of the foreign investment in developing countries is aimed at cutting production costs rather than at expanding product markets. Developing countries became competitive in world markets because of their relatively low wage structure, once they had imported sufficient capital and technology to protect and grow their industrial sectors (see Chapter 4).

The rapid growth in exports of manufactured goods from developing countries has meant that an increasing proportion of the world's labor force is engaged in activities related to international trade and capital flows. Consequently, the cost of labor has become a major factor of competition, although there is some disagreement about its relative importance compared to other factors such as technology and access to markets. Industrialized countries have responded to the challenge presented by the new manufacturing capabilities of developing countries by restricting imports (for example, the United States imposed quotas on imported textiles); by allowing real wages to decrease (for example, the erosion of fringe benefits for European workers); by switching production away from goods produced with unskilled labor (which led to unemployment among unskilled workers in Europe and the United States); and by upgrading technology and increasing productivity in order to maintain their competitive advantage (the latter is the only strategy that promotes increases in real wages and employment levels).

In sum, the competitive advantage held by developing countries because of their lower labor costs has jeopardized the job security of both union and non-union workers in industrialized countries. At the same time, the frequent exploitation of workers in developing countries by MNCs that create sweatshops, or countenance their creation by contractors, often has increased employment levels without improving the quality of life for the indigenous workforces. Consequently, workers in developed nations whose jobs have been lost or jeopardized by the expansion of operations in developing countries, and the exploited workers in those developing countries, share a common interest in the improvement in employment conditions. This common bond forms the basis for many instances of transnational union collaboration.

Governments

Capital mobility has undermined the effectiveness and autonomy of state policy-making at all levels. Time and again, governments have found that the demands of MNCs for a policy environment conducive to "competitiveness" are difficult to resist. "National, regional, and local governments have seen their traditional functions, powers, and authority leak away as the new international economic order has become established as the dominant factor in the public as well as the private sector" (Brinkerhoff and Coston 1999, 351). Consequently, the wishes of MNCs often determine national employment and labor policies (in Chapter 4, see specific instances of concessions about labor laws exacted by MNCs to assure their investment in export processing zones). Domestic firms also join the fray, threatening to move operations abroad if regulations are not relaxed and taxes reduced. According to David Jessup, "There is great irony in this situation. At the very moment in history when political democracy has triumphed in more countries than ever before, the decisions that affect people's lives are being made outside the countries' boundaries. National sovereignty, at least in the economic policy sphere, is inexorably crumbling" (Jessup 1994, 10).[4]

At the very least, movement toward higher labor and social standards may be closed off. An even greater danger is a "race to the bottom," in which governments compete against each other to see who can offer the most competitive (i.e., deregulated, low-cost, and even subsidized) environment for investment. The problem for unions is that such policies exert downward pressure on wages and other labor standards and often facilitate non-union or weak union environments.[5]

On the other hand, governments can (and sometimes do, as in northern

Europe) opt for the "high road" by raising labor productivity in order to improve national competitiveness and attract capital investment. This approach entails, for example, supporting the expansion of vocational training and cooperative forms of organization, increasing investment in infrastructure, and devoting greater resources to research and development. For unions, such an approach is obviously preferred, because high labor productivity makes high wages possible and because unions often are included in initiatives on training and labor-management cooperation. National competitiveness, as northern European countries have shown, does not have to mean weak unions—although it all too often does, as in the United Kingdom, United States, and much of East and Southeast Asia before the economic collapse of 1997–98.

Another problem for labor is the privatization of government employment, in many cases inspired by global pressures that force governments to cut spending (Brinkerhoff and Coston 1999) and by the desire to reduce the role of the public sector while expanding the influence of market-driven institutions. Privatization often lowers wages and cuts jobs. At the same time, privatization takes entire workforces out of the public sector where union representation may be established more easily than in the private sector.[6] Workers are likely to suffer losses when social protection benefits such as health insurance and pensions are shifted from one system to another, "because the old scheme does not transfer enough funds to the new" (ILO 1996, 57). Inevitably, privatizations result in a smaller government that can find itself less able to develop and implement policies for a global economy, such as training, support for displaced workers, or inspection of plants for labor law violations. Given these pressures, governments have tended in recent years to expand "individual rights," often at the expense of collective rights, again undermining union influence (Galenson 1994). As Taylor has argued, "Rampant acquisitive individualism has become the dominant creed. Worshipping the values of the free market has helped undermine social cohesion. Trade unions are seen as obstacles to competition and often barriers to improved productivity" (1998, 25).

The aforementioned 1991 Employment Contracts Act in New Zealand and the 1993 Trade Union Reform and Employment Act in the United Kingdom are examples of "individualization." In Australia, with the blessings of the government, Rio Tinto appears to be trying to deunionize its Hunter Valley No. 1 mine by insisting on individual contracts. In such cases, union influence is typically an explicit target, in order to "liberate" individuals from the tyranny of union representation.

In sum, governments are either on the attack against unions or under great pressure to reduce labor standards and union influence. Governments no longer have the power they once possessed to regulate the national or local economies. In all of these ways, unions find themselves under new pressure and in need of new strategic responses of their own.

Multinational Corporations

By the mid-1990s, 40 percent of international trade took place among the subsidiaries of MNCs (Ramsay 1997). The dominance of MNCs is based in part on their size and in part on their willingness and capacity to transfer resources from one sector or one market to another venue in order to maximize profits (Southall 1988). Although most MNCs operate from a solid national base, a number act as financial trusts that simply buy and sell enterprises and therefore possess a rootless character. The ICFTU writes, "Trade unions cannot avoid the suspicion that, regardless of their behavior, MNCs make decisions that profoundly affect their members and communities without any obligation to take their interests into account" (1994c, Agenda Item 7, Section 36). Even governments have learned that MNCs' "national commitments are, unsurprisingly, severely constrained by the calling to maximize profit" and that MNCs "accordingly play one government and one labor force off against another, cross-subsidize product lines, engage in transfer pricing and so on" (Southall 1988, 5). And there is nothing to stop unscrupulous MNCs from additional anti-union tactics: transferring funds from one country to another, for example, to subsidize resistance against union job actions.

MNCs have been at the forefront of "production sharing,"[7] a decentralized (i.e., segmented) production process that sequences stages of manufacturing in different countries. Subassemblies are manufactured in several countries, while final assembly is performed in still another, to take advantage of low wages and benign regulatory environments. Segmentation also characterizes research and development and manufacturing facilities, so that incubation of technological innovations is no guarantee of employment stability.

MNCs can and do threaten workers and unions by stating (or suggesting) an intent to relocate production to another, more "company-friendly" country, thereby enhancing their own bargaining power.[8] In all of these ways and more, MNCs have undermined the prospects for independent unionism (as opposed to unions that are controlled by an authoritarian government or by a large and powerful company), especially in developing countries, but increasingly in developed countries as well. Even where unions are strongest, as in northern Europe, MNCs have increasingly played the relocation threat card to get their way in negotiations. Where unions are not so strong, as in the United States, MNCs have used such tactics to resist unionization altogether.

Threats to Workers and Their Unions

Competitive pressures have forced many firms to restructure their operations. It is clear that employees have had to bear the brunt of restructuring costs and "they are suffering for it" (Cappelli 1997, 206). Employees have been laid off, relocated, demoted, spun off, put on temporary contracts, and otherwise dislocated. Real wages and salaries have been held down for most, benefits have been shaved or eliminated for many, while job insecurity has risen dramatically. Despite receiving less in the form of compensation and security, workers now must work harder, for longer hours (in many cases), under greater performance pressure and higher stress. In addition, many workers have been compelled to assume greater business risks: in performance-based compensation, in defined-contribution pension plans (in which employers no longer guarantee a post-retirement income level), and in many other ways.

The wages of lower-skilled workers have declined, on average, across the board, especially in advanced countries (ILO, 1997). According to Frances Stewart:

> We can thus conclude that the new international division of labor is (and to a greater extent will be) associated with a new distribution of income. The division between rich and poor may no longer occur on country lines, but on class and skill lines. . . . The professional and skilled classes of the world will increasingly share a common standard of living, no matter which side of the old North-South divide they live on. And of course the very rich will continue to be the international capitalists, whose interests and willingness to exploit them are restricted to no country or region at all. (1994, 29)

As the bargaining power of workers and unions is undermined by growing capital mobility, relocation threats by domestic firms and MNCs alike become increasingly credible. Both relocation threats and new investment strategies can force competition among workforces, as governments make regulatory concessions that often result in lower labor standards and in industrial relations concessions by unions. The ability of MNCs to ex-tract such concessions, which ultimately become costs to workers (Langille 1996), constitutes a real threat to social stability and order.

Labor's Response

Responding to the challenges of the contemporary global economy requires that unions worldwide develop new strategies. Union efforts to cope with the demands of globalization have ranged from the traditional to the highly innovative. At the most basic level, unions have sought to restrict the ex-pansion of free trade when it does not include protections for labor and social standards. For example, the umbrella European Trade Union Con-federation (ETUC) coordinated a successful campaign for the inclusion of a Social Chapter in the Treaty of Maastricht (signed in 1991, ratified in 1993) that enshrined important labor rights within the European Union while it pushed on toward economic and monetary union. The failure of the North American Free Trade Agreement (NAFTA) to provide similar protections led American unions to wage a successful campaign against ex-tension of the so-called "fast-track" provision in 1997. This measure would have empowered the President to negotiate trade agreements that could not be amended by Congress (to include, for example, labor or environmental provisions), but only voted up or down. Called "protectionist" by its op-ponents, labor's successful effort against fast-track in fact made possible a meaningful discussion of the terms under which expanded international trade competition should take place.

At the firm level, in many cases unions have developed partnership rela-tionships with MNCs, in hopes of negotiating the effects of global compe-tition, from workforce size and other personnel matters to working hours and new work organization.

> The reinvented trade unions will have to develop as mediatory bodies, seeking to reconcile economic efficiency with social justice through mutual gains bargaining with companies. . . . It seeks to reconcile the financial objectives of the company in developing competitive goods and services with employee demands for greater security and protection of their human rights at work. . . . So-called partnership agreements at the company level have been pioneered by the Metalworkers Union in both Sweden and Ger-many with companies like Volvo, Ericsson, Volkswagen and Opel. (Taylor 1998, 26)

Although the American experience of the 1980s has made it clear that partnership efforts (often referred to as "labor-management cooperation") alone cannot revive a declining labor movement, such efforts at willing firms can be an important part of a larger effort. Trade-offs have been made, for example, in which workers gain employment security guarantees in return for agreeing to greater flexibility in the organization of work.

To reverse their own decline at home, unions have developed a variety of approaches. These include, in the United States, United Kingdom, and other countries, offering new services to workers, including supplementary social benefits, group legal and other insurance benefits, union credit cards, and advisory services in work-related areas such as retraining, social security, and taxation. More militant activists may scoff at such efforts. However, when well designed and attractive, these approaches do, in fact, appeal to many members or potential members, as, for example, white-collar unions in Britain have discovered.

Many unions have addressed, or begun to address, the needs of a more diverse membership, in particular of those groups that have traditionally been outside the ranks of organized labor. Thus unions have taken on women's issues, above all equal work for equal pay, in collective bargaining and in public policy arenas. Some unions, in Chile, Peru, France, and the Netherlands, for example, have begun to focus on organizing and servicing migrant, temporary, and part-time workers.

Understanding that labor needs allies more than ever, unions have built coalitions with community organizations, churches, and women's groups. They have worked with Amnesty International to secure the release of imprisoned trade unionists. They have worked with environmentalists (thereby striving to repair an old schism that weakened both) to save the Great Barrier Reef in Australia, to defeat fast-track in the United States, and to protest environmental ruin at Rio Tinto's mining projects.

In all such alliances, labor identifies its own interests with a larger, common interest, thus answering Robert Taylor's call to "revive a more active sense of social citizenship" (1998, 26). This dynamic was apparent in the watershed success of the Teamsters' strike at United Parcel Service in 1997. The union was able to frame the conflict as a battle on behalf of part-time workers seeking good full-time jobs—an issue with great resonance throughout the American working population in the mid-1990s.

In the United States, in particular, organized labor is increasingly addressing its decline through a new focus on organizing the unorganized. The AFL-CIO has created an Organizing Institute to train hundreds of new organizers in modern techniques. The AFL-CIO and many of its member unions have shifted resources from other purposes (such as administration and servicing) to organizing. This major shift in strategy was advocated by John Sweeney when he ran for president of the AFL-CIO in 1995. Sweeney and his administration have made a massive new commitment to organizing and to a national campaign for the right to organize. To the extent that the decline of the U.S. labor movement is related to the globalization of capital, the AFL-CIO's domestic response constitutes an important international effort. Trade unions in other countries are watching closely this initiative by the AFL-CIO. In the United Kingdom, for example, the Trades Union Congress has established an Organising Academy based explicitly on the lessons of the American effort.

Finally—although this is by no means a complete list—unions have used, under a variety of names, so-called "corporate" or "comprehensive campaigns." These efforts are targeted at large companies that are generally MNCs as well. Unions learned the hard way that, when negotiating local issues in a subsidiary, they are contending "with one tentacle of the multi-national octopus" (Litvak and Maule 1972, 62) that is able to "whipsaw" (Ulman 1975, 2) lower wages and other concessions. Therefore campaigns are focused on the corporation itself in order to win a strike, defeat an adverse corporate policy, prevent a plant closing, or otherwise promote the interests of workers who may be outgunned at the local level. To these ends, unions wage publicity campaigns, speak out strongly at stockholder meetings, and link up with the workforces of other subsidiaries of the target firm, thereby demonstrating innovative ways to pressure a company from other parts of the country or world. In some instances, unions create public relations fiascoes for the company by, for example, exposing company abuses of labor's or stockholders' rights at stockholder meetings (see Chapter 11). In other instances, pressure is brought to bear on politicians and government officials to become involved and influence the company themselves. Or unions may wield the generally unused economic clout that stems from their extensive holdings in pension funds.

A Brief History of Transnational Union Collaboration

Today's union efforts build on a history of over 130 years. The first international conference of union officials, a European gathering, took place in 1864 (Beard 1968). An American union delegate first attended such a meeting in 1869, in Basel, Switzerland, seeking assistance in curtailing the emigration of cheap labor to the United States. These meetings and ties continued throughout the late nineteenth and into the twentieth centuries with no pattern of common action, but with a great deal of communication and mutual learning. What unions in one country demanded and won, unions in other countries would often demand, in some cases finding the path smoothed by employer and government knowledge of bargaining outcomes in other countries. Solidarity, however, broke down in 1914, when European workers rallied to their national flags and killed each other by the millions on the battlefields of the First World War.

Unions nonetheless emerged from the destruction of war as a more influential force than ever. The Treaty of Versailles provided for an official international labor conference to help stabilize working conditions throughout the world. The first of these world labor conferences officially recognized by the League of Nations and many national governments was held in Washington, D.C., in October 1919 (Beard 1968). While the pattern of transnational communication, largely in the absence of common action, continued through the 1920s and into the 1930s, solidarity again fell victim to the brutality and nationalism of war.

Once again, unions emerged with renewed legitimacy and vitality from the ruins of world war. With the approval of most national governments, the new United Nations founded the ILO, which began its studies of working conditions and labor policies around the world, and which started the process of defining, encoding, and winning tripartite support for commonly agreed upon minimum labor standards and rights. Beyond the ILO, however, international labor confederations and meetings fractured along the lines of the Cold War. Unions from the West left the World Federation of Trade Unions (WFTU) to the unions of the communist East, instead establishing their own rival International Confederation of Free Trade Unions (ICFTU) in 1949. These contending bodies participated in government-led Cold War efforts and fostered extensive communication among national labor federations. However, neither the WFTU nor the ICFTU did much to promote meaningful transnational collaboration among unions during the 1950s.

It was not until the 1960s that union leaders began to consider closely the operations of MNCs and possible labor responses (Litvak and Maule 1972). Early attempts at collaboration occurred under the aegis of the international trade secretariats (see Chapter 6). The International Metalworkers Federation, for example, established three world auto councils in 1966, for General Motors, Ford, and Chrysler workers, to promote solidarity, harmonize working conditions, and increase communication and cooperation regarding negotiations, strikes, and other campaigns. The International Federation of Chemical and General Workers attempted something akin to coordinated bargaining in 1969 at the multinational company

St. Gobain, establishing a worldwide strike fund, agreeing to stop all over-time worldwide in the event of a strike, and agreeing to refuse shipments from a striking country (Levinson 1972). Although the St. Gobain campaign resulted in new job security and technological displacement measures, these early efforts did not lead to greatly expanded international labor collaboration. The barriers proved too substantial.

The AFL-CIO's Internationalism

For much of the twentieth century, American labor organizations, for better or worse, have played a substantial role in international union activity. The relative wealth of American unions, as well as their access to funds from the U.S. government, often provided financial leverage to influence the structure and policies of the international trade union movement, and to underwrite labor activities abroad. Because of the special role it has played in labor relations at the international level, it is worth describing, if only briefly, the activities of the AFL-CIO in global affairs.

AFL-CIO Foreign Policy

Samuel Gompers established the basic elements of AFL foreign policy, and these did not change greatly under successive leaders of the Federation (Larson 1975). One bulwark of AFL, and later AFL-CIO, foreign policy has been its strong aversion toward labor organizations dominated by communist or socialist political parties. Gompers' enthusiasm for partnerships with European labor movements was tempered by his dislike of socialism. His aversion was manifest in attempts to found international movements that would rival the various socialist Internationals, and was omnipresent in his promotion of pure and simple business unionism, which defined the role of organized labor as a partner to business and government in a capitalist society. Gompers and his successors argued that societies that embraced socialist or communist economic doctrine often limited the civil rights of their citizens, including the right to form unions free of government interference. The demise of free trade unions after the Bolsheviks came to power in Russia in 1917, and after the Nazis came to power in Germany in 1933, strengthened the conviction of George Meany and others that free trade unions could not exist in fascist or communist societies (Godson 1976).

Following World War II, in many European countries the control of unions became a battleground for the intensifying Cold War. The AFL promoted pro-Western unions at the expense of communist unions. Although AFL (and after 1955 AFL-CIO) foreign policy blended well with U.S. State Department Cold War goals, the effect on foreign labor movements was, at times, disastrous. In France and Italy, for example, not only did AFL policy fail to prevent the consolidation of dominant communist union federations (CGT in France, CGIL in Italy—each by far the largest domestic labor federation), but the effect was also to splinter and thereby weaken the French and Italian labor movements as a whole. While the Italian labor movement recovered after 1969, to a large degree under the leadership of its predominant "Eurocommunist" labor federation, the French labor movement remains deeply fragmented to this day.

In spite of the negative effects, including a highly unfavorable reputation in some labor circles overseas, militant anti-communism guided the AFL-CIO's foreign policy orientation for almost fifty years, even after the collapse of communism and the end of the Cold War. Because its anti-left stance was congruent with U.S. foreign policy and much of its funding for foreign activities came from State Department sources, the independence of the AFL-CIO has been questioned for many years (Shorrock 1999). John Sweeney has even been criticized in some quarters for accepting government money for new types of international activities. Although it is questionable whether the AFL-CIO has had much influence on U.S. foreign policy, it is clear that the Federation has played a role in helping to implement that policy. On the other hand, while admitting to an overlap of interests with those of the government, AFL-CIO leaders throughout the post-war period have claimed to manage their own foreign policy, i.e., doing whatever was necessary to strengthen free trade unions. To a large extent, this has meant using government funds for actions where overlapping interests were apparent.

The critical problem has been that U.S. State Department interests as well as the AFL-CIO's definition of what constitutes a free trade union have all too often been at odds with the perceived interests of labor leaders in other countries. With important exceptions such as supportive AFL-CIO roles in Poland and South Africa in the 1980s, American labor's foreign policy has often appeared to those in the targeted countries (except for those actually receiving the money or other support) as interventionism rather than solidarity. The way to judge the foreign policy of the Sweeney leadership, we believe, is not by where the money comes from but rather by what purposes it serves. Is it used for widening and strengthening international solidarity, cross-border collaboration among equal partners? Or is it used in the old Cold War manner of intervening in the affairs of another country's labor movement, to serve some U.S. hegemonic purpose rather than the interests of workers and unions?

Establishment of Transnational Labor Organizations

Almost from its inception, the AFL has promoted the idea of an international organization of trade unions. Between 1909 and 1913, Gompers led the transformation of the International Secretariat of Trade Unions, an organization of the secretaries of national trade union centers that concerned itself with issues of both unionism and parliamentary socialism, into the International Federation of Trade Unions (Mandel 1963). Having banned from the IFTU all unions with ties to the Moscow-led Third International, Gompers "endeavored to capture the leadership of this world movement" (Reed 1966, 160). Nonetheless, Gompers and fellow American participants grew increasingly uneasy about the commitment to socialist policies of the majority of members, and in 1921 the AFL withdrew.

Gompers' missionary zeal to bring Mexican workers into the fold of organized labor led to the creation of the Pan-American Federation of Labor in 1917. This organization was created to promote "pure and simple" business unionism throughout the Western Hemisphere and to form one more barrier against foreign domination from any quarter in Latin America.[9] Suspicious of AFL intentions, which were viewed as intervention rather than solidarity, few Latin American unions joined the association, and collaborative activities were for the most part limited to relations with established Mexican labor leaders (Harvey 1935).

Concerns about affiliation with Communist-dominated trade unions prompted the AFL's refusal to join the WFTU after World War II, although the CIO believed that it could work in such an organization. Encouraging American unions to affiliate with the appropriate ITSs, the AFL was instrumental in thwarting Soviet attempts to bring the secretariats under control of the WFTU. With support from the Marshall Plan, the AFL organized union conferences in 1948 that gave impetus to formation of the ICFTU.

Cross-Border Activities

The central foreign policy principle of the AFL-CIO has been to promote the development of independent trade unions abroad. This view led the AFL-CIO into anti-communist battles across the globe throughout the twentieth century, as well as into battles against fascist, military, and other non-democratic governments. It is beyond our scope to examine the various institutions through which the AFL-CIO has pursued its cross-border campaigns. In every case these institutions have been controversial: viewed by some as State Department–dominated and even CIA-linked (Shorrock 1999), viewed by others as independent efforts (although State Department–funded) to promote free trade unions around the world, through financial support, training for union activists, and related strategies. The institutions include the American Institute for Free Labor Development (AIFLD), an outgrowth of the U.S. government's 1962 Alliance for Progress in Latin America; the African American Labor Center; the Asian American Free Labor Institute; and the Free Trade Union Institute in Europe.

Facing dwindling funding from USAID (a State Department agency) and the National Endowment for Democracy, the AFL-CIO under Lane Kirkland began consolidating the institutes to eliminate duplication of resources. Consolidation was well under way when John Sweeney became president, and the four institutes were replaced by the American Center for International Labor Solidarity. Many of the previously dominant "cold warriors" are now gone, in some cases replaced by their ideological opposites: former activists from the 1960s, opposed to foreign intervention while strongly in favor of new solidarity initiatives. Barbara Shailor, one such activist, now heads the AFL-CIO Department of International Affairs (which in turn governs the Center for International Labor Solidarity) (Shorrock 1999).

Beginning during the Kirkland regime, the AFL-CIO participated in pioneering campaigns in Asia (e.g., the Philippines, Malaysia, and Bangladesh) to help workers in garment and other factories. Organizers developed centers throughout the region where workers could go outside of the so-called Free Zones to get health care, take literacy classes or learn clerical skills, and receive legal assistance. Real breakthroughs occurred when workers convened organizing meetings in the centers that resulted in the formation of unions in the garment trades. The AFL-CIO and other international groups also assisted union organizers throughout Latin America, such as banana workers in Honduras and garment workers in the Dominican Republic (see Chapter 9).

The Kirkland leadership launched a major effort to link worker rights with trade, persuading the ICFTU and other labor groups to champion this cause inside the ILO and other international forums. Kirkland's focus on international affairs, however, drew fire from those both inside and outside the labor movement who believed that U.S. trade unions might best be strengthened by focusing on organizing American workers rather than on cross-border concerns. This perspective helped elect John Sweeney to the presidency of the AFL-CIO over Kirkland's handpicked successor, Thomas Donahue.

It would be a mistake to interpret the outcome of the election as a condemnation of internationalism. Rather, our reading of events suggests that the current AFL-CIO has two salient priorities: to increase dramatically the resources for innovative domestic organizing and political action, and to close down the old Cold War operations and move from intervention to solidarity. The Sweeney regime thus continues to involve the AFL-CIO in international solidarity campaigns, and these are increasingly important.

Obstacles to Transnational Union Collaboration

Obstacles begin with the attitudes, structures, and practices of unions themselves. Cross-national differences posing problems for cooperation have been widely analyzed (Helfgot 1983; Martinez Lucio and Weston 1994; Ramsay 1997; Streeck 1991; Ulman 1975). They include fear of loss of autonomy by national unions and federations; concerns about the cost of supporting foreign strikes (ranging from income loss during a solidarity strike to job loss for an illegal action); religious and ideological differences (although with the end of the Cold War these are less important); differences in union structure, collective bargaining practice, and national industrial relations systems, making particular demands or actions appropriate to one country but inappropriate in another; contrasting interests and agendas, between, for example, developed countries and developing countries; legal constraints on cooperation; and preoccupation with national and local problems, resulting in a lack of time for or interest in international solidarity. For all of the above reasons and more, analysts and many trade unionists have long doubted the viability of transnational collaboration. Even in Europe, where such cooperation has gone furthest, arguments prevail about the long-term limits or even impossibility of international cooperation (Mahnkopf and Altvater 1995; Streeck 1991).

Beyond the institutional and political barriers, an additional problem is the lack of accurate information about multinational employers. Transnational collaboration, from bargaining demands to industrial action, requires accurate information about the target firm: where it produces, how much it can afford, where it might be vulnerable, its own bargaining strategies in different locations, investment plans. Thus a first union effort in the international arena often involves the demand for information, ultimately making the MNC transparent (Latta and Bellace 1983). This can be seen, for example in the successful union push for European Works Councils as well as in more recent efforts to promote information disclosure by large firms in the European Union. It can also be seen in the proposed code of conduct developed by the Northern Telecom Workers International Solidarity Coalition (including the International Metalworkers Federation and the Postal, Telegraph and Telephone International), the first section of which calls for "timely information." Yet full transparency, with a few exceptions such as at Volkswagen with its powerful works council and social partnership ideology, remains difficult to achieve, even in Europe (Ramsay and Haworth 1990).

Perhaps the most important barrier to transnational collaboration is the opposition of MNCs themselves. By withholding information, causing workforces in different countries to compete with each other, and other tactics, MNCs have demonstrated their determination to prevent collaborative bargaining efforts and other expressions of solidarity among their various national workforces. Just as determined employer opposition is often the key barrier to revitalizing national labor movements (as in the United States), so the intransigence of MNCs is the key obstacle to transnational union collaboration. And such employer opposition makes the effort to overcome the above institutional and political barriers all the more important.

Factors Promoting Transnational Union Collaboration

Economic and political changes throughout the world have now lowered barriers that previously hindered, if not prevented, collaboration among unions in cross-border campaigns. Cooperation is now more likely because of the dwindling political divisions within the trade union movement, reflecting dissipating Cold War tensions among nations. Gone is much of the hostility between and among communist, socialist, social-democratic, and liberal or business unions. When the Cold War ended, to cite just one example, professional activity among media unions was increasingly supplemented by international industrial action (see Chapter 8).

The history of organized labor indicates another factor that will continue to provoke transnational cooperation, namely, the willingness of unions to restructure themselves to suit environmental circumstances. Over the years, pragmatic concerns stemming from changed economic conditions (for example, development of transportation systems in the United States allowed employers to move manufacturing jobs from unionized areas to non-union facilities) gave rise to new structural relationships among unions intended to strengthen labor's ability to promote its agenda (for example, national unions were created in response to transportation developments to take wages out of competition in union and non-union areas [Helfgot 1983]). Another environmental factor, viz., the increasing number and strength of multinational employers, has also provoked transnational cooperation among unions. Since local unions can only muster ad hoc responses to decisions taken as a result of policies contrived by multinational corporations, "developing a truly international force has become a condition for national trade union survival" (Levinson 1972, 141). Levinson, a former secretary general of the International Federation of Chemical and General Workers, proposed fully integrated collective bargaining as an appropriate structural response. In this vein, a German chemical, paper, and ceramic workers' union (IG Chemie-Papier-Keramik) and a British general union (GMB) agreed to extend full entitlements to each other's members. When working in Germany, all GMB members will be entitled to full support and advice from the IG Chemie, and vice versa. When the agreement was signed, GMB General Secretary John Edmonds said, "Multinational companies require a multinational response from workers. . . . Our goal will be the creation of a joint membership at the European level so as to achieve minimum standards on bargaining agreements for all workers" (ICEM Update 1997).

New sources of information and advances in communications technology offer unions high-tech tools for coordinating their efforts (Lee 1996). Shostak (1999, 230) found a new generation of labor "digerati," that is, "those eager to expand and improve creative uses made of computers," whose lives have been steeped in Information Age technologies and whose expectations for trade union renewal are limitless. Of particular fascination to this group are the possibilities for facilitating cross-border campaigns: "The vision of labor's digerati includes a quantum increase soon in the collective intelligence of 'global village' unionists in a global international. They expect unprecedented cooperation across national borders, and thereby, the first effective counter to transnational corporate behemoths" (1999, 231).

Advancement in electronic communications is one of the most important influences on the ability of unions to plan and conduct transnational campaigns. Computers now assist organizing efforts (Cantrell 1999) as well as servicing functions (Laskonis 1999). Unionists share data across enterprises and national borders to provide perspective on industrial relations problems confronting local labor officials (e.g., information may be shared about the bargaining practices and financial status of MNCs and their subsidiaries in different countries, for example). There is greater communication "in order to exchange information that will constrain management's interpretation and use of data related to its own industrial establishment; on the other hand, information is being exchanged concerning the adoption of new management practices as potential means to find ways to curb the reassertion of the management prerogative" (Martinez Lucio and Weston 1995, 245). Responses to company actions can be mobilized by website notices that encourage letter writing or phone calls to MNCs' worldwide 800 numbers. Unions have much to learn about transnational cooperation before they are likely to abandon their typically cautious approach to defending worker and human rights. But when labor's adversary is multinational, cross-border collaboration appears to be one of labor's most effective responses.

2

Know Thine Enemy:
Understanding Multinational Corporations
as a Requirement for Strategic
International Laborism

HARVIE RAMSAY

Just as the main energies of organized labor at the local and national levels have aimed at advancing the interests of workers by countering the power of employers, so the various forms of international unionism (federations, trade secretariats, bilateral union links, shop steward combines) have tried to match the powers of capital that transcend national boundaries. Almost invariably, the ultimate aim has been the transnationalization of collective bargaining to prevent multinational corporations (MNCs) from outflanking each separate local labor movement by dividing and ruling. Activities such as information gathering and exchange, solidarity campaigns such as boycotts or simultaneous strikes, and political lobbying have tended to be seen as steppingstones to this goal.

Three aspects of an international labor response to capital call for examination. The first involves the internal capacities of labor itself to network, organize, and coordinate across frontiers. Discussions of the prospects of transnational labor organization tend to focus on its internal capacities, backed by some consideration of whether reliance on (capitalist) state organizations is advisable. The second focuses on the political channels of support for labor, especially through intergovernmental organizations such as the United Nations, the International Labor Organization, or the Organization for Economic Cooperation and Development, or via governments regulating trading pacts such as the North American Free Trade Agreement (NAFTA) or the European Economic Area. International union bodies themselves have spent most of their limited resources implementing this approach, by lobbying in key centers for intergovernmental organizations such as Brussels, Geneva, or Washington to gain support and concessions.

The third approach examines the "enemy"—the MNC itself—seeking to understand the precise nature of the challenge and thereby define a more appropriate response. This analysis of MNCs themselves remains seriously underattended. The remainder of this paper will therefore focus on this dimension of the methods appropriate to labor movement internationalism.[1]

Unpacking the MNC

The prevailing conception of international unionism, particularly that which advocates transnational collective bargaining as the sole or primary mode of internationalism, tends to rely on a monolithic, "black box" view of MNCs. According to this undifferentiated view, MNCs are created from a single mold: they are all global in scale; their operations are integrated and strategically planned from the center; they are able to shift their activities from one product to another at the stroke of an e-mail; and they can relocate with a swirl of the cape and a momentary hitching of underpants worn over the corporate suit. This image, which in fact is lifted from the fantasies of economic theory, portrays the management of MNCs as almost invincible in the absence of a coordinated, countervailing labor movement that is capable of blocking management's attempts at social dumping. Two ideas flow from these assumptions. First, the monolithic view of MNCs has engendered the idea that labor need only fashion a single battle plan to deal with the actions of these corporate monsters. Second, because realistic assessments show labor in almost all sectors divided and hard pressed to make strides toward international integration, the result of such assumptions is likely to be abject defeatism.

To understand the nature and extent of international labor cooperation needed to confront MNCs thus requires a far more thorough understanding of the MNC itself. I will identify some potential resources for such an understanding, including analysis of corporate strategies, commodity chains and interfirm networks, organizational structures, and managerial dilemmas and incapacities. For the most part, these resources are derived from managerialist writings and, as such, require a number of health warnings. First, they were produced by business-oriented academics, consultants, or investment advisers and therefore reflect management priorities. These writings require critical study rather than mere absorption. Second, just as labor interpretations tend to overestimate the power of capital, so some managerial writings, because they dwell on the fears of top executives, may understate it. This underestimation applies to the organizational analyses in particular. Third, the opposite problem may apply to theories of strategy. Analysts of strategy tend to assume that in practice management has copious and accurate knowledge, plentiful time and research resources to deliberate on decisions, and tremendous capacities for rational thought. In practice, though, strategy formulation and implementation may be far less coherent and logical-sequential. Indeed, for unions to assume a rational management may even be dangerous in some circumstances. The knee-jerk fear of union recognition in many boardrooms is a good example of ideology ruling rationality.

Analyzing Corporate Strategy

Companies make choices that vary according to the exigencies of the sector or sectors in which they compete and their position in those sectors. The options and protocols for strategic analysis are exceedingly complex. However, even a scan of some of the basic approaches will clarify how consideration of MNC market constraints and strategies helps to break down the assumptions of the "black box" approach. These strategic analyses can also help to address questions immediately relevant to labor without having to reinvent the work already done by the servants of capital. For example, do MNCs all comb the world in search of cheap and compliant labor? In 1993, Hoover PLC relocated from Dijon in France to Cambuslang in Scotland. Was British Prime Minister John Major justified in interpreting the move as a symbol of the ability of the United Kingdom's low-wage, low-employment-rights, minimalist-regulation policy to attract foreign investment? If so, why has not all capital relocated long ago to the areas of the world blighted by poverty and huge reserve armies of labor?

Because educators and other putative cognoscenti espouse them, theories of corporate strategy are important. They are disseminated in MBA and similar courses worldwide, in part because most business school textbooks present the theories as received wisdom. Each consultancy embraces its own version of strategic analysis (the authors generally are consultants themselves), and business leaders tend to think in these strategic terms, whether rationally or distortedly. Thus, in explicating the theories, we are at the same time examining important facets of MNC top management perceptions of the world (though with the caveat that, being written by management ideologists, the texts do not examine political struggles for power and tend to neglect the real consequences for employees of impersonally presented strategic options).

Theories of corporate strategy overlap. Some proprietary variants do little more than elaborate and repackage existing theories. There are some simple (but often very effective) devices for analyzing company circumstances such as SWOT (Strengths, Weaknesses, Opportunities, and Threats) or PEST (scanning the environment to examine Political-legal, Economic, Socio-cultural, and Technological challenges). (Unions can sometimes usefully apply these exercises to their own activities.) Beyond these, three main types of strategic analysis prevail: generic strategies, portfolio analysis, and product life-cycles. All of them are rooted in a view of strategy as an assessment of corporate position. Consequences for the way subsidiary operations are likely to be viewed are discussed below.[2]

Generic Strategies

Michael Porter (1985) became the leading management guru of the 1980s, reputedly equaled only by Tom Peters in the awesome fee stakes, and his formulations remain widely used. Porter suggested that firms could achieve durable competitive advantage only by adopting one of three basic (i.e., "generic") strategies: cost leadership (emphasizing low-cost production), differentiation (providing something distinctive for which customers will pay a mark-up), or focus (finding a narrower market niche to exploit). The last of these may prioritize either a cost or a differentiation advantage within the niche focus.

Although Porter suggested that getting "caught in the middle" between these strategies is a risky mistake, in practice most companies try to reduce costs while making products that have (or appear to customers to have) a distinctive edge. In practice, therefore, the three enunciated strategies are more like ideal types than real choices. Management research also indicates that each strategy may be achieved by a range of methods, dependent on context and opportunity, and that different parts of the same company (regions, product divisions) may be advised to adopt different strategies. Porter's work requires additional exploration and interpretation before its implications are useful to unions. For example, a cost-leadership approach is the most likely strategy to foster a compulsive management search for labor costs savings (by cutting training, reducing contractual obligations to workers, seeking cheap locations, and the like).

Elsewhere I have proposed a similar generic analysis that concentrates on a simple classification of labor market priorities derived from competitive position and strategy (Ramsay 1995). My proposal was intended to clarify the way strategic analyses can be relevant to international labor in understanding how MNCs decide to locate their production facilities. In general, all MNCs will be happy to play unit-cost or productivity cards in the bargaining game, but whether these factors really are critical to their willingness to stay in or to leave a region depends on the MNC's strategic position. The more truly international the market is, the greater the possibility of operating just one or a few large-scale operations whose precise location in a region will then be shaped by labor and other unit-cost factors. On the other hand, the greater the variation in local demand and/or in effective access to a market, the greater the need for fragmented and localized provision of the product or service. In this case, the company's ability to supply from a single source is limited by the nature of its market.

Meantime, the importance of skilled and motivated labor will also vary with the type of product, the link from employee to customer, and so the generic strategy adopted. This implies that wage costs may well not be the primary influence on the location of much MNC activity. Labor costs are likely to count for most in highly price-competitive markets, particularly for mature products (where product distinction usually counts for less— see the life-cycle analysis below). More skillful, adaptable, and cooperative labor will tend to be more important where a differentiated product, or the quality and image of product or service, is the chief asset for the firm. A simple two-way distinction of labor costs and labor quality defines the four situations contained in Figure 2.1.[3]

Box A includes banks, up-market retail, non–mass produced electronics, and research and development functions. Box B embraces white goods and other household consumer durables, cars, electronics assembly, and clothing/textiles. Box C contains activities such as specialized financial, architectural or consultancy services and perhaps the headquarters operations of MNCs. Box D includes work such as catering, cleaning, fast food and supermarkets, and transport and other distribution. Examination of Figure 2.1 reveals that the union "black box" view of MNCs applies only in Box B. The classic low-labor-cost-location image of MNCs applies most strongly to workers making, for instance, white or brown goods in mass production firms who may well face the type of MNC decision on location that unions see as typical. Hence, solidarity in bargaining and even industrial action across frontiers remains essential for these workers.

The implications for transnational cooperation among unions are different for workers who produce food targeted on local demand. Under these circumstances, coordination ought to focus on sharing information about company bargaining techniques and human resource policies, because local union contracts remain primarily shaped by local markets. This tenet was illustrated when Hoover moved jobs from Dijon in France to Cambuslang in Scotland after dividing the unions in the two locations to gain

Importance of Labor Quality
(training/skill/motivation)

	High	Low
High	**A** Quality-driven opportunities Cost-sensitive non-mass production Unified market	**B** Mature/declining production High-volume cost competition Unified market/high-competition local market
Low	**C** Fast growth/quality driven Fragmented market	**D** Mature product/service Fragmented market Local competition low

Importance of Labor Costs

Figure 2.1. Labor Factors Affecting MNC Priorities in Locating Production Facilities

labor cost and flexibility concessions. Almost simultaneously, Nestlé moved Lion Bar production from Glasgow to Dijon, but this time because the main market was French, overriding labor cost considerations. Despite the mirror image of the shifts, rather different international labor strategies would have been appropriate in the two cases.

Portfolio Models

Generic strategies are concerned with the standing and priorities of different businesses within a large company. The portfolio approach, of which the Boston Consulting Group (BCG) growth share matrix and the General Electric/McKinsey matrix are the best known, is ultimately concerned with the overall state of the corporate collection of products, understood as in-

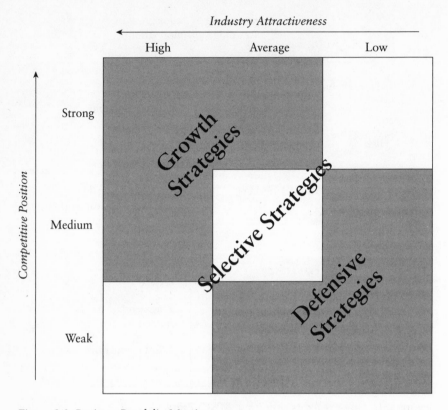

Figure 2.2. Business Portfolio Matrix

vestments. This approach suggested another 1980s management perspective: that businesses were primarily financial investments to be bought or sold as necessitated by circumstances. The product identity of corporations was eroded severely by the portfolio approach. Indeed, the wave of "unbundling" of businesses after acquisitions by selling detachable sections of surviving companies helped spark the enormous surge of mergers and takeovers that still continues to gather pace at the beginning of the millennium. Ironically, other managerial doctrines that preached developing and sticking to core competencies offset the creation of conglomerates suggested by the portfolio approach.

Figure 2.2 contains a business portfolio planning matrix based on the GE approach. Portfolio matrices have two dimensions, in this case one that reflects the attractiveness of the industry (for example, its growth rate) and one that reflects the company's competitive strength in the sector (for example, its relative market share).[4] Because profitability has been found to be statistically related to having one of the three leading brands in any market segment, these approaches place a great deal of emphasis on market share—a view that has become a mantra for many executives.

Each strategic business unit is categorized into one of the cells. Investment strategies are recommended for each of the cells: growth strategies (such as horizontal integration or diversification) for businesses where long-term industry attractiveness and competitive position are favorable, and defensive strategies (such as divest or harvest) for businesses where long-term prospects on the two dimensions are less favorable. A mix of strategies is recommended for the remaining businesses, which carry a medium investment allocation priority.

These matrices identify strategies that have important implications for labor relations. For example, it may be reckoned that fast-growth companies in an attractive industry will have high margins and rely on employee initiatives and skills to succeed. Companies with relatively strong market positions in slow-growth industries will seek stability in all phases of their operations, including labor relations, to allow the harvest to proceed as smoothly as possible. Finally, companies ticketed for divestiture are likely to experience crisis-ridden confrontation with their workers much of the time.

Whereas the full portfolio balance is of particular interest to corporate management following this approach, the single product will seem the relevant focus for labor, and so it is for everyday workplace organization. However, if they are to gain a sense of the management outlook, labor strategists must also understand the wider positioning and state of health of the entire MNC. An appropriate understanding entails knowing how each product line stands in relation to the company's overall portfolio.

Product Life-Cycles

The idea of a product life-cycle introduces the dynamics of competition. Specifically, one may anticipate that a product will evolve through a phase of development, followed by one of novelty and rapid growth, and then will reach a plateau before decline. Because the idea of a life-cycle analysis is implicit in portfolio models, the two have been fruitfully combined (Hax and Majluf 1996).

At the plateau the product's market is generally mature. Consequently, competition is expected to be plentiful because other companies will have been able to enter the market. Generic strategy analysis suggests different sources of potential competitive advantage, especially for innovators who are able to rely on differentiation in the early life-cycle stages but must face tighter competition as the market matures.

As one example, the market for personal computers has followed this path closely thus far, despite continual replacement demand generated by technological advances in chip design. Demand initially emphasized the perceived "quality" lead of market leaders, but standardized components and methods of construction later blurred differences. Recently, manufacturers have sought differentiation by means of service support quality, while cost effectiveness has come from building to order and not being caught with outmoded stocks. These strategies have fueled the rise of companies like Dell at the expense of former front-runners. When dealing with companies seeking to compete on costs in a mature market, unions will find it hard to resist reallocation of work to low-labor-cost sites. However, where more service-oriented differentiation is practiced, the odds are stacked differently, and sharing information about management tactics and weaknesses again may be valuable for the localized pursuit of agreements where international agreements remain infeasible.

Critics of the life-cycle approach point out that it is often easy to read in retrospect, but hard to decide at the time what stage a product is in, making the tool difficult to use in practice. Moreover, product cycles vary hugely from sector to sector, in overall and phase duration, as does the pattern of concentration and competition. For trade unionists, it is crucial to remember that the challenge is not just to understand how to analyze the life-stage of a product and its implications. Rather, unions must anticipate management actions toward labor in the light of what management believes to be its situation.

The Relevance of Strategic Analysis

Drawing together the three approaches I have considered here, it should be evident that they provide a basis not just for opening the black box of corporate decision-making but also for rethinking aspects of labor internationalism. Strategic analysis may clarify the extent to which access to the local market, and so location of production or service provision, binds the company to do a deal and stick around in one country or not. Such clarification is necessary to assess the viability of local union strategies and of the leverage of cross-national comparisons through distributing information on pay, benefits, and work environment. Also, considering the MNC in strategic terms produces a clearer evaluation of the likely parameters of management decisions, such as those on investment or contraction, wages and other labor compensation, or industrial relations style. In short, strategic analysis can suggest the type of internationalism required to confront MNC management. There is no reason why unions cannot heed the oft-heard management injunction to "think globally, act locally." However, the problem is that usually unions think and understand locally too, and so have either an overconfident or an over-fearful understanding of their situation.

Core Competencies

Because the strategic positioning analyses of 1980s management orthodoxy tended to see corporate activity as inherently a matter of mixing distinct businesses, these analyses had serious consequences for the security of workers. Employees often were considered only as entries on a balance sheet and consequently were traded or terminated based on management's understanding of the company's strategic situation. Recently, this type of thinking has been challenged in management circles. The watershed seems to have been a 1990 article in the temple of popular management thought, the *Harvard Business Review*, by two prominent academics, C.K. Prahalad and Gary Hamel (1990). Rather than emphasizing the firm's particular portfolio position, these and like writers stress organizational capabilities to manage products and resources, and so the internal synergies of successful corporations. This new orthodoxy was used to justify the role of corporate headquarters (as the gathering site for core competence and its application through scattered operations) and had the effect of downgrading the paramount importance attached to market share in particular products.

Core competencies represent an intriguing reversal of management thinking. In the quasi-rational discourse of management with unions, it bolsters pro-employee logic. For example, this viewpoint is compatible with a "resource-based" approach to analyzing the firm (Barney 1995) and actually lends weight to a long voiced, but rarely believed, management cliché: "Our employees are our greatest asset." In the search for sustainable competitive advantages, labor knowledge and skills increasingly are accepted as the most obvious distinctive and inimitable potential source of capability. This attitude also lends momentum to training and development approaches, such as those advocated in another popular management theory of the 1990s, that of the Learning Organization (Senge 1990).

Such a viewpoint is consistent with recent prominent disavowals of the "organizational anorexia" and other damage left by faddish and ill-planned downsizing.

For international labor, the possibilities here may be important. A grasp of the rhetoric can be an important trigger in formulating arguments for negotiation, while the cross-border pooling of information and analysis can provide the concrete proposals for international job security and upward leveling of pay and conditions. On the other hand, the idea of core competencies may add to organized labor's woes in most MNC boardrooms, where management appears deaf to reason from unions. The competence-based argument panders to management's self-importance (especially for those at headquarters) even more than other theories, and tends to insulate them from "outsiders" (which is how they continue to view unions for the most part) as sources of good sense.

Value and Commodity Chains

Value chain analysis also emphasizes linkages and synergies across corporate activities. Originally introduced as an accounting method, value chain analysis seeks to identify the main sources of profits in the various steps to supplying a product or service. Porter (1985) enlarged this idea by highlighting strategic capabilities and identifying the different activities as linked building blocks of corporate profitability. Five primary activities were defined: inbound logistics (bringing in, handling and storing factors of production), operations (turning inputs into products), outbound logistics (getting products to customers), marketing and sales, and services (supporting products in use). Human resource management, finance, product research, and quality control were viewed as support functions for these primary activities. Because MNCs are most likely to emphasize the operational costs issue in isolation when talking to their unions, an awareness of this categorization can be useful for turning management arguments back on themselves.

In the fragmentary and finance-driven view of business that prevailed in the 1980s, value chain analysis became a tool for focusing on the most lucrative parts of the business rather than for enhancing linkages and synergies. Reengineering, downsizing, and outsourcing fetishes in management circles continued this way of looking at parts of the chain in the 1990s. One result was to justify offloading the less immediately profitable parts of the process. Consequently, many companies have actually weakened synergies, losing control of areas that were crucial to competitiveness but did not themselves generate profits directly. It has also often meant the marginalization (or sometimes even outsourcing) of support activities that did not make profit, such as human resources management. Unions could thus usefully apply value chain analysis to restore an emphasis on synergy and linkage, within and across borders. This approach might also enhance the ability of workers in different parts of international firms to recognize their ties to each other.

A development with some parallels to value chain analysis, commodity chains analysis is rooted in critical social science rather than in management thinking. Commodity chains analysis represents a distinct advance in understanding some of the dynamics of contemporary international developments in capitalist production, though with both enlightening and in some cases frightening implications for labor. A commodity chain is "a network of labor and production processes whose end result is a finished commodity" (Hopkins and Wallerstein 1986, 159). The result is a picture very different from and far more inclusive than that provided by value chain analysis. A "network" is not necessarily confined to one organization—indeed, it is very unlikely to be so—and is seen as socially rooted in particular locations and groups of people. Nevertheless, commodity chains analysis demonstrates that power is distributed unevenly across the network, and that profits tend to accrue mainly to those who control and organize core "nodes" in the production and distribution of the product (Gereffi and Korzeniewicz 1994). In practice, chains tend to be driven either by buyers (such as clothing retail outlets) or by producers (as with automobile companies using just-in-time supply networks), with the drivers taking the greatest rewards and dictating the fate of others in the chain (Gereffi 1994).

The commodity chain approach has many fascinating and vital implications for labor, local and international, but here I can note only a few. First, chains are far more readily constructed and reconstructed than companies, and can often operate across frontiers with relative impunity. This provides plentiful opportunities for MNCs to extend their traditional divide-and-rule tactics, playing workers in different countries and client companies off against each other, creating what some have termed a "race to the bottom." The export of U.S. jobs to the maquiladora factories in Mexico after the NAFTA agreement is one example. Second, dealing with the linkages requires unions to confront as much of the chain as possible rather than a single organization. Third, the way MNCs are building commodity chains is shifting fast as new tricks are learned. Without extensive intelligence (which can be gained in significant part from academics, of all people!), labor will find itself left behind in its understanding of corporate and sectoral dynamics.

As commodity chains develop, they look more like the chimerical image of the all-flexible, slippery MNC that has long prevailed in the labor movement than anything real that has gone before. However, this may be a misleading picture. Many of the organizational problems of MNCs discussed later continue to apply, sometimes more fiercely than before. Moreover, most of the existing pictures of chains are based on investigations of the garment industry or come from automobiles and electronics. These are presently the most internationalized sectors, and they also tend to operate in mature product markets where labor costs are particularly important and where feasible logistics for supplying international markets exist. If one were to consider, for instance, printing, the commodity chain would look very different, with the demands of local responsiveness of supply for many print products currently limiting corporate flexibility. Very different chains might also characterize brewing and distilling, food, software development and application, or financial services. At the same time, potentials for international linkages using new technologies to transform aspects of the business can be seen emerging in each area, and are likely to be exploited increasingly over time. There has yet to be a thorough exploration of the patterns and potentials in different sectoral and product chains, but for international labor it is urgent that there should be.

Corporate Structures

According to the dictum of Alfred Chandler (1962), one of the founts of conventional wisdom in business theory, structure should follow strategy. In other words, a company should be organized to achieve its strategy, not choose its strategy to fit its structure. In practice, this bromide ignores the resilience of existing organization in the face of pressures for change. Thus there is an argument for treating structure as an important factor in its own right. Moreover, when it comes to MNCs, the structure of the organization becomes an important influence on the level and nature of decision-making—which, in turn, affects fundamentally where and how labor needs to confront management.

I will illustrate the relevance of structure by summarizing two discussions of the subject. Hill (Hill and Hoskisson 1987; Hill and Pickering 1986) developed a classification of the multidivisional ("M-form") company (typical of MNCs) according to the economies that it seeks through its multiple operations: synergistic, vertical, and financial. The connection with value chain analysis and other analyses above will be evident. A company that seeks synergy among its operations will need to plan in an integrated way,

rather than consider the competitiveness and organization of those operations separately. The operations are somewhat less tightly linked in a verti-
cally integrated company that incorporates different stages in the production chain inside the organization (for example, when a retailer seeks to
buy up agricultural producers and food processing operations to control
supply and internalize profits). Operations linked only by financial considerations are regarded as independent businesses. The three types of
economies imply progressively weaker levels of integration of management,
and so a markedly decreasing role for headquarters, common policies, and
common culture. Human resource management and industrial relations
will have a more or less centralized focus of decision-making according to
the form of integration, with synergistic integration implying the highest
degree of central coordination of policies.

Goold and Campbell (1987) offer a second structural analysis that provides a more detailed account of centralization or devolution of responsibilities. As we move from the broad category of "Strategic Planning" to the
less integrative "Strategic Control" approach, and finally to "Financial
Control," the role of the center declines.[5]

Here we see the link back to the positional, portfolio-type approach
of the 1980s, with the extreme form being the conglomerate predators who
did so much damage to long-term business viability and to employees. The
possibility for a strategy based on human resources, and the likelihood
of labor-management issues being a matter for close headquarters policy-
making attention, gets progressively less as a more finance-driven coordination system gains ground.

For a while, it was "asset-strippers" of the Hanson PLC variety that
seemed to be the future of international capitalism. This may still be the
case, but the faltering of some of these icons of modern business has at least
made this scenario less certain (see Chapter 11). On the other hand, the
penchant for shifting from a center-driven strategy to a "bottom-line" discipline of local decision-making appears to be growing.

Ironically, this debureaucratization in some respects also makes key decisions more remote from labor in MNCs, and yet makes it harder to find
some counterpart in the management structure to confront in an effort to
overcome this. For example, Paul Marginson (1992) has exploited structural analyses of this sort in his work on multinational collective bargaining. Where the business itself is fragmented into several distinct divisions
or to serve distinct local markets, and most operational decision-making
is largely decentralized, management will be more reluctant to engage
in cross-border dealings with unions. When the international management
structure is unified, the company will be more receptive to cross-border

dealings with unions because decisions about operations are also integrated across frontiers. Marginson notes that some of the pioneers of cross-border worker consultation, such as Volkswagen AG, had unified structures. The other side of the coin, though, is that where operations are linked, management may have the *strongest* reason for resisting or subverting labor unity, to minimize comparison and disruption that could come from solidarity. This notion is exemplified by the efforts of Ford to keep bargainers in different countries divided. When Ford worker representatives from around the globe gathered in Liverpool in 1985, they were able to swap notes about management's stories of why each of them should fear the others.

Management Defects

There is a huge literature on the management of international business, but it goes almost entirely unread by international labor. One of the most fascinating aspects of that literature is its exposure of just how problematical corporations find it to manage far-flung, intricate operations in culturally disparate environments. This undergrowth, off the main fairways of organization tidily laid out in the textbooks, actually dominates the terrain on which unions seek to forge effective ties across borders. Three examples of the problems are summarized here.[6]

First, MNCs find themselves beset by gaps in the communication network on which they have to rely for effective coordination. Although e-mail and other technological innovations have helped, they have not entirely bridged the distance gap, let alone those of language, culture, national frontier, legal system, and informal contacts. The spectacular failure rate in expatriate assignments in MNCs demonstrates one aspect of the dilemmas here: operating tight central control is typically associated with an ethnocentric management style that requires home country managers on the spot. Unfortunately, these managers often are unable to operate effectively locally, and they find the personal and family adjustments involved debilitating as well. Looser, polycentric organization allows local immersion, typically through managers from the particular culture. This arrangement, however, may undermine central coordination, shared corporate culture, and so perhaps the firm-specific advantages in management which were the basis of a competitive edge in the first place.

Second, constant effort is necessary to find strategic or structural solutions to these problems. Constant oscillations occur between centralizing and decentralizing priorities (Doz 1986), resulting in repeated disruption of authority lines and futile grasping at fashionable solutions that compound local disillusionment. These contrary pulls are intensified by the differing demands of different functions. In particular, finance and production seem best served by centralization, which tends to maximize economies of scale and coordination. However, marketing attempts to meet local demands and persistent nationally differentiated customer preferences often combine with the need to present an image of the "good corporate citizen" who provides jobs and prosperity in the national economy. Some feel that the distinctiveness and deep impact of national forms of legal regulation and other "business system" elements (Whitley 1994) override the global imperative.

Third, the enormous resources of MNCs are thought to allow them to identify sophisticated solutions to their problems, or to override them by sheer power. Investigations suggest that in practice it is very hard for corporations to bring resources to bear on such difficulties. Top management tends to spend little time briefing itself before making major "strategic" decisions. Studies of how managers actually use the kinds of strategic theory I reviewed earlier show that they are almost always highly inconsistent. In fact, they perceive any given situation in widely varying ways, thus guiding their actions with irregular and unpredictable mental maps of the world they are seeking to act on (Huff 1990). Research departments are swallowed up in the internal politics and personal rivalries of large organizations that further bedevil economic-rational and consistent decision-making (Ghoshal and Kim 1986).

These kinds of findings are double-edged. On the one hand, they suggest a vulnerable and anything but omniscient and omnipotent management: these people can be confronted and their rationale for barbaric decisions challenged on their own terms. This lends both encouragement and a powerful ideological weapon to the prepared international union. And it demonstrates the value of an international labor network able to analyze and challenge management idiocy.

On the other hand, the illogic of much of what passes for MNC management also makes ordered attempts to understand and predict MNC behavior using the kinds of strategy theory outlined earlier far more difficult. Opening the black box clarifies and muddies the water at the same time (to mix metaphors in cavalier fashion). The arbitrariness of the powerful may make them vulnerable to later criticism, but at the time it is implemented, arbitrary action may be worse news for the powerless than a calculated and rational management. Corporate irrationality also often pushes labor into blind survival tactics, resisting where muscle can be turned to strike at a visible enemy, i.e., locally, to the frequent neglect of international collaboration.

Conclusion

I have only begun to scan some of the resources that international labor might put to good effect in refining its response to MNCs. Other structural features of MNCs that deserve exploration are the complex forms of integration in corporations (or broader sectoral networks) that affect the power of labor to intervene at critical nodes or the ability of management to bypass labor resistance.

Hopefully the need to understand MNCs will now be apparent. An undifferentiated view leads to a search for some monolithic, cure-all labor strategy that does not actually exist. It also leads to exaggerated yet poorly focused fears about the seemingly irresistible power and inescapable logic of MNCs, and provokes misreadings of the priorities and constraints on the mobility of capital. All such misunderstandings may restrain and misdirect labor demands unnecessarily. Equally, other dangers of disinvestment or anti-union policies might go undetected until too late, and yet could afford a chance for labor to intervene in or obstruct management decision-making to progressive effect if anticipated early enough.

Unions' classic aspiration (and often pipe dream) is international bargaining across an entire corporation, but other goals are likely to prove appropriate in different settings. These may include bargaining at divisional level or maintaining an industry bargain at a more localized level, where MNCs are tied to producing in that market. Information sharing may be far more useful for guiding what remain largely local struggles than has been realized to date. Thus, for example, companies in the printing industry have hardly begun to exploit the potential for digital information transfer because of the nature of most of the markets they serve and because of their own present organizational state. In this instance, unions' ability to exchange information on staffing of new equipment, management tactics and outlook, and benchmarking on deals (e.g., working environment or training) would be an invaluable resource for bargaining. For many other national markets, such as those for many food and beverage products, shared information and labor benchmarking are likely to be worthwhile.

In global operations, such as construction machinery or industrial chemicals, more obvious advantages accrue to closer international bargaining links. Where global corporate strategies tie in with local market pressures and variations, as in pharmaceuticals, automobiles, or computers, the classic openings for transnational collaboration combined with autonomous local action are at their greatest. Meanwhile, dealing with highly fluid arrangements for exploiting cheap labor and other costs, as in the garment industry, sets a very different order of challenges. Even if unionization levels were acceptable, transnational company bargaining could not grapple easily with a company like Nike which, according to estimates, directly employs barely one in ten of those making the products that sell under the corporate brand name. Here national and international responses are likely to rest with international trade secretariats and their capacity to forge alliances with governments, intergovernmental organizations, and ethical ginger groups like Christian Aid.

Whatever the sector or company under consideration, labor intelligence involving critical analyses of corporate strategies must become far more important than unions have appreciated up to now. Networking such information and training local representatives to access and use it are imperative. Although labor should not simply shadow management strategy and organization, it must understand these factors and know at what level which sort of intervention might challenge managerial agendas.

Finally, the micro-politics and illogic of much management decision-making act both as a warning and as an encouragement to unions' challenges to MNCs, whether in direct discussion or through publicity and appeals for government support. To exploit these corporate foibles requires, once again, an international system for information gathering and critical analysis.

Opening the MNC black box, then, leads to a reinforced appreciation of the need for internationalism, and hopefully also the will to make it happen. At the same time, understanding MNCs provokes a call to reevaluate the best ways forward in different contexts. Possible approaches require detailed and constantly updated understandings of the differing configurations in different firms and sectors, as is suggested by strategic and structural theories, but also, perhaps most vividly, by commodity chains analysis. This approach will do most for the needs of labor across the world in something closer than the ever-awaited long term.

3

Labor Law and Cross-Border Cooperation among Unions

JEAN-MICHEL SERVAIS

The institutions and practices developed within the context of nation-states and national economies during the last 150 years are regularly and increasingly challenged by "globalization." Despite the increasing economic interdependence among nations, however, the systems of industrial relations remain, to a great extent, at the national level. Clearly, unions have attempted to establish and monitor working conditions that transcend national boundaries. Coalitions of national trade unions from different countries have mounted campaigns to assist one of their number to resolve a difficult labor dispute. These international efforts have resulted in a variety of outcomes, including settlement of conflicts about the terms of employment at particular work sites, or creation of more long-term policy commitments among trade unions and employers, such as codes of conduct for multinational enterprises and joint union-multinational employer statements.

Nevertheless, these efforts are still quite limited. Undoubtedly, the most advanced steps in the direction of transnational industrial relations have been taken by the European Union, with the creation of European Works Councils. The European Directive of September 22, 1994, is a legal instrument that has been used to foster labor-management arrangements.

The European Directive is a significant development because it prompts us to examine more generally how labor laws both facilitate and hinder cross-border cooperation among unions. Supranational legislation remains an exception. In most instances, national labor laws still govern industrial relations, even when they contain an international dimension. The question then is to decide which national laws are applicable and, as the case may be, which national jurisdictions are competent. Those are issues of private

44

international law. In the fields of labor they have been studied by few researchers (e.g., Bronstein 1985; Coursier 1993; Lyon-Caen 1991; Morgenstern 1984; Rodière 1987).

The purpose of this chapter is not to revisit private international law, because only a few cases are raised in practice with regard to industrial relations. Rather, I will focus on the very conditions imposed by a (normally applicable) national law that prevents unions, even if unintentionally, from establishing or increasing their transnational cooperation. To this end, I begin by discussing some serious legal impediments to cross-national cooperation among trade unions. Next, I will consider difficulties stemming from the general legal system of industrial relations in a particular country, and then other difficulties caused by inadequate implementation of the relevant legislation. Finally I will discuss briefly how supra- or international rules and regulations can overcome some of these problems.

Legal Impediments to Cross-National Cooperation

From the information available, in particular the data collected by Committees within the International Labor Organization (ILO) that supervise compliance with its Conventions, it appears that very damaging and frequent legal impediments exist, related to: affiliation with international organizations of workers and participation in international activities; international direct actions by workers, including strikes; and restrictions on trade union freedom in special areas, in particular Export Processing Zones (EPZs).

International Affiliations and Activities

The International Confederation of Free Trade Unions (ICFTU), the international trade secretariats (ITSs), and the World Confederation of Labor (WCL) and its sectoral federations are among the most prominent union organizations that were established to promote the interests of workers throughout the world. Others have been created at the regional level, as in Africa or Asia. Several states have expressed reservations about the right of domestic unions to join the major international confederations. Some, like Nigeria, have even gone so far as to prohibit such affiliation (Panford 1994, 50). More often, however, legislation restricts the right of international affiliation by limiting it to certain organizations,[1] by requiring prior authorization by public authorities,[2] or by permitting it only in certain conditions established by law.[3] These are, of course, the most direct—and very efficient—means to impede cross-border trade union cooperation.

A number of African countries, for example, have at one time or another made relations between an international confederation and its national members difficult or even impossible by forbidding national delegates to attend meetings of an international union organization, by preventing the latter's representatives from entering their country to attend or hold meetings, by prohibiting national federations from receiving financial assistance from an international federation, or by restricting the exchange of publications.[4] As another instance, legislation in the Philippines requires prior approval from the authorities before a union may receive financial aid or subsidies from foreign organizations.[5] The ILO Committee on Freedom of Association has also received complaints of cases where the authorities confiscated the passports of union officials, thereby preventing their participation in ILO meetings.[6] In practice, the pressures exerted by this Committee have proved to be one of the most efficient ways to circumvent these restrictions.

International Strikes and Other Direct Action

Nothing is more difficult to assess than the influence of the laws of a particular country on the organization and success of unions' direct actions. Historically speaking, strikes were initially outlawed in most industrialized countries, France and Britain, for example, but these job actions occurred anyway. Even today, many strikes are considered illegal according to a given law. Throughout history workers have gone on strike in order to make such job actions legal. A number of international direct actions are successful even if they are considered illegal in some of the countries involved.

This being said, restrictions on the right to strike are especially frequent in the case of sympathy strikes or other solidarity action. These restrictions are contained expressly in the labor rules and regulations, or they are interpreted as such by the courts. The effect of strikes on those not directly concerned in a labor dispute is often put forward as a justification for specific limitations in this regard (Kahn-Freund and Hepple 1972). They are more likely to exist in countries where the possibility of striking is directly linked to collective bargaining, such as Canada or Japan, than in countries where striking is recognized as a basic right of the individual worker, such as France or Italy.

In the same manner, so-called secondary boycotts are permitted only in very limited cases in countries like the United Kingdom and the United States, where that form of direct action has been used. A secondary boycott in this context is a direct action taken by a union that tries to dissuade an uninvolved employer from doing business with another employer who is in the midst of a labor dispute. In this regard, questions may be raised when an international action focuses on various subsidiaries in different countries of the same multinational corporation (MNC). As the entities are legally independent, actions taken by unionized workers to support their brethren in another subsidiary of the parent corporation may be classified as a sympathy action and considered illegal. Even if the action concerns the same corporation, the strike could be banned under the secondary boycott prohibition (Wedderburn 1995, 240–243).

Export Processing Zones

Workers in Export Processing Zones (EPZs) are experiencing difficulties in forming and joining trade unions of their choice. Labor statutes that restrict unions' activities are one reason; other reasons are based on practice and will be dealt with later.

In the first place, states have adopted legislation that exempts employers in the EPZs from having to abide by portions of the labor laws that apply to the rest of their countries. For example, some EPZs prohibit workers from joining unions or engaging in any union activity. It goes without saying that these rules and regulations may also impede any form of international union cooperation.

In Bangladesh, for example, the Export Processing Zones Authority Act of 1980 provides for the exemption of a zone from the operation of all or part of the Industrial Relations Ordinance. In Pakistan, the Export Processing Zones Authority Ordinance of 1980 completely excludes such EPZs from the scope of the Industrial Relations Ordinance, thus denying workers there the right to establish and join trade unions.[7]

Apart from specific laws, other regulations make it possible to restrict either union membership or related activities. Zone enterprises may, for example, be declared "essential services," "activities vital to the national interest," or "pioneer industries," in which strikes and other forms of industrial action will be considered illegal. Many observations and complaints charging violation of the ILO Conventions on Freedom of Association and Protection of the Right to Organize (No. 87, 1948) and on the Right to Organize and Collective Bargaining (No. 98, 1949) have, in this regard, been submitted to the ILO supervisory bodies.[8] Here again the ILO has been instrumental in restricting loose interpretations of the concept of "essential service."

Obstacles Deriving from the Legal System

The previous findings lead us to a general observation: efficient cross-border cooperation among unions presupposes recognition in the countries concerned of the right of workers to establish and to join unions. The basic principles of trade union freedom are enshrined in the constitution or legislation of most states today, but in many cases their actual operation appears more difficult (Servais 1984). I will focus again in this section on problems of a legal nature.

ILO Conventions 87 and 98 in particular reflect the conditions considered necessary for organizations of workers (as well as of employers) to further and defend the interests of their members and other workers (or employers). Some of these conditions pertain to the freedom of the workers, the employers, and their respective associations vis-à-vis the state. Governments must refrain from any interference in the creation or in the activities of the organizations concerned to defend and promote the interests of their members.

Other conditions refer to the nature of relations between unions and employers, particularly the protection against anti-union practices. Governments have an obligation to take positive action against possible abuses, such as, for example, establishing appropriate bodies that would protect the rights of these organizations as the need arises. Mechanisms to support collective negotiations also appear to be necessary. Governments are expected to promote the full development and use of voluntary negotiation, with a view to the regulation of terms and conditions of employment by means of collective bargaining. This basic obligation may lead countries to establish mechanisms to peacefully settle labor disputes on a voluntary basis. Belgium, for example, has established sectoral joint committees. They are composed of representatives of employers' and workers' organizations and chaired by an appointee of the government. Many disputes are settled and most collective agreements are concluded within the framework of these bodies. One fundamental idea underlies these generally accepted standards and principles concerning industrial relations:[9] the importance of having the employers, the workers, and their respective organizations on an equal footing in order to promote meaningful discussions of basic issues for the future of a corporation, such as the quality of working life and the efficient operation of the enterprise.

Although globalization and the resulting economic adjustments present obvious risks for the trade union movement,[10] these circumstances may also constitute a good opportunity to modernize labor-management relations in various countries. Nonetheless, too many governments appear more inclined to adopt authoritarian measures that impede the development of a free labor movement and the negotiation of employment conditions. An analysis of the cases examined by the ILO Committee on Freedom of Association highlights the following difficulties:[11]

- Restrictions on the right to establish and join workers' organizations (especially to the detriment of rural workers and public employees), including the explicit or indirect requirement for prior administrative authorization to form a union, and the prohibition against constituting more than one union (e.g., China or Viet Nam)
- Limitations on the right to establish federations and confederations of trade unions
- Suspension and dissolution of a union by an administrative authority
- Restrictions on the free functioning of unions (for example, election of officers, control of union activities, including the drafting of their rules and their internal affairs, and limitations on the protection of trade union property)
- Severe restrictions on the right to strike.

Some countries in East Asia and Southeast Asia have chosen a strictly state-controlled economic policy. These policies normally entail attempts to strictly limit union rights and to carefully monitor union activities. However, in some countries in the area, one can observe a trend to move away from purely technocratic development planning to a more consensual, negotiated approach to development that permits less restricted union propagation. For example, in the Republic of Korea labor law is moving toward convergence with the general standards of international labor law. The events of the last few years in the country seem to illustrate both the strength of the union movement and its capacity to bargain collectively. Indonesia also has moved very recently toward a closer adherence to the principles of trade union freedom.

The extent to which unions are able to bargain collectively is obviously another essential yardstick to assess industrial relations law. Here, a number of legal obstacles exist with regard to the levels of negotiation (be they enterprise, sectoral, or national level); the matters covered by collective bargaining (Malaysia and Singapore, for example, place restrictions on the topics on which the unions may bargain); the approval by a public authority of the agreement concluded; and other forms of government intervention (such as the freeze on pay increases which has been imposed in a number of countries, including Argentina).

Apart from these discrepancies, the simple fact that the legal framework of industrial relations differs from one country to another may sometimes lead to complex problems. I have already mentioned that the legal concept of a phenomenon such as the strike varies greatly between countries. The stoppage of work is recognized as a constitutional right of the individual worker in France or in Italy, while it is considered in the United Kingdom only as a freedom involving an immunity from penal sanctions. Consequently, the stoppage of work in Great Britain is not seen as a legitimate reason to suspend the contract of employment and may lead to its breach. In other words, striking workers may be fired legally.

A still clearer example of diverging national laws relates to the right of workers to negotiate their conditions of employment through collective bargaining. Main differences among countries concern the recognition of unions for the purpose of collective bargaining and the establishment of machinery and procedures to facilitate negotiations. Differences also exist with regard to the scope of the concluded agreements. Examples follow.

The recognition of a union by an individual employer or an employers' association is the first question to be settled in a negotiation process. Special provisions have been adopted in Canada, the United States, and other countries under which a union representing a certain percentage of the workers in a unit, or, in the case of competitive unions, the majority one (generally determined by means of a ballot) is granted exclusive bargaining rights for a category of workers. An administrative body or a court may review these representation decisions.

The situation is completely different in Belgium, France, or Spain, for example, where the law draws a general distinction between the most representative trade unions and other ones. The determination of the representative character is based on pre-established criteria, and in the first place on membership. Such distinctions consist, in particular, in the recognition of preferential or exclusive bargaining rights at certain levels (national, sectoral, enterprise). In these countries, collective negotiations take place very often at sector level or at regional or national level. It is therefore more difficult to leave the recognition of a union to the employers. In addition, the official recognition of the main workers' federations is considered an important factor of social stability.

National legislation also varies on the machinery and procedures to facilitate collective bargaining.[12] In some countries (for example, Belgium, Cameroon, Russian Federation, and Zambia) the legislation provides for setting up joint bodies—inside the enterprise or the branch of activity, or at the central and intersectoral level—within which collective agreements must be, or are normally, concluded. Various rules may be designed to assist in the negotiation process. For example, compulsory or voluntary mediation and conciliation procedures may be specified. Sanctions may be provided against certain practices likely to hinder the development of collective bargaining, such as unfair labor practices. Further, labor law may contain provisions to facilitate access by the parties to certain information, and in particular the communication to unions of information on the economic situation of the bargaining unit, the enterprise, or companies in the same sector. In other countries, however, these rules are completely unknown.

In some countries the nature and scope of bargaining issues are regulated by legislation, which either prescribes the discussion of certain matters or prohibits the discussion of certain items (such as some types of union security clauses). For example, in the United States, many subjects are considered mandatory topics of collective bargaining by the National Labor Relations Board. These include wages, hours of employment, health insurance, pensions, safety, the grievance procedure, and seniority. Both employers and unions are obligated to bargain in good faith about a mandatory subject if either party wishes to negotiate about the matter. Other legislation, as already pointed out, mentions certain questions as falling outside the scope of negotiation. In Malaysia, for example, the Industrial Relations Act excludes from the scope of bargaining promotions, transfers, recruitment, dismissal without notice, and assignment of jobs.[13] The Industrial Relations Act of Singapore contains a similar provision.[14]

In most countries, collective agreements have a compulsory legal effect on contracts of employment. In the United Kingdom, however, they may still be considered as a pure "gentleman's agreement." By contrast, labor laws in France and Belgium provide for collective agreements under certain conditions to be extended by the public authorities to all other firms in the industry. These regulations, of course, have a direct impact on the coverage of the agreements.

These differences in the negotiation process and the extent of coverage are a significant impediment to transnational collective agreements. If they are conceived as legally binding and not as gentleman's agreements to be implemented with good faith, it is true that they raise considerable problems as to the applicable law. Nevertheless, major breakthroughs in European law are potentially encouraging developments for the cooperation of unions in cross-border bargaining. I will return to these developments in the last part of this chapter.

These differences also show how difficult it is to argue that the legal systems of industrial relations are quickly converging.[15] Powerful MNCs are, of course, pushing forward elements of convergence, such as the new methods of human resources management. There are also ongoing attempts, at the regional or at the global level, by international trade unions in particular, to promote some basic rights of workers, wherever they live. However, the actual legal framework of industrial relations, even within such an integrated market as the European Union, is still very specific to each country. Beyond that, even the place of law in the society differs substantially from one part of the world to another. Rules and regulations have a more important role in the day-to-day life of the United States, for example, than in many countries of East or Southeast Asia.

Obstacles Deriving from Inadequate Application of the Law

Not only is the legal protection of trade union freedom inadequate on many occasions, but more often serious problems appear in the implementation of labor laws. The numerous complaints lodged before the ILO Committee on Freedom of Association as well as other reports on alleged violations of trade union rights provide ample evidence of failures to enforce existing labor laws. Anti-union practices of all kinds and violations of basic human rights in the field of labor have been documented: summary execution of trade unionists; ill-treatment; arbitrary arrest; infringement of the inviolability of trade union premises, correspondence, and conversations; violations of the freedom of movement and of the right of assembly (public and private), of the freedom of expression in general, and of the freedom of the trade union press and public speech in particular.

The responsibility for these violations of worker and human rights may frequently be traced to the authoritarian nature of the government. Quite often, also, employers seek to limit to the minimum their own statutory obligations to their workers and therefore do not necessarily favor unions and collective bargaining as major instruments of industrial relations. Worker rights also may be abused when, all too frequently, trade unions continue to follow old models of organization that either integrate them too much within the state structure or are excessively politicized. Even when trade unions are actually changing, it quite often takes some time for the employers to realize that the reforms are effective.[16]

The control or enforcement of legislation adopted in the fields of trade union freedom and industrial relations remains a major problem. The labor inspectorate, which in most countries is in charge of the supervision, is fraught with numerous problems, especially, but not only, in developing countries. These problems include lack of resources, absence of qualified staff, manifold assignments for inspectors, and limited transportation facilities to travel to widely dispersed workplaces.

Regulations concerning the creation or functioning of unions, the bargaining process, strikes, or other industrial relations matters are often too numerous, intricate, and complicated and consequently sometimes not well adapted to the needs and constraints of workers and their employers. Frequently one or both parties, whose level of education may be quite limited, do not completely understand these rules. Workers very often hesitate to lodge a complaint under the regulations because of fear of retaliation and lack of confidence in the administrative and judicial procedures available, which may be lengthy and inefficient.

In many countries a clear need exists to reorganize the structures and institutional frameworks of labor administration. Ministries and departments of labor must review and, where necessary, revise their programs. Further, given the limited resources available, labor inspectors must streamline their methods of work with a view to efficiently sanctioning blatant abuses of workers' basic rights. In some countries, a special unit has been created in the labor administration to deal with industrial relations issues.

In this period of globalization of the market economy, however, some activities in a particular country are no longer under the complete control of the nation-state. A classic example is the management of a national subsidiary that appears to be unable to agree to the proposals made in the course of a labor dispute without consulting its headquarters in another country. It may also be difficult for a national judge of country A to assess the reality of the economic reasons justifying collective dismissal when an enterprise (such as the French multinational Thompson) is closing an establishment (Videocolor) in country A (France) and transferring its activities to country B (Brazil).

Supranational Regulation

Commonly agreed international standards facilitate cooperation among trade unions. A number of such provisions have been adopted at either the regional or the worldwide level.

Regional Level

The most sophisticated body of labor provisions at this level is certainly the one adopted by the European Union, beginning at its foundation in 1958. The provisions include a joint statement by the heads of state or government called the Community Charter on the Fundamental Social Rights of Workers, adopted in December 1989, and the Protocol and Agreement on Social Policy signed at Maastricht on February 7, 1992, revised by the Treaty of Amsterdam, 1997.

The Charter, which itself has no legally binding effect, guarantees freedom of association and the right to bargain collectively. It recognizes explicitly the right to strike and the need to foster the peaceful settlement of labor disputes by means of conciliation, mediation, and arbitration.

The Agreement on Social Policy has encouraged dialogue between the "social partners" (i.e. employers' and workers' organizations, together with the governments concerned) at the community level, including, if they so wish, the conclusion of collectively bargained agreements. It has been integrated into the Amsterdam Treaty.

Finally, European Directive No. 94/95/CE of September 22, 1994, provides for the establishment of European Works Councils or for an equivalent procedure of information and consultation among the workers within enterprises or groups of enterprises having a Community scale. By "Community scale undertaking," the Directive means any undertaking with at least a thousand employees within the member states and at least 150 employees in at least two member states. While the Directive contains no explicit mention of unions, the majority of councils have included or will include unions within their structures.

Collective bargaining that results in binding agreements is still infrequent at the European Union level. However, representative organizations of employers and workers have adopted some joint statements at the sectoral level. For example, the employers' organization EuroCommerce and the commercial trade section of Euro-FIET (the European Regional Organization of the International Federation of Commercial, Clerical, Professional and Technical Employees) jointly elaborated three position papers on combatting violence in commerce (1995), on the future of social dialogue in commerce (1995), presented to the intergovernmental conference on the revision of the Treaty on European Union, and on combatting child labor (1996).

Some recent agreements, if confirmed by others of the same kind, could have a substantial impact on industrial relations at the European level. First, the ETUC (the European Trade Union Congress), the UNICE (the

European Private Employers' Organization), and the CEEP (the European Public Sector Employers' Association) signed the first European-level collective agreement on December 14, 1995. It provides all men and women workers with a personal right to parental leave on the birth or adoption of a child, to enable them to care for the child for at least three months while the child is eight years old or less. On the basis of the above-mentioned Protocol and Agreement on Social Policy, the scope of application of the agreement has been extended beyond the signatories and their members through a procedure of extension similar to those in force in several European Union member states. The signatories requested the European Commission to submit the collective agreement on parental leave to the European Council (of government representatives) for a decision to make these requirements binding in the member states of the European Union. For that purpose, the European Council issued a Directive on June 3, 1996. Other agreements of this type have been concluded since then by the same parties. They deal with the promotion of part-time work and with fixed-term employment (i.e. contracts of employment with a limit of time such as one year).

Furthermore, the purpose of European Directive No. 94/95, which created the European Works Councils, was to improve the right of workers to information and consultation. The French-based food processing group Danone has gone further and agreed to a negotiating role for its European Works Council. Negotiations will lead to joint statements and measures on issues such as employment, training, safety and working conditions, and the exercise of union rights. An agreement formalizing the arrangements was signed on March 28, 1996, by the multinational company, the International Union of Food, Agriculture, Hotel, Restaurant, Catering, Tobacco and Allied Workers' Association, and five representative French trade union confederations.[17] With a view to giving the agreement some official character, it has been filed with the International Labor Organization and with the Commission of the European Union.

Aside from European labor law, various regional instruments contain provisions on freedom of association. They include the Additional Protocol to the American Convention on Human Rights in the area of economic, social, and cultural rights (Valticos and von Potobsky 1995, 106–108), the Supplemental Agreement on Labor Cooperation to the North American Free Trade Agreement (NAFTA), and two instruments of the Council of Europe, the European Convention on Human Rights and the European Social Charter.

Although it is not a regional organization, the Organization for Economic Cooperation and Development (OECD), which includes the industrialized states around the world, should also be mentioned here. In 1976 its Ministerial Council adopted a Declaration on International Investment and Multinational Enterprises. The Declaration includes voluntary guidelines for MNCs that are intended to encourage economic and social progress (Tergeist et al. 1995, 44–50). The guidelines chapter on Employment and Industrial Relations makes a number of requests to MNCs:

- To respect the right of their employees to be represented by trade unions and to engage in constructive negotiations with a view to reaching collective agreements
- To provide relevant facilities to employee representatives which are necessary for effective negotiation
- To provide relevant information to employee representatives which enables them to obtain a true and fair view of the performance of the establishment or enterprise
- To observe standards of employment and industrial relations not less favorable than those observed by comparable employers in the host country
- Not to unfairly influence ongoing negotiations or hinder the exercise of the right to organize by threatening to transfer an enterprise or its employees between countries
- To enable employee representatives to conduct effective negotiations with management representatives who are authorized to make decisions on the matters under negotiation.

These Guidelines and their revisions of June, 2000, are not legally enforceable. However, national and international monitoring and consultation procedures have been developed to implement them that carry the moral and political weight of a joint recommendation of OECD governments. Hence, they have had some impact despite somewhat diminished interest in them in the 1990s (Tergeist et al. 1995, 50).

Worldwide Level

International instruments aimed at promoting freedom of association, collective bargaining, and the consequent cooperation between trade unions in the nation-states have mainly been adopted by the ILO. Conventions Nos. 87 and 98, referred to previously, embody the fundamental principles. They have been supplemented by a number of instruments dealing with different aspects of industrial relations, including the protection of workers' representatives in the enterprise and the facilities to be afforded to them,[18] rural workers' organizations,[19] labor relations in the public service,[20] collective bargaining,[21] examination of grievances,[22] voluntary conciliation and arbitration,[23] cooperation and communications within the undertaking,[24] and consultation at the industrial and national levels.[25]

The ILO has established very elaborate procedures to promote the ratification and application of these Conventions. Some are common to all ILO instruments and are designed to permit regular supervision. Others are only compliance provisions set in motion after a complaint has been lodged and may either apply to all conventions or deal with specific conventions, especially those concerned with freedom of association.

In November 1977, the ILO Governing Body adopted a Tripartite Declaration of Principles concerning Multinational Enterprises and Social Policies that deals, among other things, with industrial relations (freedom of association and the right to organize, collective bargaining, consultation, examination of grievances, settlement of industrial disputes). It has established a special procedure to monitor the effects of this Declaration (ILO 1977).

The limitations of the ILO's standard-setting activities have been extensively analyzed (Servais 1986). Two basic concerns underlie discussions of these limitations. First: nothing can oblige a government to ratify an ILO Convention and thereby make a formal commitment to respect it. Second, the recommendations of the ILO supervisory bodies do not constitute judicial decisions. However critical they may be, they take the form of encouragements to action and requests for dialogue, and not condemnations. The influence of the ILO supervisory machinery has been recognized in a great number of cases, including in Hungary, Poland, and Czechoslovakia during the communist era and in Latin America and Africa when nondemocratic governments have been in power. The impact of the conclusions of the ILO bodies on the countries concerned is based on the academic and moral authority of their members as well as on the publicity given internationally to their work.

It would be futile, however, to deny that genuine problems do arise in the application of standards of trade union freedom, even if the special procedure established by the ILO in this regard does not require ratification of the relevant Conventions by the state concerned. These problems of implementation explain why there have been proposals from the trade union movement (including the AFL-CIO) as well as from some governments (such as the United States and France) to add a "social clause" to international trade agreements that would impose minimum or equitable labor standards. These proposals are based on simple reasoning: a country that permits its enterprises to employ workers under deplorable conditions and to deny basic workers' rights—including freedom of association and collective bargaining—will be able to export its products at lower prices and thus take unfair advantage of its competitors. Hence, to protect fair competition the social clause would oblige all countries to guarantee their workers certain minimum rights imposed by international economic regulation. As has been seen in the 1996 meeting of the World Trade Organization (WTO) in Singapore, however, many developing countries, in particular in South and Southeast Asia, have opposed the social clause proposal, claiming that it is a circuitous but effective way for industrialized states to raise tariff barriers against developing countries.

Seldom has an issue so sharply divided opinions for so long as has the social clause. To break this deadlock, the ILO suggested a different approach that entailed reframing the issue (Servais, 1996, 79–81). Instead of questioning whether it is appropriate and possible to impose on everyone a minimum of social protection, the ILO focused on determining what conditions are necessary for those concerned to be able to enjoy an equitable share of the benefits resulting from the liberalization of international trade, while at the same time permitting each country to design its own particular social protection benefits according to prevailing national conditions. The ILO suggested a dual strategy. The first was to examine how to introduce in the international trade system minimum guarantees ensuring the social partners their share of the benefits of trade liberalization, to which they are contributing substantially. This, of course, entails some kind of link, however problematic, with the procedures of the General Agreement on Tariffs and Trade (GATT) and the WTO. The second was for the ILO to take its own specific action with a view to increasing the efficiency of its own procedures. Eventually, the International Labor Conference adopted, in June 1998, a Declaration on Basic Rights at Work, which has become a major instrument for promotion worldwide of such essential rights as freedom of association and collective bargaining, abolition of forced labor, including child labor, and abolition of all forms of discrimination.

With the exception, to a limited extent, of the European Union, the strategies of the international organizations like the U.N. have mostly been based on the commitments made by the nation-states and on the action to be taken by them. Today, however, to a varying degree nation-states have been losing their control of the instruments of national economic and social policy.[26] In particular, the rise of MNCs occasionally removes decision-making power far from the workplace or from national institutions of a higher level where collective bargaining traditionally takes place. These facts have led to attempts to ensure, worldwide, greater coherence between economic and financial policies, on the one hand, and social policies, on the other. At the World Summit for Social Development in March 1995, the heads of state called for a program of action to create a "favorable national and international political and legal environment" and to "establish conditions for the social partners to organize and function, with guaranteed freedom of expression and association and the right to engage in collective bargaining and to promote mutual interests . . ."[27] The trade union movement has, of course, a direct responsibility, together with employers, for making this statement a reality. In this respect, the ILO is a unique forum in which cross-border industrial relations issues can be debated, because it is the only tripartite body of workers' organizations, employers, and governments existing at the world level. Its regional, sectoral, and technical meetings also offer excellent opportunities for exchanging views.

Conclusion

As illustrated by a number of statements of the ICFTU's leaders there are growing efforts within the trade union movement to answer the multinationalization of the market economy with action taken at a cross-border level. The legal framework of industrial relations at both national and transnational levels is certainly a critical topic in this regard. Objective divergences between trade union and industrial relations systems (as for example between the ones of the United States and of most Western European countries) constitute without doubt an obstacle to collaboration. Much more seriously, the legal environments in some countries inhibit the growth of free trade unions and therefore also constrain union cooperation across national borders.

Cross-border cooperation between trade unions may certainly assist in making labor laws in some of these countries more compatible with the principles of free trade unionism. The difficulties in overcoming legal constraints obviously relate to the political, economic, and social environment and go beyond the capacities of any trade union movement. Because of its vast worldwide experience with labor issues and its tripartite structure, an international institution such as the ILO constitutes a natural forum in which transnational labor-management relations can be discussed.

4

Export Processing Zones

MICHAEL E. GORDON

Two men look out through the same bars: one sees the mud, and one sees the stars.

Frederick Langbridge

The globalization of the world economy has meant closer integration between industrialized countries and those in the Third World: more international trade, more foreign direct investment (FDI), and a tidal wave of cross-border financial transactions. These interrelated phenomena are consequences of economic liberalization and of technological innovations in transportation and communication that have expanded the scope and volume of goods that may be traded internationally. Export Processing Zones (EPZs) are one manifestation of these trends. From Panama to Hong Kong, indeed on all the continents of the earth, governments have established EPZs that offer foreign investors competitive costs and an array of income tax, tariff, and quota benefits, to induce them to set up factories that process imported raw materials for export.

The rapidly increasing number of EPZs is a measure of companies' success in decentralizing production capabilities to capitalize on the cost savings available in these special economic environments. However, a broad consensus has emerged that development instruments such as the EPZ must be evaluated in terms of equity, empowerment, self-determination, and sustainability (Brinkerhoff and Coston 1999). Therefore, in addition to judging the success of EPZs by their ability to satisfy the economic needs of the multinational corporations (MNCs) that invest in the zones, it is important to determine whether they are meeting the many work-related needs of the employees in these facilities.

The latter is the primary concern of organized labor. Labor regards many EPZs as havens for the exploitation of workers, made possible by the inability of unions to gain footholds because of employer opposition and the

60

complicity of local and national governments. In addition to humanitarian motives that fuel antagonism toward perpetrators of human rights violations, unions in industrialized countries are fearful that EPZs are helping to unleash new international competition based on wages and working conditions. As Thomas Donahue, former Secretary-Treasurer of the AFL-CIO, put it, "The world has become a huge bazaar with nations peddling their workforces in competition against one another, offering the lowest price for doing business" (quoted in Lee 1996, 492). Such competition could result in a race to the bottom, with a consequent decline in working conditions in the developed economies, the loss of national policy-making autonomy, and increased impotence of sovereign governments to regulate employment in the best interests of their laboring classes.

Two vexatious problems implied above complicate the description and evaluation of EPZs. First, EPZs have sprouted all around the world and assume many forms; their commercial value and their effects on people vary widely. Therefore one must qualify any conclusions about EPZs and accept them as somewhat ambiguous instruments of economic development that may or may not be beneficial. Second, employers, governments of developing countries, representatives of nongovernmental organizations (NGOs), and trade unions view EPZs quite differently. After studying the data available on the economic and social effects of EPZs, some perceive the zones as holding the promise of uplifting Third World economies, while others see them as a new form of exploitation visited upon the largely unskilled, desperately poor people who inhabit developing countries.

Although some EPZs have benefited both host country economies and populaces, there are, nonetheless, many zones that countenance Dickensian working conditions and treatment of workers. These harmful social effects are often attributed to the lack of free trade unions in EPZs. It is this fact that makes EPZs relevant to this collection of papers, two of which describe cross-border campaigns to win collective bargaining agreements in these zones (Chapters 9 and 12).

Defining Export Processing Zones

EPZs are one manifestation of strategies undertaken by many Third World countries to deal with their problems of social and economic development by promoting their export capabilities. Two of the strategies for expanding the export base of a country are to increase the production capacity of existing companies that currently supply only the domestic economy or to create entirely new facilities dedicated primarily to production for export.

Generally speaking, EPZs represent the second of these strategies, as they are designed to promote nontraditional exports by providing free trade status to products manufactured for sale abroad (World Bank 1992). By inducing foreign investment in EPZs, low-income developing countries hope to expand export capabilities, create employment quickly, and increase foreign exchange earnings.

Investment in EPZs is only a small portion of the total of FDI worldwide. However, "the dramatic growth in FDI flows in the 1990s and over time since the 1970s has brought about a greater degree of integration of the world economy than could have been achieved by trade alone" (Miyake and Thomsen 1999, 111).

In the case of the People's Republic of China, free zones were created to serve an additional purpose. Given the context of overall economic reform, from their outset China's special economic zones (SEZs) were used as "living laboratories of economic change" (Shum and Sigel 1986, 202) "in which different doses of market economy planning could be experimented upon and adapted and imported into the socialist economy of China" (Oborne 1986, 9).[1] For example, the SEZs were testing grounds for decentralization proposals that increased the autonomy of individual enterprises, such as the "factory manager responsibility system" in Shenzhen (Crane 1990).

EPZs exist in a variety of formats and are known by several different names (free trade zones in the Dominican Republic and other parts of the world, SEZs in China, and *maquiladoras* in Mexico). Many EPZs are clearly demarcated locations (enclave or "fenced-in" EPZs) that provide special incentives for companies that engage in the manufacture of goods for export (e.g., the EPZs in Jamaica and the Dominican Republic). This form of the EPZ is relatively easy to create and administer. It is well suited to the rapid clearance of imports and exports, and its small area makes it easier to provide a favorable, more lightly regulated environment than could be provided simultaneously in several different locations.

Some entire countries operate as virtual EPZs (e.g., Hong Kong and Singapore). Kenya's Export Processing Zones Act of 1990 empowered the Minister of Finance to declare any area of the country an EPZ. Sometimes individual firms that operate in several regions of a country (e.g., Tunisia) have been granted the privilege to function as EPZs (ICFTU 1996a). Finally, China's SEZs are entire cities or an entire province that offer housing, business, and recreational areas and provide a variety of health, education, and social services.

The diversity in nomenclature and structure of EPZs mirrors the variability of their economic effects on their host countries and of the working conditions provided for employees. Indeed, the "great variety of situations in which zones find themselves" was the theme for an international conference in fall 1998 sponsored by the World Export Processing Zones Association (WEPZA). Given this diversity, we rely on the following definition:

> EPZs are either geographically defined, economically extraterritorial areas or they are functional statuses in which enterprises produce almost exclusively for export. Special fiscal incentives, publicly subsidized infrastructure provisions, duty-free imports of inputs, and unlimited repatriation of profits are usual features offered to attract foreign (and when possible domestic) entrepreneurs to operate in the industrial enclave. (Roberts 1992, 2)

Unfortunately, the research on EPZs is somewhat limited and generalization is difficult. The sensitive nature of union rights and the quality of labor relations complicates investigations of these issues. Although numerous in-depth studies have been performed on EPZs in individual countries, good comparative data are not abundant (Chen, 1994; Roberts, 1992). The most comprehensive source of information is an ILO report by Auret van Heerden (1998) that was based on missions to sixteen countries and on information collected on southern Africa and the Caribbean.

History of EPZs

Writers differ about the earliest antecedents of the EPZ model, some tracing the form back to the Roman Empire, others to thirteenth century Spain, notably the city of Cadiz. There appears to be agreement that the first modern EPZs were established around 1960 as free trade zones that stored, repackaged, and re-exported goods that had been produced elsewhere. The first modern EPZ was established in 1959 in the area surrounding the airport in Shannon, Ireland, to stave off anticipated local economic devastation; the stimulus was the advent of jet aircraft that did not require refueling for transatlantic flights. In 1965, Taiwan became the first developing country to establish a zone. EPZs based on the Taiwanese model were created throughout Asian developing countries in the 1960s and 1970s as a means of launching industrial growth (Wilkinson 1994). A variety of incentives was offered to investors, including low rates of taxation and havens of cheap, disciplined labor for "transnational companies interested in exploiting the benefits of international subcontracting" (Sit 1986, 242). Many EPZs were created in the Western Hemisphere in the 1960s as well, most notably the *maquiladoras* in Mexico. EPZs were created in Eastern

Europe in the 1990s, including Poland's creation of three zones beginning in 1995 (Hallam 1999).

In sum, EPZ development has been substantial and widespread, although with a few notable exceptions (e.g., the United States, Singapore, and Hong Kong) EPZs are rarely located in industrialized countries.[2] In 1978, EPZs had stirred sufficient interest to prompt creation of the WEPZA, an independent non-profit organization dedicated to exchange of information, recruitment and training of EPZ managers, research on trade and markets, and representation of EPZs' interests before international bodies.

Early EPZ development was inspired, in part, by a strategy of many developing countries to replace imports with domestic production. However, low domestic demand limited the development of such EPZs, and these domestically produced goods typically were not competitive on price or quality with the imported products for which they were intended as substitutes.[3] EPZ creation was also motivated by the critical rate of indebtedness in many developing countries (Basile and Germidis 1984). In fact, during the 1980s some EPZs evolved into multifunctional institutions for generating foreign exchange, creating employment, and attracting foreign capital and new technology. However, these national benefits often did not offset the fact that EPZs offered an unstable employment base, generated little domestic added value, developed few labor or managerial skills, and infrequently created substantial economic ties to domestic manufacturers, that is, backward linkages (Rondinelli 1987).

Over the years estimates of the scope of EPZ activity have varied widely, although figures supplied by the WEPZA appear to have become the most authoritative source, and several conclusions appear warranted. First, the number of zones and thus the levels of employment in EPZs have increased rapidly over the past fifteen years. In 1997, 845 EPZs worldwide employed approximately 27 million people (van Heerden 1998). Employment in China's SEZs dwarfed employment in EPZs located in all other host countries.[4] Because enabling legislation for establishing EPZs is currently being prepared or is in the process of enactment in several countries, and because EPZs have been newly authorized in other countries, the numbers of zones and levels of employment can be expected to increase.

Several estimates suggest that approximately 70 percent of EPZ employees are women, although the proportion can vary from 47 percent in India to as much as 79 percent in El Salvador (Romero 1993). Women are as much as 90 percent of the workforce in EPZs that produce garments, textiles, and electronics. Indeed, employers consider women to be ideal workers in these industries (which represent the majority of EPZ employers) because they assume that women have "nimble fingers" (Dunn 1994, 21) and dispositions suited to performing boring, repetitive, and low-paid tasks. When petrochemicals, iron, steel, fertilizers, and plastics are produced (e.g., in Trinidad and Tobago), EPZ employment is predominantly male.

How EPZs Operate

The global economy has stimulated many employers to restructure their production processes into global chains, producing part of a good in one country, other parts in other countries, and assembling the disparate parts in still other countries.[5] By sequencing stages of production in different locations, a process called "production sharing" (Drucker 1977), MNCs can manufacture discrete components in decentralized entities, scattered around the world, that offer the most alluring economic incentives and possess the cheapest sources of trainable labor. Many EPZs were created in the Third World to serve as links in these global chains. In 1996, U.S. and European Union companies sent $76 billion worth of materials, components, and supplies abroad for processing and assembling that were returned with duty charged only on the value added abroad.[6]

Early development strategy required the host country of the EPZ to supply two of the three factors of production, labor and land. In order to provide exporters with a competitive advantage, governments of host countries also relaxed tariff and quota regulations and devoted foreign currency reserves to EPZ industries (Rondinelli 1987). Capital, the third factor of production, was typically supplied from abroad. Because of competition among EPZs, it soon became necessary for host countries to develop infrastructure (utilities, sanitation, and "standard design factories") and to provide services (insurance information, satellite telecommunications, finance, hospitals, and bonded warehouses) to attract investors. Typically, a government agency develops and promotes the array of incentives, and administration of the EPZ is the responsibility of a zone authority. Potential investors deal directly with the zone authority, thereby avoiding the need to work with several separate agencies on matters such as customs, industrial development, and finance. "Noticeably absent are officials from labor institutions, even though these authorities often regulate and handle labor-related matters in the zones" (Romero 1995, 248).

International organizations such as the International Monetary Fund, the United Nations Industrial Development Fund, and the World Bank, and national organizations such as the United States Agency for International Development and the United States Overseas Private Investment Corporation, have directly and indirectly promoted EPZs as a way to stimulate the economies of Third World countries. "The orthodox assumption is that economic benefits will 'trickle down' and have a positive 'ripple' effect on other sectors of national economies" (Dunn 1994, 23).

The majority of enterprises operating in EPZs are wholly foreign-owned businesses or joint ventures. The primary employers are MNCs, most of which are headquartered in Western industrialized nations.[7] MNCs headquartered in newly industrial countries also represent an important presence. For example, South Korean MNCs operate in EPZs throughout Latin America and the Caribbean. Some MNCs operate as "virtual companies" that employ only a handful of people directly. Nonetheless, MNCs are able to influence operations within EPZs by means of non-equity links involving subcontractors and supply relationships. "MNC (and non-MNC) producers and retailers in industrialized countries can contract out production to small enterprises in EPZs, while keeping a firm control on product design, marketing, quality control and distribution" (Hamill 1993, 58). For example, most big name clothing designers concentrate on designing and marketing their products, and license others to handle the manufacturing. MNCs therefore usually take little or no responsibility for the working conditions in the facilities that manufacture their products.[8]

Local entrepreneurs may also operate in an EPZ. In Asia, EPZs have attracted a substantial number of local investors, especially in Sri Lanka, India, and China. Local investors may be courted when a sufficient number of foreign investors has not been attracted to justify a country's investment in the EPZ's infrastructure and administration. This policy may raise concerns that the local economy could be destabilized if host country investors operating within the zone enjoy unfair competitive advantages in local markets over domestic firms that operate outside the zone. Such concerns led the Indian government to limit EPZs to selling no more than a fourth of their output domestically.[9] Nonetheless, with payment of appropriate customs duties, exports from EPZs to domestic markets would be less unsettling to local economies and might encourage local entrepreneurs to invest in the zones (Basile and Germidis 1984). This policy guides trade between China's SEZs and the domestic economy (Crane 1990).

A variety of products is manufactured in EPZs, including toys and shoes in China, automobile parts and assembly in Mexico, tennis rackets in St. Vincent, and textiles throughout Central America and Sri Lanka. Bangladesh is known for the manufacture of garments. Iran has recently established the Bandar Imam "special economic zone" to entice foreign investment in petrochemical businesses (Rhodes 1999). Advanced telecommunications and computer technology has made it possible to locate services such as data entry and data processing in EPZs, in Jamaica and Barbados, for example. However, EPZ production tends to focus on textiles, clothing, and electronics.

Factors Influencing the Decision to Operate in an EPZ

A variety of incentives has influenced companies' decisions to locate a production facility in an EPZ, including tax and regulatory relief and lower wage costs. It is an established commercial practice to invest abroad in order to reduce tax and regulatory burdens that are perceived to increase the cost of doing business in the home country. All EPZs offer potential investors duty-free imports and a favorable business environment that is not encumbered with many regulations and red tape (World Bank 1992).

Companies also shop around to find the cheapest, most productive, and most compliant labor forces, and EPZs appear to offer an attractive way to deal with labor costs. Field studies in the 1970s and early 1980s concurred "that labor costs play a fundamental and decisive role in any policy for the redeployment of industrial activities to EPZs" (Basile and Germidis 1984, 27). Many firms continue to use labor-intensive technology in which wages represent an important component of total production costs; reducing the bill for labor remains an important determinant of these companies' decisions to invest in EPZs (Romero 1995). However, potential investors now seem to recognize that labor cost advantages are frequently ephemeral and represent a diminishing cost of production in a number of industries ("Too Little" 1994). Instead, the quality of human resources may be of greater importance than the cost of human resources. New technology and the new emphasis on speed and quality have made it necessary for employers in certain industries to locate a trainable workforce. "The more widespread use of computers . . . requires English language proficiency because the software and operating manuals are invariably in English" (van Heerden 1998, 11).

Market access is another important consideration.[10] The time required to reach the customer is an especially important consideration when EPZ factories are integral parts of just-in-time manufacturing systems that require suppliers to be close to their customers. Market access may be influenced by trade agreements that grant privileges to their signatories (for example, the North American Free Trade Agreement and the Multifiber Agreement), thereby disadvantaging manufacturers located in EPZ countries not embraced by the pacts.

Finally, after comparing the development of EPZs in Jamaica and Mauritius, Roberts (1992) concluded that the social conditions of the host country are of greater relevance in attracting investors to an EPZ than the specific package of incentives offered to encourage foreign investment. For example, quality of life issues for foreign nationals who live in host countries are important.[11] Similarly, a stable society, notably a sound government, is an important consideration for investors.[12]

Economic Effects of EPZs

Most research on EPZs has focused on their economic aspects, but this research has serious limitations. First, only a handful of theoretical papers treats the role of EPZs in developing economies. Instead, researchers adapt conceptual frameworks developed in other contexts that may not provide appropriate models for the economic effects of EPZs (Din 1994). Second, comparing the overall economic impact of EPZs is difficult because the data are either unavailable or not standardized (Roberts 1992). Cost-benefit assessments provide only very crude estimates of the economic effects of EPZs because appropriate financial information is available for only a few zones (World Bank 1992).

The economic effects of EPZs vary greatly. For example, the World Bank (1992) reported that approximately 40 to 50 percent of the EPZs for which crude economic data were available appeared to have been financial successes (most of these were in Asia), about 20 to 30 percent appeared to be moderately successful, and about 30 percent were unsuccessful. It is not clear whether this variability is attributable to the conceptual and methodological limitations in studying the economic effects of EPZs, to the variability in the structure, location, and administration of the zones themselves, or to the complexity of the economic phenomena affected by EPZ development.

The success of EPZs may be judged in terms of several economic criteria. One obvious standard is the record of business survival in EPZs. Many EPZ businesses were unable to sustain themselves during the 1970s due to faulty decision-making about the locations of the zones and the industrial estate construction (World Bank 1992).[13] Increasingly sophisticated zone administration appears to have learned to deal with these matters so that they are less frequently identified as reasons for EPZ failures.

Because EPZs typically are located in countries with significant labor surpluses, a second criterion of economic success is the number of jobs created. "There can be a lot of discussion about the cost-effectiveness of zones as a form of employment creation, and about the quality of those jobs, but in sheer numerical terms the fact remains that zones have produced many jobs" (van Heerden 1998, 18). China's SEZs and Mexico's maquiladoras rank first and second in terms of total employment. Impressive employment growth followed EPZ development throughout the Caribbean and Central America as well.

EPZ success may also be defined in terms of the effect on the economy of the host country. Backward links to the domestic economies of host countries take a variety of forms, including the establishment of exchange relationships between zone and customs-area businesses. For example, by extending equal-footing policies to firms outside the zones, some East Asian economies succeeded in developing supplier capacity to satisfy the needs of zone enterprises, thus creating viable backward links. These successes are isolated, however. Although EPZs have promoted a great deal of investment, failure to create sufficient linkages to the domestic economies of the host countries (e.g., the local content of manufacturing is inadequate) has severely limited their overall economic benefits (van Heerden 1998). Most economists agree that EPZs have had a negative or at best a very limited positive effect on commerce in the customs sectors of host countries (Johansson 1994). "Significant backward links from exports rarely develop in EPZs" (World Bank 1992, 19). Even when increased production capacity and more sophisticated manufacturing has replaced labor-intensive technology in some EPZs (e.g., the maquiladoras), local economic development has not followed in its wake.

Another type of backward link takes the form of transfers of business acumen from professional EPZ managers to local producers in the domestic economy. This knowledge and skill transfer is especially important given that EPZs were begun in many developing countries because indigenous entrepreneurs lacked the knowledge of foreign regulations and trade practices and did not possess the production and marketing skills necessary to embark successfully in exporting. Johansson and Nilsson's (1997) research on Malaysian EPZs found evidence of a related, indirect economic spillover that they referred to as a "catalyst effect." Specifically, foreign companies operating in EPZs provided local manufacturers in the customs territories with assistance in managing their production, distribution, and sales of manufactured goods on the world market, thereby increasing the total of Malaysian exports.

With the exception of advanced developing economies such as Korea and Taiwan, and the garment industry in particular, transfers of product and process technologies generally have been small. Further, the limited transfers of management and technical skills that have been observed are a consequence of movement of people from EPZ jobs in which they received specialized training to jobs in the customs sectors. Obviously, these skill transfers are less numerous where business opportunities outside the zones are least attractive.

Lastly, the economic effects of EPZs are almost certainly attenuated by the nature of the incentive package offered to investors in the zones. Obviously, depending on the generosity of the tax relief provided, governments of host countries may forego substantial revenue from the commercial activity in the EPZs. Further, backward linkages may be less likely to develop where the structure of the tariff and duty relief provides an impetus only for importing raw materials from abroad and exporting all finished products. Finally, if tax and regulatory concessions are the primary reason for investing in an EPZ, then certain companies may well abandon their operations should a more attractive package of incentives be offered by another zone.[14]

Taking all these various economic criteria into consideration, most writers agree that the performance of the Mauritian EPZ has been spectacular.[15] In some countries such as Taiwan, Singapore, and Malysia, EPZs grew and became viable industrial communities that are integrated with the manufacturing system in the rest of the country. Indeed, about half of the Asian EPZs in the World Bank report were judged to be unequivocal successes. EPZs have had few successes in either Africa or the Middle East, with the exception of Mauritius and Cyprus (Cooper 1998; Ryan 1994). When EPZs have not performed well, failure may be due to intense competition with one another, the poor quality of labor and management, the failure to develop an outward-oriented trade strategy, and the lack of integration with the economy of the host country (Johansson and Nilsson 1997; Sit 1986).

Working Conditions in EPZs

Studies of working conditions in EPZs are less numerous than papers dealing with their economic effects. Indeed, several comprehensive reports about EPZs prepared by the OECD (Basile and Germidis 1984; Oborne 1986) and the World Bank (1992) totally ignore or barely mention working conditions. Interestingly, in 1981 the WEPZA established a Code of Conduct for its members. The Code addresses a variety of matters, including truth in advertising EPZs, fairness and impartiality in dealing with clients, and the need "to conduct itself at all times as a highly ethical professional industrial development organization so as to reflect favorably on itself and on other WEPZA members."[16] Nowhere in the Code is there an explicit reference to the treatment of workers, and it is not clear whether the quoted passage implicitly reminds members of their ethical obligations to employees.

With their dramatic growth, anecdotal evidence began emerging about deplorable working conditions in EPZs that prompted the ILO in 1981 to start publishing articles and working papers on social and labor issues in the zones. In 1996, such concerns spawned the ILO's Action Program on Social and Labor Issues in Export Processing Zones, intended to create industrial relations climates in EPZs that are both conducive to attracting and expanding investment and respectful of the fundamental rights of workers. In fall 1998 the ILO convened an important tripartite meeting about EPZs (ILO, 1998).

Working conditions in EPZs have been the focus of several surveys, but despite many precautions, it is not clear how representative their findings are. For example, it is possible that those countries that condone the least wholesome working conditions did not respond to requests for information. "Reliable generalizations about the situation in all zones cannot be made, since the scope and level of detail of the replies are not uniform and information from all major host countries is not available" (Romero 1993, 4).

Information about working conditions in EPZs has also been gathered by various human rights groups, such as the National Labor Committee (see chapter 12). These data are often very rich and compelling, and they typically reveal strikingly oppressive conditions within EPZ firms. Although the impartiality of these groups has been questioned, more important is how representative their findings are of the total EPZ population. News stories, speaking tours, and videotapes attract less attention if they present information from EPZ sites with reasonable working conditions.

Despite the limitations of the available information, several conclusions about working conditions in EPZs appear to be warranted. To begin, physical facilities may be more modern in EPZs than those in typical plants outside the zones. Nonetheless, the record of certain EPZ firms (e.g., in China and Thailand) with respect to health hazards and the occurrence of catastrophic industrial accidents is also well known.

Working conditions in EPZs generally are less favorable than in industrialized countries (hours are longer and compensation is lower), although conditions in EPZs frequently do not differ markedly from those in other industries in the host countries. "The situation with respect to standards in many EPZs is often a reflection of more widespread problems in the host country" (Romero 1995, 267). Nonetheless, when differences are reported, seldom are conditions in EPZs better than in other enterprises, and often they are worse. "In examining the characteristics of EPZs, it emerges that working conditions in many of them conflict with international labor standards established by the International Labor Organization" (Dunn 1994, 31). For example, Sri Lanka denounced its ratification of Convention No. 89 (which prohibits employment of women in night shift work) because of concerns that it would discourage investments in its EPZs, which were expected to operate three shifts. The Jamaican government acknowledged that workers in EPZ textile and garment enterprises received less compensation and endured poorer working conditions than workers in other domestic companies (Romero 1993).

Although variation exists from country to country, reports of harsh treatment of employees persist. For example, because EPZs are separate customs territories, security is tight and access is restricted for personnel and goods. It is not uncommon that body searches are conducted upon workers entering or leaving the EPZs, leading to complaints about sexual harassment (Dunn 1994). Further, strict discipline is customary in international assembly operations, and EPZ companies offer few accommodations to human needs during periods of sickness or child rearing (van Heerden 1998). Finally, writers agree that the lack of opportunity for career development is one of the most prevalent problems facing EPZ workers.

Wages

Studies reveal that EPZ wages typically fall below international standards but often exceed regional wages. For example, in China's SEZs the minimum wage is lower than in competing countries in the region but higher than pay in China proper (Crane 1990).

Wages vary substantially across EPZ employers, partly dependent on the type of industry and other economic factors. Especially in labor-intensive assembly and processing operations, firms compete on the basis of price. Hence, employers tend to view labor as a "cost to be contained rather than an asset to be nurtured" (van Heerden 1998, 12). Several East Asian governments, recognizing the importance of wages in labor-intensive export manufacturing, have taken steps to control labor costs and ensure labor peace as a means for attracting foreign investment (Deyo 1989).

Although the data are sketchy, wages in some EPZs may be exploitative. Particularly in countries with a surplus of labor, unskilled workers are likely to receive very low wages. "The crucial importance of low wages to EPZ industries can be gauged indirectly from the data on the rate of growth of employment in EPZs and the rate of growth of per capita income: the countries where EPZ employment has been growing fastest are those where EPZ wages have been growing slowest" (ILO/UNCTC 1988, 102). Not only may wage scales be lower in EPZs, but the basis for calculating earnings may be inequitable. For example, in Caribbean countries, "The wage structure is such that high production targets are established and varied upwards, but workers only get bonuses if they achieve them. This means that the company gets the benefit of this additional work without having to pay extra unless the quotas and targets are met" (Dunn 1994, 25).

The absence of unions and collective bargaining agreements appears to exacerbate the situation. For example, Romero (1995) reports that wages increased in South Korean EPZs following the lifting of restrictions against union representation.[17]

Some EPZ firms pay wages that are higher than those characterizing the local economy. Several factors have been linked to the higher wages, including the availability of overtime, piece-rate incentives, and the perceived need to pay a wage premium to attract workers to EPZ companies with reputations for harsh working conditions. It is also true that enterprises that "compete on quality and innovation (such as high-tech electronics firms running 'no fault' production lines) are invariably setting standards that are higher than national norms for wages" (van Heerden 1998, 12).

Labor Laws in EPZs

As globalization accelerates, governments increasingly compete for foreign direct investment by offering regulatory incentives. Although domestic labor laws appear to be applicable inside and outside the zones in a majority of countries with EPZs (van Heerden 1998; World Bank 1992), it is not uncommon for governments to offer "flexibilization" of labor codes within the zones (see Chapter 3). Indeed, "allegations as well as well-founded reports of the non-observance of labor standards in a number of host countries have multiplied over the years" (Romero 1995, 248). For example, when advertising the benefits of Panamanian EPZs, zone administrators state: "Labor relationships are governed by special regulations, which are more flexible than those of the Labor Code."[18] These advertisements are based on a 1992 law permitting "flexibility" of contracts and functions in firms operating in the zones. Also, night work was permitted in Mauritian EPZs despite the fact that it was expressly prohibited outside the zones (ILO/UNCTC, 1988).[19]

In many instances where labor laws are extended *de jure* to the zones, de facto working conditions do not meet the required standards. Evidence suggests that some governments consciously ignore their own labor regulations in the zones. It is more common, however, that lack of government resources such as inspectors and monitoring technology is responsible for failure to enforce labor laws in EPZs. Many reports of abuses, such as failure to pay legal minimums and social security, may be traced to a lack of government personnel to oversee compliance (Romero 1995; van Heerden 1998).

A number of countries have postponed the application of industrial relations laws to start-up firms in EPZs. For instance, in 1990, after being pressured by Asian companies, Panama decreed that investors in the export sector would have a three-year grace period free of collective bargaining, in contradiction to Panama's labor law. The governments of Turkey and Bangladesh suspended labor laws for an initial "honeymoon" period to hinder the development of unions. In the case of Turkey, labor disputes during a company's first ten years of operation must be handled by the Supreme Arbitration Committee because Turkish laws dealing with strikes, lockouts, and conciliation are not applicable within this time period (Romero 1993).

Rights to Union Representation

The most controversial aspect of EPZ operations, indeed the matter that prompted discussion of employment conditions in the zones to begin with, pertains to the rights of workers to form unions and to bargain collectively. A U.S. Department of Labor survey of EPZs in eleven countries conducted in 1989–90 found that a number had low rates of union representation (reported in Hamill 1993). For example, not a single EPZ company in Sri Lanka was organized, despite a 20 percent union density in the country as a whole. Low unionization rates would be understandable if there were normative restrictions against union formation. However, the survey did not find, in general, "special laws or regulations concerning freedom of association" (Hamill 1993, 62). Despite the fact that labor law applies equally within and without Jamaican and Mauritian EPZs, for example, and despite the fact that many companies outside the zones are unionized, hardly any union representation exists in EPZs in these countries.[20] Governments rarely challenge (and often assist) employers' actions to keep unions out of the EPZs, and free trade unionism generally is unwelcome within the zones. In this vein, the government of Pakistan admitted that some of its ordinances limiting the rights of EPZ workers to unionize were "introduced in response to conditions laid down by transnational organizations before they were prepared to invest in Pakistan" (Romero 1993, 11).

In a number of countries that permit unionization within EPZs, representation may be authorized solely for government-controlled unions. For example, only unions affiliated with the All China Federation of Trade Unions (ACFTU) represent workers in China's SEZs. Strikes are not permitted, and the ACFTU is under tight government control (ICFTU undated).

"House" or company-controlled unions are often used within EPZs to thwart genuine worker representation. Workers in Malaysian EPZs, for example, may not join the national union of electrical workers, and only company unions may be registered (ICFTU undated). In Central America, employers promote "solidarity associations"to undermine the development of truly representative workers' organizations. These associations provide savings programs and mutual assistance, such as low-interest credit and housing loans. Although Costa Rican law prohibits these associations from functioning as unions, only ten unions have been organized in the EPZs, none of which has been able to negotiate a labor contract (van Heerden 1998). Finally, Chinese authorities may encourage election of "enterprise leadership groups" (Crane 1990) within individual factories in some SEZs. These groups do not act as traditional unions, but rather as mechanisms to overcome "bureaucratic problems."

In some instances, unionization may be restricted altogether. For example, enterprises located within Indian EPZs are considered public utilities and therefore unionization is not permitted (ICFTU undated). Bangladesh law forbids unions in its EPZs (van Heerden 1998). In Pakistan, the government "entirely exempted all export processing zones from the scope of the Industrial Relations Ordinance, whilst section 4 of the Export Processing Zone (Control of Employment) Rules, 1982, deprived workers of the right to strike or to take other forms of industrial action" (Hamill 1993, 62).

Other types of government interference may hinder the formation of unions. For example, in Sri Lanka union officials are not permitted access to EPZs for the purpose of organizing workers. Likewise, EPZs in Zimbabwe are not subject to the country's labor laws, thereby effectively denying workers the right to unionize (van Heerden 1998). In response to antiunion actions, unions in several countries (e.g., Bangladesh, the Dominican Republic, Fiji, and Pakistan) have filed complaints with the ILO's Committee of Experts on the Application of Conventions and Recommendations regarding infringements on the rights to freedom of association and organizing (Conventions 87 and 98, respectively).

Conclusion

It is difficult to generalize about EPZs for several reasons. First, all EPZs are not structured or operated in the same way. Consequently, their economic and social effects are quite varied. Further complicating the possibility of generalizing about EPZs are the predictable differences in interpretation of the data on their economic and social effects. The tripartite meeting held by the ILO to discuss the findings of the van Heerden report vividly demonstrated these disagreements (ILO 1998). Union representatives felt that the report did not emphasize enough the extent to which appalling working conditions characterized the zones. Employer and some government representatives felt that the report was too harsh on this point, buttressing their arguments with evidence that conditions in the zones simply mirror those in the non-export economies of the host countries.

Because EPZs are an increasingly important element of the global economy, policies must be established to guide their development and operation. Such policy-making begins with one or two verities. First, like it or not, there is nothing inherently harmful or insidious about EPZs. Their popularity and their economic and social successes have demonstrated time and again that EPZs are viable commercial instruments for the conduct of global business. The record of their operations, rather, suggests that, like other government institutions and programs, EPZs may be managed in a manner that genuinely assists their clients, or may be run for the sole benefit of those who administer them at the expense of their clients. Consider, for a moment, the differences between the Mauritian EPZ experience that has enriched an entire country (Roberts 1992) and Central American EPZs that typically have exploited workers and failed to strengthen the domestic economies. Those who manage an EPZ can create economic opportunities that redound to the benefit of all who come in contact with it, or can create an economic entity of long-term value only to the masters of the zone (zone administrators or MNCs who dictate the terms of investment).

This suggests the second verity. Frequently, EPZs operate in a manner that benefits neither the economy of the host country nor the workers who labor in them. In too many instances, "EPZs have retained their enclave nature as isolated islands of foreign investment and have had little impact on the domestic economies of host countries" (Crane 1990, 9). The lack of backward links raises a number of legitimate questions. For example, might not the host country monies invested in the EPZs have been better used to strengthen the domestic economy by funding local industries and training local entrepreneurs and workers to compete in international trade?

Further, the number of complaints about violations of human and worker rights in the zones is alarming. In less controlled business environments, one might expect that workers would attempt collective action to relieve the most oppressive conditions. The record is clear that zone employers, often with the assistance of government officials, impede, if not prevent, the formation of unions. "The overall picture seems to be one of very low unionization, and the absence or limited presence of independent organizations, often with the acquiescence of governments" (Romero 1995, 260). The ILO was forced to conclude that "the classic model of labor regulation with a floor or framework of minimum labor standards, and free trade unions and employers (individually and collectively) coming together to negotiate binding agreements that regulate their interaction is extremely rare in EPZs" (van Heerden 1998, 20).

The ILO has attempted to begin the process of improving EPZs with a series of gentle but pointed reminders to all parties. It is the ILO's position that competitive advantages based on exploitative conditions are temporary, at best. This idea is consistent with management scholars Snow, Miles and Coleman (1995), who state that cost-based global networks, which rely on inexpensive labor or locate facilities where there is minimal concern for ecological conditions, eventually will approach an equilibrium from which it will be difficult to extract further competitive advantages. Thus employers and governments are advised that investment in the zones ought to be geared toward jobs that add substantial value to the final product. Such action will make jobs more meaningful and satisfying to workers and help to assure the long-term viability of the investment.

Poor labor relations make EPZs less attractive investments because of the potential for instability. Because adequate labor standards and a system of labor relations are lacking in many zones, the ILO concluded that instability in EPZs could be expected. Despite increasing calls for change, little progress can be expected given the severe limitations of enforcement mechanisms.

Reports of poor working conditions have been frequent enough to provoke numerous organizations to act to protect the human and employment rights of defenseless zone workers. These efforts take place at both the national and international levels. For example, local unions, NGOs, and even churches may mount domestic campaigns intended to impel employers to improve working conditions in the EPZs. These campaigns have been directed at the employers, host country governments, and domestic public opinion. At the international level, a variety of union organizations including ITSs and the ICFTU, as well as the ILO and certain NGOs (e.g., Human Rights Watch and the National Labor Committee), have been able to widen campaigns by bringing conditions in certain EPZs to the attention of the international community. In some cases governments of countries that import EPZ products, such as the United States and the European Union, have used trading privileges as leverage to win concessions on working conditions from EPZ host countries or employers. In the United States, the AFL-CIO has filed charges with the government to threaten trading advantages obtained by EPZ host countries under the General System of Preferences.

As time goes on, such organizations will undertake more campaigns to compel economic and social change in the EPZs. This must be the case as long as workers around the world ponder the intrinsic and extrinsic value of their jobs. The questions still remain for EPZ workers staring out beyond the fences that define their employment enclaves: How has their work affected their lives? What role has it played in their development as human beings? Does their job provide them with a vantage point to see the stars or only the mud?

Part II

Interorganizational Structures That Promote Transnational Cooperation

5

The International Confederation Of Free Trade Unions: Bread, Freedom, and Peace

MICHAEL E. GORDON

The International Confederation of Free Trade Unions exists to unite the workers organized in free and democratic trade unions of the world and to afford a means of consultation and collaboration between them in furtherance of the aims here set out.

> Preamble, constitution of the International Confederation
> of Free Trade Unions

As apparent from the first words in its constitution, the ICFTU is an organization dedicated to translating trade union sentiment for solidarity into a reliable system of mutual support at the global, regional, and national levels. Headquartered in Brussels, the ICFTU is the largest and most representative confederation of workers' organizations in the world; it is "the sole real organization of national labor centers" (Lee 1997, 7). Because of its large, diverse membership of national trade union confederations and because of its size and resources relative to other labor organizations, the ICFTU is a focal point for developing contacts with other unions, governments, and international agencies concerned with economic and social life. A broad-based and pluralist organization, the Confederation, in keeping with its motto of "Bread, Peace and Freedom," attempts to influence "international economic and social policy; peace, security and disarmament; and the protection and promotion of trade union and other basic human rights" (ICFTU 1988, 3).

Any discussion of international cooperation among unions would be incomplete without consideration of the ICFTU. The Confederation facilitates information exchange among its affiliates and serves as a voice of free trade unions worldwide. Over the years the Confederation has established working relationships (although not necessarily formal ties) with other democratic union associations, intergovernmental organizations (IGOs), and other nongovernmental organizations (NGOs), ranging from broad-based consumer groups to specialized advocacy groups for environmental and humanitarian causes. These relationships enable the Confederation to mobilize collaboration for campaigns that promote the union agenda throughout the world. That agenda is intended to:

i.   promote and update adequate international strategies and policies on social rights, economic policies, international trade and employment promotion;
ii. oppose the gross exploitation of working people wherever it occurs;
iii. campaign and participate in the decision-making process for the establishment of international policies and standards to stop and reverse the drift to economic, social and environmental disaster, and to promote full employment, social and economic sustainable development; and,
iv. promote the growth of trade union membership throughout the world.
(ICFTU 1996b, 6, 7)

Although magazine and newspaper articles frequently recognize the Confederation as an authoritative voice on human and union rights issues, and the ICFTU's involvement in various international congresses and campaigns is regularly reported, there are few extended discussions of the Confederation in scholarly publications. The Confederation has been the subject of only a few brief chapters (e.g., Freeman 1985; Windmuller 1967; Windmuller and Pursey 1993), none of which thoroughly describes or analyzes its structure and operations. In this discussion I will describe the Confederation with particular emphasis on the collaborative manner in which the ICFTU attempts to promote human and trade union rights.

Origins of the ICFTU

Immediately following World War II, the most important confederation of trade unions was the World Federation of Trade Unions (WFTU), founded in 1945 and headquartered in Paris. The WFTU was dominated by trade unions from the Soviet bloc that espoused Marxist ideology and supported Soviet political and economic policy. Cold War pressures, including participation in the European Recovery Program and implementation of the Berlin blockade, soon brought about rifts among WFTU affiliates. In January

1949, unions from Western democracies, led by the delegations from Great Britain's Trades Union Congress (TUC) and America's Congress of Industrial Organizations (CIO), walked out of the WFTU. This action was welcomed by several national governments that were uneasy about the associations between domestic labor organizations and the communist unions in the WFTU.[1]

In July 1949, a conference convened in Geneva that was attended by fifty delegates from thirty-eight national labor centers, including international trade secretariats (ITSs), the AFL and the CIO,[2] and a few Christian unions. The conference agreed on the outlines of a new international labor organization in direct competition with the WFTU and in December 1949 the ICFTU was born. Initially, the Confederation represented 47 million members in sixty-six affiliated labor organizations in fifty countries. Throughout the Cold War, intense rivalry raged between the ICFTU and the WFTU. The two global labor organizations often supported rival union federations within a particular country as, for example, in Nigeria in the 1960s (Millen 1963). Labor organizations that sought to strengthen relations with the Confederation might be rebuffed if they attempted to work with the WFTU as well.[3] After the Cold War, the viability of the WFTU declined significantly.

ICFTU Structure

As of June 1999, the Confederation's membership had grown to 124 million, represented by 213 labor organizations in 143 countries and territories on six continents. Although the ICFTU will consider membership for individual unions, it is composed almost entirely of national union centers, each of which represents a number of unions in a particular country.[4] Affiliated unions represent workers both in the developing world and in highly industrialized nations. The umbrella of the ICFTU is broad enough to cover both relatively small national centers, such as Swaziland's Federation of Trade Unions and Tonga's Friendly Islands Teachers' and Nurses' Association, and relatively large centers like the AFL-CIO and the TUC. Its North American affiliates constitute a near monopoly of trade union representation in the region.

The governing body of the ICFTU is its Congress, with delegates from all its affiliates. The Congress meets every four years and elects an Executive Board and a General Secretary. The Board is responsible for directing the Confederation between Congresses and for electing the President and Vice-Presidents. Administration is the responsibility of the General Secretary.

The ICFTU's income is derived largely from affiliation fees levied on member organizations by the Congress. After annual increases of five percent from 1987 through 1994, affiliation fees were frozen until 1996. Financial exigencies made it necessary for the Congress to increase fees by three percent for 1997 and by one-and-one-half percent per year until 2000.[5]

The Confederation also derives income from sale of its publications, although this income declined from 1987 to 1994 (ICFTU 1992a; ICFTU 1996c). It is not clear whether this source of income will decline even further given the amount of information the Confederation provides on its website.

The ICFTU has achieved its growth in the face of countervailing forces. On the one hand is the stark reality that unions are struggling to maintain their membership in all employment sectors in both totalitarian countries and Western-style democracies. This phenomenon might be expected to reduce the size of the Confederation. On the other hand, the ICFTU has benefited from the democratization of many governments around the world, which has created political environments more supportive of free trade unionism (for example, in Central and Eastern Europe).

The ICFTU constitution limits membership to "free trade unions," which are defined as labor organizations that are not dominated by governments, political parties, or other external forces. Nonetheless, many of the Confederation's affiliates have close ties to socialist, social-democratic, and other political parties (Windmuller and Pursey 1993), and some affiliates clearly are influenced by their close ties to national governments. In fact, foreign policy conflicts among the national governments typically have been mirrored in conflicts that arise among the Confederation's constituent labor organizations (Busch 1980).

Economic and Political Heterogeneity

The Confederation is not committed to a particular economic or political philosophy. Most influential affiliates are politically and ideologically oriented toward either American business unionism or democratic socialism. Differences in philosophy have often caused conflicts among affiliates. For example, the AFL's two-year withdrawal from the ICFTU during the early stages of the Cold War in 1951 was, in part, a result of the Confederation's unwillingness to take as strong a stand against communism as George Meany recommended.

In this vein, contact with unions in the People's Republic of China has been a subject of recent internal debate. Despite its government's protestations to the contrary, there are no independent labor organizations in China. Indeed, many Chinese trade union activists have been jailed or forced to flee the country, and the *laogai* system (literally "reform-through-labor") is estimated to intern six to eight million people in forced labor.[6] The All-China Federation of Trade Unions (ACFTU), the only legal trade union, is controlled by the Communist Party (Islam 1994/95; Williamson 1994; Zhu 1995).

The Executive Board of the ICFTU attempted to marginalize the ACFTU by publicizing and supporting the activities of Shen Yinhan and Han Danfong, founders of the Beijing Workers' Autonomous Federation, and by adopting a firm no-contact policy after the Beijing massacre of June 1989. The Confederation reaffirmed its no-contact policy in 1994 over the objections of some important affiliates in the region, who cited national interest as a reason for favoring recognition of the ACFTU. Policy toward the ACFTU promises to be a continuing source of friction among the affiliates.

Regional Organizations

As a way of increasing its presence throughout the world and particularly to assist developing unions in Third World nations, the ICFTU was the first international union organization to successfully establish regional organizations that were solely operated by union officials from the regions themselves (Peterson 1963). The Confederation created a decentralized structure with three major regional organizations: the African Regional Organization (AFRO) headquartered in Nairobi, Kenya; the Asian and Pacific Regional Organization (APRO) headquartered in Singapore; and the Inter-American Regional Organization of Workers (ORIT in Spanish) headquartered in Caracas, Venezuela.[7] Consolidation within the regional organizations has proceeded at different rates. For example, the development of AFRO was hindered by the suppression of unions by many one-party governments. With the collapse of some of these regimes, AFRO began to grow and managed to re-establish its headquarters on African soil in 1994.

In theory, the regional organizations operate within a framework provided by the ICFTU's policies, although relationships between the regional organizations and Brussels have never been either uniform or strictly hierarchic (Windmuller 1967). The regional organizations have their own officers and enjoy a wide measure of autonomy, a subject of periodic and at times heated controversy. Due to the presence of strong national union federations in their areas that can offer financial support and leadership, APRO and ORIT have become relatively autonomous organizations. Nevertheless, the ICFTU still provides significant financing to both these regional organizations which, in turn, are required by statute to submit regular reports on their activities and financial transactions to the Executive Board.

Because of their proximity to the affiliates, the regional organizations act as channels of communication between affiliates and the ICFTU as a whole and are the Confederation's primary means for implementing programs. For example, from its outset the ICFTU provided financial assistance and faculty members to the regions to train union leaders at all organizational levels. The regional organizations also promote mutually supportive activities among affiliates. For example, issues surrounding the emergence of democracy on the African continent—the strengthening of political parties, representation in legislative bodies, and the independence of the judiciary—are matters of special concern within AFRO (ICFTU—AFRO 1995).

Among the most important responsibilities of the regional organizations is to support affiliates that are asserting union rights, especially in countries with undemocratic governments or political systems that are in transition from a military government to one-party rule to democracy. To this end, the regional organizations offer both moral and practical support to victimized labor organizations and trade unionists. Finally, the regional organizations discuss economic, political, and social policy in their respective areas with other concerned bodies (e.g., AFRO holds discussions with representatives of the Organization of African Unity), and they confer about trade union affairs with other regional labor organizations (e.g., APRO is in regular contact with the South Asian Regional Trade Union Council, the ASEAN Trade Union Council, and the North Pacific Trade Union Forum).

Standing Committees

A good deal of the ICFTU's work is performed by standing committees. The Steering Committee and the Finance and General Purposes Committee deal with administration. The Economic and Social Policy Committee advises the Executive Board on problems such as full employment, deficit spending by national governments, the behavior of multinational corporations (MNCs), and minimum standards for working conditions. The Human and Trade Union Rights Committee, established by the Executive Board in 1992, promotes cooperative union activities. This Committee brought together the different committees that dealt with rights violations in the regions in order to promote coordinated responses, while being sensitive to the views of the concerned national centers. It uncovers and publicizes violations of human rights and trade union rights, examines and makes recommendations on alleged violations, and assists in mobilizing the international labor movement for solidarity actions and campaigns. Many affiliates contact the Committee at the same time that they make appropriate representations to their own governments about violations. Communication has increased steadily each year; the number of contacts was approximately eight times greater in 1995 than in 1991 (ICFTU 1996a, 9).

ICFTU Campaigns

The ICFTU generally tries to avoid undertaking actions on its own. Rather, the Confederation attempts to mount multilateral strategies that involve other organizations with overlapping interests on particular issues. Hence it is customary for the ICFTU to operate as part of a variety of transnational social networks, each of which is defined by a particular trade union or human rights issue of concern to the cooperating organizations. The ICFTU typically mobilizes support for its campaigns by disseminating information about human and union rights issues, developing an alliance of concerned organizations, generating political and financial resources for the campaign, and conducting the action.

Information Clearinghouse

Because of their familiarity with the situation on the ground, unions are well placed to monitor the human condition throughout most of the world and to provide early warnings about emerging rights violations. Through contacts with its affiliates, the ICFTU maintains an international clearinghouse of information and research on problems of trade union organization, wages, working conditions, labor legislation, and collective bargaining.

The ICFTU acts as a spokesperson for international labor by discovering and publicizing injustices committed by governments or employers against the rights of unions and their members. To the degree that it is perceived to be vigilant and to have a credible voice, the ICFTU is a visible reminder to violators that their actions will not go unnoticed. It is unclear whether such anticipated attention has any power to deter rights violators and, indeed, there is ample evidence that, at least in the short run, some governments have not been influenced whatsoever by the Confederation's negative publicity. For example, the incarceration of trade union officials Frank Kokori and Milton Dabibi continued for approximately four years despite regular calls for their release by the Confederation and a number of ITSs, and only ended with the death of the Nigerian dictator, General Abacha.

ICFTU publications tend to report in a selective and partisan fashion. In the interests of solidarity, the Confederation's publications typically conceal controversies among its affiliates and internal factions. Rather than describe the opposing points of view, the Confederation's publications customarily ignore this dialectic process and postpone formal discussion of issues until authoritative positions have been formulated and adopted.

For many years, the ICFTU acted as an information base through its monthly newspaper, *Free Labour World*, its weekly telex news, and its press releases and publications. Today, greater use is made of the internet and the World Wide Web. The ICFTU's homepage[8] has links to pages that, for example, explain the main functions of the Confederation, list affiliated unions, and share educational resources about forming and strengthening unions. ICFTU publications are also available on the Web, including the *Annual Survey of Violations of Trade Union Rights*. The website is critical for mobilizing support for particular ICFTU campaigns. Under the "Trade Union Rights" link, sample letters of protest are provided that describe instances of rights violations. These letters are pre-addressed to government officials who allegedly are empowered to take action to end the violations. In 1996 the ICFTU launched a daily on-line news service to provide up-to-date information about labor issues around the world.

The *Annual Survey of Violations of Trade Union Rights* is the most widely circulated ICFTU document dealing with human rights issues. The Surveys are by no means exhaustive in their coverage of alleged violations of human and trade union rights. Rather, they focus on blatant violations of the ILO's Conventions 87 and 98 that pertain to freedom of association and collective bargaining, respectively (ICFTU 1995a, 1996a, 1997). Data are supplied by regional organizations, affiliates, ITSs, human rights groups, and the media. The ICFTU is attempting to improve both the reliability and the comprehensiveness of its monitoring system by creating an international network of national-center rights specialists and correspondents. Many of the specific complaints identified in the Survey are brought to the ILO's Committee on Freedom of Association by the ICFTU, one of its national affiliates, or an ITS. Such action may result in hearings during which governments are asked to respond to the charges. Parties that are found to have violated the ILO's conventions will be asked politely to bring labor practices into conformance with the Conventions.[9]

The largest portion of each Survey is devoted to reports on individual countries in which alleged violations have occurred. The number of countries cited for violations in either the public and private sectors has increased steadily since 1991, when fifty-three countries were named. By 1999, that number had expanded to 119. The increase appears to be due to current global economic conditions that stress the unfettered operation of commercial markets, the tendency toward a more hostile industrial relations environment, and improved reporting capabilities of the ICFTU's network of correspondents.

Collaborators

Over the years, the Confederation has collaborated with other organizations to amplify its voice on human and trade union rights. The ICFTU has consultative status with the United Nations system, the International Monetary Fund, the World Bank, and the World Trade Organization (WTO) and has worked with other NGOs when there has been a congruence of goals. International alliances often are formed to create "epistemic communities" (Haas 1992), transnational sets of experts in the fields of human rights, the environment, and the global economy. For example, a clear common interest exists between the Confederation and Amnesty International (AI) because many prisoners of conscience are trade unionists. Common interests have been defined with NGOs concerned about the environment, such as Greenpeace International and the World Wide Fund for Nature. Relationships with environmental groups typically are somewhat tenuous because of abiding union concerns that the expenses incurred by employers to improve environmental protections could threaten jobs.[10]

The ITSs
ITSs are international labor organizations composed of national unions concerned with a particular trade, profession, or industry (see Chapter 6). The ICFTU and the ITSs long have recognized the importance of cooperation and joint activity. The Milan Agreement represents a pledge by the ICFTU and the ITSs that they are in fact part of the same international trade union movement and that they intend to cooperate in all questions of common interest. The Agreement was created in 1951 and revised in 1969 and 1992. Each revision has provided for greater engagement between the

Confederation and the ITSs by increasing joint consultation and mutual representation in each other's governance structures. The Confederation (represented by the General Secretary) may take part in the General Conference of the ITSs as well as the important meetings of individual ITSs. In return, representatives of all ITSs are invited to participate in the Confederation's Executive Board meetings in a consultative status. Revisions of the Milan Agreement identified appropriate divisions of labor between the ITSs and the ICFTU that avoid duplication of activities and waste of resources. The Sixteenth World Congress in 1996 committed the Confederation to develop new partnerships between the ICFTU and the ITSs. Because the Confederation and the ITSs are supported by virtually identical labor constituencies, implementation of the Milan Agreement has rarely been a problem.

ICFTU/ITS working parties have operated for years to deal with MNCs, youth, women, education, and occupational health and safety. The two groups also mount joint missions to defend trade unionists. For example, an ICFTU-ITS delegation visited South Korea in February 1997 to visit workers imprisoned by the government for union activities occasioned by controversial changes in labor laws enacted during a quasi-clandestine session of the National Assembly. Included in the delegation, led by the president of APRO, was a representative from the ICFTU's Trade Union Rights Department and an official of the International Federation of Building and Woodworkers.

The ICFTU jointly sponsors with ITSs local and regional programs on human and trade union rights. For example, on the eve of the 1996 European Soccer Championships, the International Textile, Garment and Leather Workers Federation, the International Federation of Commercial, Clerical, Professional and Technical Employees, and the ICFTU pressured manufacturers of soccer balls in Pakistan to recognize basic ILO standards. The cooperative effort focused on the $750 million industry located around the city of Sialkot where three-quarters of the world's top-quality soccer balls are hand sewn and where 8,000 children worked in sporting goods factories (Islam 1997).

The United Nations

Collaboration between the Confederation and the UN was an outgrowth of the first significant successes of NGOs in lobbying for amendments to the world body's Charter in 1945. Article 71 was written to provide consultation arrangements for NGOs with the Economic and Social Council (ECOSOC) and to broaden the UN's objectives to include the promotion of human rights (Willetts 1996). The 1966 UN international covenants on

Economic, Social and Cultural Rights and on Civil and Political Rights make extensive reference to the right to organize and the right to strike, thereby enlarging the commonality of interests between the Confederation and the UN. Today the ICFTU has general consultative status with the ECOSOC, with the right to address the Council and its subsidiary committees, such as the Commissions on Human Rights and on the Status of Women.

The Confederation participates in major UN activities, such as the 1995 World Summit for Social Development, by preparing written and oral statements for consideration by the delegates, by lobbying delegates, and by following up to determine whether decisions made were implemented and had their intended impact. The ICFTU has also worked with a variety of UN commissions on women's and children's issues. For example, the Confederation helped to prepare, conduct, and evaluate the activities associated with the UN's Decade for Women 1975–1985, Year of the Child (1979), and International Youth Year (1985).

The ILO is a UN agency of special significance to unions (see Chapter 3). The ILO has a tripartite structure of delegates representing workers' organizations, employers, and governments. Although the composition of the delegations changes every year, the vast majority of workers' delegates represent unions that are affiliated with the ICFTU. WFTU affiliates from Cuba, Cyprus, and Vietnam and a handful of unions affiliated with the WCL also send worker delegates in any given year. The ILO is an important forum in which the Confederation defends human and trade union rights, which is one reason that the ICFTU maintains a full-time staff in Geneva. The Confederation has helped to formulate the ILO Conventions against which a country's observance of fair labor standards and union rights may be measured, has supported ILO initiatives to get more countries to ratify the Conventions, and regularly presents complaints against governments that violate Conventions 87 and 98, updates those charges as subsequent events warrant, and publicizes the ILO's decisions on those complaints.

Financial Support

The International Solidarity Fund was created to support actions that require financing on a scale greater than the normal means of the ICFTU. The Fund is derived from voluntary contributions, both responses to general appeals by the Executive Board and to special requests for earmarked projects. The original motivation for the Fund was to assist educational and organizing activities and to support ITSs, but it has been used to promote international solidarity and to offer temporary relief to individuals or families suffering as a result of their union activities.

The ICFTU provides financial aid from other sources as well. For example, special funds from a variety of budgetary sources were allocated in 1990 to support an ICFTU program to strengthen democratic union movements in Central and Eastern Europe.[11] This aid helped unions participate in the economic, social, and political transformations under way in the region. However, because of its own financial difficulties and increased reliance on grants from various governmental agencies, the ICFTU has had "to convert itself, for almost half of its income and activity, into a state-subsidized development-funding agency" (Waterman 1998, 354,355).

Campaigns for Basic Human Rights

The ICFTU has consistently advanced the idea that democracy and the observance of international labor standards are the foundation for successful and open economies. To that end, it has supported democratic movements in a number of countries that have denied basic human rights to their citizens.

South Africa and the Campaign against Apartheid

Beginning in 1948, the South African government introduced a variety of repressive measures known collectively as apartheid, to maintain control over the country's black majority. Intended as a mechanism to overturn apartheid, the Coordinated Program for South Africa was the ICFTU's single largest assistance program during the 1980s and early 1990s. Because of their role in promoting the civil rights of blacks, South African unions were regular targets of government repression. The headquarters of the Congress of South African Trade Unions (COSATU) and the National Council of Trade Unions (NACTU) were raided by the police, and restriction orders were placed on a number of trade union officials. Industrial action (work stoppages and demonstrations) were met by police violence, the killing of trade unionists, and mass dismissals.

The Confederation's program embraced several types of coordinated action. The ICFTU campaigned against new legislation intended to further restrict the rights of people of color and unions. The Confederation lobbied the governments of the European Community (EC) which in turn helped to prevent passage of the Promotion of Orderly Internal Politics Bill, which would have forced the disclosure of foreign financial aid received by labor organizations. In conjunction with COSATU and NACTU, in 1988 the ICFTU contributed to a massive campaign against a proposed Labor Relations Amendment Act that would have rescinded most rights possessed by South African unions.

The ICFTU fought for the release of imprisoned black leaders and trade union officials. It coordinated appeals for clemency for the Sharpville Six and the Alexandra Five. The ICFTU sent observers to these trials and provided funds for the legal defense. To publicize human rights abuses in South Africa, the ICFTU prepared a short commercial film, "Don't Buy Time for Apartheid," which won the Gold Lion Award at the 1987 Cannes Film Festival.

Perhaps most important in terms of the demise of apartheid, the ICFTU helped world organizations and governments to monitor the embargoes against the import of South African products. The ICFTU's South African Monitoring Unit was created in 1987 to supply information to affiliates in their campaigns for comprehensive economic sanctions and alerted them to instances of sanction-busting by a number of companies headquartered throughout the world.[12] The Unit also monitored violations of the UN Security Council's resolution on an arms embargo, the United States' Comprehensive Anti-apartheid Law, and other sanctions adopted by countries and organizations such as the EC.

In sum, the actions of the ICFTU and its affiliates helped bring about the downfall of apartheid. Not only did the ICFTU help to mobilize world opinion against discrimination against blacks, it provided direct support to South African unions that were in the forefront of the fight against apartheid.

Support for the Rights of Women

Full participation of women is essential to democratic societies and to democratic unions. Consequently, the Confederation's constitution was amended in 1983 to establish a special Women's Committee, with the right to elect two persons to the Executive Board. The constitution was amended again in 1992 to permit the Committee to nominate five members of the Board. The Committee prepares policy on equality and women's issues for adoption by the Executive Board and Congress (ICFTU 1994d). These policies are aimed at improving the living conditions and employment opportunities of women and at ensuring the representation of women workers within various international forums.[13]

The Confederation has organized a number of collaborative activities around women's rights. It has a permanent representative on the UN's Commission on the Status of Women and has contributed to the drafting of UN conventions on the rights of women (Connors 1996). The Confederation and its regional organizations regularly present workshops on union education and technical assistance on women's issues and organize and participate in world conferences on women's rights.

Members of the Women's Committee often participate in cooperative campaigns with affiliates and ITSs in solidarity with women workers and to protest violations of the rights of women trade unionists. These violations include death squad threats in Central America, murder of female union officials in Indonesia and Columbia, and arrests and beatings by Moroccan police of women workers protesting their dismissal for union activities (ICFTU 1996c, 178,179). *Free Labour World* publishes a supplement on these matters four times a year.

Support for the Rights of Children

The scourge of child labor (which is frequently, in fact, child slavery) is widespread and shows signs of increase in an alarming number of industrialized and developing countries. Because many of the most exploited and endangered working children go unnoticed (Leipziger and Sabharwal 1996), estimates of the amount of child labor vary and assessments of the participation rate differ from one country to another, but all are shockingly high. Enacting and enforcing laws that ban child labor is problematic due to the paucity of special interest groups that would support such legislation. Therefore unions, which have vested interests in all government and employer actions that affect employment, are important in mobilizing a constituency to defend children's rights.

In 1975 the Eleventh ICFTU World Congress adopted a Youth Charter that outlined the rights and conditions of working children, and subsequent Congresses have amended this Charter to expand the Confederation's commitment to dealing with child labor. The Charter has been used worldwide as a guide for unions attempting to establish the necessary minimum conditions for the advancement of the position of young people. Also, since the 1970s, an ICFTU/ITS Working Group on Young Workers' Questions has held programs to introduce young workers to the principles of unionism.

The Confederation has organized concerted actions for children's rights among its affiliates. For example, in 1992 and 1993 the Confederation organized a global union network with the financial support of its Norwegian affiliate, Landsorganisasjonen i Norge, to investigate and document child labor in a manner that was sensitive to labor market and other local conditions. The findings of this survey appeared in *Child Labor: The World's Best Kept Secret* (ICFTU, 1994b), a booklet published to help launch the

Confederation's Campaign Against Child Labor. Finally, the ICFTU has stressed the importance of trade-related measures in combatting child labor, including verifiable trademarks such as the RUGMARK that certifies that production of a carpet did not involve child labor.[14] A number of the Confederation's affiliates, including those in the United States, Germany, Norway, and Sweden, helped to introduce the RUGMARK to their countries.

Campaigns for Trade Union Rights

The primary function of the ICFTU is defending the right of workers to join the union of their choice. The threat to union rights is not a new circumstance, but the ICFTU believes that "our movement is now under attack on a global scale and with an intensity never before experienced in its history" (ICFTU 1996d, 5).

Given the number of complaints received by the ICFTU about rights violations, it has neither the time nor the resources to respond with concerted action to all requests for assistance. Therefore, after consultation with its regional organizations and affiliates, the Confederation has established standards and priorities for undertaking "targeted campaigns" in a limited number of situations. These decision criteria include "the gravity of the trade union rights situation; the commitment of the trade unions concerned to combating violations; the real potential for the campaign to bring improvements; and the presence of multinational enterprises which would facilitate the application of effective international leverage" (ICFTU 1994e, 26,27).

The ICFTU has been involved in two types of union rights campaigns: those designed to change the industrial relations environment worldwide and campaigns directed at specific employers.

Campaigns for International Labor Standards

The Confederation continues its long-running campaign for the acceptance of minimum labor standards throughout the world. This battle has been fought under the banner of the Social Clause. Trade unions that subscribe to the concept of a Social Clause typically support the version promoted by the ICFTU that would guarantee workers freedom of association, the right to collective bargaining, a minimum age for employment, nondiscrimination and equal remuneration, and prohibition of forced labor. Efforts to assure conformance with these minimum labor standards have been linked to initiatives on regional and world trade. For example, the Confederation continues to lobby the WTO for the imposition of minimum labor standards as a condition for international trade.

At the moment, many governments, especially among Asian nations, oppose the Social Clause or trade sanctions for labor rights violations. Nonetheless, lobbying by the U.S. affiliates of the ICFTU and ITSs and by key human rights activists in Washington has influenced the United States to raise the issue of labor standards at international conferences on trade and to exert pressure on other governments to improve working conditions. The ILO is presently considering a Confederation initiative that would make observance of core human rights standards a constitutional requirement for ILO membership and establish new supervisory mechanisms to promote this aim.

Campaigns for Union Rights Focused on MNCs

Both the Organization for Economic Cooperation and Development and the ILO have adopted codes of conduct for multinational corporations with respect to industrial relations. Despite the ICFTU's vigorous efforts to defend them, the codes have not substantially influenced MNCs to conform more closely to the requirements of the ILO Conventions.

The ICFTU and the ITSs have pledged a new partnership that will combine their separate strengths with those of other trade union centers to identify, publicize, and oppose MNCs that refuse to adopt decent pay and working conditions. A Working Party established by the ICFTU and the ITSs to explore approaches for dealing with MNCs has existed since the 1970s. The Working Party has considered establishing global trade union councils to represent the interests of workers in all the companies in which a particular MNC has holdings. The councils would try to achieve some type of working arrangement with the MNC headquarters, mainly to exchange information about the operations and future investment plans, matters that create considerable uncertainty and inhibit the development of good collective bargaining relationships. Another goal of global councils would be to provide mutual support to gain leverage on the MNC in specific situations. Such councils would have to be sensitive to the interests of the unions representing employees of the MNC, the relevant national centers, the various ITSs, and the ICFTU. A number of obstacles have interfered with the creation of MNC councils, including the high cost of international meetings and the lack of resources available to service all the global councils that would be necessary to deal with even just the very largest MNCs.

Campaigns for Union Rights at Particular Employers

The ICFTU has a long history of helping labor organizations enforce the rights of workers involved in struggles with their employers. One campaign involved the Pittston Company. In June 1989 the ICFTU responded to a request from the United Mine Workers of America (UMWA) and the Miners' International Federation (MIF) for assistance in a long and bitter lockout that threatened the economic security of both the workers and entire coal mining communities.

The ICFTU made a direct appeal to Pittston representatives to resume good-faith bargaining with the UMWA. The Confederation, the MIF, and affiliates in countries that imported Pittston products contacted Pittston's customers and asked them to persuade the company to resolve the disagreement. Officials from the ICFTU, MIF, and International Metalworkers Federation (IMF) met with representatives of Pittston, the UMWA, the AFL-CIO, several elected U.S. government officials, and the Secretary of Labor. Shortly after this mission, the Secretary appointed William Usery, a noted mediator, to help reach an agreement between the parties, Usery's recommendations were accepted and a new agreement was concluded.[15]

The ICFTU's Working Party on Multinational Companies carefully studied the Confederation's role at Pittston as a model for future cooperative efforts. The success of the ICFTU's involvement was attributed to several factors:

> First was the strong commitment of the national center and union directly concerned and the direct link between the dispute and the principles of freedom of association and the right to bargain collectively. Second, the personal involvement of the U.S. Secretary of Labor was important, as was the thorough research undertaken by the United Mine Workers, and the careful preparation for the mission. Third was the ICFTU's involvement as part of a plan for resolving the dispute, and the fact that the company's activities were international and spanned more than one industrial sector. (ICFTU 1992b, 55)

Conclusion

A much lengthier tome would be required to describe all the ICTFU's cooperative campaigns, such as its efforts to promote peace in the world and to improve occupational safety and health and the majority of its education and training activities. Despite my selective reporting of ICFTU activities, it is possible to draw certain conclusions about its work and its role in the future.

If the Confederation did not exist, trade unions would have to create a similar organization to deal with international matters on behalf of workers and national unions, which typically are organized to deal with local problems. Forums must be organized in order to identify and explore the common interests of trade unions and to develop relevant international policies that promote the viability of organized labor. Also, the activities of national centers must be coordinated prior to consultations with governments or IGOs. Over the years, unions worldwide have flocked to the Confederation's banner because it has become the institution best able and best positioned to coordinate the activities of national centers on behalf of free, organized workers.

Although the challenges it confronts are complex, the ICFTU must continue to encourage those who attempt to improve human and trade union rights in this turbulent economic era. Short of the start of a world military conflict, it will be impossible to put the global-economy genie back into its bottle. Market forces will continue to pressure employers to cut labor costs, thereby threatening the social fabric of some countries. Combined with its ideological commitment to democratic employment conditions, the Confederation's instrumental commitment to reform based on the economic self-interest of its members is likely to inspire more assiduous oversight of the workplace than that of politicians, well-meaning employers, or agencies solely driven by humanitarian agendas. Given these union commitments, it "is inconceivable that existing institutions or others that might be created could take over the functions of unions" (Sugeno 1994, 519).

A paradox underlies the activities of the ICFTU. On the one hand it is moved by an unshakable faith in the liberal principle that governments in both developed and undeveloped nations can serve the interests of society. On the other hand, the Confederation often finds itself at odds with governments when it attempts to advance its causes. In these situations the ICFTU has limited options for handling the disagreement. Neither the Confederation nor other NGOs have the capacity to compel a response from any government or other internal power holder such as employers or national union center, and none can order an intervention from powers outside (MacFarquhar, Rotberg, and Chen 1996). Indeed, unless it has been able to enlist the support of a major national or international power, the Confederation and its collaborators typically enter the fray with less economic and political clout than that of their government and MNC adversaries.

The Confederation's actions are confined primarily to formal protests to authorities, public demonstrations, missions of inquiry to put pressure on governments, or submission of cases to the ILO's Committee on Freedom of Association. These actions typically are frail levers with which to weaken or abolish the deeply embedded economic and political barriers to greater freedom for workers around the world. Diplomacy is essential in theory but too often unsuccessful when (as is common) no international or supranational mechanisms are available to constrain contending parties to negotiate or, especially, to stop governments or employers from persecuting labor leaders. Hence the ICFTU and other international NGOs must continue to rely on their ability to sway public opinion that often is fickle and to win political commitments that, just as frequently, may be ephemeral.

Despite its good efforts, the ICFTU has not been immune to criticism, much of which stems from the fact that the Confederation must contain "diverse political currents" (Southall 1995, 363). When the Confederation's stance on a particular issue does not satisfy the sometimes conflicting, if not incompatible, interests of its affiliates, complaints may be heard among its members. However, all national centers that attempt to represent unions with diverse interests (e.g., the AFL-CIO) are the targets of similar complaints.[16] The ICFTU's membership is steadily increasing, suggesting that, on balance, the benefits of Confederation membership are perceived to outweigh their costs.

The ICFTU, other NGOs, and IGOs have also been criticized for the slow pace of their campaigns and their uncertain outcomes. In part, the size of the Confederation and the diversity of interests that it represents militates against prompt action. In this vein, Dan Gallin, the General Secretary of the International Union of Food, Agricultural, Hotel, Restaurant, Catering, Tobacco and Allied Workers' Associations, believes that the Confederation "lives far too much in a bureaucratic and abstract world where form takes precedence over substance and preoccupations with turf, jurisdiction and status overshadow the original purpose of the exercise" (quoted in Lee 1997, 148). Given the pace of change in the global economy, one wonders whether any organization structured like the ICFTU can be nimble enough to lead labor's battles.

Although the Confederation is constantly searching for methods to react more quickly and effectively, it faces two fundamental problems. First, conflicts that involve the distribution of wealth are rarely settled without prolonged economic, political, legal, and/or military struggles. Second, given world order and domestic political realities, neither the IGOs (including the UN system) nor even powerful nations possess accepted means to intervene within a sovereign jurisdiction in order to settle partisan conflicts (Rotberg

1996). Consequently, the ICFTU must rely on slower and less certain methods to achieve its goals, including floating new ideas and approaches and pushing and embarrassing governments and IGOs to do their jobs.

Skeptics view the ICFTU as a relatively powerless organization that is remarkable only for its good intentions, its lengthy paper trail of disquieting but disregarded reports, and the numerous international junkets taken by its officials. These comments are understandable: admittedly, the ICFTU cannot impel action on the part of employers and governments despite the urgency of its message, and its worldwide constituency necessitates extensive travel. However, given the increasing significance of union cooperation at regional and global levels, some critics have reconsidered "both the symbolic significance (and the volume of the message to management) from international combine gatherings, even though the substance of policy formation at these is usually thin, and also the important potential even of merely informational exchanges" (Ramsay and Haworth 1990, 292).

Some criticisms of the Confederation may result from the fact that its accomplishments are often not reported in the global media. Recognizing the ICFTU's accomplishments is difficult for several reasons. Because of the collaborative nature of much of its work, it is often difficult to isolate and evaluate the impact of the Confederation's individual contributions to the outcome of a campaign. Its meetings with employers and government officials during labor disputes are often considered less newsworthy than the job actions taken by the troops on the ground, the local or national unions. Similarly, the Confederation's participation at trade conferences and meetings of IGOs may not receive coverage in the media because the most notable delegates at these events are government representatives and because many of the ICFTU's most significant contributions may involve behind-the-scenes preparation of position papers. Lastly, ego or political considerations cause some parties to fail to mention the collaboration of other participants in successful multilateral campaigns. Spokespersons for employers or governments may downplay or totally ignore the role of unions, the ILO, and human rights groups in bringing about highly publicized changes in employment relations.[17]

It is becoming more apparent that the cries of local and national unions need to be amplified by labor organizations with international constituencies and that "mass-based organizations can yell louder and with greater effect than more narrowly focused groups, however worthy" (Rotberg 1996, 264). The fact that the Confederation represents 125 million workers increases expectations that its pronouncements will receive attention, especially from public officials who do not have any particular constituents of their own. By taking up the chants of activists who are struggling to win or expand human and trade union rights, the Confederation provides an international presence that may be a source of hope. "It assures them that they are not alone, that their work is important, and that their suffering will not go unnoticed by the outside world" (Mahony and Eguren 1997, 2). Without hope for a better human condition, futility wins the day and people meekly accept their circumstances.

In conclusion, it is necessary to provide men and women with a framework to mobilize themselves in favor of the great ideals of human and workers' rights. To this end, the Confederation acts as a "universal labor conscience" (Windmuller 1967, 89) by presenting a generalized trade union position on current affairs before IGOs and governments. The ultimate goal of the ICFTU is to convince the peoples and governments of the world that promoting worker and trade union rights is in their self-interest. The Confederation's challenge for the future is "to show that full respect for trade union rights is good for working people, good for societies, and indispensable to successful development and social justice in all countries, regardless of their economic and social system, their geographical location, their culture, or their level of industrialization" (ICFTU 1994e, p. 30). The Confederation helps these aspirations to take form and, in some cases, to flourish.

6

The International Trade Secretariats

JOHN P. WINDMULLER

International trade secretariats (ITSs) are the international associations of national trade unions representing workers in specific industries, industry groups, occupations, professions, or other sectors of employment such as the public services. They originated to help national unions represent their members' international interests through exchanges of information, solidarity actions, publicity, research, and liaison with other organizations, both national and international, governmental and private. Because of the remoteness of most secretariats from the day-to-day concerns of North American unions, it is remarkable that over two-thirds of American national unions are affiliated with at least one ITS. Economic interest is one reason, but political considerations and a sense of international solidarity, especially among top leaders, also play a role.

Economic interests hinge on the belief that the secretariats, as coordinating bodies, are at least to some degree able to help improve labor standards in countries where wages are appreciably lower than in the United States, thus improving the competitive position of American industry in world markets and protecting the jobs of American workers. Obviously self-interest is a stronger motivation in the case of unions operating in highly competitive international markets (textiles and automobiles, among others) than in more protected or even immune sectors (civil service, teaching, construction).

American unions also frequently subscribe to the notion that by belonging to the proper ITS they are strengthening the forces undergirding political democracy and free trade unionism in the world. That may well be the case, although the massive collapse of Communist-led societies, including Communist-led trade unions, has diminished the plausibility of the political factor as a cementing element.

Historical Background

International unionism is mainly a product of the late nineteenth century. At that time, a set of international (i.e., European) trade union organizations was founded. In several trades reciprocity agreements had long existed between unions in different countries, to assist members traveling abroad in obtaining work and having their membership cards honored by the local organizations. In some cases the unions had exchanged informal mutual aid pledges to prevent the recruitment and cross-border transport of strikebreakers. But the effectiveness of these arrangements often suffered from the lack of sustained contact. Eventually it became obvious that improvements depended on creation of formal organizations. The first to unite were several unions of shoemakers, which in 1889 founded the International Federation of Boot and Shoe Operatives. Others followed, notably the miners (1890), clothing workers (1893), typographers (1893), metalworkers (1893), textile workers (1894), lithographers (1896), glove makers (1896), transport workers (1896), tobacco workers (1897), hatters (1900), and several others. By 1914 almost thirty organizations had been founded, each one based on a particular trade, sometimes an industry. Collectively they were known as the international trade secretariats.

Although their national affiliates were almost always part of the socialist movement in their own countries, from their beginnings the ITSs devoted their efforts chiefly to prosaic rather than ideological aims: exchanging information on wages and working conditions, combatting international strikebreaking attempts by employers, extending aid to traveling journeymen, encouraging reciprocity agreements by their affiliates to ensure the mutual recognition of union cards, and mobilizing international support in periods of grave industrial conflicts.

When World War I ended, several of the weaker secretariats decided to merge. For instance, in 1920 the three ITSs in bakeries, breweries, and the meatcutting trades formed a single organization for food and drink workers (today it is the International Union of Food, Agricultural, Hotel, Restaurant, Catering, Tobacco, and Allied Workers Associations—IUF). In general, the mergers undermined the original craft or "trade" basis of most secretariats and moved them toward a more industrial-type structure. The trend reflected parallel developments at national levels in most countries during the 1920s and 1930s. No significant changes in the aims of the ITSs occurred during the inter-war period, although many were weakened by the decline and ultimately the destruction of important affiliates in countries under dictatorship rule or foreign occupation (especially Italy, Germany, Austria, Spain, and Czechoslovakia). The outbreak of World War II in 1939 forced most ITSs to suspend their work, though not necessarily their existence.

In 1945, a large majority of union federations in the allied countries established a new and all-embracing World Federation of Trade Unions (WFTU). East-West coexistence in the WFTU did not last long, and most Western trade unions disaffiliated in 1949 to a new body, the International Confederation of Free Trade Unions (ICFTU; see Chapter 5). Contributing substantially to the split in the WFTU was a sharp difference of opinion over the proper place of the secretariats. From the beginning the Communist affiliates proposed the integration of the ITSs into the WFTU structure, which would have meant the end of the secretariats as independent organizations. Most ITSs vigorously opposed integration as making them permanently subordinate to and dependent on the WFTU. Of considerable importance in bolstering the resistance of the Secretariats was the massive entry of previously unaffiliated American unions, especially AFL national unions, which had formerly shown little interest in international labor affairs.

Since the 1970s the ITSs have changed in several important ways. First, their membership is now much more widely distributed among the various regions of the world. Although most still rely chiefly on their affiliates in Western Europe and North America, others have set up bases in Japan, Australia, and New Zealand and increasingly in the less developed countries of Asia, Africa, and Latin America. To service them effectively and respond quickly to specific regional needs, most ITSs have established regional administrative subdivisions, even though the relationship of the regions to the center is not likely to be smooth.

Second, while aggregate ITS membership increased during the 1990s, the trend toward mergers has reduced the number of secretariats to eleven.

Third, almost all ITSs have become industrial and multi-industrial organizations. Only a few still represent a craft or occupation, although the original craft and trade bases live on in the functional sections and departments that many ITSs have established.

Fourth, many ITSs have tried to meet the challenge of the rise of multinational corporations (MNCs) by creating countervailing structures and adapting their policies. The ability to respond to requests for help from their constituents in the less developed countries is a particularly important item on the ITS agenda.

Fifth, the collapse of Communist rule in Central and Eastern Europe has created opportunities for growth. While learning to distinguish genuinely independent union organizations from adherents of the discredited old order, the ITSs have initiated trends toward democracy, opened their membership rolls to new affiliates, and instituted extensive education and training programs.

Organization and Structure

ITSs are autonomous organizations. Each one operates under its own constitution and determines its own policies, governance, and activities. In almost every instance their funds are contributed by the affiliated unions, mostly in the form of fees based on the number of individual members. Decision-making authority is vested in the governing bodies and officers of each secretariat, and in theory there is no superimposed or overarching organization to which the ITSs are accountable.

In this vein, the relationship between the ITSs—as individual bodies or as a group—and the ICFTU is not entirely one of equals, for reasons of structural and functional differences. Whereas the ICFTU is composed of national union federations, individual national unions comprise the ITSs. Whereas the secretariats tend to emphasize their specific sectoral problems, the ICFTU claims to speak on behalf of all workers, whether organized or not, and aspires to do so at the broadest levels of social, economic, and political policy. The basic terms of the ICFTU-ITS relationship are laid out in the Milan Agreement originally adopted in 1951 and since amended. Both sides to the original Agreement affirmed that they were constituent parts of a single international trade union movement, that they would cooperate in matters of joint concern, and that on major policy issues the secretariats would follow the general line of the ICFTU.[1]

Notwithstanding the considerable differences in size, resources, effectiveness, leadership, and cohesiveness that imbue each ITS with a specific character, the secretariats share a wide range of interests and problems, certainly wide enough to make a regular exchange of views profitable. The ITSs meet annually in a General Conference, and in recent years a second meeting has been held in conjunction with the annual meetings of the International Labor Organization (ILO). Agenda items include labor education and training (especially in less developed countries), technical services for affiliated unions, infringements of trade union rights, and program coordination, including dealings with multinationals. The ICFTU is always in attendance and usually represented by its leading officials.

Contrary to downward union membership trends in virtually every country (Scandinavia excepted), most ITSs seem to have been spectacularly successful in attracting new members from the end of the 1970s to the mid-

1990s, especially in the realm of white collar employees. The ITS for teachers, the Education International (EI), has become the largest secretariat, with 24 million members, exceeding even the 20-million–member Public Services International (PSI) and the Chemical, Energy, Mine, and General Workers (ICEM). Impressive increases have occurred in most other ITSs, but not in all. The Transport Workers Federation (ITF), once one of the two or three largest, has not grown appreciably since 1979. The IUF has grown at a more measured pace.

One factor accounting for the growth of the ITSs is the emergence of acceptably free and independent unions in Eastern Europe, some with roots in the pre-Communist period. This has sometimes resulted in the emergence of a large number of "recruitable organizations" that need international recognition and expect the kind of technical and educational assistance that the better-staffed secretariats can provide. To illustrate: in 1990, the International Federation of Commercial, Clerical, and Technical Employees (FIET) had one affiliated organization in all of Eastern and Central Europe. In 1994, it had nineteen.

Most ITS growth, however, can be traced to consolidation. Gradually, merger by merger, the ITSs have transformed themselves from single-craft organizations into multi-craft or industrial unions, and nowadays most may be regarded as multi-industrial unions. An apt example is the International Textile, Garment and Leather Workers' Federation (ITGLWF), which assumed its present shape in 1970 when the International Textile and Garment Workers' Federation merged with the International Federation of Boot and Shoe Operatives and Leather Workers. The two organizations were themselves the outcome, years earlier, of mergers by their predecessor organizations. The Union Network International (UNI) provides another example of mergers among ITSs that created a more heterogeneous industrial secretariat from unions with a somewhat narrower craft focus. Launched in 1999 by the merger of FIET, Communications International, and Media Entertainment International, UNI represents 15.5 million members from more than 140 countries worldwide. The 900 affiliated unions is the largest grouping of individual trade unions of all the ITSs, and among its members are actors, graphic artists, writers, hairdressers, technicians, members of a variety of clerical occupations, and postal and communication workers. (See Chapters 8 and 11 for additional information about mergers in the media and telecommunications industries.)

Growth by expanding the types of industries represented is exemplified by the International Metalworkers' Federation (IMF), whose own rules define the organization's jurisdiction as manual and non-manual workers "in metal producing and processing industries and the metal trades." This deceptively simple definition encompasses an enormously wide range of industries, including basic steel, iron and nonferrous metals, automobiles, shipbuilding, electrical and electronic machinery, aerospace, fabricated metals, and several others. Similarly, the membership of the ITF includes, according to the organization's own claim, all forms of transportation—by rail, road, air, ocean shipping, and inland navigation—as well as fisheries, dockside work, and even travel agency employees.

Conflicting principles of organization have created problems between ITSs. For example, the occupation-oriented claims of FIET to represent all white collar and managerial employees, no matter where they work, collided with the industry-centered claims of other ITSs to represent all employees in a particular sector regardless of occupation. Potentially even more troublesome have been overlapping territorial-industrial claims. The ITGLWF and the ICEM both have a proprietary interest in the man-made fiber industry. The Chemical Workers (ICEF) and the Miners' International Federation (MIF) both claimed to represent workers in the energy sector. The PSI and FIET both had an interest in representing the employees of national social insurance administrations, whereas the Postal, Telegraph and Telephone International (PTTI) and the PSI both claimed certain categories of public employees. Almost all conflicting assertions have been resolved through negotiations or mergers, such as the merger of the ICEF and MIF to create the present ICEM.

Failures of mergers are rare, but they do occur. The most stubborn jurisdictional dispute in the last few decades involved the former ICEF and the former International Federation of Petroleum and Chemical Workers Union (IFPCW). Both claimed rights in the petrochemical and petroleum-producing and refining industries. An attempt to settle the dispute through merger ended in failure. Eventually the IFPCW ran out of funds and suspended operations. Some of its affiliates later joined the ICEF.

Membership: Rules and Trends

Each secretariat follows its own rules for the acquisition, maintenance, and loss of affiliates. Although there is considerable diversity, certain rules are virtually standard. For instance, in order to become or remain an ITS-affiliated organization, a union almost invariably must be national in scope, must subscribe to the general policies of the secretariat, must meet its financial obligations in a timely manner, and must abide by the decisions of the ITS's governing bodies. Failure to comply with the rules could lead to penalties, including suspension and expulsion. But penalties are rarely imposed. In fact, even in serious financial delinquency cases most secretariats are prepared to negotiate a rescheduling of dues payments.

All secretariats are committed to support political democracy, and some of them stipulate in their constitutions that member unions are expected to conduct their internal affairs democratically. The question of what to do about membership applications from unions affiliated with a Communist-led trade union federation was raised frequently during the 1980s, particularly with regard to the Italian CGIL and the Spanish CCOO, both being under Communist control.[2] Some ITSs were quick to admit unions from former Communist countries; others first wanted applicants to give a convincing demonstration of their independence from state and political parties.

ITS constitutions often entitle affiliates to consultation when a union from an already-represented country applies for membership. Although most actions on membership are uncontested, occasionally an application leads to controversy, as in the case of the building workers secretariat (IFBWW) and a group of American building trades unions.[3] At one time it was the rule that an ITS could have only one affiliate per country, but this provision became untenable when the secretariats abandoned their trade or craft structure and turned themselves into industrial or even multi-industrial organizations. Conversely, it is by no means rare nowadays for a national union whose domestic jurisdiction cuts across several sectors to be affiliated with more than one ITS. Payment of dues to the respective ITSs usually is proportional to the distribution of that union's membership among the industries and occupations represented in its ranks.

Internal Government

The secretariats show certain similarities of governmental structure. Supreme power is invariably vested in a congress, whose composition is designed to be representative of the various industrial and geographic interests. All affiliates in good financial standing are entitled to be represented by delegates, whether in proportion to the number of individual members for whom affiliation fees have been paid, or according to a regressive scheme of representation that is usually intended to increase the weight of the smaller affiliates vis-a-vis the larger ones.

Most ITSs nowadays hold their congresses every four years. Not very long ago the intervals were considerably shorter—two or three years. The high cost of holding a congress was a major factor in the shift to a four-year cycle. Other reasons were the development of regional meetings at fairly regular intervals and the vast improvement in international communications. Both made possible closer contact between secretariat headquarters and the affiliates.

In most secretariats the congresses deal chiefly with economic and social problems affecting the industry or occupation concerned, especially proposals for protecting and improving the terms of employment through internationally coordinated action. Congresses also elect the organization's officers and executive bodies; review staff reports of activities; debate, adopt, or reject (rarely) resolutions on current political, social and economic issues that sometimes seem peripheral to the central concerns of a secretariat; set the level of financial contributions; and confirm or redefine the organization's direction.

Reducing the frequency of congresses has probably increased the importance, and almost certainly the size, of the executive bodies. Some of the larger secretariats with highly diverse constituencies, whether geographically or industrially, have expanded their boards substantially to become more representative. In years past, most board seats were reserved, either by constitutional provision or informal understanding, for Western European affiliates, in keeping with the overwhelmingly European identity of the membership. Pressure from more recent non-European affiliates for a stronger voice in decision-making led many ITSs to adopt the most politically acceptable solution, namely enlargement of the boards rather than redistribution of a fixed number of seats.

Each ITS is headed by a general secretary who is the highest-ranking full-time official and invariably the key person in the organization. Until some time after World War II, the general secretaries of virtually all ITSs served only on a part-time basis. As late as the 1960s, the IMF, then already one of the two or three leading secretariats, was still administered by a part-time general secretary who served concurrently as secretary of the Swiss Metalworkers and Watchmakers Union. Such an arrangement would be out of the question nowadays. In the larger organizations the staff may easily consist of thirty or more employees, among them research and education specialists, field representatives, translators, and clerical and technical personnel.

With one short-lived exception the ITSs have always made their headquarters in Europe.[4] The choice of location within Western Europe has usually depended on a few key factors: the ability to work unhindered by the public authorities, the presence in the host country of a strong and internationally oriented labor movement, and a reasonably central location. Since the beginning of the postwar period, Geneva and Brussels have emerged as the two favored locations. ITS headquarters in Geneva have ready access to the ILO, the intergovernmental body of greatest importance to their work. Brussels has become the nearest thing to the capital of Europe and also serves as headquarters for the ICFTU and the ETUC.

The effectiveness of a secretariat is determined above all by its general secretary. The most successful general secretaries have a keen political sensitivity, adaptability in dealings with heterogeneous constituencies, and a gift for administering a complex multinational and politicized organization. Some general secretaries owe their positions to a record of long experience in international trade unionism, though not necessarily with a particular secretariat. Others have come directly from elective or appointive union office, usually in an affiliated national union.

A general secretary can expect to remain in office until he reaches retirement age, provided only that his performance is considered at least adequate. Open contests for filling a general secretaryship are infrequent. The most influential affiliated unions generally secure informal agreement on a successor and the election becomes a formality. Absent an obvious first-choice candidate, the outcome may have to be negotiated. If that fails, open competition will probably be allowed, although that is not certain. Most unions, whether national or international, fear the divisive effects of hard-fought electoral campaigns on organizational cohesiveness and try to avoid genuinely open contests. If a contest does occur, the consequences can be costly.

Trade Groups and Regional Bodies

In view of the diversity of industries and occupations represented in their ranks, and also because of the strength of regional identities, most ITSs have established a corresponding administrative structure. Trade groups are of longer standing and are based on industrial-occupational considerations; regional bodies were formed along territorial lines only after World War II.

In multi-industry secretariats, trade groups disseminate information useful to their national union affiliates in a particular industrial sector. In some secretariats, trade groups also function in the ITS's internal government. Thus seats on the executive committee of the ITGLWF for a time were allocated to the three industrial sectors (textile, garment, and leather) in proportion to their share of the total membership. In some ITSs the trade groups hold their own meetings and elect their own officers.

Regional ITS structures are usually formed in response to some combination of internal pressures and centrifugal forces. Affiliates in less developed countries have demanded more autonomy and more representation in the decision-making bodies of their ITSs, and quite a few secretariats have formed regional organizations with their own regional executive committees, convened regional conferences, and established regional offices. Some ITSs, however, have, done considerably less, at least for the time being, perhaps going no further than setting up a regional bureau staffed by a field representative or advisor from the central office and accountable only to it. Indeed, some ITSs have not done even that much. The response to regional concerns and strivings has varied.

Finances

Rare exceptions aside, the secretariats depend for their income on annual affiliation fees paid by their member organizations. Only a few ITSs have ever required substantial subsidies. The most important was the former Plantation and Agricultural Workers Secretariat (IFPAAW), whose members were and still are among the lowest paid. The IFPAAW received sizable support, mainly from the ICFTU, after it was founded in 1961. Its merger with the IUF in 1993 resolved its financial difficulties.

Each secretariat determines its own schedule of membership fees and the variations are considerable. Probably a majority levy a fixed sum per individual member per year; others express their membership fees in percentages. Indeed, paying an affiliation fee is not a negligible item for most unions. The amount can become too much even for a relatively well-financed union in a wealthy industrialized country. Under particularly adverse circumstances, for example a change in currency exchange rates, the burden can become quite formidable. For these reasons, many secretariats grant sizable fee reductions to their member unions, sometimes even full waivers. But waivers must be requested. Frequent failures by affiliates claiming poverty to apply for dues reductions have led at least one secretariat, the ICEM, to stipulate that, if an affiliated organization has neither paid its fee nor applied for a reduction as of a given date, it will be considered to have disaffiliated.

Although affiliation fees constitute by far the largest source of income for virtually all ITSs, quite a few obtain additional income from special levies, voluntary contributions from the wealthiest affiliates, and grants by public agencies and private foundations. Grantors, whether wealthy affiliates or government agencies, typically monitor the uses to which their contributions are put to ensure that their funds are used only for agreed purposes. The most important grantors subsidizing the regional activities of the secretariats in less developed countries are the German Friedrich-Ebert-Stiftung Foundation, the Solidarity Center of the AFL-CIO, the Scandinavian trade union centers, and the principal Dutch trade union federation, FNV. These organizations, however, are not necessarily the original financiers of assistance projects. Rather the funds may well come from the foreign aid allocations of national governments that have decided to channel assistance payments in part through unions, foundations, or equivalent bodies. Most secretariats see no obstacle to accepting funding from governments.

Aims and Activities

Trade unions tend to proclaim their aims in language that combines idealistic elements with practical considerations. The secretariats are no exception. They too pledge to strive for a just and humane social order, to engage in unrelenting defense of human rights and democratic institutions, to wage a continuing struggle for peace and freedom, to foster the permanent abolition of all forms of dictatorship and military regimes, to eliminate excessive disparities in wealth and incomes, to advance international solidarity among workers, and to promote faithfully the interests of their constituents.

It is of course the last item which most nearly reflects the day-to-day concerns of the secretariats; in most ITS constitutions the sections outlining activities deal almost entirely with ways of defending and promoting the interests of their constituent unions. It has generally been agreed that concentration on tangible matters must be the primary task of the secretariats.

Information and Research

Before the end of the nineteenth century, most internationally oriented trade unionists already understood that one of the most important tasks of the secretariats, if not the most important one, was promoting a steady exchange of information about conditions of employment, country by country. That has been the case and still is.

An example of information dissemination is the survey conducted every few years by the International Graphical Federation (IGF) among its affiliated unions. The results appear in special issues of the organization's publications. They include data on negotiated maximum and minimum wage rates for skilled and unskilled workers, differences between negotiated rates and actual pay, maximum and minimum weekly hours of work, number of annual vacation days, premiums for overtime, shift, and holiday work, manning tables for various kinds of machinery, and mandated health and safety provisions. Over the years, new items have been incorporated into the survey, such as those dealing with the health impact of video display screens.

Like most secretariats, the IGF does not have the resources to do more than present its findings in an orderly way. Consequently, the largely unevaluated information, though still useful for comparative purposes, is likely to be of only limited value for the affiliates' collective bargaining. Some of the larger and financially stronger secretariats have computerized a considerable body of information, such as general employment conditions in their industry, employment trends, and data on the major companies. Because it was one of the first of the ITSs to become literate in today's communication technology, the ICEM claims to be receiving over a thousand requests for information and help from its affiliates each year (as well as many more requests for data from non-affiliated organizations). The ICEM has combined several of its data bases with several commercial data bases that deal with the financial status of companies into a single centralized source of information.

Most ITSs have given increased attention to occupational health and safety and to protection of the environment. These concerns have led to studies, publications, conferences, and other means of calling attention to the issues. Over the years, several secretariats have collaborated in a joint venture, such as a successful 1984 conference on the effects of visual display units on worker health. In June 2000, the PSI and IMF were among a number of ITSs that participated in an unsponsored review of the outcomes of the Copenhagen Social Summit.

Support in Industrial Disputes

A secretariat's ability to intervene supportively in an industrial dispute is determined by the invariably modest resources available, by its ability to mobilize support among affiliates in other countries, and, most of all, by the extent to which an affiliate expects results from ITS assistance. Most disputes run their course without any request for ITS involvement, but sometimes unions under pressure do seek international support. This is the case particularly where a company, most likely an MNC, is vulnerable to pressure exerted on subsidiary enterprises or is sensitive to threatened restrictions on the movement of its products in international markets.

Although the secretariats have long sought to be recognized as coordinators of international action on behalf of their members, the actual scope of such efforts has almost always been modest. Mobilizing significant financial support has been infrequent. The secretariats do not maintain their own strike funds and even if they did would probably not be able to collect substantial sums. Nevertheless, an ITS endorsement of an affiliate's call for support from organizations in other countries can be useful. Such an endorsement signals to other unions that the ITS has investigated the dispute and found it deserving, a finding that fraternal organizations in other countries are usually not well equipped to make by themselves.

Under some circumstances, international assistance may take the form of a boycott conducted or supported by a secretariat. Examples from the past would include the strike and boycott actions initiated by the former Amalgamated Clothing and Textile Workers in the United States against the Farah Manufacturing Company and the J.P. Stevens Company. In both cases the ITGLWF responded effectively to its American affiliate's request for international expansion of the domestic boycott. It must be noted, however, that ITS solidarity appeals to fraternal sentiments do not always automatically draw a favorable response, nor do individual unions invariably place such appeals at the top of their own agendas.

Regional Activities

For the past several decades, organizing drives, education, and training in less developed countries have been major items in the budgets of almost every ITS. The aim has been to strengthen labor organizations in less developed countries to the point where they can operate independently, represent the interests of their members effectively, support democratic institutions, and contribute to the modernization and advancement of their societies.

The needs that regional activities are intended to meet do not differ much from one country to another. Regional ITS activities include training union officers, providing guidance in organizing, consolidating fragmented and competitive union structures, identifying urgent needs for social and labor legislation, and preparing negotiators for participation in collective bargaining and complaints procedures. To carry out these tasks the secretariats have stationed field representatives in target areas, organized courses and seminars, made grants available to local leaders for observation and

advanced study in other countries, supplied financial support for administrative needs (such as maintaining an office), and, ón occasion, provided the
funds for day-to-day operating expenses.

The work has not been free of obstacles, and results have often been
slower to materialize than expected. The governments of most less developed countries are usually unenthusiastic about attempts to strengthen the
unions, which may constitute a potential political threat to their authority (or at least represent a serious nuisance). Governments also fear that
strengthening unions could discourage foreign and domestic investment
capital and further widen the urban-rural income gap.

Government hostility is only one of the problems. In many countries, legislation—often stemming from the colonial period—impedes union activity and facilitates employer resistance to organizing (see Chapter 3). Other
obstacles include linguistic and ethnic divisions, illiteracy, the backward
state of the local infrastructure, the susceptibility to corruption of officials
in various walks of life (including the unions themselves), and the over-
whelming role of government.

Assistance to Special Groups

Most secretariats consider it part of their social responsibility to pay
particular attention to the problems of certain groups, notably women and
young workers but also migrants and pensioners. As regards women workers, many ITSs, including the ITF and IFBWW, have established a Women's
Committee. The minimum position is a formal, on-the-record expression
of support for equal treatment in all aspects of employment, including
pay, job security, training, promotional opportunities, and participation on
equal terms in union activities. It may also include an endorsement of special measures for women: pregnancy and maternity leaves and provision of
child care at the workplace. A number of ITSs have organized women's
conferences or conducted special training for women members. Altogether
the ITSs have devoted significant attention to the place of women in unions.

ITSs have also paid attention to the special problems faced by young
workers in the labor market, but the work does not quite match the efforts
made on behalf of women. Some youth conferences have dealt with education, vocational training, health and safety at the workplace, and attitudes
toward unions, but on the whole young workers have received more attention from the ICFTU than from the secretariats.

With exceptions, that observation also holds true of immigrant workers.
Even in the best of times this is a difficult subject for the ITSs because of the

almost inevitable clash of interests (and cultures) between domestic and immigrant workers and because of the ensuing reluctance on the part of many unions to become aggressively outspoken advocates and protectors of immigrant workers. Even in those relatively few cases where an ITS has made a special effort to alleviate the problems of "guest workers," notably the IMF, the accent has been on items of quite general importance: worker solidarity, equality of treatment, acceptance of cultural differences, and the need for more information programs.

Relations with Intergovernmental Organizations

Most secretariats maintain ongoing contacts with IGOs operating in their domains. Thus the trade section for Plantation and Agricultural Workers within the IUF cultivates links with the Food and Agricultural Organization of the United Nations; the ITF frequently deals with at least half a dozen IGOs such as the International Civil Aviation Organization; and the EI keeps abreast of developments at UNESCO. In a world of proliferating international agencies such liaison work may become a taxing effort, especially for the more thinly staffed ITSs, but it is a necessary one if IGOs are to take into account the interests of wage earners and their organizations. For example, establishment and enforcement of minimum safety-at-sea standards is of such vital concern to the ITF that it must stay abreast of the perhaps obscure intergovernmental Maritime Organization.

For the ITSs as a whole, the ILO has the greatest significance because of its constitutional mandate to develop a body of international social and labor policies and legislation. The ITSs have attached special importance to the ILO's tripartite Industrial Committees and have frequently, but not very successfully, urged the ILO to establish committees in more industries. The committees' meetings often are characterized by a certain amount of de facto bargaining between employer and worker members, especially over the formulation of non-binding resolutions on hours of work, safety standards, vocational and apprenticeship training, employment security, productivity, and labor-management relations. The ITSs brief the worker members of the committees, who for the most part are also their constituents, on issues coming before the meetings, handle the staff work, and try to maintain a unified front of worker members.

Transnational Labor-Management Relations

One of the most important activities of the ITSs has been to support the collective bargaining goals of their affiliates by making available information relevant to negotiations and by mobilizing supportive efforts by other unions. As long as collective bargaining remains a national rather than an international activity, a supportive role is about as close to the actual negotiating process as most ITSs are likely to get. For a few ITSs, however, the proliferation and growth of MNCs together with accelerating developments in the European Union have opened up wider prospects. Because of the large number of MNCs active in their sectors, the IMF, the ICEM, the IUF, and perhaps the ITGLWF are likely to be among the ITSs most active in approaches to transnational bargaining.

Past initiatives for confronting the multinationals have come from both the ITSs and their affiliates. In the domain of the IMF it was the United Automobile Workers, one of its key affiliates, that promoted the formation of world auto councils in the 1950s. Although not widely supported at the time, this was the first attempt to create an employee representation structure potentially capable of being a countervailing force to the auto MNCs. A renewed effort in the 1960s was more successful. In other instances, as in the case of the former Chemical Workers (now ICEM), the impetus came from the ITS's central office. Whatever the instrument, the formation of corporation councils has been one of the more tangible responses by the ITSs to meet the challenge of the corporations. In the IMF, which is still one of the pacesetters, the councils now exist in other industries besides auto, especially in electrical and electronics. The ICEM has created online networks of unions at the national, regional, and local levels who negotiate with Bridgestone tire company and the Rio Tinto mining corporation.

While they facilitate coordination and cooperation among unions in different countries, neither the corporation councils nor the ITSs have yet been able to obtain employer recognition as bargaining agents in the conventional meaning of that term. Measured against that objective, they are not sufficiently strong and homogeneous. Nevertheless, they do perform some useful functions, particularly in information exchange, international solidarity actions, intervention at corporate headquarters on behalf of unions in subsidiaries, and submission of complaints alleging employer violations of international norms or guidelines promulgated by an international agency, such as the ILO or the OECD.

None of these activities, however, has resulted in actual participation in collective bargaining by an ITS. Negotiations between an MNC and the several organizations representing its employees cannot get under way without employer participation. If recognition and bargaining rights are not voluntarily granted, they would have to be obtained either through the power of government or through the strength and determination of the employees' side. Currently neither of these conditions exists—which, of course, does not imply that the situation cannot change. However, not all the obstacles are on the employer side. National unions may from time to time welcome the assistance of an ITS to bolster their positions in conflicts with employers, but they have not shown much readiness to delegate to an ITS (or to a world corporation council) the authority or the resources required for participation in genuine collective bargaining. Nor is there any likelihood of such a delegation being made without, at the very least, a convincing demonstration of its benefits.

Before a labor agreement can be negotiated between an MNC and unions in different countries, many disparities have to be resolved. Some of these are inter-country differences in bargaining structure, lack of uniformity in legal frameworks, and lack of agreement among unions on bargaining priorities. Hence establishment of multinational collective bargaining is necessarily a slow process, with few spectacular results and many setbacks and frustrations. A major role in transnational bargaining for the ITSs is not a serious prospect in the foreseeable future.

Such history suggests a more modest but perhaps still useful line of development. Some ITSs already coordinate an increasing flow of information that affiliates find helpful in bargaining. The French-based BSN Company, an MNC in the food industry, has entered into an arrangement with its unions in several European countries. The agreement provides for periodic meetings and exchanges of information, although it is not the "full access" to information on company activities, investments, and strategies requested by the IUF.

At a time of increasing international takeovers and cross-national mergers of companies, some national unions have enlisted the help of their ITSs in establishing relations with parent companies, whose influence on the recognition and bargaining policies of newly acquired subsidiaries may be of considerable importance. It is at least conceivable that in the future affiliates will make more use of the secretariats to coordinate assistance in major industrial conflicts, but admittedly there are at present no strong indications of such a development.

The European Union now requires the formation of supranational European works councils in enterprises meeting certain criteria (a minimum of a thousand employees, establishments in at least two different member states, and at least 150 employees in each establishment). About twelve hundred firms will be affected. Inevitably, difficult questions will arise about the role that the ITSs and/or their European counterparts (i.e., the European Industry Federations[5]) will play in this scheme. Will they act as a unifying or coordinating force for a heterogeneous group of employee representatives whose experiences, loyalties, and expectations will differ widely, or will their resources be put to best use if they serve chiefly in a consultative or expert capacity? Or, unlikely as it may be, will they be kept out of any significant participation? Given the measured pace of developments in European Union social affairs, it should take several years for answers to these questions to emerge.

Prospects

As a group, the autonomous ITSs will likely continue to be a useful but limited element among international labor organizations. They will face some difficult challenges, beginning with the decline of unions in most industrialized countries. ITSs whose affiliates operate in particularly vulnerable economic sectors will be the major losers. Although unlikely, these ITSs might disappear and new international union centers could emerge, notably in the public and civil services (which may, however, themselves be hurt by privatization) and among white collar and service occupations. In any event, the historic predominance of the manualist unions in manufacturing, as represented by the IMF, seems to be on the decline.

A strong possibility exists of more mergers among the ITSs. Consolidation or absorption by a stronger or more fortunate ITS may be the only answer for financially and organizationally weak ITSs to rising costs of operation, member resistance to dues increases, and jurisdictions increasingly blurred by economic and technological changes.

Relations between the globally oriented ITSs and their strong European regional organizations still suffer in some instances from competitive or conflicting assertions of authority, particularly with regard to the position of the European industry committees. Changes in organization and personnel, however, could resolve most of the unresolved issues.

Only the most tentative steps have been taken to develop relations between the secretariats and their counterparts among employer organizations. Collective bargaining in its conventional form is not a likely prospect between these two groups in the near future. Given the new regulations approved by the European Union's Council of Ministers requiring the establishment of works councils in most of the larger companies, the ITSs will probably claim a key coordinating role in serving the employee side (unless such a role is also claimed by their counterparts, the European Industry Federations). It remains to be seen whether the works councils can become the cornerstone of a genuinely European industrial relations system.

7

Fo 2
JS1
JS3

European Integration and the Europeanization of Labor

ANDREW MARTIN AND GEORGE ROSS

For trade unions, as for national states, the regulation of markets becomes more difficult as they extend across national boundaries. Historically, as markets expanded unions had to enlarge their strategic domains to keep workers from being played off against each other, undermining wage and labor standards. Never easy even within national boundaries, it is still more difficult to do so when markets transnationalize. In Europe, transnationalization has been carried very far by a half-century of economic and political integration. European trade unions consequently have especially strong reasons to develop the capacity for transnational action. In important ways, the political form that European integration has taken offers unions much better possibilities for doing so than in other regional arrangements, such as the North American Free Trade Area, not to speak of global arrangements such as the World Trade Organization. But in other ways, European political institutions limit the possibilities and discourage the development of Europe-wide union structures and strategies. This chapter describes the contradictory implications of integration for European trade unions and their responses to the challenges they pose.

So far, European integration has resulted in what is now called the European Union (EU), to which 15 countries belong, and a European Monetary Union (EMU) to which 11 of the 15 belong.[1] Economic integration has gone further in the EMU than in the EU. In the latter, there is a single market in which there is, in principle, free movement of goods, services, capital, and labor across the boundaries of the member states. In EMU there is also a single currency, the Euro, and a single monetary policy carried out by a single central bank, controlling the general level of economic activity in the Euro area ("Euroland") by setting interest rates just as the Federal Reserve Bank does in the U.S.[2]

120

The single market is governed by a complex set of intergovernmental and supranational institutions. In the successive treaties that in effect serve as the EU's constitution, power over specified policy areas is distributed among those institutions while power over the other areas is reserved to member states.[3] The resulting political structure, like no other in the world, is difficult to describe. In some respects it comes close to being a federal state, in many others it is considerably less centralized, and in few others it is more centralized. The essential point is that the EU institutions have been given the power to enact laws (regulations or directives) on specified subjects which the member states are obliged to implement, by changing their own laws if necessary.

However, this legislative power is partly vested in a kind of legislative body, the Council, which consists of cabinet ministers of the member governments who pass legislation either by unanimous vote or a qualified majority (QMV)—i.e., more than a simple majority—so the member states have a strong say in the rules by which they are to be bound.[4] On the other hand, this legislative power is shared with two supranational bodies, the European Parliament and the European Commission. The Parliament, elected directly by citizens of the member states, has been given increasing power to determine the fate of proposed legislation. The Commission is a kind of executive body, consisting of 20 members nominated by the member states, appointed by the Council, and now approved by the Parliament for five-year terms, but whose duty is to implement the integration objectives set in the treaties rather than to represent the member states from which they come. The Commission members each head administrative departments—Directorate Generals—staffed by European civil servants. As "guardian of the treaty," the Commission alone has the authority to propose the legislation which the other bodies enact. Yet another supranational institution, the European Court of Justice (ECJ), consisting of 13 judges appointed jointly by the member states, adjudicates disputes over compliance with the treaty or EU laws by EU institutions, member states, or private parties, and its decisions are binding on courts in the member states. In addition to these EU institutions, monetary policy within the EMU is carried out by the most centralized, supranational body in the EU, the European System of Central Banks (ESCB), consisting of the European Central Bank (ECB) and central banks of the member states, as described more fully later on.

In this new European political economy, the strategic challenges faced by trade unions have been transformed. The national employers with whom they bargained in the past now face competitors and themselves increasingly operate throughout the single European market. In many policy areas important to unions, the national governments which they influenced through political action in the past have surrendered their power to the EU's governing bodies. Unions therefore have strong incentives to develop their own capacity for action throughout the European market and political arenas. The unions' possibilities for such transnational action are also made much greater than in other regions or the global economy as a whole by the existence of the European-level political institutions that set the rules for that market. Relatively greater intra-European similarity in institutions and development levels also enlarge the potential for cross-border union action.

Yet, there are serious limits to what unions could expect to accomplish at the European level. Transnational governance in Europe is limited in precisely those fields that most directly concern unions. Core industrial relations matters such as pay and the rights to organize and strike are explicitly excluded from the EU's jurisdiction by its treaty/constitution. Social policy generally also remains the prerogative of the member states. At the same time, much of the power to regulate the economy which has been taken away from them in the process of creating a single market has not been re-established at the EU level. Moreover, EMU institutionalizes restrictive monetary policies insulated from political accountability at European as well as national levels, raising formidable obstacles to reducing Europe's high unemployment.

The limits on market regulation at the EU level built into its political institutions give unions strong disincentives to invest resources in the Europeanization of their structures and strategy. As long as industrial relations and social policy are left in member state hands, unions still have to act in national arenas, relying on familiar national resources and practices. These disincentives reinforce chronic obstacles to transnational action, including cultural and language barriers and the institutional differences that persist despite the similarities. Conflicts of interest among national labor movements, perceived and real, often paralleling those of their governments, remain strong. In general, European unions—like unions elsewhere—have become profoundly integrated into their national societies in the twentieth century.

Accordingly, while European integration gives national unions reason to transnationalize, multiple factors induce them to "stay home." Nevertheless, a thickening network of transnational union activities has been developing, largely within the framework of the European Trade Union Confederation (ETUC). Founded in 1973, the ETUC is a peak organization of 68 national trade union confederations and 13 sectoral union federations, covering some 60 million union members in 29 countries, including all EU members and some potential members. By the 1990s, as discussed more fully below, the ETUC had become a limited but genuine participant in European policy formation, and its significance for its member organizations was growing. A European trade union structure with some potential for becoming a European labor movement was emerging.

Why, despite the obstacles, did this Europeanization of labor occur? The renewal of European integration itself provided much of the impetus. But an important part of the answer lies in incentives offered to unions by European political institutions, principally the Commission and Parliament, to reconceptualize the unions' strategic interests. Consequently, the unions have "Europeanized" more than could be expected, largely in response to what European-level policy-makers have offered them. But those policy-makers had their own purposes, not always congruent with unions' interests. The result was a particular form of Europeanization that arguably failed to equip unions to cope with the challenges posed by integration.

Integrating Europe: The Economic Approach and the Subordination of Social Policy

For the EU's founders in the aftermath of World War II, European integration was a geopolitical imperative, securing peace by binding Germany to its neighbors as well as uniting Europe in the face of the Soviet threat. They chose to proceed by a strategy of incremental economic integration. This economic approach meant that integration had to be consistent with the interests of those whose support was decisive, namely, European capital and national governments coping with economic problems. The fact that social matters were basic sources of domestic political support for governments meant that social policy, labor standards, and industrial relations institutions were largely excluded from Europe's scope. To this day, therefore, European integration has primarily been about "negative integration"—the creation of a European market by eliminating barriers to cross-border economic activity—rather than "positive integration"—the replacement of national regulation by regulation at the European level. For the most part, social and labor matters have been regulated at that level only when doing so seemed instrumental to market creation.

The EU began as a narrowly trade-oriented adventure. In its first phase, following the 1957 Treaties of Rome, the goal was a "common market" compatible with national models of economic development. Member states retained their industrial, macroeconomic, social, and industrial relations policy prerogatives. Timid attempts by the first European Commission to

go beyond this mandate were stopped in the mid-1960s by French Presi-
dent General de Gaulle. The outcome, the 1966 "Luxembourg Compromise" that governed EU institutional life into the mid-1980s, allowed each
EU member to invoke "national interest" on essential matters, making una-
nimity necessary on all controversial issues. In the Rome Treaty, issues of
employment and remuneration were considered national in essence, ex-
cepting only equal pay for men and women, enshrined in Article 119. The
free mobility of labor had to be a counterpart to free movement of goods
and capital, leading, in time, to a small body of rules. The major "social"
clause was Article 118, which spoke of the need "to promote improved
working conditions and an improved standard of living for the workers"
but established no instrument beyond the "functioning of the Common
Market" for so doing. Broad matters of "social citizenship" remained the
responsibility of member states.

The Common Market phase of integration thereby reached a post-war
boom equilibrium. European national economies thrived within a Keynes-
ian-welfare state framework as they entered the consumerist era. The EU's
customs-free zone and common external tariff gave them space needed to
regulate themselves, strike viable domestic political deals, and trade with
one another while being reasonably well insulated from the outside world,
particularly the United States. They needed and wanted little more.

Economic difficulties and rising unemployment in the 1970s stimulated new preoccupation with national economic policies and resistance to
Europe-wide solutions. Growing pains from the expansion from six to nine
members after 1973 also led to chronic budgetary conflicts, paralyzing European decision-making. Proposals for workers' participation (the Vredel-
ing Directive of 1980) were stopped by concerted business opposition, as
were a number of proposed regulations on part-time and temporary work
in the early 1980s.

After a period of "Europessimism," integration was renewed in the mid-
1980s. The June 1985 White Paper laid out the "1992 program" to establish a single market with free movement of goods, persons, services, and
capital but made little mention of social policy matters. Member states then
quickly renegotiated the Rome Treaty to fit the new program, resulting
in the Single European Act (SEA, signed in 1986, ratified in 1987). To prevent "1992" from being blocked by a small minority, the SEA provided for
decision-making by "qualified majority voting" (QMV) for most White
Paper areas. It also presented an extended list of new European "competencies"—areas in which the Community acquired a legal basis to act—in
research and development, the environment, foreign policy cooperation,
and "economic and social cohesion" (regional policy). Reliance on QMV

was expanded in some areas of existing competence, notably workplace health and safety. Finally, it put EMU back on the agenda, though without setting any timetable for further action.

The post-1985 renewal of European integration ignited business and public enthusiasm and allowed key European actors, the Commission in particular, to move forward boldly. Commission President Jacques Delors hoped that movement toward completing the internal market would promote "spillover" of integration from the economy into new areas (Ross 1995).[5] Social and industrial relations policy matters still carried a relatively low priority, however. The SEA preserved unanimity rules over most social and labor law measures, even if it did allow QMV on health and safety issues. Finally, in a new Article 118b, the Commission was encouraged to promote a "social dialogue" between capital and labor at the European level.

"Market building" continued to take strong precedence, and social matters were broached only after the Single Market program was well under way and EMU was in the pipeline. The 1989 Community Charter of Basic Social Rights for Workers was the centerpiece of the Commission's social policy program. Rather than laying down a set of enforceable rights, however, the Social Charter was a "solemn commitment" on the part of member states—eleven, given British rejection—to a set of "fundamental social rights" for workers. The Action Program of November 1989 promised legislative initiatives to implement the Charter where the EU's existing treaty base allowed them. However, except for health and safety measures, which rapidly became strong transnational regulations, the degree of new regulation was modest.[6]

The 1991 Maastricht Treaty on the European Union (TEU) provided for the establishment of Economic and Monetary Union (EMU), the most far-reaching step toward economic integration, in a three-stage process to be completed, at the latest, in January 1991. EMU replaces the national currencies of the member states with a single currency, the Euro, managed by a European System of Central Banks (ESCB). The ESCB consists of the European Central Bank and the member state central banks, whose governors sit on the Governing Council of the ECB along with a six-member Executive Board, appointed jointly by the member states. The ECB is given exclusive power over monetary policy throughout the Euro-area and a mandate to use that power to maintain price stability, as the ECB itself defines it. To assure that it pursues that goal, regardless of its consequences, it is given complete independence from all political authorities, at both national and European levels. The member state central banks are similarly required to be independent of national governments, and simply carry out the ECB's monetary policy. To join EMU, states were required to meet stiff "convergence criteria." In addition to central bank independence, these included tough targets for lowering budget deficits, public debt, inflation rates, and exchange rate instability. A "Growth and Stability Pact" incorporated into the 1997 Amsterdam Treaty extended, and further toughened, the deficit and debt requirements into the period when EMU is in operation. In short, EMU tied economic integration to a highly restrictive macroeconomic policy, putting top priority on price stability, without establishing any equivalent commitments or institutional arrangements aimed at reducing unemployment. For this reason, as we shall see, the ETUC was sharply critical of the particular design of EMU while strongly supporting a single currency and integration more generally.

Maastricht did bring unions some gains in the form of a "Social Protocol"—so designated because the British government refused to sign it while the eleven other member states at the time agreed to it, so that it was attached to the Treaty rather than being part of it (the Labour Government under Tony Blair subsequently ended the British opt-out so the text is now part of the Treaty). The Protocol modestly expanded the scope for EU legislation on social standards by extending QMV to "working conditions" and "information and consultation."[7] In addition, and more interestingly, it opened up the possibility for standards to be set through negotiations between the European-level "social partners"—i.e., the ETUC and the two employer organizations, the Union of Industrial and Employers' Confederations of Europe (UNICE) and European Confederation of Public Enterprises (CEEP). Agreements reached in such negotiations could then be enacted by the Council into binding European law. Negotiations between the union and employer organizations were thereby turned into a formal part of European social policy formation, enhancing the importance of European-level interest representation in the process.

Introduced by the Commission, the proposal for such negotiated legislation was supported by the ETUC because it promised to open the path to European-level collective bargaining. UNICE supported it to hedge its bets: it expected the Commission's attempt to expand this scope of EU social legislation to be blocked, at least by the UK. But if not, and there would be more social legislation after Maastricht, then UNICE preferred bargaining because the employers' bargaining strength could soften Commission proposals. The result was the October 31, 1991 Agreement between ETUC and UNICE which, to the latter's surprise, entered the Treaty as a Protocol despite the UK's objections.

Action under the Social Protocol was delayed because of unanticipated difficulties in ratifying Maastricht. Thus the Commission did not make the first proposal under the Social Protocol until the second half of 1993: to establish European Works Councils (EWCs) in multinational corporations (MNCs). Failure to achieve a negotiated agreement on EWCs led eventually to an ordinary legislated Directive in 1994 that mandated works councils in all MNCs above a certain size and with facilities in at least two member states. We discuss this important development later on.

The Commission used the Social Protocol again in early 1995 to propose action on parental leave. This time, the social partners reached agreement on the "first European bargain," officially signed in December 1995 and given legal force with a Directive in June 1996. Substantively, the measure made very modest progress in the realm of parental leave, but it did establish the political precedent of negotiated legislation under the Social Protocol. Since then, two other agreements, providing for equal treatment of workers with "atypical" employment contracts, were reached and then turned into EU law. One, in 1997, applied to part-time workers and the other to workers with fixed-term rather than indefinite contracts. Currently (mid-2000), negotiations have begun on an agreement dealing with temporary-agency workers.

The Commission's 1995–1997 Medium Term Social Action Program anticipated few new legislative measures, however, and signaled the end of the Delors-type activism in social policy. It advocated shifting the emphasis to a "process of collective reflection" by European institutions, member states, and social partners. This process was aimed at creating jobs, the "top priority" of social policy, for which responsibility lies mainly with individual member states. The role of European institutions is now conceived as facilitating coordination and pooling of experience and ideas rather than establishing binding common standards.

The Tentative Europeanization of Trade Union Structure

While there were multiple factors militating both in favor and against the Europeanization of structures and strategies from the European perspective of European trade unions, those actors most committed to fostering European integration sought to tip the balance in favor of such a shift. This was particularly true of the European Commission. From the outset, the architects of European integration such as Jean Monnet, the French economic planner and designer of the ECSC, believed that the route to political integration was through economic integration. They expected the creation of European institutions to receive the most powerful support where they served economic interests. Once in place, such institutions could themselves provide further impetus to integration, mobilizing support for its extension to functions instrumental to those initially assigned to the institutions, successively spilling over into support for a widening role and eventually for broader political integration and a European political culture. The development of Euro-level representation by societal interest groups was an integral part of this "functionalist" logic, which the Commission followed by using its resources to induce interest groups to invest themselves in Euro-level processes.

The pattern of such investment by the "social partners" was at first quite asymmetrical. Business formed the Union of Industrial and Employers' Confederations of Europe (UNICE) in 1958. Some trade unionists also saw a need for a new Euro-level organization, but union divisions delayed the establishment of the ETUC until 1973. The new ETUC, open to all EFTA and EEC unions, Christian, Communist, or ICFTU branches, was a broad organization with a strong claim to be the representative of all unions at the European level. With insufficient support for European-level action among its members, however, the ETUC could not do much more initially than act as a liaison and lobbyist for national union confederations.[8] Moreover, the diversity of the ETUC's affiliated organizations made it hard to reach agreement on policies and action.

The ETUC's early attempts at exerting influence were largely confined to the rarefied and small Brussels arena and dissociated from the members it nominally represented. The new Confederation initially had high hopes for "proto-corporatist" initiatives by the Commission, but it quickly withdrew from most in 1978 after concluding that neither employers nor governments were interested in serious commitments.[9] By then, though, the impetus for broader European integration had all but disappeared as governments reverted to national solutions to the economic crisis that had set in. The appointment of a new Commission headed by Delors in 1985 and the launch of the "1992" project brought new momentum to integration, and with it new efforts by the Commission and now Parliament to promote Euro-unionism which eventually revitalized the ETUC and enlarged its influence.

Delors had succeeded in making "social dialogue" between union and employer organizations an explicit Community objective in the SEA's Article 118B. But the discussions between them he initiated did not get very far.

Social dialogue was relaunched in 1989 in the glow of the Social Charter. The contradictory purposes of the participants again made discussion frustrating and produced few results. UNICE was opposed to meaningful discussions and was in a position to defend an intransigent position. ETUC, on the other hand, wanted European-level labor market regulation, and if it could get it through European-level bargaining, so much the better. But ETUC was very weak. Because the stakes and resources of each of the major social partners were different, the Commission adopted an asymmetrical approach, seeking first to strengthen ETUC. The Commission recognized that strengthening European-level unionism required resources beyond those that might be generated from its national constituents alone and that, therefore, European-level resources might help. A stronger ETUC, partly dependent upon Commission resources, might be a useful ally for the Commission in broader political matters and might cause UNICE to reconsider its negativity.

Delors took the lead by giving speeches to various European labor organizations to promote a new European commitment and by supplying money to fund ETUC's internal activities.[10] The small costs involved allowed ETUC to hire new staff and build a larger, more autonomous headquarters organization endowed with new capabilities. The Commission also carefully nourished privileged networks of communication between itself and ETUC, while Delors devoted precious time to cultivating relationships with ETUC leaders. Financial support from the Commission and Parliament also strengthened European union structures at the level of the company and of the economic sector. Funds were provided to enable union representatives from different subsidiaries of European multinational companies to meet and form committees to press the companies to set up European works councils in anticipation of EU legislation requiring it. These meetings were organized with the help of the European Industry Committees, or Federations (EIFs) as they are now called. The EIFs are organizations of unions in the same sector, such as the European Metalworkers Federation (EMF) which covers the all-important metal manufacturing sector. There were fifteen of them at the time. They became member organizations of the ETUC with the same status as the national confederations, but because they are transnational organizations directly controlled by their member unions, they are more likely to be given mandates for actions like collective bargaining than the ETUC itself which is one step removed from direct union control.[11]

The post-1985 relaunch of integration and the Single Market contained both threats and opportunities for unions. As member states and business grew more receptive to European solutions to their problems, the settings that ETUC constituents faced began changing rapidly. The inevitable transnationalization of markets results from the "1992" stimulated a new willingness among unions, increasingly on the defensive in their national contexts, to consider transnational strategies. These two facts—the Single

Market and the willingness of the Commission and Parliament to support them—encouraged trade unionists to develop European-level action.

Serious efforts to rethink ETUC did not really begin until after the 1988 ETUC Congress, when the confluence of impulses toward change coming from the Commission and from within ETUC became clearer. At the Congress, Delors asked unions to join him in defending the "European model of society." Delegates urged that the ETUC become a united and coherent proponent of true social and contractual European policies and also proposed strengthening structures and increasing membership, enhancing efficiency, and improving cooperation among EIFs, thereby implicitly increasing the authority of the ETUC.

The Congress authorized the preparation of broad proposals for reform of the ETUC to be put to the 1991 Congress. Although encouraged by Delors, change was an internal matter and could be brought about only by the national confederations. The German DGB, the most powerful European labor movement, and the Italian confederations, which strongly desired a more supranational ETUC, requested a working group on ETUC organization. In December 1989, the ETUC Executive Committee established such a group, chaired by Johan Stekelenburg, president of the Dutch Confederation of Labor (FNV). The "Stekelenburg Report," "For a More Efficient ETUC," adopted at the end of 1990, recommended that the ETUC "become a genuine confederation with appropriate competencies and tasks." This implied the transfer of some areas of authority from national to European level, including the establishment of priorities to "coordinate collective actions, build up international trade union countervailing power and organize solidarity through actions promoting common objectives." The report proposed a new Steering Committee, giving more power to the ETUC leadership, and urged a larger role for the EIFs. Previously composed of national confederations, the ETUC would have a dual membership base consisting of cross-national sectoral organizations, the EIFs, as well as national intersectoral ones, the confederations.[12]

After discussing the report, the 1991 Congress announced a higher priority to European transnational union action and emphasized that the ETUC would be its organizational vehicle. Its new tasks would include the formulation of joint strategies in collective bargaining and the representation of joint interests in the EU legislative arena. It selected Emilio Gabaglio from the Italian CISL as new General Secretary and Jean Lapeyre, the French master of the Delors-Commission connection, as the first Deputy General Secretary. Structural and procedural changes were meant to draw the member organizations into closer collaboration with the ETUC's new officers.

The Congress did not reflect consensus on new goals, however.[13] Deciding what competencies should be transferred from national to European level was left to the Executive Committee, where obstacles to a stronger ETUC were rooted in the diverse structures and interests of national constituent bodies. Quite as important, the ETUC's financially strapped members were in a difficult position to provide more resources, and so the ETUC would remain a small organization, its six-member secretariat backed by a staff of thirty. Resource poverty was a still greater problem for the EIFs.

Commission support for European labor representation was uneven, however. While the Maastricht Social Protocol reflected a clear effort by the Commission to join with the ETUC to overcome employer resistance to negotiations at the inter-sectoral level, the Commission's commitment to bringing employers to the bargaining table at the sectoral level was more uncertain and ambiguous. Employer resistance to sectoral negotiations was facilitated by their European organizational structure at that level. Specifically, the largest number of sectoral business organizations are industry rather than employer associations. This industry-based structure typically is invoked to justify refusal to enter into social dialogue, leaving it to UNICE to discuss social dimension matters. UNICE has sought to reinforce its resulting virtual monopoly of representation on such matters by confining social dialogue to discussion among European-level intersectoral organizations, where it can count on blocking proposals.[14] Sectors accounting for about half of Europe's jobs, including the core metal manufacturing sector, have not entered into even minimal social dialogue.[15]

The support the EIFs have received from European institutions has been concentrated on their organization of trans-border labor representation at the MNC level. The establishment of European Works Councils has already had very important effects in extending the structure of European unionism down to company level. The number of companies covered by the Directive is uncertain, but one estimate is a little over twelve hundred. If all set up EWCs with thirty members (the maximum under the Directive unless companies and employees agree on something larger), and if the unions are involved in forming and operating them, several tens of thousands of workplace activists will be drawn into transnational union work. The ETUC itself has had to generate the intellectual and financial resources to help train EWC members and the EIFs are developing the capacity to support them.[16]

There is thus a definite bias in European union structure. There are many more works councils than EWCs resulting from the intervention of European institutions. It has cultivated intersectoral levels, where the ETUC leadership operates, and MNC level, where EWCs are being formed. It has given least support to the intermediate, or sectoral level, which is the EIFs' turf, except insofar as they organize EWCs rather than attempt to engage employers at the sectoral level. Because employer resistance to dealing with unions at the sectoral level is virtually complete (and no employer counterpart group in any form exists in some sectors) and because Commission efforts to overcome this resistance are so meager, it has been difficult for EIFs to avoid concentrating their activity on the works councils.

Even the ETUC's support for the development of sector-level negotiations has been ambiguous. The ETUC has described such negotiations as an important part of the European industrial relations system it seeks, and recently echoed the EIFs' complaints of inadequate Commission support of sectoral social dialogue. But the ETUC has not supported the EIFs in some situations where the potential for sectoral agreements opened up. This structural bias raises issues about which strategies may be facilitated and which inhibited by the kind of structure that has developed.

Despite numerous obstacles, a significant Europeanization of labor representation has occurred. The 1991 ETUC Congress was a milestone. Relations with national constituencies were created by the new units established prior to the Congress, the Trade Union Technical Bureau and the European Trade Union College, and expanded by the links to EIFs through the formation of trade union committees in MNCs. A multi-level structure began to emerge through which the ambitious federalist vision of the ETUC potentially might be realized. Since the 1991 Congress the most important change has been the establishment, after much controversy, of procedures for ETUC conduct of negotiations under the Social Protocol. The ETUC's organizational resources have also been strengthened considerably.

Significant developments occurred on sector and local levels as well. The EIFs remain small and unevenly effective. Much of their effort continues to be focused on MNCs. The availability of funds has nevertheless enhanced their status and resources. In fact, per capita dues of some EIFs have recently risen to three to four times those to the ETUC. This is solid evidence of increasing member union commitment to the EIFs and of their decreasing dependence on European institutions for resources, with the increasing strategic room for maneuver that this permits. The EIFs have intensified cooperation among themselves, developing a collective identity through regular joint meetings and joint organizing work on European Works Councils.[17] Largely with their help, the formation of EWCs has accelerated. EWCs are creating European networks of union activists at company level, providing channels for direct cross-border links among unions in addition to those at sectoral and intersectoral levels.

All in all, then, ETUC, no longer a "head without a body," has extended its scope downward to draw national and local union officials into transnational activities of various sorts. However, this has been largely a top-down process driven by the interplay of actors in the European institutions and by European-level trade union organizations with common stakes in legitimating a European union structure. Less apparent in the ETUC's development has been the conviction of national-level trade unionists of the need for Eurolevel action. Nor is there evidence of any pressures from below, from the level of the rank and file. Thus, as one observer suggested, the story of the Europeanization of labor has been one of "structure before action" (Turner 1996).

It can also be seen as one of structure before strategy. Indeed, the process by which the structure has been developed poses fundamental strategic issues for unions. Clearly, many unionists and influential EU actors such as Delors had common stakes in the Europeanization of labor. However, the purposes of unionists who supported the Europeanization of labor and the purposes of EU actors who provided the incentives that influenced the development of that structure do not necessarily coincide. Moreover, there are diverse conceptions of the strategies that structure should serve, both within and among different levels of that structure and among different national labor movements. We turn now to a discussion of those issues.

Strategic Dilemmas

The ETUC has consistently articulated an expansive vision of its role as the instrument for mobilizing and orchestrating the resources of unions throughout Europe and bringing them to bear on the course of European integration. In the words of a 1995 Congress statement:

> The emergence of new economic and political power systems at European level calls for the establishment of countervailing force by the unions. This necessitates common objectives and common negotiating strategies, mechanisms for European trade union action to back up these objectives in the event of dispute, and real cross-border coordination. Building up trade union counter-pressure in Europe is thus essential in order to ensure that European construction pursues the objective of sustainable and lasting development, capable of creating jobs for all men and women, as well as that of social progress and solidarity. As a Unitarian and pluralist organization and the representative of the labor movement in all its breadth and diversity, the ETUC sees itself as the instrument which will serve that purpose.[18]

These aspirations meant going well beyond "Brussels lobbying" to become a player in European-level policy deliberations and an organization that negotiates binding agreements with employers at the peak level of a multi-tiered European industrial relations system. In short, ETUC sought to do at the European level what the most powerful national union confederations did, or aspired to do, in their own countries. The ETUC leadership's strategic ambitions were not completely shared, however. Issues about the ETUC's bargaining role thus became the focus of a long internal controversy.

Bargaining

The most enthusiastic Europeanizing trade unionists hoped that social dialogue would develop into European-level collective bargaining. As a genuine confederation the ETUC would negotiate binding "framework agreements" with its intersectoral employer counterparts and coordinate European-level sectoral bargaining strategies. This hope was not very realistic, however. The German DGB and British TUC, ETUC's two largest member confederations, themselves had very limited bargaining roles, and some confederations that had had significant collective bargaining roles in the recent past, most notably Sweden's LO, were losing them. The question of distributing bargaining authority and subjects among different levels was brought to the top of the ETUC's agenda by the Maastricht Social Protocol. Protracted internal controversy followed among the ETUC Secretariat, some of the member confederations, and the EIFs.

The ETUC leadership convened a conference on "European Collective Bargaining—ETUC Strategy" in June 1992, at which the Secretariat staked out ambitious claims to a collective bargaining role for itself. Support for this was inversely related to the strength of the unions in their national contexts, with the weaker unions looking to European regulation to compensate for their lack of national resources. German participants opposed this claim, urging a "bottom-up" approach to European-level bargaining. According to this view, collective bargaining presupposed bargaining power, so national unions first had to be strengthened before national collective bargaining could be coordinated and an independent European union counterforce developed at sectoral level. ETUC might provide the context within which such coordination would occur, but could itself only engage in bargaining at the intersectoral level some time in the future. Collective bargaining, conceived as contingent on genuine bargaining power, accordingly had to be distinguished from the negotiation of agreements on legislation contemplated in the Social Protocol. The DGB was even skeptical about the latter, but was willing to see the ETUC negotiate when given case-by-case mandates. The strong Nordic unions would not go even that far, rejecting negotiated European labor market regulation altogether and insisting instead upon legislation. On the other end of the organizational-strength continuum, most Mediterranean participants as well as the TUC supported negotiations by the ETUC.

The ETUC leadership responded with a draft position paper to the October 1992 Executive Committee meeting, again laying out an ambitious agenda. Stressing the importance for democracy of rights of association, collective action, and bargaining, it called for explicit recognition of these rights at European level. The leadership argued that the effective exercise of these rights required ETUC to play a key role that would not replace or weaken what happened at national level, but give it a new dimension. ETUC's constituent organizations then could coordinate national and transnational bargaining issues to counteract the deteriorating effects of economic integration on national collective bargaining. The ETUC further proposed that European-level agreements be framework deals to be completed and made binding at national, sectoral, and transnational levels.

This expansive view of ETUC's role was resisted again. Instead, the Executive Committee established a set of guidelines authorizing ETUC to negotiate exclusively within the framework of the Social Protocol under strict supervision by its affiliates. The leadership's supranationalist ambitions ran up against strong resistance from national actors, paralleling federalist versus nationalist struggles over the integration process more broadly. Despite the ETUC's considerable revitalization as a consequence of the 1991 Congress, its constituents were not ready to let the Social Protocol turn ETUC into a collective bargaining agent. In any event, while UNICE refused to bargain, the question of ETUC as bargainer was moot.

A second phase of the controversy involved use of the Social Protocol to promote sectoral as well as intersectoral negotiating. This phase was triggered when the employer organization for commerce, Eurocommerce, declared that it was not bound by the parental leave deal because UNICE did not represent Eurocommerce. The corresponding EIF, EURO-FIET, therefore felt it necessary to negotiate a separate agreement on parental leave. In response, the Secretariat renewed its efforts to establish authority over sectoral negotiations, which the EIFs as a group staunchly resisted.

The Secretariat's position revealed a tension between the ETUC's avowed support for cross-national bargaining at all levels, including the sectoral, and its stake in protecting its monopoly of representation of labor at the intersectoral level as well as the binding status of agreements reached there. Given the ETUC's earlier declarations, it could have been expected to welcome any precedent-setting opportunities for sectoral bargaining that arose. Nonetheless, it opposed separate sectoral agreements for a variety of reasons. In this instance, ETUC seemed wary of supporting Eurocommerce's claim that UNICE was not representative, lest it open the door to claims by minor union organizations that ETUC was not representative either.

Although the Council's later adoption of the parental leave agreement as a directive rendered the issue moot, the Secretariat tried to gain statutory control over future sectoral negotiations. Concerned with their own problems in maintaining their positions in national union structures, most of the confederations supported the ETUC's efforts. All the EIFs strenuously resisted. Faced with the prospect of a sharp split between the EIFs and the confederations, the Secretariat backed off, agreeing to rules assuring the EIFs' autonomy at the sectoral level.

In both phases of the controversy the Secretariat had to settle for less than it initially desired. By 1996, it was left with a role as bargainer in intersectoral negotiation under the Social Protocol, a process of negotiated legislation that is collective bargaining only in a very special sense. This role had already been established in practice in the initial Social Protocol negotiations over European Works Councils and parental leave. In the Protocol process, therefore, the ETUC's role is now accepted by its affiliates. Quite as important, getting to this point involved national affiliates and their member unions being drawn into taking European-level activity more seriously than ever before. By demonstrating that significant matters could be at stake, Social Protocol negotiations compelled union leaders with responsibility for collective bargaining at the national level to become engaged in the controversy, even if they were often concerned mainly with heading off what they saw as threatening in the European-level activity.

Since the bargaining role affiliates allowed to the ETUC was confined to the Social Protocol, it fell short of the ETUC's vision of a European industrial relations system in which cross-border collective bargaining would play a significant part in regulating the European labor market, and in which it would negotiate binding framework agreements at intersectoral level and coordinate bargaining strategies at sectoral and national levels. The potential for moving toward this vision through Social Protocol negotiations is limited as long as the employers will not negotiate except when under the shadow of law. The range of subjects over which that shadow can be cast is narrowly circumscribed by the constitutional limits of the EU's legislative authority. Moreover, even within those narrow limits everything ultimately depends upon the initiative of the Commission, currently disinclined to propose new legislation. Finally, the Social Protocol did little to enlarge the possibilities for sectoral negotiations. These, as we saw, were severely limited by employer opposition that neither the Commission nor ETUC consistently tried to overcome.

European Works Councils

The 1994 EWC Directive seemed to open new possibilities for transnational bargaining that, on closer examination, turned out to be quite contradictory. Having pressed for an EWC directive for nearly a quarter century, the ETUC could plausibly hail it as "a major breakthrough" for European unions. UNICE, having resisted equally long, warned that unions would now use EWCs "as a major step toward realizing their ambition for pan-European structures and collective bargaining." But EWCs will not necessarily serve that purpose. Indeed, in particular circumstances they might even become new obstacles to it, fostering a "transnational micro-corporatism" at the MNC level, detached from any collective bargaining structures above company level, national or European.[19]

The potential effects of the EWC Directive are ambiguous. On the one hand, management is required to "inform and consult" with employees once a year, with consultation defined as an "exchange of views." It does not enjoin consultation on any continuing basis or require management to respond to employees' views. The Directive provides no mechanisms for suspending decisions until management responds to employees, and does not require negotiations dealing with matters about which the employees are informed. Further, even EWCs were set up in all covered companies and there was a union presence in all of these (neither likely), this would amount to company-level, cross-border representation for only a small portion of the European labor force.[20] Even with union involvement, however, employers can still prevent any metamorphosis of EWCs into collective bargaining institutions by insisting upon the minimum legal observance of the Directive's terms.[21]

On the other hand, EWC meetings could create a dynamic leading to European-level company bargaining, despite employer intentions. Although central management typically prepares the information it has to provide, this is more than employee members can count on getting at the individual sites they represent. Moreover, management has to explain and justify decisions it otherwise would not have to. Probably more important, companies are obliged to pay for meetings that facilitate cross-border communication among employees (especially in pre-meetings held without management). Once such communication is established it can be continued and expanded, sustained by a cross-border network that probably would not exist otherwise, thereby enabling unions to compare situations between different sites and verify management claims about other sites. Beyond that, the information can be funneled into established national and local collective bargaining, calling bluffs, bolstering demands, and putting new issues on the agenda.

Assuming that the second dynamic emerges at least in some circumstances, MNC managers will find it increasingly difficult to unilaterally implement company-wide "human resource management" strategies. This might prompt some MNCs to try to coopt the EWCs, to legitimate or even secure "framework agreements" on various company-wide workplace issues, such as organization and training. Even if wages are kept out of the purview of EWCs, it could be a short step from such workplace issues to pay systems. Negotiating with employee members of EWCs could have the additional benefit of strengthening the company's European corporate identity. Thus by embracing EWCs to use them for collective bargaining, MNC managers might find them handy for regulating industrial relations company-wide throughout Europe.

This scenario need not necessarily lead to more Europeanization of collective bargaining, however. Indeed, in the worst case it might further weaken national-level unions and their ability to affect industrial relations, without any offsetting European-level gains. Whether there is a danger of such "transnational microcorporatism" is unclear. Depending on their strength, national industrial relations institutions have constrained MNCs, providing unions with resources to resist the construction of company-specific employment systems that deviate from national patterns. Precisely because EWCs might be used to overcome resistance to such deviations, workers in MNCs might well put more trust in their national unions to protect their interests, particularly when the distribution of investment and jobs at different sites is at stake. Such conflicts of interest could paralyze EWCs, making their atrophy more likely than transnational microcorporatism.

On the other hand, where MNC managers are in a position to distribute mutual gains while spreading "best practice" among subsidiaries, they might be able to forge cross-border productivity coalitions with their own employees through EWCs.[22] MNCs might thereby gain employee support for decentralizing collective bargaining to company level at the expense of multi-employer bargaining by national sectoral unions. This could reinforce common trends toward more decentralized, company-specific deals, further undermining national unions' ability to aggregate workers' interests at more inclusive levels.

Such complex situations are unlikely to emerge for some time, indeed not before EWCs have been widely established and tested. The most immediate dilemmas are more likely to come from EMU and a single currency.

Economic and Monetary Union

EMU is bound to have a major impact on unions because it concentrates the burden of adjustment to variations in economic conditions among the member states heavily on labor costs. EMU turns what used to be national economies separated from each other by their national currencies into regions within a single economy with a single currency, thereby eliminating the possibility of using changes in exchange rates to adjust to "asymmetrical shocks"—changes in the relative competitiveness of companies in the different regions that can result from a variety of causes, external or internal. These include the effects of changes in export markets that are uneven because of differences in export dependence or the composition of exports, the effects of variations in wage growth rates because of differences in the tightness of labor markets or the organization of wage bargaining, or the effects of differences in economic development.

In principle, fiscal mechanisms could offset such effects in place of exchange rate changes. One such mechanism is fiscal federalism, through which the taxes flowing from the relatively disadvantaged regional units into a central budget decline while expenditures flowing from the central budget back into those regional units increase, as in the U.S. Another is changes in the relationship between taxes and spending within the regional units themselves. But neither of these mechanisms can play much of a role in the EU. With a budget corresponding to little more than one percent of EU GDP, the EU is incapable of more than token fiscal federalism.[23] At the same time, the member states' fiscal policy discretion is also quite limited by the Stability Pact. This leaves adjustment primarily to the labor market, which can achieve it in basically two ways. One is by workers moving from regions where employment is adversely affected by the uneven changes in economic conditions to regions which are relatively advantaged and where there is greater demand for labor; the other is by making labor costs lower in the former regions relative to what they are in the latter. But even though free movement of labor is one of the four kinds of freedom of movement prescribed by the SEA, durable barriers of language and culture and differences in employment-related institutions such as social security have kept labor mobility much lower in Europe than in America. This puts most of the burden of adjustment on changes in relative labor costs—non-wage costs such as social security payroll taxes as well as wages.

As a result, unions in affected areas are likely to be pressed to acquiesce in nominal wage reductions or at least low increases and to accept cuts in non-wage costs that erode the financing of bargained or statutory social benefits. Because unions' capacities to resist such pressures vary, regions with stronger unions could lose competitiveness to regions with weaker unions, putting stronger unions under pressure to accept cuts.[24] The potential is clear for a vicious circle of labor cost dumping that could cumulatively lower aggregate income, demand, and employment throughout the Community.

Monetary union accordingly confronts unions with a new situation. Some argue that it makes development of a European structure for collective bargaining necessary and unavoidable (Keller 1995). Others argue that although monetary union makes such Europeanization necessary, it also makes it impossible (Mahnkopf and Altvater 1995). From a neoliberal standpoint, that is exactly what monetary union is supposed to do. In the past, national or sectoral unions could dampen wage competition within national labor markets separated by different currencies. With EMU, the separate national unions within a single European labor market will be in direct competition with each other. Common ground will be difficult to find precisely insofar as labor cost competition becomes the only available mechanism to protect jobs. Creating a currency area too large for "an effective wage cartel" thus creates a highly decentralized European wage bargaining structure (Busch 1994).

The danger that unions will be pitted against each other in a vicious circle of competitive concessions to save jobs is accentuated by the highly restrictive macroeconomic policy regime built into EMU. Because EMU makes monetary policy (the control of interest rates) the only instrument for influencing growth in the Euroland economy as a whole and places it in the hands of a completely independent central bank mandated to use that instrument to maintain price stability, there is a strong risk that the bank will not allow the economy to grow enough to bring unemployment significantly below the Great Depression levels it reached in the 1990s. Under these circumstances, unions would be under enormous pressure to save jobs wherever they can, not just within sectors but in individual companies, straining solidarities even within the latter. Under these circumstances, the prospects are extremely slim for constructing common cross-border cross-company collective bargaining strategies, not to speak of mobilizing the bargaining power to implement them effectively. Instead of providing the impetus for a Europeanization of union strategy that could avert the threat of microcorporatism that EWCs may pose, monetary union, as designed, could well reinforce that threat. The political choices embodied in EMU thus emerge as potentially decisive for the course of European trade unionism.

The Political Arena

Possibilities envisioned by the ETUC for building up trade union counter-pressure in the European market arena rest ultimately on the trajectory followed by European integration. Influencing that trajectory to create more favorable conditions is the most fundamental strategic challenge facing the ETUC and its member unions. The ETUC's persistent position has been that political integration is essential to assure the survival of the welfare state and industrial relations institutions that distinguish the European model of society in an economically integrated Europe. Within the EU, the ETUC has shared with the strongest supporters of European integration the idea that political union could be achieved only through successive installments of economic integration, a belief buttressed by confidence in "spillover" from economics to politics. However, the gaps between the ETUC's "spillover" hopes and the actual course of integration since the mid-1980s have thrown into sharp relief the difficulties of relying on the "economic approach" to political integration.

While welcoming the promise of growth and employment embodied in a unified Europe, the ETUC has also noted "serious dangers for workers." The ETUC has called repeatedly for measures to make sure that economic integration fosters upward convergence of social and labor standards rather than a race to the bottom.[25] The ETUC's view of the needed measures was most fully elaborated in its 1988 "European Social Programme" and its proposal for a "Community Charter of Fundamental Social Rights." To avert social dumping, rights had to be guaranteed at European level through the "two channels" of legislation and negotiation. Social legislation was needed to establish the general principle of "fundamental social rights," defined as rights of workers to organize, bargain collectively, and strike, and to have their employment conditions regulated by collective agreement or law. Additionally, other guarantees were needed on health and safety at the workplace and equal treatment regardless of gender. They would also include "completely new standards such as the right to information or participation in the introduction and application of new technologies," cross-border representation structures for European MNCs, a "framework for European industrial relations," and rights to further training, recognition of credentials, and educational as well as parental leave.

Once it was established that these rights were enforceable, it was up to the Commission to propose separate legislation spelling out how each of them was to be assured. Anticipating the Social Protocol, the ETUC called for negotiation of agreements between the European-level social partners, to lay the basis for additional legislation as well as to secure compliance at all levels.[26]

The ETUC's quest for a social dimension has seen mixed results. It failed to achieve the principle of an enforceable set of social rights: the 1989 Social Charter ended up being no more than a "solemn commitment." The measures in the Action Program following the Charter all lay within areas where a clear treaty base already existed. Most Action Program legislation was on workplace health and safety, where qualified majority voting had been prescribed by the SEA in 1986. To be sure, the October 31, 1991, Agreement and its incorporation into the treaty/constitution through the Maastricht Social Protocol was a breakthrough for the ETUC. And the Social Protocol made possible the Directive mandating European Works Councils, the parental leave and atypical work agreements, and hopes for passage of a few more items.

The ETUC achieved these modest successes in the EU's highly segmented policy arena largely through the social dialogue mechanism, where it could be part of alliances, often led by Delors and deftly managed by his lieutenants, with substantial member-state support. Such political constellations were few and far between in the post-Maastricht period, however. In particular, the ETUC and national union movements were shut out of the arena in which the fateful decisions shaping EMU have been made.

The ETUC has consistently criticized EMU's design, and especially the inflexible interpretation of the convergence criteria, stressing the social costs and the political resistance they have generated. It has pointed out that no amount of "supply-side" reform, the current orthodoxy, can do much to bring unemployment down without the demand stimulus that EMU has ruled out. Despite all this, ETUC continues to support the strategy of integration of which EMU is part. It reasons that monetary union in itself is needed. Although its formulation may be faulty, EMU still may prevent competitive devaluations and blunt the constraints imposed by international financial markets, thereby creating the necessary conditions for a coordinated macroeconomic stimulus. The ETUC also contends that EMU is needed politically to keep the integration process going, and that if it failed, Europe would be in an even worse situation. The ETUC's present position, then, is not to reject EMU but to remedy its flaws, although it is quick to recognize that it has not been able to deflect the course of integration via EMU from its dangerous path.

The ETUC's pro-EMU commitment ultimately rests on its view that the development of transnational union capacity in Europe depends on strengthening European political institutions. This puts the ETUC in the excruciating bind of being tied to the *particular* strategy for political integration that has been adopted despite its flaws and contradictions from a labor perspective. Official support for EMU is still fairly widespread among member confederations, for diverse reasons, but support is fraying in the face of rising popular disenchantment.

Contrary to the functionalist hopes ETUC has shared with many of Europe's builders, there is in fact nothing automatic about the extent to which social and political union accompanies economic integration: that is determined by political choices. So far, the ETUC and its national affiliates have had limited impact on those choices. Whether their positions reflect realistic political judgments is open to debate. Our analysis suggests that the success of Delors and the Commission in mobilizing ETUC support for their own integration strategy may have had more influence on ETUC's positions than the latter have had on the choice of integration strategy. It is not clear that ETUC support for Delors's version of integration has been the price paid for European institutions' support for the Europeanization of labor, but it is a question that has to be faced.

Summary and Conclusion: How Do Transnational Industrial Relations Systems Develop?

European integration has involved the creation of transnational markets in a context of national industrial relations systems. As integration progressed, it would have seemed logical for unions, central actors in these national systems, to follow their market adversaries and transnationalize to avoid exposure to new and threatening pressures. Yet a number of obstacles to such restructuring seemed to stand in the way. Trade unions were deeply rooted in their national societies. Their resources were national, as were their ideas about how to use them. The payoffs from the national use of these resources, if dwindling, still seemed greater than foreseeable returns from transnationalization, which risked diluting national union power. Moreover, the cumulative differences among national economic structures, union organizational patterns, industrial relations systems, and "cultures" (including languages) created further pressures to "stay at home."

The institutions and strategies of European integration reinforced these incentives. The "economic approach" to integration militated powerfully in the direction of transnational liberalization and deregulation—"market building"—and discouraged the relocation of regulatory activities and social policies to European level. In addition, the intergovernmental character of policy decision-making in European institutions made it rational for unions to try to use their influence on national governments.

European unions thus needed to transnationalize to follow market integration but faced a strong set of disincentives. Nevertheless, the unions have transnationalized considerably more than such disincentives might have led one to expect, largely through the growth and changing scope of the ETUC. A large part of the explanation, we suggested, was that particular European institutions—especially the Commission—had set out to provide incentives to unions to invest more at European level. These incentives also favored the goals of those union leaders who themselves advocated further Europeanization of union strategies.

However, the pattern of union Europeanization that resulted was ambiguous for unions themselves. The ETUC was strengthened and changed in response to both market integration and the growing role of European legislation in regulating the market. Some of this legislation, in workplace health and safety, for example, is very important. This interaction of the Commission and Europeanizing union leaders led to the Maastricht Social Protocol and its enticing promise of European-level collective bargaining. The products of the Social Protocol have been relatively slim, however. The parental leave agreement was a huge precedent for intersectoral bargaining at European level, but its substance was weak. The EWC Directive could, in the best of circumstances, foster a substantial development of genuinely transnational unionism, but it could also foster a transnational micro-corporatism that would further weaken national unions' capacity. Apart from the recent agreements on atypical work, which are significant, there seems little likelihood that the precedent established by the Social Protocol will be followed in any important areas.

Organizations and industrial relations systems are shaped in the interactions between strategic actors at specific historic junctures. Thus interactions among national union movements, "Europeanizing" elements emanating from those movements, and European institutions have played a central role in structuring the ETUC, its goals, and its strategies. One significant effect of these interactions has been the commitment of the ETUC to the general vision of European integration held by the Commission and other institutional players. An important tradeoff followed. The ETUC prior to the "1992" period was a weak Brussels lobby. Those in charge of ETUC may have "gone native" in the rarefied atmosphere of Euro-discourse, but it mattered little because ETUC was not very influential. Changes in Europe after the mid-1980s meant that the ETUC became more important. As this happened ETUC's leaders began to desire and claim roles broader than simple lobbying; in the process they developed deeper commitment to what one might label the "European ideal." Beyond details of structure and strategy, this may be the most significant consequence of the fostering of ETUC by European institutions.

ETUC insiders in the later 1980s must have understood that the use of resources offered from Brussels was one way to generate the new prominence that they needed to promote their urgent message about the importance of transnational action among European unions. They could rely on additional support from their more "European" contacts in different national movements. The cost of these resources from Brussels was significant ETUC support for the initiatives of those supplying them, particularly in the Commissions headed by Delors. In this exchange there was an implicit promise to the ETUC that the Commission's particular European strategies would lead to a real expansion in European social regulation and the foundation of a genuine European industrial relations system. The Commission was unable to produce as much as it promised. Perhaps ETUC was naive in expecting such things. Perhaps Delors and his Commissions were naive in thinking that the market building they promoted would lead to spillover into new European regulatory activities. Perhaps some parts of both the ETUC's and the Commission's hopes were dashed by changing circumstances.

As a consequence, ETUC found itself restructured along lines that were only partly its doing and not always clearly to its advantage. It also had to commit, albeit often critically, to the deeper trajectories of European integration sketched out from the Single Market through Maastricht to EMU. This might have made some sense during the Social Charter period, when it seemed as though the dam against European-level social policy was about to give way to compensate for the liberalization brought by the Single Market. This did not happen. Committing to Maastricht turned out to be an even larger leap of faith. Economic and Monetary Union, as designed, is arguably inimical to the interests of European workers and unions. Yet all good "Europeans"—and the ETUC has to be seen as such—have had to line up behind EMU, although many, including some of the more central architects of EMU itself, now do so with heavy hearts. The transition to EMU has already cost jobs while making it virtually impossible for governments to confront the consequences.

The future will bring more of these contradictions. EMU may be a clear step backwards in the European Union's lifelong struggle to overcome its deep "democratic deficit," because it removes policy options from member states and gives them to unelected and statutorily independent central bankers. Yet if EMU fails, it could be a big enough setback for European integration to change the directions that Europe has set over these past decades ETUC and many other actors have managed to put themselves in a position of being damned if they do support EMU and damned if they do not.

Yet, now that EMU has been established, these contradictions have been reshaped. Some features of European integration still drive unions to Europeanize while others reinforce their reliance on national strategies, and some continue to threaten the European social model of which unions are an integral part while others offer possibilities of defending it. But the specific nature of these opposing incentives and the strategic challenges and opportunities facing unions are being altered. The ETUC consequently is in a new situation, bringing with it new threats but also new possibilities.

The transition to EMU has paradoxically reinforced reliance on national organizational resources. To satisfy the tough requirements for entry into EMU and find ways to maintain competitiveness when exchange rate changes are no longer available, many governments have forged national "social pacts" with unions and employers. In essence, unions, in their various weakened states, have been called upon to agree to wage restraint, increased flexibility in hiring and firing, and cost-saving changes in health, pension, unemployment and other welfare state benefits. What they have gotten in exchange is as much political as economic: they have won renewed recognition as key players in national economic policy. This reflects the recognition by governments and employers that, even though unions have been weakened, wage moderation and institutional changes cannot be imposed without the risk of serious conflict that could jeopardize adjustment to EMU—the downfall of recent French and Italian governments that attempted to impose changes in the face of union opposition offers strong testimony to that. This gives unions opportunities to secure commitments from governments and employers to serious training programs and flexible forms of employment security instead of savage dismantling of employment protection, and in reforms in social benefits that improve their equity and efficiency instead of ruthlessly rolling them back. Moreover, to the extent that their consent eases adjustment, jobs may be saved and even increased. In the renewed opportunities for national bargaining given to unions by social pacts, their proliferation in the shadow of EMU gives strong impetus to a "renationalization" of union strategies.[27]

This development could run counter to the ETUC's efforts to create a European industrial relations system in which it would have a leading role, undermining the EU level intersectoral bargaining and lobbying strategies on which it has relied since the later 1980s, along with its claims for its own significance. For example, "pactism" and renationalization pose danger to national unions. Narrow national agreements to make economies leaner and meaner for EMU could lead to intra-European competition that results in a race toward the bottom. Individually, the national unions might be unable to avoid such a self-destructive course. They might slip into a collective action trap from which they could escape only if an outside actor enables them to act jointly. It is precisely this essential "public good" that the ETUC is in a position to provide. The function of coordinating its national constituents' strategies (which it had envisioned but was denied on traditional wage bargaining) would thus become indispensable to national unions in the new context of negotiating terms of national adjustment to EMU.

In performing this role, the ETUC could also enter into new coalitions with European institutions. New initiatives from the Commission and Parliament reflect a search for ways to foster "upward" emulation among national responses to the constraints and opportunities of EMU. The 1997 Amsterdam Treaty's employment clauses were quickly translated into the proposal of the Luxembourg Summit for annual National Action Plans (NAPs) for employment (the first of which had been produced by late spring 1998). This "Luxembourg Process," as it is called in EU jargon, does two things. On the one hand, the NAPs set out specific sets of measures for increasing the number of jobs that result from a given level of demand in the economy on which a consensus can be reached among government, unions and employers within each national context. Given the need for consensus, the plans reflect the process of negotiated rather than imposed change, so that they tend to focus on measures like active labor market policies rather than labor market deregulation. On the other hand, the process is Europeanized because the NAPs are reviewed by the Commission and Council, which comment on the plans. This exercise, if carried out effectively, could make different national strategies for employment creation more vigorous and transparent, and also make clear when any member state seems set on pursuing a "beggar thy neighbor" version of "competitive corporatism." The whole procedure not only gives the ETUC greater legitimacy both with the other actors and its own constituencies but also the potential for playing a significant new strategic role for its constituent unions. It could coordinate national union responses to demands for wage restraint, labor market flexibilization, and social policy reforms made in the course of negotiating national social pacts and formulating the NAPs, thereby setting a broad Europe-wide union agenda for negotiated reform of the European social model. The ETUC can then back up the common elements of the union position at those points in the review of NAPs in the

EU institutions where the European level union and employer organizations present their views.

The flaw in this "Employment Strategy" as originally formulated at Luxembourg is that it is focused on supply side measures while accepting as given the level of demand set by the ECB, at least for the EMU member states. Yet, opportunities for remedying this flaw are opened up by linking the NAPs with the Commission and Council procedures for formulating and reviewing national compliance with what are called the "Broad Economic Policy Guidelines" and, for the EMU members, fiscal policy programs for compliance with the Stability Pact. Whether these opportunities are used to push the ECB to allow growth to be fast enough to substantially lower unemployment is contingent on domestic politics in the member states and how that is reflected in the interaction among the governments, the Commission, the ECB, and now the EU level union and employer organizations. The latter have been formally brought into the EU economic policy arena by the establishment of the so-called Macroeconomic Dialogue at the June 1999 European Council meeting in Cologne, under the Presidency of the German coalition government headed by the Social Democrats. It involves two pairs of meetings (at "technical" and "political" levels) a year at which the ETUC and its employer counterparts discuss macroeconomic policy with finance ministers, the Commission, and the ECB. While this does not alter the ECB's power to decide monetary policy unilaterally, it (together with meetings of the EMU member finance ministers with the ECB in the informal so-called Euro-eleven council) contributes to a political context in which the ECB has to take into account and respond to economic policy goals broader than its mandate.

In fact, securing more expansionary macroeconomic policy in Euroland than the very restrictive regime prescribed by the Treaty, as the ECB interprets it in its public statements, is probably the central challenge on which the rest of the ETUC's strategic possibilities depends. If unemployment is significantly reduced, it will substantially improve the chances of implementing a common union agenda for a negotiated renewal of the European social model; if it is not, it will be difficult to keep tendencies for renationalization of union strategies from turning into a self-defeating vicious circle of competitive corporatism. The prospects for more expansionary economic policy are better now than during the transition to EMU because of the very fact that the separate currencies have been replaced with a single one since the financial markets can no longer play the separate currencies off each other. Moreover, the single currency eliminates the problem of coordinating monetary policy, and because it makes the monetary conditions known, it in turn facilitates the coordination of fiscal policies. All these aspects of EMU create the potential for a concerted expansion that did not exist before.

Whether this new potential is realized depends on the political and economic context within which the ECB operates, and how pragmatically the ECB responds to it in practice. That context has been significantly reshaped by the series of elections that have replaced conservative and neoliberal governments by social democratic and center-left governments, reflecting widespread voter concern about unemployment and economic insecurity. The employment chapter in the Amsterdam Treaty, the Euro11 council, and the Macroeconomic Dialogue are direct results of the resulting changes of government. This political shift may justify cautious optimism about the prospects for a progressive Europeanization of the European labor movement.

How could a transnational industrial relations system develop in Europe? The question is unanswerable. To begin with, national industrial relations systems took a much longer time to take shape than the brief period surveyed. If the development of such national systems is a precedent, though we have no reason to think that it is, then we must take care to avoid premature conclusions. It may turn out that the trajectories begun so tentatively by ETUC and its constituents lead to something resembling a real European-level industrial relations system with capacities to protect and sustain workers' interests in the new global economy, although this seems wildly optimistic now.

A pessimistic outlook may be more realistic. To this point the development of ETUC as a "movement" has not really followed the historic lines of most national labor movements, where long decades of debate, mobilization, and struggle made unions strong and confident enough to oblige states and employers to concede their legitimacy. The ETUC has so far developed largely by borrowing resources from European institutions to gain legitimacy with its own national constituents and by using the openings provided by these European institutions to try to change employer behaviors. ETUC, in other words, has developed from the top rather than as a mass organization built from the bottom out of a broader social movement. EMU and the changes that it will engender offer new opportunities and new threats. It remains to be seen whether ETUC will be able to build upon these and the experiences we retrace in this chapter to become a different kind of transnational unionism in the new millennium.

Part III

The Practice of
Transnational Cooperation

8

From "Solidarity" to Convergence: International Trade Union Cooperation in the Media Sector

JIM WILSON

Campaigns in defense of freedom of expression and human rights, multinational industrial actions to force recognition of unions or to support media workers confronting employer intransigence, lobbying before intergovernmental bodies such as the World Intellectual Property Organization, and dialogue, sometimes even international agreements, with transnational media groups—these are some of the actions that media union internationals are carrying out. Many people in the labor relations field have been convinced that such coordinated and large-scale actions were impossible in the media sector because the national and inter-professional interests among its workers are so diverse and the job structure and organizational contexts are quite complex. A few skeptics have even been overheard to say that the workers are too "independent-minded." Though international cooperation in the media sector has traveled a long and rocky road, such coordinated actions are becoming stronger and more effective.

In this chapter I will describe the motives for and history of structural changes in worker associations in the media sector. These changes have made it possible in certain instances to coordinate job actions across international boundaries. Although cooperation among unions on this scale generally is difficult because of the short duration of the contract work that typifies much of the industry (crews of technicians may be assembled for a two-day shoot for a television commercial, for example), I will conclude by providing evidence that media workers are capable of transnational coordinated action in order to protect the human and job rights of their members.

153

Media Labor Market Exceptionalism

Dealing as it does with the availability and content of communications in society, the media sector plays a crucial role throughout the world. Media workers include technicians and staff in broadcasting and film, writers, directors, performers, journalists, and related workers in the arts and entertainment. The unionization of these workers is somewhat unique. There are many labor organizations but relatively few members, because of the small populations of workers in the sector. Nonetheless, like unionized workers in other sectors, media workers have found it advisable to create national and international associations.

A peculiar sort of trade unionism exists in the media sector, at both the national and the international levels. Professional associations and interest groups abound, although sometimes with confused identities (a given association may include both amateur and professional workers, other interested parties, and sometimes even employers) and sometimes with unusual purposes that overlap with traditional labor questions (encouragement of the industry, sponsoring festivals and awards, setting standards for quality of work, or training). These diverse associations often arise spontaneously within the sector to defend workers' rights, and sometimes they develop because of other influences, such as political motives, purely professional ends, or to encourage production in a city, region, or country.

It is doubtful that media trade unionism would have taken the exact forms and adopted the programs it has in many countries were it not for the example of traditional trade unionism. Imitating traditional trade unions has, on occasion, resulted in trying to square circles and force ways of thinking that were somewhat artificial. For instance, a "local" (or "branch") of a national film technicians' union might, in fact, have been a national professional group without geographical boundaries. Miners or even office clerks would have a hard time recognizing a strike among screenwriters, although some of these strikes have been quite successful. In Germany even sculptors and painters have gone on "strike"—organized demonstrations at government ministries in support of their demand for a public exhibition right. Meanwhile, journalists' organizations in some Latin American countries have promoted traditional bargaining goals such as wages, hours, and working conditions, although their primary objective was jurisdictional: convincing employers (and governments) to refrain from hiring anyone to do bargaining unit work who did not have the approved education and titles. Finally, even defining the existence of a job and the nature of work may be problematic. Consider the following types of employment in the media sector: a Hollywood star who did only one six-week film shoot a year but still earned millions, and a "student/trainee" working fulltime at a local cable operation who not only earned little or nothing, but might even pay tuition at a local junior college for the right to hold the "job."

A certain amount of fiction always underlay the notion that every labor organization in the media was simply a derivative of the generic union concept and that industrial relations in the media sector could easily be fitted into the law and practice of the rest of society. But this is not to say that the fiction did not serve its purpose. On the contrary, media trade unionism at many times and in many places was extraordinarily successful in defending and advancing the interests of its members. It was primarily the organizations that approximated the trade union model most closely, even if more careful examination revealed that they were still something quite different from most trade unions, that made the greatest gains for media workers and maintained themselves, often with help from the rest of the union movement. On the other hand, organizations that did not show great creativity in adapting to the special circumstances of the media, or that acted too rigidly in trying to apply a generic model of trade unionism to the sector, usually failed to attract serious support from the people they were supposedly serving. Nonetheless, many of the spontaneous, unclassifiable organizations mentioned above were notoriously ephemeral and, even when successful, could often only be counted so in ways quite apart from the economic or social interests of the workers.

In the past, industrial relations and unionism in the media might have been considered a case of "exceptionalism" and therefore dismissed as of limited illustrative value by all except those involved in it or those specialists who studied it. Today, however, the situation is changing. Especially in an era that is starting to call itself the "new information society," such exceptionalism may soon become, if not the norm, at least a system shared by very large portions of the labor market. It may make sense to study the media sector, because its lessons may soon be relevant to many others. I begin with developments at the national level that help to explain the halting progress made over the years toward genuine cooperation at the international level.

The Idea of Common Interest among Media Workers: Ups and Downs at the National Level

As was true throughout the world, media union organization in the United States long has been and remains highly fragmented. In New York City alone, as many as a dozen national unions represented area locals that convened as a regional coordinating body, the Conference of Motion Picture and Television Unions. Sometimes national unions were not unified either. For instance, the International Alliance of Theatrical and Stage Employees, which represented the largest share of "non-creative" workers in theater, film, and commercials production, had more than a dozen relevant locals in the Hollywood area. Each was largely autonomous and represented a single, or limited number of crafts (e.g., stage hands, camera and lighting people, and wardrobe mistresses).

As a result of this fragmentation, the motion picture and television locals were constantly embroiled in jurisdictional disputes, despite the fact that all were affiliates of the AFL-CIO (except the Directors, the West Coast Writers, and, for a time, the Teamsters, which represent the drivers). For example, when a small programming unit at Manhattan Cable Television came under pressure to join the International Brotherhood of Electrical Workers (the IBEW represented the rest of the staff), the members of the unit approached the National Association of Broadcasting Employees and Technicians (NABET) as a way of avoiding representation by the same union that acted in behalf of the installers and subscription personnel. Even so, two IBEW locals vied to represent them. There were interregional disputes as well. For example, the New York camera local was in open conflict with the one in Hollywood.

Nonetheless, a strong feeling of solidarity existed within each of these unions. Were it not for this solidarity, the unions would have disintegrated (though some groups did collapse and others emerge). In fact, in the more important parts of the sector the unionization rate was high and union control was strong. Virtually all theater workers and, in the larger markets, most broadcasting workers were unionized.

Great divisions and kaleidoscopic union organization have existed in many countries, where media workers were every bit as confusingly organized as in the United States. In the United Kingdom, journalists, actors, musicians, writers, broadcasting staff, film workers, and theater staff each had their own union. In the Nordic countries and Germany the structure was similar, though the lines were not always the same. In Austria virtually all broadcasting, film, and theater workers, journalists, actors, and musicians had been together in a single umbrella organization called the Culture, Media and Independent Professional Workers' Federation (KMfB) for decades. The KMfB was created by the national center, the Austrian Trade Union Confederation (ÖGB). Special conditions in Austria allowed the ÖGB to force the KMfB to stay together, sometimes against the apparent desires of one group or another (most recently, the journalists).

Fragmentation was even more apparent in Latin America, where the tendency existed to establish unions, if only on paper, that resembled the unions in other sectors. Some of these organizations had few obvious members, resources, or activities, but were perpetuated for years nonetheless.

In Africa, media unions frequently emerged along with centrally organized national labor centers in the wake of anti-colonialist victories. Often these unions did not behave like traditional unions and were not always considered trade unions. However, when they became active in attempting to represent workers, as among journalists, the unions and their leaders were sometimes punished or co-opted by the new regimes. (Of course, the colonial powers had not allowed unions to exist at all.) A major exception was South Africa, where anti-apartheid unions emerged, aided initially by media colleagues in the United Kingdom and later by media internationals and others around the world.

It is difficult to generalize about Asia and the Pacific. India, a highly important media country, had perhaps the most diverse and complicated media union structure in the world. Almost any generalization could be proved or disproved there. At the extreme north and south of the western Pacific, Japan and Australia/New Zealand reflected many of the media union trends of most other industrial countries: traditionally fractured organizations resolutely attempted to look and act like regular unions but still differed from them significantly. In Japan, for example, most of the media unions stayed out of mainline national centers. After what they considered a bad experience of over-politicization of their association, Japanese actors insisted that they were not members of a trade union at all, and, indeed, they did not negotiate collective agreements.

During the 1990s, many attempts were made around the world to bring media workers together at the national level. The most publicized and, in the minds of many, most hopeful attempt at unity has been in Germany. Traditional media workers (journalists, broadcasting, film, and visual artists, and commercial theater workers) joined with the graphical workers (printing and publishing) to form a single union called IG Medien. Within months, however, large blocs of journalists, actors, and musicians broke off, some of them leaving the labor movement entirely, while the writers remained members, although highly autonomous ones. There is still turmoil within the organization. Nonetheless, IG Medien, which has over 200,000 members (and has absorbed media workers in the former German Democratic Republic as well) remains perhaps the bravest attempt yet at national-level media trade union unity. By late 1999, IG Medien was on course to merge with the public employees union, the white collar workers, and the telecommunications and postal workers to form a new union to be called VER.DI. With three million members, VER.DI will become the world's largest union.

In a series of mergers among unions in the United Kingdom, nearly all organized non-performer, non-journalist media workers (broadcasting, film, theater, visual artists, and cinema staff) are now in the relatively new Broadcasting, Entertainment, Cinematograph and Theatre Union (BECTU). The performers are unlikely to go the same route in the foreseeable future, but it is not inconceivable that the National Union of Journalists and BECTU could merge.

One of the most interesting processes toward unity has been among the affiliates of the Netherlands Federation of Trade Unions (FNV). Media workers there were dispersed across the Kunstenbond (performers, theater staff of all kinds), the Journalists, the Dienstenbond (broadcasting workers), and the Graphical Workers. Hoping to avoid the woes of IG Medien, which were attributed to over-theorizing and rigidity, the Dutch put together a working party for cooperation on projects, leaving structural issues for later (if at all). Early on the Journalists opted out, but the remaining unions established an organization for Culture, Information, Entertainment and Media (KIEM), which the Dutch described as a type of joint venture. At first, KIEM investigated the problems of organizing and representing workers in new or unorganized sectors of the media, especially freelance or other workers who had not been unionized before. A popular hot-line information service was established for all media workers, aimed especially at independents. The experiment seems to be holding its own, thanks to the unusual sensitivity of the leaders involved. By 1999, KIEM had formally consolidated from a merger of the other groups into a regular union.

Curiously, in much of the developing world media union structures seem to be changing little, if at all. Brazil is an exception. A new, revitalized labor movement largely associated with the militant confederation Central Unica dos Trabalhadores (CUT) has promoted similarly dynamic and militant media organizations. Close association in CUT has meant close cooperation, if not always unity, among the sub-sectors of the media, especially on common issues such as mobilization against private monopoly in the media.

In Australia, nearly all sectors of the media (except those in public service broadcasting, who remain in two public service workers' unions) have been brought together in a single organization, the Media Entertainment Arts Alliance (MEAA). Often mentioned as another example of growing media worker unity, MEAA was a direct result of an anti-labor law that withdrew collective bargaining rights from any organization with less than five thousand members, forcing a shotgun marriage among a number of small media unions.

Somewhat surprisingly, in the 1990s the United States became one of the places where greater cooperation and even mergers between media unions are now most visible and discussed. This trend was based not on ideological grounds but on pragmatic factors: financial problems of smaller groups, recognition of rapidly changing ownership, and technological trends. For example, a new factor has been the gigantic (in media workers' terms) Communications Workers of America's (CWA) plan to bring as many media workers under its tent as possible. Thus far, the CWA seems to be following this philosophy and is attracting considerable interest. NABET and The Newspaper Guild have joined the CWA's, which was previously mostly telecommunications workers.

Sometimes it seems that for every example of merger and successful cooperation at the national level there is an opposing example of conflict and break-up. One of the most spectacular break-ups occurred in Canada. The Association of Canadian Television and Radio Artists (ACTRA) was created in the 1970s to represent actors and screenwriters, many broadcasting journalists, and some other media groups. Early in the 1990s, ACTRA broke up into its various constituent parts, each of which now looks somewhat acrimoniously at the others.

The break-up trend is especially strong in Latin America. The return to democracy in Chile has led to the re-fragmentation of some media unions. In Venezuela, the Caracas regional body of the so-called national organization FEDERATEL rejects the latter's authority and philosophy. Unity around the CUT banner for most Brazilian media unions has driven others toward total independence. The relaxing of state control on union structures has resulted in similar break-ups in Central and Eastern Europe.

In sum, it almost seems as though trade union organization in the media sector is like the structure of stars. No totally stable example exists. National organizations implode or explode, centralize or break up. In cases of extreme particularism, the negative aspects become so apparent that various groups start joining together. After they reach a certain point of centralization, the nature of the workers and the work appear to make such a structure unpalatable, hence explosion again. The answer, obviously, would be a large degree of both: centralization for efficiency and federalism and autonomy for professional identity. But finding the right balance at the right time (for the context is also variable) is extremely difficult.

Impulses toward and against Cooperation at the National Level

Looking back at the constantly changing nature of cooperation among media unions, it is possible to discern a number of motives that have fostered greater cooperation as well as other impulses that have prevented cooperative relationships from beginning or have destroyed existing forms of collaboration. A variety of ideological and pragmatic impulses were responsible for the trend toward cooperation among media unions. First and foremost was the belief that workers could be united on the basis of common interests. Naturally communists, socialists, and their allies were the most avid proponents of this belief. They tried to apply this notion to organize mining, industrial, and other sectors (where it made sense in many cases) as well as to media workers (where it often fit the situation quite poorly). Even so, common interest was and remains a powerful motive. For example, it was a strong motivation underlying the formation of the Cultural Workers in the Soviet Union and the Social-Democratic-led IG Medien in West Germany.

One did not have to be anti-socialist to realize that personalities, creative ambitions, desires to work independently, and work structures placed a deal of strain on the belief in common interests among media workers. Nonetheless, even Christian Democrats and Liberals perceived unity in the media sector as an ideal, partly because it increased their political strength against their more leftist enemies, but also because it seemed to be the efficient and reasonable thing to do. On paper, if you are drawing up a scheme for a national trade union movement based upon a federation of homogeneous groups of industrial workers, it seems logical to put all media workers in a common group. This was the scheme often followed in southern European countries.

A second impulse toward greater cooperation was inspired by practical motives. By the mid-1980s, multinational conglomerates had been created in the media sector. Privatization and deregulation had also arrived. New technology that cut across national borders and across traditional subsectors was creating a growing sense of common fears, although not always a clear sense of common interests. What a growing global market had started (threats to job security and employment conditions, among others), satellite communications, cable, and other technologies were completing. National work standards, intellectual property rights, and other protections media workers had taken for granted were under threat. By the mid-1990s, starting in the most advanced countries but quickly becoming part of the consciousness elsewhere, the concept of convergence became apparent. Broadcasting, computers, and telecommunications were, it seemed, destined to become a single industry. Hence in many places the logic took hold of bringing together traditional media workers, sometimes already joined with graphical workers, and the more numerous and organizationally powerful telecommunications workers.

Meanwhile, many media unions, even relatively strong ones, at that moment happened to be confronting financial and organizational difficulties. Even in the best of circumstances media unions are more precarious than most. In many countries, perhaps most, media workers are just not numerous enough to form effective unions at the sub-sectoral level. Further, the 1980s were hard times in many countries for all unions because of political environments created by conservative governments such as those of Margaret Thatcher, Ronald Reagan, and Helmut Kohl. Changing notions of class in contemporary society also affected societal norms in a manner antithetical to trade unionism. Ironically, at the moment some media workers were becoming somewhat more class conscious, their chances of organizing effectively were becoming weaker. Many media unions lost ground and some went broke during this era. However, labor organizations rarely ever completely die or fade away; rather, they generally merge first. From this perspective, not every trend toward "cooperation" is entirely positive, though it may be no less necessary.

Unfortunately, the impulses that reinforce media workers' particularism do not go away just because objective conditions change. If given the choice, a large percentage of media unions, often for some very good reasons, have preferred less effective and divided organizations to efficient and centralized ones. The greatest resistance to unity has usually been the fear, sometimes imagined but often real, of one group losing its identity and not being serviced well should its interests become submerged by those of other workers in a merged union organization.

Thus many media unions, especially in the more "creative" categories, are quite unenthusiastic about the recent trends toward unity. Organizations that result from mergers are not necessarily stronger than the sum of their parts, and it is more difficult to organize some of the most particularist groups or individuals. For example, screenwriters, audiovisual directors, and visual artists in many countries, especially if their numbers allow it, tend to seek to form their own, often rather isolated, organizations. They argue that to have all or most of a single craft—like screenwriters—in a single country gives greater bargaining power than to have thousands of allied workers behind them. The problem is that the creative workers may not be numerous enough to sustain organizations. The creative groups alone may seem practically invisible or at best of little importance to larger groups—hence the potentially problematic relationship of media workers with their numerically larger and relatively more powerful new allies in the formerly separate graphical and telecommunications sectors. However, these particularist groups may constitute a very large portion of media workers in the future and, indeed, in society as a whole.

IG Medien in Germany, the KIEM "joint venture" experiment in the

Netherlands, and the CWA in the United States demonstrate that intelligent approaches to cooperation are possible. Whether these will be effective enough to maintain and extend high levels of organization and unity in the media sector remains to be seen.

Beginnings of International "Solidarity"

Although international trade unionism developed over a hundred years ago in many sectors, this was not true in entertainment and media, for three reasons: First, compared to mining, transport, or the metals industry, the media sector was (and still is) small, especially the organized sector. Second, as already described at the national level, the sense of common interests was weaker among media workers than in most sectors. Despite the fact that performers often traveled around the world and immigrants might be numerous in supporting and technical positions in any country, the concept that media was an international economic activity was very slow to develop. And third, when it came along, broadcasting in most industrialized countries, especially television, was established as a public service (with obvious exceptions like the United States) and thus was purely a national entity. Figure 8.1 indicates when the various international labor organizations in the media sector were founded and how they have combined to form more inclusive associations.

International labor cooperation in the media was a post-World War II development concurrent with the Cold War, and was both weak and complicated. The International Federation of Journalists (IFJ) considers itself descended from some conferences and organizational attempts of journalists that took place between the two world wars. The IFJ was actually established in the 1950s as a response to the takeover by pro-Moscow sectarians of the International Organization of Journalists (the IOJ was international in scope but not always considered a trade union body). It was not until the mid-1980s that the IFJ applied for and was recognized as an international trade secretariat (ITS).[1]

The first conscious attempt at international union organization was the International Federation of Musicians (FIM) in 1947. Shortly thereafter, the International Federation of Actors (FIA) was created. These two organizations soon encountered problems of Cold War conflict similar to those confronting the IOJ. But their affiliates in the West, of whom the British were the most influential in both cases, handled the situation quite differently from the journalists. They declared themselves nonaligned and, without losing support from a number of real and independent unions in

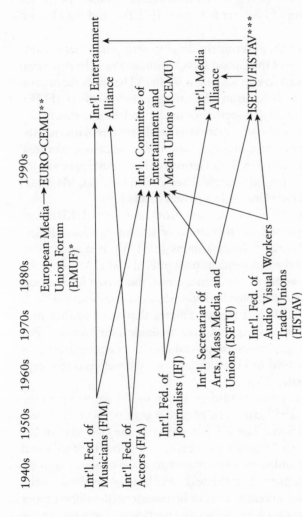

1940s 1950s 1960s 1970s 1980s 1990s

European Media → EURO-CEMU**
Union Forum
(EMUF)*

Int'l. Fed. of
Musicians (FIM) → Int'l. Entertainment
Alliance

Int'l. Fed. of
Actors (FIA)

Int'l. Fed. of
Journalists (IFJ) → Int'l. Committee of
Entertainment and
Media Unions (ICEMU)

Int'l. Secretariat of
Arts, Mass Media, and
Unions (ISETU) → Int'l. Media
Alliance

Int'l. Fed. of
Audio Visual Workers
Trade Unions
(FISTAV) → ISETU/FISTAV***

* A forum, rather than a formal organization, for discussions among European representatives of FIA, FIM, FISTAV, IFJ, ISETU, and IGF.

** When ICEMU was formed, EMUF was renamed EURO-CEMU which, in turn, became the European dimension of ICEMU; in the late 1990s, CI was admitted to ICEMU and EURO-CEMU.

*** Renamed Media and Entertainment International (MEI).

Figure 8.1. Evolution of International Trade Union Organizations in the Media Sector

the West, concentrated on professional issues. This strategy enabled the affiliates to continue working with Soviet-bloc unions (which differed substantially from the free trade unions common in Western nations) and carry
out limited but continual activity for decades that frequently involved appropriate American unions. However, because of their willingness to deal
with Soviet-bloc unions, the FIM and FIA forfeited recognition by the International Confederation of Free Trade Unions (ICFTU) and the ITSs associated with it.

Aided substantially by U.S. government development funds that became
available as a consequence of the Cuban Revolution, in 1963 the American
media unions took the lead in establishing a Western Hemispheric organization, the Interamerican Federation of Entertainment Workers (FITE).
This organization covered all sub-sectors of media and entertainment, including technicians and other staff, performers, and, less often, journalists.
Later, a loosely organized European organization of broadcasting workers'
unions emerged, headquartered in West Germany. These developments led
to the founding of ISETU, the International Secretariat for Arts, Mass Media and Entertainment Trade Unions in Brussels in 1965.[2]

In 1973, left-wing media union leaders from the United Kingdom,
France, and Italy championed the formation of the International Feder-
ation of Audio Visual Workers Trade Unions (FISTAV) as a counter to
ISETU. FISTAV followed the independent path of FIM and FIA, eventually
establishing a loose cooperative arrangement with those two federations.
Thus FISTAV brought in Eastern bloc affiliates while expanding in the West.
Though never large, FISTAV had many affiliates that were neither pro-
Communist nor even left-wing (Belgian Christian unions, for instance). But
in fact, its political message was more defined and more aggressively presented than that of either FIM or FIA, although one did not need to accept
the party line to participate.

The international trade union landscape in the media sector up to the
end of the Cold War in 1989 consisted of media organizations that performed a variety of functions. The IFJ was probably the strongest of the
groups. Journalists held world conferences every two years that facilitated
the exchange of ideas, afforded the opportunity to make contacts, and reinforced participants' identity. The IFJ was also heavily involved in the
defense of press freedom (representation in broadcasting developed more
slowly) and of independent trade unionism and participated in a number of
solidarity campaigns. For example, the IFJ organized important actions in
defense of journalists in Chile, South Africa, and later Palestine. Following
successes by more traditional ITSs, and with assistance from Nordic, German, and other funding sources, the IFJ became deeply involved in devel-

opment programs that helped journalists' unions in Third World countries. The IFJ always emphasized professional as well as trade union issues. However, toward the end of the Cold War period, "industrial" activity (which we might define as mutual self-help among the wealthier affiliates who were the financial basis of the organization, as opposed to solidarity in distant countries) also began to be important.

Similar activities were carried out, though on a lesser scale, by the FIM and FIA. These organizations functioned as exchange centers and advocates for professional identity and intellectual property rights. But they were also involved in solidarity activities; FIA's support for Chilean actors during the Pinochet regime was an important example. Because they were denied assistance from ICFTU-connected funding sources, FIM and FIA did little direct developmental work of the sort that the IFJ had begun.

FISTAV was weaker than FIM and FIA and never progressed much beyond the coordinating, exchange-center level. It held occasional congresses and conferences, mostly in Europe (alternating between Eastern and Western sites). FISTAV had a high level of internal political consciousness, passed resolutions that helped to educate trade unionists across borders, and was committed to solidarity, particularly with media unionists whose ideological tendencies were strongly to the left (e.g., some film unions in India or the militant broadcasting workers in Colombia).

ISETU, especially in its first years, devoted itself almost entirely to presenting seminars and other events in developing countries. The unspoken consensus was that this would help unions in these areas to build support against communism, although no ideological test was posed for those seeking assistance. In contrast to all the other media internationals in this period, ISETU's development activities (though they dwindled for long periods) were probably greater than its role among its main paying affiliates as a point of contact, discussion, or identity reinforcement.

In retrospect, during most of the Cold War period these organizations lacked a real sense that international activity was an extension of national "industrial" activity by the affiliated members. This is in marked contrast with the large and growing industrial ITSs that were increasingly concerned about multinational corporations and other transnational issues.

Starting in the 1980s, structural changes that had emerged at the national level of media trade unions began to occur at the international level as well. Beginning in Europe, always the strongest center of international trade unionism, the impetus at first was more political than economic, springing more from idealism than from the intent to carry out common industrial action.

In the late 1980s, FIM, FIA, IFJ, ISETU, FISTAV, and the IGF started meeting together under the name European Media Union Forum (EMUF). In fact, it was the European sections of these organizations, rather than the internationals, that started this process. The immediate objective was to cooperate in lobbying within the European Common Market, which was establishing the more thoroughgoing Single Market. This move toward greater cooperation was brought about by the declining intensity of the Cold War during the Gorbachev years and the periodic calls within ISETU, FISTAV, FIM, and FIA to find a way of dealing with one another. Not least in driving this process was pressure from European national unions such as IG Medien and several Southern European countries' unions that had merged some sub-sectors.

EMUF concentrated on public policy issues in Europe and on defense of trade union rights in the media. A common statement was adopted opposing privatization and deregulation, calling for intellectual property rights to be protected in the new technologies, and seeking safeguards against too much private cross-media concentration within the emerging Single Market. The Murdoch group's attacks on trade unionism in the British newspaper industry were singled out for special condemnation.

The imminent collapse of communism in eastern Europe began to overshadow even the growing unity of Western Europe as an impetus for greater cooperation, and almost overnight the divisions among some of the media internationals appeared totally out of date. The new, positive atmosphere was indicated by discussions among unionists who had never before officially met together, most notably a representative of the AFL-CIO (ISETU's vice president) and a representative of the French communist-oriented CGT (the general secretary of FISTAV).

Not coincidentally, just after the failed coup against Gorbachev and the final break-up of the Soviet Union in late 1991, FIM, FIA, ISETU, FISTAV, and IFJ signed an agreement to establish the International Committee of Entertainment and Media Unions (ICEMU). The same agreement provided for a European component called EURO-CEMU. Given the complex history and discussion leading up to this action, the actual agreement was only moderately explicit on the common principles that were being adopted, and it was extremely short on actions to be undertaken. The most explicit commitments were contained in an appendix: FIM and FIA were to be the "internationally recognized bodies for performers," without prejudice to ISETU's maintaining as members those performers who already belonged to its affiliated unions; FISTAV and ISETU would discuss the future of audio-visual workers.

The most concrete and immediate result of the ICEMU agreement was a plan to establish an office in Brussels, to be financed jointly by the five bodies, that would serve as ISETU's European and world secretariat. This agreement was a subtle compromise since it was implicit that by helping ISETU the other organizations that had conflict with it could expect eventual resolution of those conflicts as part of the settlement. It was informally agreed that the new office would actually function within the IFJ's secretariat. Although complicated, this agreement was immediately endorsed by the European Trade Union Confederation (ETUC) and by the ICFTU. The latter backed up its endorsement with substantial financial assistance for the new office for the first two years (later extended to three).

The IGF had not been a part of the original ICEMU discussions, but it was highly supportive of the process. When its possibilities for greater involvement became clear, the IGF also was admitted following a proposal by the IFJ. Thus EURO-CEMU superseded EMUF.

The individual programs of most of ICEMU's members did not change much after its founding. Rather, ICEMU brought the various internationals' leaders together from time to time, creating something of a sense of a common movement. It drew those who had never had relations with the ICFTU or ETUC into a new, as yet undefined, ad hoc relationship with those organizations. A variety of common campaigns, mostly letter writing and related activities, was carried out in support of causes taken up by the individual internationals.

Curiously, one of the most unifying experiences within the new group occurred when the PTTI, the telecommunications international, started organizing broadcasting workers in Latin America. This organizing was a logical result of the convergence of the telecommunications industry with the media, and it was consistent with PTTI's new ideas of how it should react to convergence. ISETU and FISTAV both felt threatened by this turn of events. First ISETU and FISTAV, and then all ICEMU members together, protested strongly about PTTI's testing of the media waters. Various communiqués indicated that while lines might still be fuzzy between the media internationals, collectively they considered their jurisdiction to be the entire sector. (This position was to be modified within a couple of years, as will be seen below.)

The most tangible result of the establishment of ICEMU and its Brussels office was the eventual outright merger of FISTAV and ISETU, first called ISETU/FISTAV, in a Unity Congress in London in December 1993. Although creating ICEMU brought cooperation to new levels, it also highlighted jurisdictional conflicts about representation of performers. Long negotiations between ISETU/FISTAV, FIM, and FIA eventually resulted in a new agreement that established still another cooperative body called the International Entertainment Alliance. It confirmed that FIM and FIA would represent performers "in public fora," but no performers would be forced out of ISETU/FISTAV who were already there. The agreement called for recognition of the new Alliance as the ITS associated with the ICFTU that covered the field formerly represented by ISETU alone; the same was to be sought for Europe at the ETUC. (The European component was the European Entertainment Alliance.) It called for closer association between the three entertainment internationals in a number of areas. In this vein, it proposed that the inter-Americas region of ISETU/FISTAV (PANARTES) be reorganized as the common representative there of all three organizations, although the agreement did not specify how this arrangement would be implemented.[3]

A similar, less emotionally charged agreement on cooperation was signed between ISETU/FISTAV and the IFJ, setting up the International Media Alliance. Since opening the ICEMU/ISETU office within IFJ's secretariat, these two organizations had begun to work together. Outright merger, however, did not take place because of ISETU/FISTAV's uncertain financial base and because of strong resistance from some journalists' groups to giving up their "journalists only" identity. This alliance was changed in 1999 to a more pragmatic arrangement based primarily on the commitment that neither organization would compete with the other's area of activity.

By early 1995, ISETU/FISTAV had reached an accommodation with PTTI. PTTI mollified ISETU/FISTAV (backed up by the rest of ICEMU) by, in principle, agreeing not to intrude on ISETU/FISTAV's "jurisdiction" (a concept not entirely understood by many of PTTI's members previously). The two organizations agreed to cooperate to organize the unorganized at the international level, especially in the areas where ISETU/FISTAV could not be very active. After tacitly recognizing PTTI's representational role in the media sector, ISETU/FISTAV proposed that PTTI become a sixth member of ICEMU. In mid-1995, the other ICEMU members accepted this proposal and PTTI was accepted into the organization. At its 1998 congress PTTI renamed itself Communications International.

At its second world congress in Washington, D.C., in December 1995, ISETU/FISTAV was renamed Media and Entertainment International (MEI). In 1999 MEI agreed in principle to merge with FIET, CI, and IGF to form a new ITS called Union Network International (UNI). This ITS would have fifteen million members, of whom only 250,000 would be from MEI. About 800,000 would be from IGF. As of this writing, FIET and CI have held congresses endorsing the merger and MEI and IGF have scheduled congresses to deal with it. In 1999, MEI voted to merge with FIET, CI, and IGF to form a new ITS called Union Network International (UNI), with fifteen million members, of whom only 250,000 were from MEI. About 800,000 were from IGF. This merger became effective January 2000.

ICEMU's secretariat, without any joint financial support, was moved to the IGF office in 1994 and to FIA's office in London in 1995. Although still more cooperative structures may develop among media internationals, including a possible merger or two at some point, no one is suggesting that ICEMU is going to become a unified body. But neither is it going to go away. Its existence as an anomaly on the international trade union scene now seems confirmed: a half-way body, neither a single trade secretariat nor a new international center, with real but limited programs and aspirations.

Conclusions about Structure

The nineteenth-century socialist American labor theorist Daniel DeLeon is generally credited with developing the concept that trade unions must develop their structures and programs according to the structure of the industry in which they find themselves. In our sector only the Dutch media unions have come right out and proposed limited arrangements, "joint ventures," that will carry out certain activities in conscious imitation of media employers' structures. On the other hand, many media unionists, being almost invariably drawn from idealistic backgrounds, dream of One Big Union. In actuality, media unions throughout the world have created some of the most complex forms imaginable.

At the national and international levels, the complex structure of media unions has arisen for a number of reasons, some of them purely due to personalities or subjective reasons. The most important influence on structure, however, has been the growing complexity of the industry itself. Even the most casual observer quickly notices that world famous film studios, whose productions are increasingly bought from outside independents, are subsidiaries of little-known production companies. Joint ventures, alliances, and transitional mergers are now the rule. On the broadcasting side, U.S. networks supply many more affiliates with products than they have owned-and-operated stations.

In Europe newly emerging private television already has a complicated ownership pattern that even intricate charts covering an entire wall fail to explain fully; the same is developing in Asia. Finally, in advertising much of "Madison Avenue" is in fact owned by London-based global conglomerates. Advertising is structured into chains or networks, the ownership of which is often distinct from everyday operating connections.

In sum, those who would like neater paradigms of union structure should look elsewhere. Those neater paradigms are probably more identifiable in the past than in the future, as what was media sector exceptionalism becomes much more common in many other industries.

If Not Solidarity, at Least Convergence

The endless discussions about structure, and the emphasis given here to institutional evolution at the national and international levels, tend to obscure the fact that existing structures have enabled media unions to defend their members' interests (though it must be admitted that sometimes the structural talk has received more attention among trade union leaders and observers than the activities). I turn my attention now to examples of the concerted actions that were made possible by the interconnectedness of media unions. Much (hopefully most) activity of the internationals in the Cold War period was at least ostensibly professional, although clearly some measures were inspired by anti-Western on the one hand or anti-Communist on the other political considerations.

It happens that two of the earliest examples of international labor agreements anywhere were in the media sector. In the early 1950s FIM and FIA negotiated agreements with the European Broadcasting Union (EBU) concerning payments to performers in international exchanges of programming, first in radio and then in television. This negotiation resulted from lobbying and pressures that were organized by FIM and FIA around the "Eurovision" song contest program. Eurovision is the simulcast agreement of members of the EBU. Eurovision's annual song contest for decades has had the largest audience (first for radio, now for radio and TV) of any simple transmission in the world. It is known like no other program almost everywhere around the world (except in the United States). In the same decade IFPI, the London-based international federation of phonogram producers, signed an agreement with FIM on similar lines. However, both the EBU and IFPI agreements were only recommended to the national organizations affiliated with them and could not really be enforced unless employers voluntarily complied.

As the Cold War drew to a close, professional activity came to be increasingly supplemented by attempts at international "industrial" action in this sector. The experience of ISETU/FISTAV is an example.

Before its merger with FISTAV, but with their reasons for conflict already fading, ISETU, almost by accident, got involved in one of the most purely industrial actions it had yet undertaken. The circumstances were the finals of the 1991 European (soccer) Cup, to be held in Barcelona. The Spanish media unions had been involved for some time in inconclusive negotiations with the national broadcasting system, RTVE. The issues were economic and, less conventionally, the unions' desire to impose limits on how many freelance, as opposed to regular full-time workers, RTVE could hire. The latter was (and is) a major concern of broadcasting workers around the world and can quickly arouse a good deal of emotion.

One of the Spanish unions contacted the ISETU secretariat and reported a secret plan to call a joint job action in Barcelona to try to force RTVE to take negotiations more seriously. In the forty-eight hours before the start of the tournament, the Spanish hoped that ISETU could reach the unions of most other media workers who would be at the stadium, inform them of the situation, and urge them to take such solidarity actions as they could.

One critical factor was that both ISETU's and FISTAV's Spanish affiliates were involved and that both sought help from both internationals. On the day of the event, an unprecedented international job action took place. The Spanish journalists and technicians went on strike while those from other countries demonstrated their support. Viewers in Italy and Switzerland watched in amazement as their nationals' cameras turned to the sky the moment play began. In France, viewers saw a blank screen with an explanation about a "labor dispute" superimposed. Elsewhere in Europe transmission by national crews was affected in various ways.

The Spanish unionists had originally asked only that no colleagues from unions in other countries be left uninformed as to what they were doing and why, and they were especially concerned that no one else take over their jobs that day. But the journalists and technicians used the opportunity to show direct support for the Spanish strikers and also to express their own concerns about the lively issue of freelancers. The result was international action that contributed to management's accepting several of the Spanish unions' demands.

A second example of international industrial action occurred just before the Summer Olympics in 1992, also by chance in Barcelona. This action combined older-style "solidarity" with newer convergence issues. The union involved was the Media Workers' Association of South Africa (MWASA), representing most of the workers, journalists, and other staff of the South Africa Broadcasting Corporation (SABC). MWASA was an affiliate of both ISETU and the IFJ.

In this instance, the unions had more time to prepare. For some months, MWASA had been in negotiations with management to assure that pay and opportunities for black workers were equivalent to those for whites. Although many blacks were doing exactly the same jobs as whites, they were receiving much less pay. MWASA warned that there would be labor difficulties in Barcelona if no agreement was reached. ISETU and the IFJ asked their affiliates to contact South African embassies or interests in their own countries and to warn their own national broadcasting operations that were going to Barcelona that there could be problems. The ICEMU took over coordination of the campaign. The ICFTU was brought in, which in turn drew in important national centers, notably those in Spain and the United Kingdom. Press conferences were held in London and Barcelona, and U.S. media workers prepared to demonstrate in Washington.

Just hours before the Barcelona games began, SABC and MWASA reached an agreement in Johannesburg that was highly favorable to the union's position. The effectiveness of the ICEMU/ICFTU efforts was indicated by management's demand for a primary clause in the agreement that MWASA would end all international organizing around the racism issue and would request its fellow ISETU and IFJ affiliates to drop all their activities in this regard.

Once the ISETU/FISTAV merger took place, the new organization, with assistance from the ETUC, started focusing much of its "industrial strategy" around social dialogue (social dialogue is the program of the European Union that seeks to establish at least rudimentary levels of consultation between workers and employers who operate in two or more EU member states) within the European Union and around implementation of the European Works Council Directive in the media sector (see Chapter 7). ISETU/FISTAV and its successor, MEI, held separate conferences in Europe for freelance film workers, advertising workers, cinema (exhibition and distribution) workers, public broadcasting workers, and theater workers. Even a gathering of visual artists was organized. All these events were intended to promote social dialogue, but getting to that point proved difficult.

To be sure, some employers' representatives were induced to attend some of the meetings and to participate in some discussions. For example, the European advertisement producers' association, the European theater producers' group, the international film producers, and others participated. Although it was not part of the EU official program, the most successful dialogue occurred among the European Broadcasting Union, MEI, and IFJ regarding defense of their common interest in public service broadcasting.

Identifying single employers and starting some sort of relationship with them was often an illusive goal. However, ISETU/FISTAV underwrote two successful conferences among its German and French affiliates that represented workers at the bi-national ARTE broadcasting operation in Strasbourg. As a consequence of these conferences, a new international collective agreement for ARTE workers was negotiated between management and the French and German unions. Later a conference was called in Lyon that would involve French, Spanish, and Italian unions connected with Euronews. These instances of greater cooperation were unusual, but by 1999, formal social dialogue had been established by EURO-MEI with European broadcasters, live performance employers, and other employers' groups.

Transnational Activities of MEI

Early in 1996, MEI and its Italian affiliates identified four European private broadcasting groups that theoretically could be fitted under the difficult (for media workers) requirements of the Works Council Directive. These were Canal Plus (France), CLT (RTL) (Luxembourg), Finnivest (Berlusconi) (Italy), and the Leo Kirch group (Germany). Attempts were made to establish cross-border works councils in these companies. To date, however, only one council has been created, in CLT, a success for media workers but very small potatoes compared to other industries in which many more such councils have been established.

Another cross-border campaign took place in 1995 when MEI organized support in France for American workers at NBC. For many months, these workers had been unable to get even a minimally acceptable contract renewal. The NBC workers (members of NABET, which had recently merged with CWA) had for some time demonstrated outside the window of the "Today Show" studio in New York during the broadcasts in order to publicize their demands. When NABET learned that the show was going to be produced in France for several days, the union sent a representative of the bargaining committee there to surprise NBC by continuing to display the signs. MEI organized logistics for the NABET-CWA demonstrations, both in the south of France and in Paris. The French unions are known for great militancy in their own way. Although surprised by American-style job actions *during* broadcasts, French unions participated until forced back by the police. Because NBC continued its refusal to reach an agreement, it appears that the action was probably more of a Franco-American learning experience regarding styles of action than anything else.

Early in 1996, during negotiations with the International Olympic Committee (IOC), American media unions once again asked the help of the MEI and other members of ICEMU, to strengthen the unions' negotiating position on the hiring of technical workers for the Summer Games in Atlanta. MEI affiliates, especially those in Europe, and affiliates of other media internationals pressured their own national broadcasting organizations, with little success. The U.S. unions blamed the IOC for a certain amount of bad faith and concluded that national and international unions would have to be much better organized prior to the 2000 Olympics in Sydney.

After just two years in existence, MEI's report on solidarity activity at its December 1995 congress identified twenty-eight distinct actions in which the International and its affiliates had been involved. Included on this partial list were interventions of protest to Nigerian authorities over the hanging of a noted playwright, filing a complaint at the ILO against the Venezuelan government for collusion with a private broadcaster to set up a yellow (i.e., employer-dominated) union, supporting workers' defense of the arts in post-communist Poland, and mounting a successful international campaign to support a hunger strike by Romanian trade unionists promoting independence of the media in their newly democratized country. Other MEI actions involved support for striking French dubbers, protests against an anti-union U.S. broadcaster for investing in South Africa, and interventions with a Mexican broadcaster who used anti-union tactics in Peru. Admittedly, most of the solidarity actions do not differ greatly from the activities carried out by various internationals during the Cold War period. However, recent action is intended to address a larger share of "industrial" issues. Awareness appears to be increasing that these actions will produce modest but real effects.

Although MEI has demonstrated its willingness to campaign around contract issues, particular employers, or human rights, it is also occupied with several topics of more general concern. Probably the greatest single issue for MEI has been support for public service broadcasting. Australian, British, Canadian, Colombian, Belgian, French, Japanese, and Spanish unions are just a few of the MEI affiliates that have undertaken campaigns of varied magnitude to support public services challenged in their countries.

A second major activity was a comprehensive study of working conditions of freelance film workers, initially in Europe and then in other regions. The purpose was to prepare for discussions with employers about observing minimum conditions, no matter where productions take place. These conditions would probably not include wages or social benefits, which would be difficult to harmonize from one country to another. Rather, the focus was working conditions, such as the minimum number of hours of rest required between shoots on two different days. Experience suggested that it was probably more practical for the workers, through their unions in MEI (which probably represent most professional freelance film technicians in the world in one way or another) to agree on such minimums (very unambitious ones at first) and try to follow them unilaterally. A similar process was being considered for the theater sector.

The freelance film worker activity was suggestive of the fact that MEI, like other media internationals, can very rarely work on projects that are aimed at single companies across borders or that can be considered industrial in the usual sense. The IFJ, FIM, and FIA accepted this premise long ago. The fact that MEI has come to some of the same conclusions is an indication of convergence in yet another sense.

One touchy question illustrates both the limits to international cooperation in the media sector and the extent to which MEI's members yearn to go further. That is the "national production issue"—that is, whether governments should require certain amounts of media content to be produced locally. This issue touches on quotas vs. free market, subsidized vs. commercial production, and countless other complicated questions of national culture. Because the European region of MEI adopted diametrically opposed positions to those held by the U.S. affiliates, the matter was considered to be so threatening that the organization consciously avoided dealing with it for some time.

Ultimately, a small but internationally representative conference was convened in Paris in mid-1996, and an internal dialogue was begun on the issue of "International Audio-Visual Production and Trade: Culture and Commerce?" The focus was discussion only, and no conclusions were articulated or distributed. Predictably, the discussions identified certain interests that were shared by media workers in different countries and other interests that divided media unions. Participants appeared to agree that MEI could exist only if it emphasized the commonalties and downplayed divisive matters at international meetings. Consequently, future MEI discussions would deal with matters in which international producers' interests were against those of all production workers and with sharing of information on regulations for the use of foreign technicians in each country. This meeting certainly did not end with the singing of "Solidarity Forever." Few meetings more clearly exposed the ambiguities of international cooperation in the sector. But these divisive issues could not be ignored. "It would be like having an elephant in the room, but no one mentioning it," remarked the representative from the Hollywood Screenwriters' Guild.

Transnational Activities of Other Media Federations

The activities of FIM, FIA, and IFJ in the new period have expanded, especially those of the IFJ. These media federations function very differently from internationals in other sectors, even more so than MEI does.

FIM and FIA have survived the reorientations of the end of the Cold War, a traumatic event for the two federations even though it was welcomed by a majority of their members. FIM and FIA seem to have stabilized again. Contrary to the predictions of some, although they have lost certain income from eastern countries, they have gained greater acceptance among mainline trade unions. Both FIM and FIA are still concentrating their efforts on performance rights issues, but have increased their involvement in union-building activities in developing countries. They now are seen as eligible for funding from such groups as the Nordic international programs that formerly would not have felt at ease with them. In conjunction with MEI, FIM and FIA are involved for the first time in serious plans for joint activities on issues such as cross-border social security questions for freelancers.

The IFJ has increased its size and activities in the recent period. In part this growth might be attributed to the increasing importance of independent media in much of the world where they were absent before, to especially good leadership in the IFJ, and to greatly increased outside assistance (thanks more to the organization's important activities in media than to its standing as a trade union). It might also be argued that the IFJ was already at the take-off stage when this new era of good feeling arrived, while the other media internationals (not considering PTTI or IGF for the moment) may only now be reaching this stage of development.

Probably the IFJ's biggest commitment at the moment is to presenting a workers' point of view on the new information society. Its Media for Democracy program promotes both independent unions and independent media in many African and Central and Eastern European countries. By increasing its activity in Europe, the IFJ has become an important lobbying voice at the European Commission and Parliamentary levels on a number of issues such as freedom of the press. The IFJ is involved in all sorts of special projects, including helping the Palestinian broadcasting authority get off the ground and playing a big part in establishing a new broadcasting system in Sarajevo. Finally, for years the IFJ has issued international press cards and more recently has publicized lists of journalists killed on the job or as a result of their work.

From most trade unionists' point of view, it is curious that the list of IFJ activities includes few examples of "industrial" action. Now and then, the IFJ supports striking affiliates. It also promotes a worldwide boycott of *USA Today* because its owners also own a Detroit newspaper that has treated its striking workers scandalously. But there is even less talk of strategies for confronting multinational corporations within the IFJ than within MEI (though perhaps more than in FIM or FIA). As a matter of fact, in no multinational media company do the IFJ's affiliates represent even half the workforce. The IFJ is strongly committed to working with other groups to try to bring some influence to bear on such companies. However, the record of its activities clearly suggests that the IFJ does not perceive its role to be exerting pressure on multinational media companies by itself.

In sum, recent years have witnessed the emergence of more complex, perhaps less idealistic, but maybe more enduring types of transnational activities. There is little room here for "all for one and one for all," fully consistent with the ideology of international solidarity. But there is a growing sense of convergence of interests. The final irony may be that, at least in the media sector, these new forms of cooperation may be more effective than solidarity of the old type. In a period of lower expectations, it is perhaps in the sectors where organizational unity was already the most problematic and complex that new ways of thinking and working may have a good chance. Whether that is for better or worse, history will decide. For our part we must play the hand we have been dealt.

From Convergence to Real Solidarity?

The IFJ as of late 1999 claimed an affiliated membership of over 400,000, while the other three internationals each had perhaps half that number, and sometimes even these were overlapping. Certainly, the total number of members in the media internationals, not counting the IGF or PTTI, did not reach one million (compared to more than a million for the IGF alone, four times that for the PTTI, and twenty times or more that number for education or metal workers, among others). But for the first time since international union organization was attempted in the media sector, a real, if complex, base now exists.

Can this base continue to evolve into a truly effective instrument for international solidarity? The need for such solidarity is much more apparent now than in the past because global media enterprise can no longer be controlled by national action alone. The continuing development of new technologies that undermine the entire system of intellectual property rights at the international level, the increasing concentration in the media, and, most recently, the growing convergence of traditional media with the computer and telecommunications industries are issues that demand the creation of some sort of international countervailing power to defend workers' rights and to safeguard independent media. The trade union movement is the only entity with an abiding, long-term interest in maintaining a countervailing force that is in any way capable of providing the required assistance. Indeed, unions may, by default of other institutions, bear the burden of building pluralism and democracy at a world level because the national state can no longer assure it. That is a pretty tall order for such a small and, so far, only modestly effective community of organizations.

In 1998 ICEMU held an international conference on the new international alliance of British Telecom, MCI, and News Corporation. The conference was a small step, but quite different in kind from anything else the internationals had tried collectively. It resulted in a commitment to work more closely in dealing with communications/media conglomerates and was one of the common actions that led to the emergence of the UNI concept later.

World councils and other activities at the level of the multinational corporation have been attempted by union internationals in other sectors for years with only partial success, and those in sectors where organization and discipline have been greater than anything that can be expected of media unions. Nonetheless, the media sector does have characteristics that enhance its ability to promote and implement cooperative activity. First, numbers alone are not as important here as in many industrial sectors. Weak and divided media unions at the national level have known that all along. It is the media unions' ability to convince the public that others are not acting in the public interest that magnifies their power. And this they have often been able to do.

Second, as often happens at the national level, when a time of crisis starts becoming apparent to all, union activity, which might not be so important at other times, can sometimes step into the breach and have a tremendous impact because of the absence of other credible players. We may be approaching such a moment at the world level with the arrival of the new information society. The new Union Network International is clearly conscious of this possible role and its founding documents show that it intends to play this part.

But if these special characteristics of media unions are to bear fruit, the growing unity of the international media union community must somehow learn its lessons from the past by resisting the temptation either to fragment or to attempt to become too centralized. Ironically, it may only be through emphasizing the limitations of cooperation in this sector, and accepting convergence rather than more idealistic goals, that something comparable to solidarity may eventually emerge. And that solidarity may accomplish a few things on behalf of media workers, in such a way that this "peculiar" sector could demonstrate some lessons that other sectors in a brave new (but also very dangerous) world might apply.

9

Organizing in Export Processing Zones: The Bibong Experience in the Dominican Republic

DAVID JESSUP AND MICHAEL E. GORDON

For twenty-five years the sprawling maquiladora "free zones" in the Dominican Republic (D.R.) were known as havens for transnational companies. They could set up shop with the assurance that their workers, mostly young women, would be denied the fundamental right to bargain collectively to improve their working conditions. In 1994, that image began to change. On July 22, 1994, employees at the Bibong Apparel Corporation won the first collective bargaining contract in the history of export processing zones (EPZs) in the D.R. Their achievement capped a three-year struggle in which scores of workers paid a heavy price of dismissals, threats of violence, bribery, sexual harassment, arrests, and blacklisting.

In this chapter we will describe the coordinated international campaign spearheaded by unions in the D.R. to organize workers at Bibong. This campaign is significant for several reasons. First, the EPZs in the D.R. are considered typical of those in zone-operating countries (van Heerden, 1998). Second, the success of this campaign set the stage for greater militancy among workers in EPZs throughout that country and led to other victories that established collective bargaining rights. The consequences of the Bibong campaign have had a significant influence on the democratization of the D.R., the empowerment of women workers, and the ability of unionists to effectively represent their members. Third, the Bibong success is important because working conditions in many EPZs in the Caribbean and Latin America are among the harshest in the world. The opportunity for collective representation offers the approximately one million EPZ workers in this region the prospect of taking direct action to improve their conditions. The significance of the Dominican EPZ experience is underscored by the fact that it was one of only a handful of cross-border union campaigns reported in the International Labor Office's *World Labor Report, 1997–98* (ILO 1997, 40).

We begin with a brief background sketch of the D.R. and a description of the EPZs in that country, followed by discussion of the campaign at Bibong. We conclude by suggesting several principles of international cooperation that appear to increase the success of union organizing in a country that chooses to ignore its own labor laws in order to promote its export industries.

The Dominican Republic

In contrast to highly industrialized nations, both the political and the economic environments in the D.R. are unpredictable.This longstanding situation of uncertainty has worked to the detriment of the formation of unions. For most of its history, the D.R. has been ruled by other countries or by dictators. Troops from the United States occupied the country twice in the twentieth century to halt fighting between rival political factions. Although an elected president serves as the head of state, the constitution had to be modified in 1994 because of widespread voting irregularities reported by opposition party officials as well as international observers. Dominican and foreign investors have alleged judicial and administrative dishonesty in government, and there have been complaints that settlements of business disputes are frequently influenced by corruption (American Embassy 1995).

The D.R. has a narrow economic base. It has limited natural resources, and its economy traditionally has relied on the export of agricultural products, especially sugar. Because it does not produce these commodities in sufficient quantity to influence global price or demand, the country's economy is quite sensitive to changes in the international market for these products. Tourism now accounts for almost one billion dollars annually, mostly from European visitors. The overall financial position of the country has been weakened by ineffective fiscal management, inadequate brakes on government spending, and high tax evasion (Thomson Bankwatch 1997). Government investment is focused on public works, thereby making the country's infrastructure more appealing to foreign investors. However, human capital investment has received relatively little attention and has left the country with an undereducated work force (American Embassy 1995).

Because management skills and experience were in short supply in the D.R., and because of the country's institutional/infrastructural shortcomings, the government played a major role in attempting to stimulate the export portion of the economy. Because high-level government officials participated in the D.R.'s export promotion organizations, policy directives tended to be clear and authoritative (Seringhaus and Rosson 1990). Consequently, Dominican trade promotion organizations had a high or moderate degree of influence on a variety of activities to enhance exports, including the preparation of trade information and market profiles, the presentation of trade fairs, and the creation of EPZs.

Economic Status of Dominican EPZs

EPZs have been a rapidly growing sector of the Dominican economy (Wiarda and Kryzanek 1992). In 1968 enabling legislation was passed that provided for their creation. The first EPZ was established in La Romana in 1969, built and managed by Gulf and Western Americas Corporation. EPZs were created in San Pedro de Macoris and Santiago in 1972 and 1973, respectively.

Two factors aided the rapid increase in EPZs during the 1980s. First, the World Bank channeled $36 million to private developers in the D.R. during this period (World Bank 1992). Second, the 1980s witnessed profound socio-economic transformations throughout the Caribbean and Latin America that impelled women to enter the labor market in order to maintain their household economies and, on a wider scale, the national economies in the region.[1] It was during this period marked by extreme worker vulnerability and consequent adaptability that the Dominican EPZs began to flourish.

At the end of 1995, there were 469 factories in thirty-three free zones in the D.R. (Medina 1998), the majority in the garment industry. Next to Mexico's, the Dominican EPZ sector is the largest in the hemisphere. About half the firms in Dominican EPZs are from the United States and approximately 15 percent are owned by South Korean and Taiwanese investors. The zones witnessed a trend towards the "Dominicanization" of EPZ capital, and by 1995 Dominicans owned approximately thirty percent of the total investments in the country's EPZs. Despite this broadening ownership base, the country's economy remains vulnerable because 96 percent of zone output is exported to a single international customer, the United States (van Heerden 1998).

Growth of the EPZ workforce has been particularly dramatic. EPZs have been the fastest growing sector of the economy and play an important role in new job creation, the inflow of foreign exchange, and the generation of new economic activity (Mortimore, Duthoo, and Guerrero 1995). Between

1986 and 1990 employment more than tripled, from 36,000 to 120,000 (Romero 1993). Employment appears to have peaked at 176,000 workers in 1994 and declined through 1996, in part due to global conditions that made investment in capital-intensive industries more attractive (van Heerden, 1998).[2]

Most of the production jobs entail ordinary assembly work characterized by low-skill, repetitious tasks (Mortimore et al. 1995; Willmore 1995). Approximately 60 percent of EPZ workers are female, and almost 95 percent of women workers are production workers, whereas only 88 percent of male workers hold this type of job.

The National Council of Free Zones of Exportation (NCFZE) is the government agency with the authority to regulate EPZs. Its members include both government officials (such as the Secretaries of State for Finance and for Industry and Commerce) and employer representatives. No workers' organizations are included. The NCFZE has the authority to enforce compliance with Law 8–90, which was created in 1990 to regulate activities in the EPZs by defining both the rights and the obligations of employers. In addition to its regulatory function, the Dominican government also plays a management role in the country's EPZs. Through its Corporation for Industrial Promotion (CFI), the state owns and operates fourteen EPZs.[3]

Law 8–90 entitles companies that operate in EPZs to one hundred percent exemption from almost all taxes, including corporate income tax, construction taxes, taxes on loan agreements, the tax on creation of corporations, municipal taxes, taxes on exports or re-exports (except for exports into the local market), taxes on inventory or assets, and the tax on transfer of industrialized goods and services (American Embassy 1995). Further, these companies are completely exempt from paying import duties on transportation equipment or on equipment and utensils for the installation and operation of cafeterias, health services, medical assistance, child care centers, or "other equipment for the well-being of the working class." These exemptions are available for a renewable period of fifteen years from the first day of production.[4]

Authorization from the Directorate of Investment and registration with the Central Bank is not required of companies interested in undertaking new operations in the EPZs. Firms licensed to operate there may produce any type of product, good, or equipment, provide almost any type of service, introduce any required means of production into the EPZ, and transfer virtually any tangible asset (including labor) from one EPZ to another. Customs authorities rarely permit EPZ companies to export to the customs territory of the D.R. and EPZ workers are not permitted to consume any goods that they produce (Willmore 1995).

Opinions differ about the economic effects of the Dominican EPZs. Willmore (1995) reported that Dominican EPZs have been successful because exports have been promoted without threatening producers in the protected manufacturing sector, jobs have been created, and income has increased. He argues further that many of the problems besetting the EPZs are a consequence of unwise government policy, but that these may be easily rectified given a change in government. On the other hand, Kaplinsky (1993; 1995) stated that Dominican EPZs were economic failures because of immiserating growth (employment growth that is contingent upon wages falling in international purchasing power), the absence of transfer of technology, and the failure to develop backward linkages.

One matter about which there appears to be agreement is the enclave status of Dominican EPZs. In contrast to several East Asian countries that have been able to integrate the economies of their EPZs and their customs territories, the Dominican EPZs have failed to develop backward linkages (Mortimore et al. 1995). This is a significant failure given the fact that Dominican law encourages backward linkages, particularly with regard to local materials.[5] Although the Dominican EPZs have performed well in terms of attracting foreign investment and achieving high export volume, their enclave status appears to have made it more difficult for them to have a beneficial effect on non-EPZ companies and, consequently, total exports from the D.R. For this reason, a comparative study of total exports for eleven countries with large EPZ employment found that the growth of EPZs in the D.R. was negatively related to total exports (reported in Hamill, 1993). To some extent it is the D.R.'s trade relationship with the United States that limits opportunities for backward linkages.[6]

There also appears to be agreement that the D.R.'s competitive advantage, that is, the low cost of its unskilled labor, may be easily replaced in other Third World countries.

Finally, investments in EPZs in the D.R. and other Caribbean Basin countries have been threatened by the North American Free Trade Agreement, which permits exports from Mexico to enter the United States free of all duties. Failure to win approval in the U.S. Congress of the Interim Trade Program (commonly referred to as the "NAFTA Parity" bill) means that parity does not exist between textiles manufactured in Mexico and Caribbean-made goods, which continue to be taxed on a value-added basis.

Working Conditions

Working conditions in the Dominican EPZs have not progressed beyond those found in many of the manufacturing firms in the customs territory

(Kaplinsky 1995; Willmore 1995). Although the Employers Confederation has long contended that pay and benefits are usually better at multinational corporations (MNCs) than in local industry, compensation in the EPZs was either similar to, or in some cases less than, that offered by domestic enterprises (Romero 1995). "The best of the EPZ employers provide terms and conditions of service which are relatively good, although few appear to offer facilities such as literacy classes and other perks which progressive domestic employers such as Cartonera Dominica (which operates outside of the EPZs) provide to their workforce" (Kaplinsky 1995, 537).

Proponents of EPZs predicted that the zones would provide jobs and income that, over time, would enable workers to escape poverty. Thus far, however, the employment statistics from the region tell a different story. Kaplinsky (1995) reports that, far from fueling a process of rapid increase in per capita income in the D.R., the expansion of its EPZs took place during a period of declining incomes. Real per capita incomes in 1992 were 8.2 percent lower than those in 1989. In December 1992, the Apec Foundation of Educational Credit (FUNDAPEC) conducted a National Labor Force Survey (Apec 1992). Wages fell from $1.33 per hour in 1984 to $.56 per hour in 1990, which is less than what workers made in 1977. In 1995, the hourly wage in the zones was $.57, according to the NCFZE (Medina 1998).[7] Another study released by the highly respected Centro de Investigación Económica para el Caribe (CIECA) in May 1993 stated that the minimum wage had fallen to 58 percent of its 1970 level. These data do not prove that EPZ development caused the decline in income. But because more than half of manufacturing jobs are located in the zones, EPZ wages have had a substantial influence on the figures for the country as a whole.

The D.R. has a single minimum wage for its EPZs that differs from the eleven-tier national minimum wage outside the zones. The EPZ minimum wage is lower than that of large private sector companies and higher than that in small private companies and in the sugar industry (van Heerden 1998).

According to Dunn (1994), workers in Dominican EPZs reported that their pay was based upon only those hours devoted exclusively to production, although others noted that they were not paid for overtime work. Absenteeism and tardiness were not tolerated. This rigid work environment also included severe restrictions on visits to the bathroom. In this vein there were complaints that management removed toilet doors in some factories in San Pedro de Macoris, ostensibly to reduce the probability of theft.

Working conditions in the EPZs are particularly burdensome for women. Many employers fire women who become pregnant, despite laws prohibiting the practice. Sexual harassment is also commonly reported. A recent study involving Dominican medical doctors at the Occupational Health

Unit of the Autonomous University of Santo Domingo compared the health of women who work in the EPZs with that of those who work outside the free zones (cited in Abreu 1994). Women who work in the EPZs are nineteen times more likely to suffer from menstrual complications, two-and-a-half times more likely to suffer miscarriages, two times more likely to have children with low birth weight, and three times more likely to have children with congenital defects. The research team attributed these findings to "repression against pregnancy on the part of employers."

Unions and EPZs

The Dominican labor movement was suppressed for many years under the dictatorship of Rafael Trujillo and was tightly regulated and controlled under a succession of elected presidents, notably Joaquin Balaguer. For example, in 1978, a mass rally in the stadium in La Romana was brutally broken up by police, who arrested hundreds of workers. Until 1992, labor matters in the D.R. were regulated by the Trujillo labor code that essentially permitted employers to fire any worker at any time for any reason. Given these powers, employers in EPZs found it easy to destroy union organizing attempts. No penalties or costs were imposed on employers, who virtually had a free hand in dealing with workers.

Although there was some unionization outside the zones, the ILO's Committee of Experts reported that only five out of the approximately two hundred EPZ firms were unionized, based on documents supplied by the Dominican government. "Moreover, between 1989 and 1990, three applications to register unions in the free zones were refused under section 349 of the Labor Code, while for the same period more than 80 unions representing workers outside those enclaves were registered" (Romero 1993, 11). A Department of Labor survey encountered widespread allegations of collusion between the Ministry of Labor and EPZ employers to "ensure a union-free environment in the zones" (Hamill 1993, 63). For example, union organizers were not allowed to meet with, or distribute literature to, workers in the EPZs.

One consequence of this repressive environment was that Dominican workers were splintered among six small, ineffective labor groups. These labor organizations competed for members and influence. In the early 1990s, "the cutthroat competition among the confederations . . . left the labor union movement not only divided but also weak and unable to effectively challenge the new working conditions found in the export processing zones" (Wiarda and Kryzanek 1992, 75).

The leader of the National Confederation of Dominican Workers

(CNTD), Mariano Negron, had tried to help workers in the free zones to organize. In August 1991, the CNTD assisted a group of maquila workers to form a new Federation of Free Zone Workers (FENATRAZONAS) under the leadership of a determined young unionist named Jacobo Ramos. By July 1992, FENATRAZONAS had succeeded in organizing and gaining legal recognition for unions in eighteen factories, including the Bibong Workers Union (BWU).

The AFL-CIO had been concerned about labor conditions in Latin America for many years. Since the late 1980s, the AFL-CIO has used the U.S. Generalized System of Preferences (GSP) law to combat worker rights violations in a number of countries in the region, including Chile, Paraguay, El Salvador, Guatemala, Panama, Haiti, Nicaragua, and Costa Rica. In 1989–90, at the request of the AFL-CIO, the U.S. government undertook a review of the D.R.'s trading privileges under the GSP because of worker rights violations.[8] As a result, the Trujillo code was exposed as being out of compliance with ILO Conventions. Because of the pressures of that GSP case, the Dominican government changed its labor regulations.

In May 1992, a new labor code was approved for the entire D.R. One of the prime movers for change was the Secretary of Labor, Dr. Rafael Albuquerque, who appeared to take some pride in showcasing the new legislation that made it illegal for employers to fire workers for engaging in legitimate union activities. This step forward helped the government to avoid GSP sanctions.

In September 1992 Secretary Alburquerque negotiated a pact between the business leaders of the Dominican Free Zone Association (ADOZONAS) and the country's six labor confederations. The pact, hailed as a major breakthrough at the time, committed the EPZ companies to respect the new labor code and to refrain from firing union organizers. Most important, the pact established a new system of conciliation and arbitration to settle disputes outside the court system. However, the ADOZONAS member companies objected to the pact and pressured the leadership to refuse to ratify it.

Problems arose immediately because the new code was not enforced. Although the Ministry of Labor promptly recognized scores of new unions, EPZ companies continued to fire union leaders with impunity, resulting in what Dominicans called "headless unions." Of the nearly one hundred new unions that were registered during the next two years, all but a handful were rendered nonfunctional, and none was allowed to negotiate a collective contract. Secretary Alburquerque criticized the Dominican judicial system for not punishing companies that violated the new labor code. Although 222 firms had been cited for violations, only two had been subject to a court decision.[9] Alburquerque was quoted in the Dominican press as stating that the new labor code was worthless because "the labor judges don't apply sanctions when the [labor] secretary brings a case."[10]

Jose Manuel Paliza, president of the Association of Industries, responded by admitting that there were a few violations of trade union rights in the EPZs. He attributed these, however, to a lack of familiarity with the new code rather than to a systematic attempt to undermine unionism. He called for Alburquerque to remain neutral in disputes between employers and workers and to keep in mind the number of jobs generated by companies in the EPZs.

Unmoved, Alburquerque told the press that EPZs' continued resistance to unionization could eventually lead to trade sanctions by the United States: "Mr. Paliza must realize that if I make declarations of this type, it is because resistance to trade union freedom will damage our country and the firms in the free zones."[11] Alburquerque encouraged Paliza to help sound the alarm among employers.

The AFL-CIO filed another GSP petition in June 1993 to encourage the Dominican government to implement its new labor code. By that time, a new approach to organizing was being implemented, and the Dominican labor movement was in a better position to deal with the tremendous resistance to unionization that pervaded the EPZ business community.

Organizing at Bibong

The Bibong Apparel Company was a small transnational whose Dominican operations in the Bonao EPZ assemble pre-cut pieces of raincoats. Although the owner, Hwan M. Ryu, lived in New York City, he was, nonetheless, a "hands-on" manager. London Fog, Capezio, and British Mist were among Bibong's customers, and Misty Valley, a New Jersey company, was its most important one.

The organizing campaign was centered not on wages but on the abusive treatment of workers. Supervisors would yell at the workers, throw clothing in their faces, or slap them. Workers often were forced to work overtime with no compensation, and they were unhappy with inadequate sanitary facilities and sexual harassment. Finally the firing of activists was added to the list of grievances that Bibong workers wanted to redress by forming a union.

On June 29, 1992, the company was notified of the Bibong Workers Union's registration. Two hours later, the BWU's general secretary and another of its leaders were fired. The Ministry of Labor was asked to mediate, and the company signed an agreement to recognize the BWU and re-hire the illegally fired workers. Within eight days, however, the company abruptly and unilaterally cancelled the agreement and fired three more leaders and eight activists.

This early experience illustrated two fundamental roadblocks to union-ization in the D.R. One was failure to enforce the new labor law, and the other was a flaw in the organizing strategy of the Dominican unions.

Before the change in labor law in 1992, the Ministry of Labor and the employers had acted in collusion. After 1992, the Ministry began to act more independently by filing complaints on behalf of workers and regis-tering unions, thereby providing legal recognition. Employers continued to fire organizers and occasionally were fined. The new law made it more costly for employers to destroy union organizing drives. It did not, how-ever, secure the right of Dominican workers to organize and bargain collectively.

As in many countries, the Dominican Ministry of Labor's role is to con-duct investigations, host mediation sessions, and issue findings. To enforce compliance with the law, the Ministry must submit complaints to the labor courts, which had a reputation for corruption and inefficiency. Even when the courts act with relative speed, firms often appeal or simply refuse to comply with court orders. In the Bibong case, due largely to the interna-tional attention it aroused, the lower court issued an order for reinstate-ment and levied a fine within three months of receiving the complaint from the Ministry. The company promptly appealed, and the appeal process dragged on until early 1994. After a number of delays caused by the com-pany's refusal to attend hearings, the Appeals Court finally acted in favor of the fired workers. Bibong management refused to comply, even after the higher court took the unusual step of imposing an "embargo" on the com-pany's equipment, prohibiting its sale or removal. Clearly, a stronger mea-sure was needed to force compliance with the law.

The second roadblock resulted from the traditional Dominican union or-ganizing strategy of prematurely filing for legal recognition before achiev-ing sufficient organized backing from workers inside the plant. Before 1992, the minimum number of members required for legal recognition of a union was only twenty. Unions would normally file for recognition as soon as that number was recruited. When these lists of union members were pre-sented, first to the Ministry and later to the company as a form of legal notification, the employer could quickly fire the union leaders without con-cern about any organized response from the rest of the workforce. Further-more, the traditional methods for recruiting workers were leafleting out-side the plant and inviting workers to educational meetings. Little thought was given to building a structure of support inside the various departments and production lines of the factory. A new approach was sorely needed because the new labor code made union registration easier but raised the threshold for obtaining bargaining rights to 51 percent of the workforce.

Changing the Organizing Strategy

The organizing campaign eventually won because of a unique, multinational organizing agreement involving several union organizations in the United States, Europe, and Latin America. FENATRAZONAS and its parent body, CNTD, solicited the help of the AFL-CIO's American Institute for Free Labor Development (AIFLD), the International Ladies' Garment Workers Union (ILGWU), and the Amalgamated Clothing and Textile Workers Union (ACTWU). The project was supported by the International Textile, Garment and Leather Workers Federation (ITGLWF)[12] and was led by its Americas' regional organization, the International Federation of Textile, Garment, Leather, Shoe Workers (FITTVCC-ORI). By means of a consultative committee, this group of labor organizations was able to communicate on a weekly basis to coordinate activities and offer support to the Bibong workers. The multinational effort was to prove decisive in the ensuing battle.

To help craft a new approach, a two-week training course for organizers was held in Santiago in March 1993. The course was designed and conducted by Jeff Hermanson, the ILGWU's organizing director, and a team of instructors from his union and from ACTWU. The course provided approximately twenty-five young people with an intense experience of role-playing and problem solving. FENATRAZONAS leaders participated alongside the organizers they supervised, ensuring that there were no gaps in understanding and that a more cohesive and egalitarian organizational culture could be created. Participants learned the skills of home visits, company analysis, persuasion techniques, creation of an internal organizing committee, building a majority, and countering company repressive tactics. Above all, they learned not to make the campaign public until after a solid majority of workers was committed to the union and organized into a structure that could effectively communicate and appropriately respond to employer repression. At training's end, a new model of organizing was internalized, and the participants gained a new commitment to the cause and to each other.

Ten of the best trainees, four of whom were women, were selected to become the organizing team. One of these, Ignacio Hernandez, was assigned to assist the Bibong workers' campaign, which had languished for more than nine months. Organizing began anew, mostly by means of home visits. On September 20, the BWU held its first major assembly, thereby becoming visible and public. During the next two weeks, Hernandez, working with the largely female leadership of the BWU and the entire team of organizers from the rest of the D.R., undertook a recruiting "blitz" that resulted in the recruitment of 318 workers out of approximately 565. A cohesive and committed organizing committee was established with access to all production lines and departments in the factory. The company responded by temporarily laying off 140 workers, ostensibly due to a "lack of primary materials."

On November 11, 1993, after conducting a meeting to approve bargaining demands, the union filed a formal request for bargaining with the Ministry of Labor, accompanied by a membership list containing the names of 56 percent of the Bibong workforce. This action triggered a battle that was to last for nearly eight months before the BWU emerged with a contract. During this contest, the young leaders of the union were to be tested by reprisals, bribery, arrests, legal delays, and a widely publicized sexual harassment incident.

Maintaining Worker Morale and Cohesion

The intensive training of organizers, plus an unprecedented series of frequent follow-up visits and consultations provided by ACTWU and ILGWU staff, helped sustain worker morale and cohesion during even the most troubling times. The organizers had forewarned about anticipated company tactics, thereby inoculating BWU members to the threats and preparing appropriate collective responses. For instance, at perhaps the lowest point in the campaign, when several union leaders including one of the original founders were swayed by the company to denounce their brothers and sisters, the remaining union leaders quickly convened an assembly to elect new officers to continue the struggle. When the company tried to pressure members to sign blank pieces of paper that later would be attached to petitions renouncing union membership, and when groups of leaders were held incommunicado in sweltering rooms to isolate them from members, the workers responded with short work stoppages or a "day of the blouses" (wearing the same color t-shirts) to demonstrate solidarity. Toward the end of the campaign, when the company tried to sponsor an alternative company union, few workers took the bait. The ongoing preparation by the organizers and union leaders enabled members to anticipate most of these tactics and to rehearse various responses.

Avoiding the Election Trap

In early March 1994, after having previously rejected a proposal to hold an election to determine the union's majority status, the company suddenly changed course and demanded that the Ministry hold such an election. Management justified its refusal to bargain on the grounds that the union did not have a majority of workers. The union, in a major blunder, agreed to an election, which the Ministry scheduled for April 23.

After consulting with attorneys and advisors, the union leaders realized that the labor code did not require an election. The law states that a union may be authorized to represent the workers of a company in contract negotiations if its membership is a majority of such workers. It specifies no method for determining such a majority, thereby allowing the Ministry to certify a union for bargaining, as it had many times in the past, based solely on a comparison of members' notarized signatures with the company payroll list. The BWU had already fulfilled this requirement on November 11, 1993. Thus there was thus no legal reason for further delay of negotiations on the company's part, and no justification for holding an election. The Secretary of Labor, union leaders argued, was obligated to bring the conciliation process to a conclusion and declare that an "economic conflict" existed, paving the way for a legal strike, if necessary.

The union also did not want to establish a precedent for using a vote to determine majority status in future campaigns. Under conditions of free choice without fear of reprisals and harassment, elections would fairly reflect the views of workers about union representation. But such conditions did not (and still do not) prevail in the EPZs. Therefore the BWU, CNTD, and FENATRAZONAS lobbied the Ministry intensively to cancel the scheduled election and certify the union for bargaining based on the previous submission of its membership list. Actions by the company made the Ministry's decision easier.

In late March, the company attempted to discharge seven union leaders for bringing copies of the labor code into the plant. At the same time, a manager began pressuring employees to sign papers renouncing the union. To top things off, on April 8 a worker named Wendy Lima was sexually assaulted, then fired allegedly for refusing to submit to a supervisor's advances. When Aurelia Cruz, General Secretary of the BWU, denounced these actions on a local radio station, the company accused Cruz of defamation and persuaded the local police to enter the plant to arrest her.

Already on the brink of a public relations disaster, the company went over the edge on April 21, two days before the scheduled election. Five union leaders were held incommunicado all day in a closed, sweltering room. One of them, Maria Romero, lost consciousness and had to be taken to an emergency room. With calls and letters of protest pouring in from the United States, and U.S. Embassy and media personnel calling to find out what was going on, Secretary Alburquerque dispatched a phalanx of ten labor inspectors to Bonao to investigate the Bibong situation and prepare a report. The next day, Alburquerque agreed with the inspectors' recommendation that the April 23 election be cancelled on the grounds that the "necessary conditions did not exist." A new mediation (bargaining) session was called for April 28.

Changing the Legal Climate

A critical problem for the campaign was finding a way to persuade the company to abide by the various court orders to reinstate illegally fired workers and to cease violations of the labor code. The workers who had been fired at the beginning of the campaign nearly twenty-two months earlier were still unemployed and, along with those of more recently fired workers, their cases were still unresolved. New violations were occurring daily in a mounting wave as the election approached. Even after the election was cancelled, the problem remained of persuading the company to allow the union to function normally without further reprisals and to break the stalemate of refusal to bargain.

To improve enforcement of the labor code, the AFL-CIO had filed a new GSP petition in June 1993. The new petition focused on the fact that even though Dominican labor law was in technical compliance with ILO Conventions, its application was not. The AFL-CIO charged that the Dominican government was either unable or unwilling to apply sanctions that effectively forced employers to rehire workers who had been fired for legitimate union activity.

U.S. Trade Representative (USTR) Mickey Kantor accepted the petition and a new component of the campaign was begun. The GSP review lasted for over a year, marked by rebuttals and counter-rebuttals presented in hearings held in Washington, D.C., in pre-hearing and post-hearing briefs, and in a series of visits and letters designed to influence the U.S. decision on the case. For example, Douglas Payne, an official of Freedom House, the

U.S. human rights organization, wrote an exposé of the situation in the Dominican EPZs for the *Journal of Commerce*.[13] Alarmed by the negative publicity, and further stimulated by Dominican newspaper accounts of the dire consequences of losing GSP benefits, the government of the D.R. began looking for steps it might take to avoid sanctions.

At the GSP hearings in November, Dominican employers and the government tried to argue that the existence of a hundred registered unions in the EPZs disproved the AFL-CIO's accusations. That argument began to unravel when the AFL-CIO pointed out that these were all "headless" unions and that there was not a single functioning union or a single collective contract anywhere in the zones. The USTR signaled through the U.S. Embassy in Santo Domingo that he did not find the existence of paper unions to be persuasive evidence of respect for worker rights. A decision to suspend GSP benefits was due at the end of April 1994.

Two months before this deadline, on March 2, two women workers, including Aurelia Cruz, visited Washington to meet with members of Congress about the plight of free zone workers. In a press statement, the workers described their concerns:

Many of the multinational companies who profit from our hard work and our country's hospitality treat us inhumanely inside the walls of their factories. At their whim they lengthen our work time to 10, 12, even 14 hours a day, often without paying the meager overtime wages required by law and without considering our family responsibilities. When workers' energy flags, we are pressured to do more, more, more. In some factories we are even physically abused. As for our wages, we have steadily lost income and purchasing power. Our average is 56 cents per hour, which is less than what workers were making in 1977! We are given a half-hour break for lunch, and we often have no place to eat except on the street. We are timed when we use the rest room facilities, and such facilities are often unsanitary and inadequate. We are sometimes forced to disrobe when we leave the plant, and suffer the indignity of body searches even when there are no grounds for suspicion that anything has been stolen. When we get sick, we often have no clinics within the free zone, and our employers are reluctant to allow us time to visit the doctor. When we do visit public health facilities, we sometimes are denied treatment because our employer has avoided paying the required social security taxes, so our accounts are not paid up.[14]

Congressional inquiries following this visit helped escalate the pressure on the Dominican government to take more forceful action to avoid GSP sanctions. One way to do this had been suggested some months earlier by

Al Moore, AIFLD's representative in the D.R. He had discovered that Articles 41 and 45 of the Free Zone Law 8–90 made it incumbent upon companies receiving the benefits of investment in the EPZs to comply with the labor code.[15] Failure to comply could be punished with the loss of an EPZ company's export license, which is its lifeblood, or even its operating license. By using the administrative remedies available with Law 8–90, even without reliance on the judicial system the Dominican government could impose significant penalties if it became serious about enforcing labor law.

The AFL-CIO sought to make the application of Law 8–90 in the Bibong case a key test in the GSP process, which was entering its final stages of deliberation at the same time that the turmoil surrounding the proposed Bibong election was occurring. In a submission to the USTR, the AFL-CIO stated:

> The Bibong case is an important test. Workers have clearly demonstrated over a two-year period, through meetings, rallies, and signatures, that a firm majority wish to belong to a union and negotiate a collective contract. The union has carefully abided by all the requirements of the new labor code and is the first in the free zones to arrive at the stage of attempted negotiations. Yet its first group of leaders remain fired, and the company refuses to even begin the process of negotiation, successfully using delaying tactics in court and with the Labor Ministry to avoid its legal obligation to bargain. Despite its being cited by the Labor Ministry and found guilty in a lower court for violations of worker rights, the Bibong Company has never even paid a fine, and it continues to violate worker rights with impunity. Recently the company has fired more union supporters and has used bribery, extortion, and threats of blacklisting to force plaintiffs to drop a legal case against it. If the government will not enforce its own labor and criminal laws and apply its free zone Law 8–90 to suspend the Bibong Company's export license in a case as clear-cut as this one, there is little hope for other workers in the free zones.[16]

At first the USTR and the U.S. Embassy resisted the export license suspension, as being incompatible with "free trade." But when Jay Mazur, president of the ILGWU, contacted Kantor to complain about violations of worker rights just prior to the scheduled representation election, the U.S. view began to change. Mazur wrote that "this violent abduction of union leaders, in addition to the firing of eight other union leaders in the past week, just days before what all parties understood to be an historic vote in the process of establishing labor rights in the Dominican free trade zones, strongly suggests that the Dominican government is either powerless or unwilling to enforce its own labor laws."

The USTR immediately contacted the Dominican government to inquire about these charges. Although Dominican officials contended that their government had acted properly in this dispute, there was no doubt that the issue of Law 8–90 had now reached the highest levels of both governments and was being viewed as an important test of the GSP process.

Faced by these pressures, and with the GSP decision deadline fast approaching, the government of the D.R. decided to act. At a meeting in late April at the Dominican Embassy in Washington, David Jessup of AIFLD was informed that the Dominican government was prepared to close down Bibong and deny its owner an operating license if this would bring an end to the GSP case. Jessup expressed concern that such an action would cost five hundred workers their jobs and suggested that a less drastic action — a temporary suspension of Bibong's export license under Law 8–90 — would be preferable. The Dominican government agreed. On April 26, 1994, the NCFZE notified Bibong that its export license was suspended until it stopped violating worker rights and obeyed court orders. Almost immediately, the company allowed the union leaders to function freely inside the plant. An effective enforcement mechanism had been found, and real negotiations now became a possibility.

Blunting the Political Attack

Throughout the entire GSP review period, employers and their political allies in the media mounted fierce and unrelenting political attacks against the AFL-CIO and Dominican unions. Dominican unionists were accused of being "unpatriotic" and of "selling out to gringo unions," whose only interests were said to be preventing investment in the D.R., shutting down the EPZs, and returning all the jobs to the United States. Dominican unions, especially the CNTD, worked hard to defuse these attacks. They pointed out that the umbrella group for international support was not a U.S. organization but the Western Hemisphere affiliate of the ITGLWF. They also mounted a press campaign to argue that the true violators of Dominican sovereignty were the employers who tried to operate without respect for the laws of the D.R. If the government was concerned about "outside interference," the unions argued, it could simply enforce the law so that Dominican workers would not have to ask for international solidarity.

The visit of Aurelia Cruz and the free zone workers to the U.S. Congress especially inflamed passions among zone officials in the D.R., who harshly berated them upon their return and accused of them of harming their country. In anticipation of these attacks, the worker delegation distributed a statement, which said in part:

> We have decided to visit the U.S. to defend the people of the Dominican Republic against exploitation and worker rights violations by companies that don't respect our country and its laws. We want to make sure that the U.S. Congress, the U.S. government, and the U.S. news media know the truth about what is happening to workers in the Dominican free zones. We want to protect our country's trading privileges under GSP and CBI, which are being jeopardized by the companies that flout our laws and violate our rights. We want to make sure that the worker rights conditions included in the GSP and CBI laws are properly enforced. . . . No country should have to choose between investments and citizens' rights. No worker should have to choose between a job and workers' rights.[17]

Internationalizing the Campaign

In New York, Hermanson and his ILGWU staff tracked down representatives of the companies that did business with Bibong. Their purpose was to inform these customers about working conditions imposed by their Dominican contractor and persuade them to pressure the company to change its ways. For example, one customer, London Fog, which had signed union contracts with ACTWU in the United States, was apprised of the violations at Bibong in a letter from ACTWU's president, Jack Sheinkman. This correspondence was shared with Bibong's president, to convey the warning that the U.S. unions were serious about trying to provoke cancellations of customer orders if violations continued.

Bibong's largest customer was Misty Valley. Although a campaign to embarrass Misty Valley with the help of the ITGLWF would have been possible, such action was postponed for fear of putting Bibong out of business with a consequent loss of jobs for the Dominican workers.

Hermanson and other union representatives, including Francisco Chang, a Korean-American organizer from the ILGWU, met several times with Bibong's owner in New York. The presence of the Korean-speaking representative seemed to demonstrate that the ILGWU was serious about the campaign and willing to spend resources on it. This message was reinforced when, after their meetings in Washington, Aurelia Cruz and the other maquiladora workers traveled to New York to speak with union leaders, human rights groups, and journalists.

Toward the end of the campaign, on May 3, Charles Gray, director of the AFL-CIO's International Affairs Department, wrote to Seung-Soo Han, the South Korean ambassador in the United States, expressing solidarity with the Bibong workers. Gray asked the ambassador to persuade Ryu to abide by Dominican labor law. The South Korean ambassador in the D.R. was similarly contacted, and a meeting was held in his offices on May 9. At the same time, AIFLD's sister institute, the Asian American Free Labor Institute, contacted Korean union activists to explore ways of pressuring Bibong from Korea. By this time, however, the company had changed its behavior and collective bargaining had begun.

The Contract

The 1994 collective bargaining agreement was very short and modest by standards of industrial unions in the United States and the European Union. The union won recognition, dues check-off, a May Day contribution from the company, a bulletin board inside the plant, on-the-clock meeting time for union leaders, two water fountains, and a grievance committee. In return, the union had to promise that it would not strike nor make demands for higher wages, that it would support the achievement of production quotas, and that it would use "restraint" in taking actions harmful to the company. The union also agreed to allow the company to pick five workers each year to receive bonuses for outstanding work.

In 1996 a second three-year agreement was negotiated at Bibong.[18] Perhaps the most important gain was agreement that the company would continue to pay 50 percent of workers' salaries whenever work was suspended due to lack of materials or orders. Other benefits included a union-administered credit union, co-op, and loan fund; company-paid time off for personal necessities; extension of family and maternity leave beyond that provided in the labor code; increased vacation time and personal days off; inclusion of dinner time and shift-changeover time in the calculation of overtime pay; and eight scholarships for workers' children (selected by the union-management committee). The contract established a worker-management health and safety committee with the task of installing more drinking fountains, providing better chairs for the workers, improving lighting and ventilation, and establishing a dining room and a first-aid station. The union negotiated a much more effective grievance committee, more days off for union meetings, and the extension of "fuero sindical" (protection from firing) to more leaders than provided for in the labor code.

The union also got rid of the no-strike, no-salary-demand clause. The productivity clauses now gave the union a voice in the selection of workers for bonuses and in the extension of bonus pay to entire production lines rather than individual workers. The contract provided that productivity incentive schemes could not result in salary cuts, only in increases. All in all, the second contract represented a great step forward that made material improvements in workers' lives.

Consequences of the Campaign

The organizing victory at Bibong was soon replicated at several other factories. Informal agreements to improve health care and sanitary conditions have been signed at several factories and other companies have signed formal contracts. By 1997, there were ten collective bargaining agreements signed by FENATRAZONAS covering approximately five thousand workers. Although various Dominican unions claim to be increasing their memberships in the EPZs, not all have been able to negotiate collective bargaining agreements.

The success of the Bibong campaign must be measured in other ways besides counting the number of workers covered by contracts. The rise of FENATRAZONAS as a major new force in the D.R. has benefited all maquila workers, not just those directly involved in unions. Employers exploit and abuse workers less because they are now highly conscious that the workers have defenders. Minimum wages were raised with union pressure and the government took several new initiatives to protect EPZ workers. A pact between the government, the NCFZE, and the unions (CNTD and \FENATRAZONAS), brokered by the Catholic Church, was signed in 1994 to establish mediation procedures to resolve conflicts in the zones (van Heerden 1998). In 1997, another tripartite pact was created to explore ways of providing health care, transportation, day care, and lunch facilities to workers. In addition, the Bibong project has increased respect for the rule of law by pressuring the courts and regulatory system to implement the labor code more effectively. In October 1997, for example, the NCFZE suspended the export license of J.P. Industries, a Korean company, which had been ignoring court orders to reinstate illegally fired workers. Shortly thereafter, the workers were reinstated and collective bargaining was begun.

Although Bibong was a breakthrough, the campaign for worker and trade union rights is not over. Indeed, each new campaign requires a protracted struggle. Even though the Dominican government and the Ministry of Labor are behaving more responsibly than they did pre-1992, they are still reluctant to enforce the labor code unless they are pressured from outside the country. In the case of J.P. Industries, the company's export license was not suspended until after a meeting between the AFL-CIO and the Dominican ambassador.

The Dominican government's reluctance to acquiesce to further demands for better working conditions is based, in part, upon competition among EPZs. The world probably now has too many EPZs for the manufacture of clothing, so the multinationals have the option to shift production to the most employer-friendly environment. Host countries do not want to drive business away by being stricter on labor law enforcement.

Buoyed by the success at Bibong, the ITGWLF has established an organizing program covering seven countries in the Caribbean Basin and Central America, headquartered in San Jose, Costa Rica. It is hiring staff and developing plans. Time will tell whether this new organizational framework will be successful.*

Principles Derived from the Bibong Campaign

In the garment industry, organizing campaigns limited to factories in a single country are doomed to failure. Such an approach confronts only one small part of a worldwide production system. Even if a group of workers successfully organizes, it is relatively easy for the contractor as well as its customers to shift production to another plant, another industrial park, another country. To succeed requires a global strategy. The experience in the Dominican Republic has helped to define one type of multinational organizing strategy, whose success appears to depend on four interrelated factors. These might be called the "four pressure points" for multinational organizing campaigns. To apply these pressures simultaneously requires an international effort sustained by separate organizations that must put aside traditional differences in style and culture in order to create a new mechanism for cooperation. Each organization has certain strengths and certain distinct roles to play.

Pressure from Below

Dominican workers on the front lines proved unusually resilient and persistent in pursuing their goal of having their own union. They made many sacrifices along the way. Each time the company frightened away potential leaders or fired existing ones, others arose to take their places. Nurtured by months of meetings and home visits, this commitment was essential to success. Building this pressure requires hands-on training and follow-up work with a team of organizers. In the D.R., beginning with an intensive two-week training course for organizers, the U.S. garment unions provided staff for monthly visits, consultations, and follow-up training programs. FENATRAZONAS now has a fine young team of skilled, professional organizers with access to advice and information from abroad. Without such professionalization and preparation, organizing work in this industry is unlikely to succeed.

Pressure from Above

U.S. garment unions contacted Bibong's corporate customers to inform them of the company's labor rights abuses. The communications that resulted were used to raise the specter that Bibong's customers would withhold future contracts unless working conditions were improved in the D.R. Since then, the growing sensitivity of multinational corporations, to protect the image of their brand names, provides an even greater opportunity for exerting pressure on maquiladora garment firms, most of which produce for the U.S. market. That market, along with the one in Europe, has become educated on the issue of worker exploitation, especially of women and children. As explained in ILGWU testimony before the Clinton Administration's Commission on the Future of Worker-Management Relations, chaired by Prof. John Dunlop, "there can be no excuse for American manufacturers, who design and own virtually all the so-called 'imported' apparel coming into this country, to ignore the brutal and exploitative conditions under which much of that apparel is assembled."

Many of these manufacturers have signed codes of conduct that commit them, on paper at least, to respect worker rights. Numerous human rights groups and other NGOs are seeking to hold them to their word by means of independent monitoring. To be effective, however, such pressure must be exerted carefully. If it causes wholesale cancellation of contracts resulting in massive layoffs, the union can be blamed for destroying jobs. And if independent monitors lack a clear sense of their proper role, their efforts, however well intentioned, can become a substitute for unionism. For example, in our opinion, the intrusion of NGOs actually impeded organizing efforts in Honduras and El Salvador. There is no doubt, however, that carefully applied pressure on corporate customers is a vital component of any multinational organizing drive.

Pressure from the Legal Arena

Governments seeking global investors are under great pressure to relax implementation of their labor laws (see Chapter 3). Counter-pressure is needed to promote enforcement. In the Bibong case, the threat of losing duty-free trade benefits under the GSP and the Caribbean Basin Initiative (CBI) served this purpose. The AFL-CIO has also used the GSP law to pressure for reform of labor codes or to improve enforcement of existing law in Costa Rica, Chile, Panama, Honduras, Nicaragua, Paraguay, Guatemala, and El Salvador.

The GSP law has been fairly effective in small countries that are dependent on the U.S. market, but using the threat of unilateral trade preference sanctions against larger countries is another matter. Indonesia and Malaysia, where U.S. businesses have much more at stake and where retaliatory actions by those countries would affect more of our own exports, have effectively resisted GSP pressures. Acting alone, the United States government will find it difficult to improve worker rights in these larger countries. In any case, as new trade agreements are negotiated at regional and global levels, trade preference legislation will become moot. Thus it is incumbent upon all the world's democracies to develop standards for global workers' rights rules, linked to international trade. Without such enforceable standards the success of future organizing campaigns is in doubt.

Pressure from the Political Arena

Public opinion can be crucial in a multinational organizing effort. The involvement of outside organizations inevitably leads to accusations of outside interference and appeals to national pride. Unions undertaking the organizing effort on the ground must be prepared to counter these attacks. Perhaps it is appropriate, therefore, to end this chapter with a quote from the Dominican workers who visited the United States, who defended their appeal for international help in these terms:

> When we ask for help from other trade union organizations outside our borders, or take our complaints to the International Labor Organization, or provide information about worker rights violations to the U.S. Trade Representative, we are vilified for being "unpatriotic," for "endangering the jobs of workers" and for serving as "mercenaries for the AFL-CIO." Our government and business leaders rush off to Washington, claiming they are "defending the country" against these threats. But they are not defending our country. They are defending the multinational companies' efforts to exploit Dominican workers. They are defending these companies' refusal to obey our laws and respect our people. They are defending these companies' investment rights, no matter how degrading they are to the laws and citizens of our country. They are the unpatriotic ones.[19]

10

Globalization and De-Unionization in Telecommunications: Three Case Studies in Resistance

LARRY COHEN AND STEVE EARLY

As they globalize, they de-unionize. Anti-union strategies are almost a defining characteristic of multinational corporations (MNCs) in today's global economy. To confront the multinationals, union members in different countries must find ways to overcome the barriers of organizational bureaucracy, geography, nationalism, and language that separate them. Traditional forms of labor solidarity can be helpful, but they are no longer sufficient to deal with the problems confronting unions today. International conferences, speech-making, and resolution-passing by high-ranking union officials are no substitute for cross-border activity that unites workers at the grassroots. The new labor internationalism required to meet the challenges of organizing and bargaining in the twenty-first century must be built from the bottom up as well as the top down. We will describe the new internationalism practiced by the Communications Workers of America (CWA).

We begin by discussing the telecommunications industry, with special attention to structural changes and worsening union-management relations. The problems confronting the CWA are not unlike those facing other telecommunications unions, and CWA's organizational responses may provide ideas and models useful to unions elsewhere. Then we will describe CWA's steps to strengthen its ties to workers abroad. The CWA's cross-border work has involved labor organizations in North and South America, Europe, and Asia. It flows out of the more activist approach the CWA has pursued at home in response to the court-ordered divestiture of AT&T—the old "Bell System." The break-up required the CWA to deal with multiple telephone companies in a competitive environment rather than a single, regulated monopoly employing nearly five hundred thousand workers under one national contract. During the last sixteen years, the CWA has faced the combined threats of deregulation, technological change, massive job losses, corporate restructuring (including re-combination of the "Baby Bells" created by divestiture), and the emergence of aggressive, anti-union firms in telephone manufacturing and services.[1]

The Telecommunications Industry

The growth of the global economy has been led, in part, by the telecommunications industry, which provides services vital to economic development. In 1999 telecommunications firms generated worldwide revenues of $1 trillion. Among the largest companies are Nippon Telephone and Telegraph of Japan, with market capitalization of $190 billion, revenues of $100 billion, and 225,000 employees; AT&T, with capitalization of $150 billion, revenues of $65 billion, and 150,000 employees; and Deutsche Telekom (DT) of Germany, with capitalization of $120 billion, revenues of $45 billion, and 180,000 employees.[2]

The services offered by the telecommunications industry are diversifying rapidly, driven in part by changes in the regulatory environment. The liberalization policies adopted by many countries in the 1980s spurred competition in the provision of terminal equipment, long distance and wireless services, Internet access, cable television, satellite communications, and submarine cables. By 1997, within the framework of the World Trade Organization (WTO), sixty-eight countries had agreed to allow competition in voice, data, and fax transmissions.

Governments around the world have become more inclined to sell off their telecommunications facilities following the 1984 privatization of British Telecom (BT), and many telecommunications companies that once were under public domain and operated in regulated markets are now competing in the private sector. New services seem to be launched on a weekly basis, and traditional definitions of telecommunications employers have become outdated by technological developments. Because deregulation and liberalization of the market are occurring in almost every region of the world, telecommunications companies are restructuring. The merger trend ultimately will transform the industry so that only four or five global telecommunications companies will exist, in a fully integrated global network.

New agreements between private or public companies and governments, joint ventures, and alliances are being created to take advantage of the liberalized environment.[3] American companies, in particular, are creating joint ventures abroad. "Our market isn't this country any more," explained former Bell Atlantic Chairman Ray Smith. "It's the world."[4] Foreign investment by U.S. telecommunications firms has expanded in both industrial and developing economies. In New Zealand, for example, two U.S. "Baby Bells"—Bell Atlantic and Ameritech—played a key role in the sell-off and reorganization of Telecom New Zealand (TNZ), acquiring a $2.5 billion stake in TNZ when it was privatized.

Deregulation in other countries has created many opportunities in service markets that American companies could not enter at home because of remaining regulatory restrictions. For example, two other Baby Bells—U.S. West and NYNEX (now part of Bell Atlantic)—entered the United Kingdom market, offering combined cable television and local telephone services in competition with BT before they could do so in the United States.

In the United States and other industrialized economies, telephone service is nearly universal. Additional domestic growth must rely on the sale of other information services such as video and electronic publishing and extra lines for fax and Internet services. On the other hand, in most developing countries less than 10 percent of the people have access to residential service. Hence the big profit potential in Third World markets lies in extending basic telephone service to those without it or, in the worst of cases, focusing development primarily in highly profitable markets such as wireless.

The governments of developing countries expect privatization of telecommunications to be a quick source of cash for balancing budgets and improving currency valuations. On the other hand, companies that invest in developing countries expect a high rate of return because the government typically guarantees a continued monopoly over basic telecommunications services for a fixed time. All too often, the private investors expect to recoup their initial investments quickly by means of job cuts, price hikes, or market growth—or all three methods. Under such conditions, SBC Communications, originally known as Southwestern Bell, bought a stake and management role in Telmex, the former national telephone monopoly in Mexico, and a multinational consortium led by GTE now operates the Venezuelan phone system.

The most profound effect of privatization has been the loss of local control over telecommunications resources. In exchange for promised modernization and cash, public entities around the world have readily surrendered their ownership or regulation of their nation's only telecommunications system and primary distribution channel for future information services. Globalization thus reduces the influence that any one nation has over the MNCs operating within its boundaries. In the past, local, state, or national governments could set some operating standards. Today's global telecommunications firms are well positioned to dictate their own terms of business, especially on working conditions and labor-management relations.

Labor Relations

One common result of these international investment strategies has been the lowering of labor standards in an industry where, under private or public ownership, strong unions had previously been able to achieve good wages and benefits. Invariably, the host country's workers are made to pay for the new investment facilitated by privatization and/or deregulation, through job loss or less favorable conditions. For example, just five years after Bell Atlantic and Ameritech acquired 49 percent of TNZ and took over its day-to-day management, the company's workforce was reduced by 75 percent. Real wages shrank and pension coverage was reduced. Aided by the anti-union legislation enacted by New Zealand's conservative government, TNZ management first thwarted worker organization at its new business ventures and then reorganized TNZ itself in such a way as to eliminate collective bargaining almost entirely. As another example, NYNEX and U.S. West, before selling their U.K. cable TV subsidiaries in 1996, introduced employment practices into Britain that were patterned on the worst practices of predominantly non-union cable operators in America.[5] These new cable systems farmed out their entire network construction and maintenance to contractors who, in turn, employed workers as individual subcontractors. The latter were paid for each task they completed. Thus employees of these firms were denied workers' compensation when injured and had no right to collective bargaining since, in theory, they were self-employed. Since taking over from the two American companies, Cable and Wireless Communications (CWC) has maintained their anti-union stance.

For telecommunications workers and their unions, the bottom line of industry restructuring and ownership changes invariably has been bad. Employment in some of the leading telecommunications companies has declined noticeably. Between 1982 and 1992, 289,931 jobs were eliminated in telecom enterprises in OECD countries alone (OECD, 1995). Centralization and technological change have been a major factor in these job losses. For example, in the United States, AT&T's creation of national service centers for customer support resulted in the closing of many smaller customer service sites around the country. New technology has had its greatest impact on telephone operators' jobs. Complex switching systems for long distance calling and voice recognition technology reduced the number of AT&T operators by 75 percent between 1950 and 1996 (Kohl 1993).

Throughout the world, the telecommunications industry had been one of the most highly unionized industrial sectors prior to the 1980s. With a limited number of companies and employers in any country, this high level of unionization undoubtedly enhanced the ability of unions to defend their members and to influence the direction of the industry. In several cases, this influence was manifest in negotiated reductions in force that minimized the disruptive impact on the lives of workers and communities. However, as telecommunications monopolies have been broken up, traditional unionized companies now constitute a smaller portion of a much broader, more competitive industry with many new players. Workers at most of the newer companies are not unionized. Consequently the overall level of unionization has been declining and, concomitantly, the ability of unions to affect public policy and corporate decision-making is also decreasing.

Union power is at risk even within highly unionized companies. Many of these firms are investing abroad and now generate a significant percentage of their revenues in other countries. In 1993, for example, one of AT&T's strategic goals was to ensure that more than half the company's revenues were generated overseas. U.S.-based firms attempt, wherever possible, to operate non-union in their foreign ventures (as NYNEX did with its multibillion-dollar cable television venture in Britain) or to operate with the benefit of company union arrangements (as Lucent Technologies—formerly part of AT&T—does at its Mexican maquiladora plants).

Meanwhile, the MNCs headquartered abroad that have expanded into the United States, such as the Canadian-based equipment manufacturer Nortel Networks, have largely succeeded in operating free of collective bargaining agreements here. The $3.7 billion capital infusion that CWA's bitter adversary, Sprint, received in the mid-1990s from DT and France Telecom (FT) greatly strengthened its market position and its ability to spread anti-unionism abroad through Global One, a jointly-owned international subsidiary. In sum, union leverage in collective bargaining tends to decrease as employers are able to rely on revenues derived from non-union international operations.

Finally, adoption of increasingly automated technology has also weakened unions. Telecommunications companies can withstand strikes better than in the past because fewer people are required to maintain and operate telephone systems. A union postmortem on CWA's lengthy 1989 walkout at NYNEX concluded that it was two months before the strike had much impact, because of the company's high degree of automation and ability to maintain service using managers, retirees, and temporary workers.

Mobilizing Begins at Home

The CWA is the world's largest union of telecommunications workers. During the last fifteen years, when more than a hundred thousand jobs were eliminated in its traditional jurisdiction, the union has undergone considerable diversification and amalgamation. It now includes more than eighty thousand health care and public employees, forty-five thousand newspaper and printing industry workers, and fifteen thousand workers in cable television and broadcasting. Some of this growth has been the product of mergers with the remaining independent telephone unions or smaller AFL-CIO affiliates, including the Newspaper Guild, International Typographical Union, and National Association of Broadcast Employees and Technicians. But much of the growth, particularly in health care and the public sector, has been the result of aggressive outreach to non-union workers.

Nationally, CWA now allocates 10 percent of its budget to membership recruitment, while a network of two hundred "organizing locals" also contributes a growing share of local union financial resources to this task. The union has emphasized the recruitment and deployment of its own members as organizers, rather than hiring extensively from outside its ranks. Around a thousand rank-and-file activists have received CWA organizer training and participated in campaigns. Within companies where it retains significant bargaining clout, the union has been able to facilitate organizing by negotiating agreements that provide for management neutrality, union access to non-union workplaces, and recognition through card check procedures rather than Labor Board elections. A five-year struggle with SBC Communications secured such an agreement covering the company's cellular phone subsidiaries; more than four thousand SBC wireless employees now belong to CWA.

To build strong union majorities in workplaces where management actively opposes unionization—still the norm in the private sector—CWA emphasizes one-on-one recruitment of activists, creation of "in-plant" committees, extensive training and leadership development, and encouragement of direct action on the job to give workers a sense of their own collective power.

By the late 1980s, it was clear that this type of approach was needed not only in organizing drives but also in long-established CWA bargaining units where management was seeking contract concessions and displaying a new willingness to take strikes to get them. The union responded by developing a union-wide program called "CWA Mobilization" that applies the lessons of successful external organizing to contract campaigns. Employed in each round of telephone bargaining since 1989, Mobilization seeks to strengthen the union through systematic internal organizing and greater membership participation in the negotiating process. The program's goal is to make strikes, where necessary, more effective, and give CWA members the ability to pursue in-plant and corporate campaigns as an alternative or supplement to striking.[6]

One of Mobilization's earliest victories was a militant contract fight with NYNEX in 1989 that resulted in a four-month walk-out in New York and New England. The company's plan to shift health care costs to workers united the CWA and the International Brotherhood of Electrical Workers (IBEW). The forty local unions involved in this struggle prepared for more than eighteen months, creating a network of four thousand stewards and workplace mobilization coordinators who distributed literature, organized displays of solidarity, and countered company propaganda about the need for increased employee payments for medical coverage. When negotiations deadlocked and the old contract expired, a high-impact strike ensued. The strikers employed mass and mobile picketing, civil disobedience, rallies of up to fifteen thousand people, and a sophisticated community-based campaign of political pressure focused on the company's rates and its relationships with regulatory agencies. The dispute was finally settled when management withdrew its proposal for health care cost shifting, thereby making the strike one of the few successful anti-concessions struggles of the decade.[7]

Mobilizing Globally

Despite the continuing ability of some unions to mount impressive job actions, telecommunications firms are changing rapidly in ways that make them less vulnerable to strikes or other forms of workplace and community pressure in their traditional lines of business. Consequently the CWA's success in future bargaining and organizing involving MNCs depends on its ability to develop joint ventures of its own, enabling American workers to act in concert with their brothers and sisters abroad.

When MNCs attempt to boost their power and profits at the expense of workers, unions must mobilize long-term cross-border campaigns based on careful research and analysis, membership education and involvement, organizing, and international solidarity. The CWA and other communications unions have developed such campaigns through a Working Group on Multinationals formed in 1991 by the Postal, Telephone, and Telegraph International (PTTI), which is now part of Union Network International (UNI).[8] As information services, including telecommunications, television, and data, were privatized and sold to MNCs, PTTI promoted greater cooperation among its affiliates that were dealing with these firms. In particular, the Working Group has focused on the behavior of Sprint, AT&T, the Baby Bells, FT, BT, CWC, and Telefónica de España.

We turn now to descriptions of three international campaigns implemented by CWA and its allies between 1989 and 1997 to deal with global telecommunications companies. Each case study illustrates the importance of cooperation across borders to make union organizing or bargaining within a multinational more effective.

The Northern Telecom Campaign

One of the CWA's first cross-border campaigns involved Northern Telecom (or Nortel) and grew out of the crucial international assistance that CWA members received during a five-week strike in 1989. Now known as Nortel Networks, Nortel produces telephone equipment in factories throughout North America, Western Europe, and the Third World. It began as the manufacturing arm of Bell Canada but in the 1980s increased its worldwide workforce by 80 percent and its sales by 400 percent. The percentage of its unionized workforce declined by half in the same period.

In Canada, Nortel has closed plants and laid off workers, but about 40 percent of its twenty-two thousand Canadian employees remain union-represented. Nortel's U.S. workforce is about the same size, but the unionization rate is less than 5 percent. Although some equipment installation and maintenance technicians are organized, none of its American manufacturing plants has a union contract. In 1982, Nortel's bad faith bargaining and other unfair labor practices drove the CWA from the only factory where the union had ever been able to win an NLRB election. Following this victory in Nashville, Tennessee, the company's de-unionization campaign was extended to the smaller groups of workers that install Nortel equipment around the country. Between 1984 and 1989, five out of seven CWA installer units were decertified.

By the summer of 1989, the CWA's largest remaining Nortel field technician unit consisted of about five hundred workers in eight northeastern states. Nortel was clearly preparing to press for concessions that would force a strike and set the stage for yet another union decertification drive. The members of CWA Local 1109, headquartered in Brooklyn, New York, readied themselves by creating an active mobilization network, issuing regular contract bulletins, and engaging in on-the-job actions before walking out three weeks after their contract expired. Almost immediately, management deployed replacement workers, who were confronted at key customer locations by teams of mobile pickets and their supporters from other CWA locals. The ensuing five-week strike was militant and well organized, but it almost certainly would have failed if CWA had not lined up international allies as well.

Prior to Local 1109's bargaining, the CWA approached leaders of the company's two main Canadian unions, the Canadian Auto Workers (CAW) and the Communications Workers of Canada (now known as the Communications, Energy, and Paperworkers Union or CEP). Soon after the U.S. installers struck, both the CAW and CEP intervened. Then-CAW President Bob White and CEP President Fred Pomeroy sent letters of protest to Nortel's chief executive officer, copies of which were widely distributed among members of all three unions to inform them about the emerging cross-border solidarity campaign. The Canadian unions immediately launched their own grassroots mobilization in support of the strike. Leaflets distributed in CAW and CEP workplaces throughout Canada recounted Nortel's history of "anti-worker, anti-union activities in the United States," which were linked to the southward export of jobs. Strikers from Local 1109 met with Nortel's Canadian workers.

The unions also conducted a coordinated public information and press campaign that proved to be very embarrassing to a firm widely regarded as the crown jewel of Canadian high-tech manufacturing. Pomeroy personally joined the CWA's negotiations with Nortel in New York, signifying that Canadians would not stand idly by while one of their major employers abused the rights of its U.S. workers. As a direct result of Canadian labor's solidarity work, Local 1109 was finally able to settle the dispute without concessions or the loss of any striker's job.

The partnership among the three unions forged in 1989 achieved another victory one year later. In the course of a lawsuit against Nortel, the CWA uncovered dramatic evidence of the company's systematic and illegal invasion of workers' privacy during the long campaign to prevent unionization and negotiation of a first contract at its Nashville plant in the early 1980s. Copies of tape-recorded telephone conversations, wiretapped from pay phones in the employee cafeteria, were provided to the union by a former security officer in the plant. Additional tapes had been made from listening devices in the sprinkler system. The surveillance had occurred over a number of years during which Nortel workers had been trying to form a CWA local and negotiate a contract.

White and Pomeroy called a press conference in Toronto, Nortel's world headquarters, to denounce the company's conduct. The matter received wide coverage in Canadian television, radio, and newspaper reports and prompted calls for a parliamentary inquiry into Nortel's behavior. The combination of the wiretapping revelations and related legal pressure helped bring about a settlement of the CWA's lawsuit. As part of this settlement, Nortel agreed to become the first telecommunications firm in the United States to ban all secret monitoring of employees, including unannounced eavesdropping on their work-related phone calls (which is not illegal in this country).

In October 1991, a coalition of unions that represented Nortel workers in North America sponsored a conference in Toronto for Nortel unionists from around the world. More than 150 workers and union officials attended, including delegates from Ireland, England, Germany, Turkey, Malaysia, and Japan. The participants developed an "Education and Action Plan" that called for coordinated rank-and-file activity. A campaign brochure was produced in eight languages, describing the company's global expansion strategy and its record of labor law violations and union-busting throughout the world. (In Malaysia, for example, Nortel secured an agreement with the government barring unionization of its plant for at least five years after it opened.) Upon their return home through the early part of 1992, conference participants began a petition drive aimed at building worker support for the group's central demands: management neutrality and non-interference in all organizing drives; negotiations with a multinational union committee on a global code of conduct. Many participating unions also organized local press conferences, rallies, picketing, or solidarity button-wearing in Nortel workplaces.

On July 19, 1993, a joint delegation representing the CWA, CAW, and CEP presented petitions signed by thousands of workers to the company's vice-president for global labor relations. Nortel agreed to exchange some information on its business plans and to discuss its labor relations practices with this joint union group. It flatly rejected the unions' demand for management neutrality during organizing campaigns and recognition of new bargaining units based on signed authorization cards demonstrating majority support. However, after the unions' ongoing campaign was launched, Nortel did appoint a new vice-president and North American director more respectful of collective bargaining in existing units. In an exchange of letters with CWA President Morton Bahr, the company pledged that respect, trust, and mutuality of interest would be the basis for future company dealings with the union. Subsequently, both local union officials and members noted some improvement in labor-management relations. Many members attributed the change to the union's development of a cross-border strategy.[9]

Alliance South of the Border

The CWA's ongoing relationship with Mexican telephone workers provides another example of how international solidarity can and must be a two-way street. The 1990 privatization of Telmex, SBC's management role with the company since then, and the creation of "free trade" links between Canada, the United States, and Mexico have led telephone worker unions from all three nations into a joint venture of their own. This alliance was formalized in an agreement signed by the CWA's Bahr, the CEP's Pomeroy, and Francisco Hernandez Juarez, General Secretary of the Sindicato de Telefonistas de la República Mexicana (STRM). STRM represents fifty thousand workers at Telmex and is among the largest independent unions in Mexico. The joint venture commits the participating organizations "to defend union and workers' rights" through "joint mobilization" of members in Mexico and throughout North America.[10]

High-level representatives of the CWA and STRM have met periodically with SBC to discuss mutual concerns about new technology, downsizing, deregulation in Mexico, and the company's stance toward organizing efforts at its new cellular phone subsidiary in the United States. But, as in the case of its cross-border work within Nortel, the CWA has tried to cement its relationship with STRM through direct worker-to-worker contacts. In September 1995 fifteen CWA organizers and eighteen from STRM spent three days together at a training and strategy session in Laredo, Texas. All the U.S. participants were bilingual and had experience organizing immigrant workers from Mexico and Central and South America. The STRM activists were eager to learn about the CWA's organizing work, including its efforts in firms that have entered the telecommunications field since deregulation.

As a follow-up to this meeting, two STRM organizers spent a week working on a CWA campaign in Los Angeles among five thousand Spanish-speaking truckers who transported freight from the city's harbor. By 1999, as part of its own expanded organizing program, STRM had succeeded in winning bargaining rights for three thousand workers at a customer calling center run by Techmarketing, a Telmex contractor.

Other Mexican companies have recently been allowed to provide local phone service, cellular service, and cable television access in competition with Telmex. The former state-owned company's hold on long distance customers is also being challenged by new competitors from north of the border such as AT&T, MCI, and Sprint. The problem for STRM is that many of these firms would rather not deal with the independent telephone workers' union, preferring instead to install company unions or to arrange contracts with affiliates of the three-million member Confederation of Mexican Workers (CTM), the government-dominated labor federation. CTM has one such deal with Iusacel, a Bell Atlantic-controlled mobile phone company that is now the second largest in Mexico. A similar CTM "sindicato blanco," or ghost union, exists at Lucent's big manufacturing plant in Matamoros. A group of CWA members visited that facility in 1991, when it was still part of AT&T, and found that its employees were low-paid even by Mexican standards. The company had granted immediate recognition and automatic dues deduction to the CTM, which was providing little or no protection to the workers. CTM leaders were not at all interested in developing joint strategies with the CWA.

STRM, on the other hand, is a different kind of union, as demonstrated by its leading role in the National Union of Workers (UNT), a new alliance of unions outside the CTM that is seeking greater internal democracy and political independence for Mexico's labor movement. STRM is also trying to give workers in the expanding Mexican telephone sector a real voice on the job. Now facing some of the same employers that the CWA has bargained with or tried to organize over the years, STRM understands the importance of developing a united front, north and south of the border. Beginning in 1995, STRM played a key role in an important CWA solidarity campaign on behalf of workers fired by Sprint, the non-union long distance carrier which then ranked third in size behind AT&T. The CWA, in turn, has taken up the cause of Mexican workers victimized by union-busting.

Anti-union Activities at Sprint

Everywhere that U.S. workers have tried to organize as part of a CWA-backed Sprint Employees Network, they have been threatened, harassed, spied on, or dismissed. At La Conexion Familiar (LCF) in San Francisco, the company staffed an entire facility with Latinos to help target Spanish-speaking customers. Backed by CWA Local 9410, a strong majority of the $7-dollar-an-hour LCF service representatives and telemarketers signed CWA authorization cards, openly supported the union, and petitioned for a National Labor Relations Board (NLRB) election. On July 14, 1994, one week before the scheduled vote, Sprint topped off a brutal anti-union campaign by closing the entire office.

This mass firing of 177 workers, in conjunction with many other illegal management activities, caused the regional director of the NLRB to cite Sprint for forty-eight separate violations of federal labor law. NLRB lawyers then tried to get a federal court order reinstating the workers immediately and ordering Sprint to bargain with the union. The request for injunctive relief was denied. A Labor Board administrative law judge (ALJ) who heard the case thirteen months after the shutdown found Sprint guilty of almost every allegation of illegal conduct. He concluded, nevertheless, that LCF was closed because it was losing money, not because the office was unionizing. As a remedy, the ALJ proposed that Sprint send a letter to all former LCF employees admitting its violations!

A three-member Labor Board panel in Washington, D.C. reviewed the ALJ's ruling. Its decision on December 27, 1996—two-and-a-half years after the scheduled union representation vote—was a much stronger vindication of the workers' position.[11] The panel, which included NLRB Chairman William Gould, cited the falsification of documents by a Sprint vice-president at corporate headquarters in Kansas City, who attempted to create a "paper trail" indicating that management was more concerned about LCF's financial performance than actually was the case. Just prior to the July 1994 closing, the NLRB noted, Sprint had hired a new manager for LCF and was making other long-term plans for this unique Spanish-language marketing center. The panel's decision ordered Sprint to rehire all LCF workers into "substantially equivalent" jobs elsewhere in the company, provide moving expenses, if necessary, and pay the group more than $15 million in back wages and benefits. In addition, because of the company's widespread misconduct and general disregard for employee rights, the NLRB ordered Sprint to "cease and desist" from threats of plant closures if any of its facilities become unionized, and that it stop engaging in other illegal acts of coercion.

Sprint immediately appealed the Board's ruling. The case dragged on until 1997, when a U.S. Court of Appeals panel upheld the company's position and overturned the NLRB's decision. This legal setback was outrageous but not unexpected. Aware that any relief provided by the NLRB might ultimately be denied by an increasingly conservative federal judiciary, the CWA had, from the very beginning, also tried to build a wide-ranging protest campaign aimed at making the LCF workers a labor *cause célèbre* at home and abroad.

Within weeks of their firing, for example, eighty of the former LCF workers marched on a meeting of the San Francisco Board of Supervisors and secured a resolution censuring Sprint and demanding full reinstatement. The fired workers conducted a round-the-clock vigil in front of Sprint's downtown office building. They set up tents on the sidewalk, gave press interviews, and hosted visiting delegations from churches and other unions. In the city's Mission District, LCF workers and their families went door-to-door to persuade Latino-owned businesses to display signs supporting the solidarity campaign. Dozens of Congressmen signed a letter to Sprint's Chief Executive Officer condemning management's behavior.

San Francisco Bay Area community groups were also enlisted to bombard the company with angry mail. Trade unionists active in Jobs with Justice coalitions in other cities joined the fray by picketing Sprint locations elsewhere. The CWA asked telephone worker unions in Canada, Mexico, Brazil, and Nicaragua to take action within their own countries. On July 14, 1997, the third anniversary of the LCF firings, CWA locals and their allies in other unions and community organizations held protests at Sprint facilities in sixteen cities throughout the United States, as well as in Ireland and Puerto Rico.

STRM went further than any other LCF supporters abroad when it filed the first formal complaint ever made by a Mexican union under the NAFTA "labor side agreement" (known formally as the North American Agreement on Labor Cooperation or NAALC). This move attracted considerable publicity on both sides of the border in 1995. It had previously been assumed that NAALC's complaint procedures—a sop to NAFTA foes in the United States—would mainly be used by American unions complaining about lax labor law enforcement in Mexico that gave MNCs an incentive to relocate there.

But Sprint's entrance into the long distance market in Mexico as part of a joint venture with Telmex gave STRM its own good reason for challenging the company's violation of the "basic norms of labor rights" in the United States. STRM's complaint demanded that the National Administrative Office (NAO) established in Mexico under NAFTA bar Sprint from operating in the country until it reinstated all the fired LCF workers and agreed to recognize unions on either side of the border whenever a majority of them chose to be represented. The Mexican union charged that the absence of any prompt remedy for the denial of LCF workers' rights demonstrated "the ineffectiveness of U.S. law."

In June 1995 the Mexican NAO issued an eighteen-page report upholding the STRM complaint. NAO Secretary Miguel Angel Orozco expressed concern about the adequacy of U.S. labor law enforcement and called for ministerial consultations between the labor secretaries of the two countries about the disposition of the LCF unfair labor practice case. STRM reiterated its demand that the NAO develop clear remedies to address violations of Mexican workers' rights while they are employed in the United States by companies seeking to do business in Mexico.

In February 1996, labor ministry representatives from Mexico, Canada, and the United States convened a widely publicized hearing in San Francisco on the STRM complaint. Sprint boycotted the event. But testimony from STRM, the CWA, PTTI, sympathetic elected officials, academics, and—most effectively—the fired Sprint workers themselves demonstrated the need for stronger action against international labor law violators. Following the San Francisco hearing, the labor ministers asked the Commission for Labor Cooperation (CLC), another tri-national body spawned by the NAALC, to conduct a study of the effect of plant closings on the principle of freedom of association and the right to organize in the three countries involved.

The purpose of the inquiry was presumably to determine whether Sprint's actions were an aberration or reflected a pervasive pattern of employer behavior in the 1990s. Among the academic researchers retained to explore this question was Kate Bronfenbrenner of Cornell University. After collecting and analyzing data on hundreds of U.S. union organizing efforts in recent years, Bronfenbrenner concluded that "plant closing threats and plant closings have become an integral part of employer anti-union campaigns." She found that the rate of plant closings after NLRB elections "has more than doubled in the years since NAFTA was ratified," indicating "that NAFTA has both amplified the credibility and effectiveness of the plant closing threat for employers and emboldened increasing numbers of employers to act on that threat" (Bronfenbrenner 1997).

This was not the kind of findings that the U.S. Department of Labor was eager to release right before the Clinton Administration sought Congressional approval for "fast track" expansion of NAFTA to include Chile and other Latin American countries. The DOL delayed release of the CLC report for many months. When it was finally issued in June 1997, Bronfenbrenner's findings were buried or otherwise watered down in a bland 191-page document that mainly confined itself to describing employment law provisions in the three countries and that failed to single out Sprint for any criticism whatsoever. As a CWA press statement noted at the time, the report is "a huge disappointment . . . the recommendations offered address bureaucratic issues, not the real needs of workers."[12]

Nevertheless, the NAO complaint initiated by STRM succeeded in exposing the glaring limitations of labor side agreements, which provide aggrieved workers with little effective international recourse. Labor lobbyists

frequently cited this experience under the NAALC as part of their successful campaign to block the extension of NAFTA in late 1997.

CWA Returns the Favor at Maxi-Switch

In 1996, the CWA and STRM also collaborated on a NAFTA labor side
agreement complaint involving Maxi-Switch, a U.S.-based subsidiary of a
Taiwanese company called Silitek. Maxi-Switch is a manufacturer of high-
technology keyboards, including Gameboys and various Nintendo game
products. Maxi-Switch maintains a "bag and ship" operation in Arizona,
160 miles from its assembly plant in Cananea in the state of Sonora. Products are made in Mexico by workers earning $3 a day and then shipped
across the border to Tucson, where a smaller number of higher-paid employees operate a U.S. distribution center.

The workers in Sonora were led by Alicia Perez Garcia, a 19-year-old
woman who spent two years quietly building support for the "Union of
Workers of Maxi-Switch," an affiliate (like STRM) of the Federation of
Unions Of Goods and Services Companies (FESEBS). After gathering the
support of over 70 percent of their six hundred coworkers, Perez Garcia
and other in-plant activists petitioned the government for official recognition of their new union's majority status. The very next day, she was
punched and shaken up so badly by a supervisor that she had to be taken
to a hospital. All the union leaders were fired or forced to resign. To further emphasize its opposition to unionization, Maxi-Switch also dismissed
other workers and implemented a pay cut—even though wages in the plant
were already low and benefits barely met minimum legal requirements.
Later, the workers learned that the assault on their leader—for which the
supervisor was later fined—and the retaliatory firings had both been triggered by a government official who had alerted the company about the
recognition petition. The workers, in turn, were notified that their petition was invalid because Maxi-Switch already had a CTM-affiliated "sindicato blanco," although none of the workers were aware of its existence.
When the workers asked to see their "contrato fantasma" (or "ghost contract"), management refused.

Members of CWA Local 7026 in Tucson learned of this situation and
in June 1996 brought a letter of support for the Maxi-Switch workers to
a cross-border meeting in Hermosillo that was sponsored by STRM and
other unions involved in the UNT.[13] According to Local 7026 President
Michael McGrath, a worker at U.S. West, about one-third of the local's

members has family or roots in Mexico. Led by vice-president Randy Clarke, the CWA delegation met with Perez Garcia and gathered information about conditions in her factory, which included fire hazards and workers as young as thirteen. Based on their report and information supplied by STRM, the CWA went to its own National Administrative Office (NAO) and filed a complaint in October 1996, alleging that a NAFTA signatory— the Mexican government—was failing to protect workers' right to organize (just as STRM had done in the Sprint case). The CWA argued that Maxi-Switch, in collusion with government officials, representatives of the CTM, and the Conciliation and Arbitration Board of the state of Sonora, had consistently violated Mexican law to prevent workers from joining a union of their own choosing.

This instance involving Maxi-Switch was not the first time that the Mexican government's failure to live up to its own Federal Labor Code and treaty obligations had been challenged in a freedom of association case involving an MNC. In three earlier complaints, American unions had tried to get the U.S. NAO, which is part of the Labor Department's Bureau of International Affairs, to challenge mistreatment of Mexican organizers at Honeywell, GE, and Sony. Each time, hearings were held but there was no effective redress for the fired workers—and sometimes not even a nonbinding ruling in their favor.[14] However, four days before the April 1997 NAO hearing on CWA's case, the Mexican government agreed to issue a legal registration of the independent union at Maxi-Switch and to hear the reinstatement appeals of its fired leaders. This was the first time that a signatory to a NAFTA labor side agreement proceeding was ever forced to make concessions—and agree to follow its own laws—in response to a pending complaint. Unfortunately, follow-up enforcement was weak and as of 1999, the insurgent union at Maxi-Switch had still not succeeded in negotiating a real collective bargaining agreement.

Joining Forces in the United Kingdom: The Atlantic Alliance

The Americanization of labor relations in the United Kingdom's telecom industry has fostered closer ties between CWA and its counterparts in Britain. The Thatcher government's sell-off of BT in the 1980s and the company's subsequent downsizing weakened both the 300,000-member Communications Workers Union (CWU) and the 27,000-strong Society of Telecom Executives (STE). Like STRM, the CWU and STE were confronted with the task of recruiting new members at the growing number of new cable television and telecom companies—including U.S.-based ones—that are now competing with the former state-owned monopoly. For example, U.K. cable TV providers now employ more than thirty thousand non-union workers, many of them hired, American-style, as independent contractors.

The CWA's relationship with CWU and STE began modestly, with an exchange of information about the problems of organizing new members in a privatized, deregulated environment. The formal cooperation agreement that was then developed, known as the "Atlantic Alliance," states that whenever members of the three unions are bargaining with a common MNC, they will establish some form of direct "communication and joint education." In addition, "a contract mobilization timeline" will be developed and the resulting "joint action will be more an expression of basic union strategy in negotiations and less an exceptional example of international solidarity." The agreement declares that "joint organizing strategies" will be developed for key information-sector firms operating in both countries.

Even as the CWA prepared to send three members to Britain to work with CWU on their initial joint organizing venture in the summer of 1997, the corporate configurations that triggered the "Atlantic Alliance" were rapidly changing. This experience (repeated many times around the world) illustrates how little time it takes for capital to move in new directions compared to the long process of developing labor counter-moves in response. CWA had made its initial overtures to the British union when BT became a 20 percent owner of MCI, the second largest long-distance carrier in the United States. The hope was that CWU's remaining influence within BT could be leveraged in a manner that might someday restrain MCI's anti-union behavior in the United States. But MCI, including BT's share, was bought by WorldCom, then a relatively small and entirely non-union Mississippi telecom firm.

Meanwhile, just as BT was in the process of withdrawing from its major U.S. investment, some of the North American firms that had been active in the United Kingdom were selling out to the U.K.–based CWC. NYNEX Cablecoms, once wholly owned by NYNEX and more recently 50 percent publicly traded, was acquired by CWC along with two Canadian cable subsidiaries, BCE and Videotron. These transactions made CWC the largest cable systems operator in the United Kingdom. About 25 percent of all British cable subscribers got their telephone service via cable rather than through BT. As the operator of Mercury Communications, CWC now ranked second to BT in the provision of business and residential phone service. Telewest—managed jointly by two giant U.S.-based firms, U.S. West and Telecommunications, Inc. (now part of AT&T)—had become the United Kingdom's second largest cable TV operator.

With their multinational character, large concentrations of Americans in top management positions, and large non-union workforces, CWC and Telewest thus became the logical targets for the Atlantic Alliance's highly unusual joint organizing project in 1997. Three CWA organizers—Shannon Kirkland from Detroit, Andrea DeMajewski from Seattle, and Hank Desio from Tulsa—spent four months working with CWU branches in Manchester, Brighton, and London. Kirkland and DeMajewski both had been involved in cable organizing in the United States at firms like TCI. They wanted to learn more about the British practice of recruiting dues-paying members prior to making any demand on the employer for recognition. Like most U.S. unions, the CWA's private sector organizing usually focuses on building the majority support needed for card check recognition or certification via an NLRB election victory, rather than touting pre-contract benefits or services to individuals. Desio, however, had spent ten years helping to build CWA-backed organizations among state workers in Texas and Oklahoma, where weak public sector bargaining laws do not permit recognition or formal contract negotiations. In these campaigns, long-term membership recruitment and non-contractual servicing is the norm.

During their 1997 stay DeMajewski lived in Manchester, while Desio worked in Brighton and Kirkland stayed in the London area. All three roomed with union families as part of their "cross-training" experience. The members providing their housing received a stipend from the CWU. Although these living arrangements sometimes created additional adjustment problems, it increased the organizers' credibility among CWU activists and ultimately deepened their connection to the people with whom they were working. The most important outcome of their stay was the development of greater organizing capability in twenty different CWU branches, whose membership is still almost entirely based within BT. CWU organizers learned the usefulness of developing small groups of organizers in branches who, in turn, support committees inside locations without union recognition, thus providing a base of support for a subsequent recognition campaign.

Desio helped promote this grassroots approach in the Brighton branch, where a committee of five worked with him on CWC cable organizing. They signed up new members and developed a leadership committee among technical workers at CWC. The newly trained in-plant leaders helped focus their co-workers on the importance of a drive for collective recognition, rather than stressing, in traditional fashion, the benefits of individual union membership. The CWU's Brighton branch committed to appointing a full-time "external organizer" to continue this type of work after Desio returned home. DeMajewski encouraged a similar approach in Newcastle where Telewest was the target. In sum, CWU branches learned that recruitment had to take forms other than periodic leafleting and distribution of membership forms. Rather, organizing required working with new members on an ongoing basis to encourage them to build their own organization.

In December 1997 the CWU brought in-plant leaders from various CWC companies to London to launch a national campaign for recognition. The union's goal was to get 60 percent of CWC employees around the country to sign a petition demanding union recognition. Workplaces with high enough levels of membership planned to seek local recognition as well. As part of this effort, CWU, CWA, and STE have asked UNI affiliates to put pressure on CWC in other countries where it operates. By 1999, however, neither national nor local recognition of the CWU had been achieved yet at CWC in Britain.

Conclusion

A decade ago members of CWA had few opportunities to be directly involved in the union's international work. Since then, the union's cross-border initiatives have moved from high-level meetings and conferences to much deeper participation by organizers, local officers, and rank-and-file workers. Aided by the new technology of the information age—communications tools like e-mail and the World Wide Web—some CWA activists are now networking with unionists overseas just as if they belonged to another local in the United States. A growing number have had the chance to talk face-to-face with their counterparts abroad: telephone workers from Mexico, factory workers in Canada, and cable TV technicians in England. By joining forces, they have tried to enhance union strength, defend wage and benefit standards, and influence public policy.

However, if major changes are going to occur in the balance of power between labor and capital in the new global economy, far more union resources will have to be devoted to grassroots organizing and rank-and-file activity. The budgets of the ITSs such as UNI total millions of dollars a year. More of that money ought to be spent on joint organizing projects like the 1997 CWA-CWU experiment and coordinated solidarity campaigns involving workplace protests and direct action by workers within the same transnational firm. More union members must be encouraged to act locally to be effective internationally because real solidarity—as opposed to symbolic gestures—often requires the exercise of shop floor power at home. If that power has been eroded because a union has no program for internal organization and membership mobilization to meet day-to-day challenges by management, its members will be less able to help workers elsewhere.

Today, even some of the best organized, most innovative cross-border initiatives by unions are clearly too little, too late. That's because the pace of labor's work at the international level does not match the great speed with which transnational corporations are restructuring themselves and redirecting the flow of investment. Our adversaries are like giant "shape shifters"—the alien beings of science fiction fame—who can combine, divide, and assume new physical forms almost instantaneously. If unions, in response, pursue a business-as-usual approach to building their own international alliances and actions, they will be outmaneuvered and marginalized.

Worker representatives must themselves feel and convey to their membership a far greater sense of urgency about the global anti-union trends that are undermining collective bargaining and workplace protection for millions of people. Unions must be willing to break more rules, take more risks, ignore protocol, and change long-established modes of organizational behavior so that workers can better unite and fight. If we fail, the telecommunications revolution will end up forging, for our members, a new set of chains.

11

Solidarity across Borders:
The UMWA's Corporate Campaign against
Peabody and Hanson PLC

KENNETH S. ZINN

In 1993 a dispute broke out in the American coalfields that brought with it echoes from the coal industry's tumultuous past—and also reflected the tough new labor-management conflicts characteristic of the age of the globalized economy. At the heart of the dispute was job security for unionized mine workers. In the fiercely competitive conditions of the American and world coal markets, the large companies organized in the Bituminous Coal Operators' Association (BCOA) had devised a long-term strategy to eliminate the United Mine Workers of America (UMWA) from their operations. The BCOA wanted to escape from the requirements of the industry's leading wage agreement, an agreement that has its origins in the heady days of legendary UMWA president John L. Lewis.

The union leadership prepared its ground well, amassing a huge strike fund and preparing the membership for a long battle. The union's leaders carefully researched their adversaries and developed strategies to confront them at all levels and wherever the companies were doing business. This chapter describes the corporate campaign against one of these adversaries, Peabody Holding Co., and its parent, Hanson PLC.

The World Coal Market and Company Strategy

The U.S. coal strike occurred against the backdrop of the tough competition that had been taking place in the coal industry worldwide. Energy companies had opened many new mines in response to the oil shocks of the 1970s and had become engaged in an increasingly ferocious battle for mar-

223

ket share as these facilities came on stream. With the world market awash in coal, and a severe decline in the price of oil and natural gas, serious price undercutting ensued, including, in some cases, systematic dumping of coal on the world market below its cost of production. As part of their corporate strategy many coal operators attempted to drive labor costs down and to undercut working conditions negotiated by miners' unions throughout the postwar period.[1] The major companies were on the attack in all the main producing and exporting countries where they owned key mines.

Hanson is an Anglo-American conglomerate that early in the 1990s became a major player in the energy industries on both sides of the Atlantic. Headquartered in London, Hanson was the sixth largest industrial corporation in Britain, with revenues in 1992 of £8.8 billion ($15 billion). A conglomerate involved in everything from making bricks to tobacco products, this huge and highly political corporation was infamous for its global asset-stripping practices and its aggressive management techniques. The company's chairman, Lord James Hanson, and his partner in the United States, Lord Gordon White, had made millions in the merger-and-acquisitions spree of the 1980s. Typically, they bought targeted companies, which they would then break up, keeping only those parts that were highly profitable or that fit into their corporate strategy. In fact, Hanson's corporate headquarters was staffed with people who were expert in buying and selling companies and exploiting changes in the currency markets, rather than adept at running a business.

In Britain, Hanson was known as a leading opponent of the social and labor rights enshrined in the European Union's Social Charter and Social Chapter. The company and its subsidiaries had direct influence with the top echelon of the British Conservative government and cemented that tie with the appointment of former Conservative Party Chairman Ken Baker to its board of directors. For their fealty, both James Hanson and Gordon White were rewarded with peerages.

Hanson made its first foray into the coal industry in 1990 by buying Peabody, the largest coal producer in the United States, for $1.2 billion. By the time of the strike, Peabody had become Hanson's second largest profit earner, its fastest-growing division, and its largest money maker in the United States. In 1992 Peabody made Hanson $237 million in profits.

Hanson's role in the 1993 U.S. coal strike was inspired by the tough and ruthless campaign fought by Lord Hanson's personal friend, former British Prime Minister Margaret Thatcher, against Britain's miners and their union, the National Union of Mineworkers (NUM). The NUM had fought that strike at a time of declining world coal prices that were about to fall much further after the oil price collapse in 1986. Consequently, miners and other energy workers in the United States and Britain found common cause in each other's plights.

The Corporate Strategy to Weaken the Union

The coal companies comprising the BCOA began a systematic effort to weaken the UMWA years before the 1993 strike. Taking advantage of deficiencies in U.S. labor law, many began establishing a complex web of paper subsidiaries to escape their obligations to their unionized employees. The companies transferred assets, coal reserves, and supply contracts from their unionized subsidiaries to these paper subsidiaries, a practice known as "double-breasting."

The unionized sector of the coal industry declined as a result of these corporate practices and the non-union sector expanded. "They drew a box around the unionized mines," then-UMWA President Richard Trumka explained. As the union mines' coal became depleted, the companies would open new mines, hiring non-union workers instead of laid-off UMWA members. The "box" of unionized mines thus became smaller and smaller over time, as union mines closed down and the industry viciously fought the UMWA's attempts to organize. The companies' goal was to make the union no longer a force in the industry.

Tragically ironic for the miners in this scheme was the fact that by working harder, unwittingly they made it easier for the companies to discard them more quickly. From 1979 to 1992, UMWA members employed at BCOA mines increased their productivity nearly 200 percent. But the harder they worked and the more coal they produced, the sooner their mines would close. In a growing resource extraction industry like the U.S. coal industry, such a situation would not necessarily have to be a bad thing, because employers routinely open new mines to replace those that have been depleted. In these circumstances, the union's demand was simple: miners who lost their jobs should have the right to be hired first at any new operations opened by the same company—operations that were possible only through the profits generated by the hard work of UMWA miners. Given that the average age of the union's members was forty-four and that unionized mines, on average, had only seven years of productive capacity remaining, the vast majority of the union's membership was forced to contemplate almost certain unemployment in their early fifties—too young for retirement but too old to start over.

The union attempted to address this issue in its 1988 negotiations with the BCOA. The companies agreed to fill the first three out of every five new jobs at any new operations with laid-off UMWA members. However, no sooner had the ink dried on the 1988 agreement than the coal companies refused to abide by it, declaring that the contract did not apply at the other operations owned by the companies' parents. The companies' apparent violation of the 1988 agreement forced the UMWA to pursue a lengthy and expensive legal action that was unresolved in 1992, when a successor agreement had to be negotiated. The job security issue was back on the table.

BCOA Stonewalls

Trumka wrote to the BCOA in August 1992, urging that bargaining begin soon. Trumka had made a name for himself in the industry by successfully resolving the 1984 and 1988 BCOA negotiations without union concessions and without national strikes, although he had demonstrated that he was prepared to fight, if necessary, in the union's victorious 1989 strike against the Pittson Co. This time he urged the companies to leave enough time to negotiate a new agreement before the old one expired on February 1, 1993. The BCOA did not respond. Trumka continued to press the companies through September and October, but the BCOA's negotiators waited until November before agreeing to meet with the union's team, which included then-union vice-president (now president) Cecil Roberts and secretary-treasurer (now vice-president) Jerry Jones.

Following standard procedure at the beginning of any contract negotiation, at the November meeting the UMWA negotiators submitted a lengthy request for information. Among the questions were the critical ones involving intra-corporate relationships. Put simply, the union needed to know with whom it was bargaining. Was just one corporate subsidiary, several subsidiaries, or the entire parent company at the bargaining table? The union was determined not to be caught in the companies' shell game again. Trumka sent a clear signal to the other side. If the companies would respect their unionized employees' rights to job security, then the union's wage and benefit demands could be moderated. If, on the other hand, the companies intended to jettison their unionized employees as quickly as possible, the union would have to make much higher demands on wages and benefits for its members—a golden parachute of sorts for miners whom the companies were denying a long-term future in the industry they had built.

Negotiations never began, because the BCOA refused to supply the union with the requested information, which the union claimed was a violation of federal labor law, and the union refused to bargain in the dark. As a result, on February 1 the UMWA waged a selective unfair labor prac-

tice strike against Peabody's Midwestern and Appalachian mining operations. The union believed that Peabody, the nation's largest coal company,
was primarily responsible for the BCOA's stonewalling strategy and thus
targeted Peabody for the initial strike. Six thousand UMWA miners at
seventeen underground and six surface Peabody mines began walking the
picket line.

Peabody complained that, unlike Consol Energy, the second largest coal
company, it had not double-breasted its operations and that the union's
singling out of its operations was unfair. Consol had been the leader in the
double-breasting strategy, but Peabody was following suit and probably
believed it had more to lose from any *future* obligations by the industry to
transfer rights for UMWA miners. For example, Peabody had already pur-
chased two large non-union mines in Wyoming's Powder River Basin and
planned to shift more production to that region because of its high seams
of low sulfur coal and its non-union tradition.

In addition, Peabody had created a new, wholly-owned paper subsidiary
in Indiana, Premier Coal Corporation, that had not yet opened any mines.
Peabody intended to lease five thousand acres from its unionized subsidiary
to Premier and mine some forty million tons of coal over a sixteen- to
twenty-year period with nonunion miners instead of Peabody's UMWA
miners. Peabody's negotiator feigned ignorance about Premier's existence
and the company's intention.

This initial strike against Peabody continued for four weeks (and was
briefly expanded to several other companies) before the BCOA companies
agreed to respond to the union's requests for information and to bargain in
good faith. On March 3 the companies signed an extension of the old
agreement until May 3, and the UMWA suspended its strike.

The BCOA companies once again failed to live up to their agreement.
The sixty-day period came and went, and the companies refused to provide
all the information the union had requested. The UMWA resumed its unfair labor practice strike in early May, and escalated it almost every week
to cover ever more BCOA mines. Peabody's mines were struck again on
June 2. When the strike reached its peak, some eighteen thousand miners
had stopped work in seven states.

Building the Campaign

The UMWA's bargaining problems were magnified because Peabody and
many of the other BCOA companies were not simply coal companies but
rather subsidiaries of very large multinational corporations. From the start,

the UMWA's leadership was aware that a strike was simply not enough to win a just agreement from Peabody and the other companies. If the union confined its battle with Peabody only to the picket lines, Peabody's parent, Hanson PLC, would prevail because of its tremendous resources that would enable the company to wait the union out. This should not imply that the strike was unimportant. On the contrary, the strike forced the company to absorb real costs and it engaged the union's rank-and-file membership in the battle. In 1990s America, however, with the playing field so slanted against unions, waging a strike without another complementary strategy would have been foolhardy. Therefore the UMWA's leadership was determined to move this strike from its own backyard in the U.S. coalfields to Hanson's backyard in Britain and any other place Hanson was doing business. "We will take our case from Main Street to Wall Street," Cecil Roberts declared, and the union sent rank-and-file strikers to targeted cities across the United States to organize support.

Early in the dispute, the UMWA systematically began reaching out to the unions at Hanson's other operations in the U.S. and around the world to build a network of solidarity. On April 26, in an action coordinated by the AFL-CIO's Industrial Union Department (IUD), nineteen thousand workers, members of ten different unions, engaged in a "UMWA Solidarity Day." The participants wore solidarity ribbons on the job at eighty Hanson facilities across the United States and told local management that Hanson should settle with the UMWA. IUD President Elmer Chatak said the protest was "only the beginning of a broader mobilization of union and community support for the Mine Workers."

That spring, the UMWA received further support from the Venezuelan national union federation, Confederación de Trabajadores de Venezuela (CTV). On April 27 José Gomez, CTV president, wrote to Lord Hanson that, failing a settlement with the UMWA, Venezuela's powerful labor movement would oppose Hanson's entry into the Venezuelan coal market.

The global campaign was taken to a new level on June 2, 1993, the day UMWA miners struck for the second time against Peabody. Nearly a thousand miners at Peabody's Ravensworth and Warkworth mines in Australia, members of the Construction, Forestry, Mining and Energy Union, went on a twenty-four-hour solidarity strike. The Australian miners knew that in the future they could be subject to what had happened to the American miners.[2] The same was true for four thousand miners in Colombia who struck on September 22 in support of the UMWA. "We think it's urgent that we, as workers with a common cause, strengthen the links between us," declared Jorge Gomez, president of the Colombian mine workers' union, Sintercor.[3]

Simultaneously, the UMWA reached out to the British Trades Union

Congress (TUC), the national federation of British trade unions represent-
ing seven million workers, to build the campaign in Hanson's backyard.
Five TUC affiliates represented workers at Hanson operations in Britain.
The UMWA received considerable assistance from two international trade
union federations, the International Federation of Chemical, Energy and
General Workers' Unions (ICEF) and the Miners' International Federation
(MIF), both of which urged their British affiliates to support the UMWA.
The AFL-CIO also provided support for the campaign against Hanson.

The UMWA already had considerable experience in corporate campaigning but the TUC was new to the idea. Whereas a few of its affiliated
unions had organized successful campaigns (in two instances to stop Hanson's hostile takeovers of other companies), the TUC itself had not really
become involved, especially on the scale that was to develop in the Hanson
campaign. During the sixty-day spring lull between strikes, the TUC sent
its first signal to Hanson that it would be involved in the UMWA dispute.
In April Norman Willis, then TUC general secretary, visited Hanson's headquarters to meet company secretary Yves Newbold. Willis delivered a letter addressed to Lord Hanson from leaders of the five TUC unions that had
contracts at Hanson's British operations. The gist was that British unions
wanted to see a just resolution of the U.S. coal dispute and that Hanson
should expect the British labor movement to stand by the UMWA.

When the U.S. strike resumed in June, the British media, and especially
the business press, began to follow Hanson's financial performance much
more carefully. Given that Hanson was the largest British conglomerate
on the London stock exchange and, consequently, that its stock was held
by most major investors, the City of London (Britain's Wall Street) and its
large institutional investors could not ignore what was going on across the
Atlantic. The UMWA's strategy was to bring the fight into the heart of the
City itself.

The Shareholder Campaign

From the outset of the dispute, the UMWA reached out to Hanson's institutional shareholders. This effort began on March 3, 1993, when President
Trumka addressed a meeting of Wall Street investors in New York sponsored by Shearson Lehman Brothers, Inc. He told the investors that the economic self-interests of the shareholders and the workers were inextricably
linked: "Without labor, there is no coal industry and without capital investment, the industry simply cannot exist. The workers' prosperity and
that of the capital investors cannot be separated."

Trumka explained that management's plan to deny UMWA members job security made increased productivity the workers' enemy, and that this situation worked against shareholders' interests. He elaborated the UMWA's proposal for a new cooperative relationship between labor and management in the coal industry whereby workers would participate in making critical decisions with managers for the long-term profitability of the enterprise. The investment community responded favorably to the address and several shareholders expressed their concern to top management at Hanson and several other BCOA companies.

Meanwhile, Lord Hanson scheduled an extraordinary shareholders meeting on June 25 to vote on several proposals. Buried in these proposals were amendments to the company's articles of association that would have severely limited shareholder rights, among them the right to nominate candidates to the board of directors and to participate fully in shareholder meetings. Because of where the proposals were situated in the company's proxy materials, the press and the institutional investors failed to notice them.

The UMWA, itself a Hanson shareholder, joined forces with the London-based Pensions & Investments Research Consultants Ltd. (PIRC), which advises several British public employee pension funds, to oppose the company's proposed amendments. The union and PIRC engaged in a major solicitation of shareholders in both the United States and Britain, the first transatlantic proxy fight ever. The union's stake was made greater by the large investment in Hanson held by the UMWA 1974 Pension Trust, whose beneficiaries are the union's members. The campaign took place against the backdrop of the Cadbury Committee's work to introduce better corporate governance practices among British companies. The Cadbury Committee, created in 1991 by the London Stock Exchange and the Financial Reporting Council and named after its chairman, Sir Adrian Cadbury, had produced a code of practice to protect shareholder rights that, while purely voluntary, had had significant influence and cachet.

The British press (including even the very conservative newspapers that had traditionally backed Lord Hanson's financial escapades) responded with unusual force to the UMWA-PIRC efforts, giving the "vote no" campaign excellent coverage and condemning Hanson on its editorial pages. For example, an editorial in *The Times* of London stated, "Hanson's draconian counter-measures are the equivalent of a military coup in the world of shareholder democracy."[4] The *Daily Telegraph* editorialized, "For a man who thrives on takeover battles, Lord Hanson seems to have an irrational fear of facing his shareholders."[5] The *Financial Times* wrote that "the proposals have provoked a storm of protest."[6] The *Daily Mail* offered, "Were he not so smart, so rich, so famous, you could almost feel sorry for

Lord Hanson as he stumbles from one corporate gaffe to another."[7] Both shareholders and the press saw Lord Hanson's move for what it was—an overreaching "power play," in the words of the *Daily Mail*—and seemed determined to bring Lord Hanson's arrogance into check.[8]

As the UMWA and PIRC contacted other Hanson shareholders, a growing number of large investors in both countries agreed to oppose the company's initiatives. Commenting on the growing momentum against Lord Hanson, UMWA Secretary-Treasurer Jones told the press that shareholders from around the world were, for the first time, uniting to oppose an attempt by an entrenched management to appropriate their rights. The cross-border solidarity effort that had begun with Hanson's workers had now spread to its owners.

After the UMWA and PIRC successfully mobilized institutional shareholders owning more than 230 million shares to vote no, Hanson saw that he would lose the vote. On June 17, he withdrew the onerous proposals, accepting an ignominious defeat of a kind rarely suffered by British executives. The press in both countries headlined Hanson's retreat: "Hanson gives in to shareholders"; "Hanson loses to institutions"; "Hanson bows to investors' campaign"; "Hanson backs down over proposed rule changes."[9]

In an editorial the *Times* wrote, "Now that institutional shareholders have discovered they can bend the will of the mightiest company in the land, the power might go to their heads."[10] The *Wall Street Journal* noted that Hanson "has become the latest company to bow to increasingly forceful muscle-flexing by institutional shareholders."[11] The press gave the UMWA and PIRC credit for forcing the company to back down. Declaring a victory for shareholder rights, the UMWA's Jones told reporters that the episode showed that "Hanson's management cannot run our company like their personal fiefdom."

The UMWA followed up this victory by participating in Hanson's shareholders meeting in London on June 25 (the meeting was still necessary to vote on the proposed executive stock option plan). The company tried its best to defend its actions, including having Peabody CEO Irl Engelhardt fly to London to explain the coal dispute at length. Engelhardt's defense motivated no supporting speeches from the shareholders at the meeting. Instead, shareholders were becoming increasingly mindful of the continuing, huge, strike-related losses at Peabody reflected in Hanson's performance. Pressure began to build on Hanson's top management in London to intervene to force a settlement in the U.S. coal dispute.

As the union's special project's coordinator, I also attended the London meeting to address Lord Hanson and the shareholders publicly. Commenting on the unseemliness of the company's proposal to give its top executives large bonuses while the UMWA's members were being mistreated, I told the meeting that the chairman's lack of concern for shareholders mirrored his disregard for employees. The union's leaflets to participants called the strike "a tonne of trouble for Hanson shareholders." For his part, Lord Hanson defended Peabody's handling of the strike but was forced to apologize for offering such onerous and disenfranchising shareholder proposals. It was a rare public humiliation for a man used to riding so high.

The London press coverage of the meeting highlighted Lord Hanson's shareholder defeat and the company's problems with the ongoing UMWA strike. The *Daily Telegraph* compared Lord Hanson with Shakespeare's Coriolanus, who unsuccessfully attempted to deny the plebeians their votes. In the play, the plebeians complain about Coriolanus: "He mock'd us when he beg'd our voices."[12] *The Times* said Lord Hanson looked "distinctly ill-tempered," and was "clearly angered by the impact the strike is having on Hanson's profits."[13] The *Daily Mail* wrote "that coal was the main issue at the meeting as representatives of striking U.S. miners made their case."[14]

The union continued its outreach to investors by inviting the City's corporate analysts to a briefing at which the UMWA provided a detailed analysis of the strike. The questions that followed the union's presentation were not only searching but well-informed. The room was packed with analysts from most of the large brokerage firms, who seemed eager to understand the dispute and to know how and when it might end. *The Guardian* called the UMWA's briefing of London's financial analysts an "intriguing development" and a "cunning manoeuvre."[15]

Political and Religious Support

At the end of June the UMWA's campaign team won the support of Martin O'Neill MP, the Labour Party Energy Spokesperson, and Malcolm Bruce MP, the Liberal Democratic Party Energy Spokesperson, for an Early Day Motion in the House of Commons. Organized by former miner Mick Clapham MP, over a hundred Members from different political parties joined this parliamentary motion calling for proper negotiations in the U.S. dispute. They expressed their concern that a British company was part of the problem rather than part of the solution. That motion read:

> This House expresses its deep concern that Peabody Holding Co. in the U.S., owned by Hanson PLC, is currently in the throes of an all-out strike as a direct result of a management policy to deny job security and transfer

rights of unionized workers to new mines; it believes that such tactics suggest British management is seeking to export confrontational methods which are neither good for the image of British industry abroad nor ultimately for the shareholders and customers affected; it calls upon Lord Hanson to respond positively to appeals for a negotiated settlement with the United Mine Workers of America.[16]

The Early Day Motion was spotlighted at a press conference at TUC headquarters.

Religious leaders from many different denominations and faiths in the United States expressed their support for the UMWA. More than six hundred religious leaders across the country, including the heads of ten national faith groups and 132 bishops, signed an April 29 letter to the BCOA expressing support for the miners. The letter reminded the coal operators that the miners should be treated with dignity and respect and not as disposable property. The clerics affirmed the collective bargaining process and the moral right of workers to form and maintain effective unions. The BCOA was urged to refrain from hiring striker replacements and to negotiate a settlement that would bring justice to the coalfields. This statement of the religious leaders was reported widely in the U.S. press.[17] The Commission on Religion in Appalachia and its then-director, Rev. Jim Sessions, organized the clergy throughout the coalfields to provide outstanding leadership.

The British churches also became involved. Michael Szpak, a Methodist minister and religious outreach coordinator for the AFL-CIO, and Reverend Jim Lewis, an American Episcopalian Canon, made contact with their opposite numbers in Britain. Many British churches, including the Anglicans, Roman Catholics, Methodists, and Baptists, became supporters of the UMWA cause. Besides their concern for social justice, many of these churches had considerable investments in Hanson as well.

Church support was typified by a letter sent to Lord Hanson on June 7, 1993, by Archdeacon Michael Bourke, chairman of the Christian Ethical Investment Group of the Church of England. The letter wondered aloud whether trade wars might erupt—harmful to British and American workers—if Peabody could produce cheaper coal by employing non-union labor, further undermining the competitiveness of British coal. The Church of England was important to the campaign not only because of is moral influence but because it is Britain's official state church whose bishops sit in the House of Lords alongside Lord Hanson. The work with the Church of England culminated in an unprecedented meeting in Washington between the Archbishop of Canterbury, George Carey, and the UMWA's Trumka.

The meeting was publicized in Britain and brought extra pressure to bear on Hanson and the other BCOA companies to settle the dispute.[18]

Campaign at Home

During this activity in Britain, the stateside campaign continued to build. Holding Hanson's U.S. decision-makers accountable was central. These decision-makers included Lord White (the playboy head of the conglomerate's U.S. operations), Peabody CEO Engelhardt, and Charles Price II, a member of the Hanson board of directors, a prominent banker in Kansas City, and Ronald Reagan's U.S. ambassador to Britain. Lord White's office in his Beverly Hills mansion became a regular site of informational picketing by California activists. At one point early in the strike, Postal Workers President Moe Biller and Chemical Workers President Frank Martino joined several hundred people for a rally at the mansion's gates. That action followed a similar demonstration at Lord Hanson's winter home in Palm Springs, California, led by Machinists President George Kourpias.[19]

Peabody's headquarters in St. Louis was the site of daily informational pickets by UMWA strikers and community activists. At an April rally, St. Louis mayor Freeman Bosley, Jr., received a standing ovation from hundreds of union supporters when he said, "You are here for a just cause. As the mayor of the city of St. Louis, I appreciate that."[20]

Religious and labor activists in Kansas City spoke up often throughout the strike, urging banker Charles Price to use his influence as a member of the Hanson board of directors to settle the dispute. Community leaders held regular vigils at Price's Mercantile Bancorporation branches, and union locals in Kansas City pulled nearly $200,000 out of Mercantile in protest.[21]

Critically important to the success of these efforts was the union's decision to send rank-and-file strikers to these cities to assist in organizing the campaign. No one could tell the miners' compelling story better than the miners themselves. Working with experienced organizers, the miners were able to reach out to labor and community organizations and build local support in cities outside the coalfields.

The campaign at home and the one overseas were joined in July when the UMWA, supported by the AFL-CIO, invited top leaders of the international labor movement to speak to striking mine workers in a tour of the U.S. coalfields. The delegation consisted of Enzo Friso (general secretary of the 113 million-member International Confederation of Free Trade

Unions), Peter Michalzik (general secretary of the MIF), Michael Boggs (general secretary of the ICEF), and David Lea (assistant general secretary of the TUC). The officials told rallies of enthusiastic Pennsylvania and Illinois miners that world attention was focused on their strike.

The international delegation also held private meetings with B.R. Brown, CEO of Consol Energy and chairman of the BCOA, and Irl Engelhardt of Peabody. Michalzik told the coal executives that his organization would make sure coal mined by non-union labor "would not be welcome in other countries." The delegation then traveled to Washington to meet with Secretary of Labor Robert Reich to let him know the strike was in the international spotlight. Union leaders from Australia, Ukraine, Japan, Colombia, Venezuela, Chile and Peru followed soon after with solidarity visits to the union's picket lines.[22]

The UMWA also received assistance from South Africa. Seven hundred fifty workers at Hanson's Ever Ready battery factory in Port Elizabeth delivered a message to local management expressing their support for the UMWA—and then stopped work for twenty-four hours. "Workers in South Africa cannot fight the apartheid practices by Hanson in South Africa without also fighting the exploitation by Hanson of mine workers in the U.S.," said Bimba Mangabashana, Eastern Cape Regional Secretary of the National Union of Metalworkers of South Africa. "In our experience, an injury to one really is an injury to all, and we stand by our brothers and sisters in the United Mine Workers of America."[23] In a separate development, the union also received the support of Nobel Peace Prize laureate Archbishop Desmond Tutu, the Anglican Archbishop of Cape Town. "I support your struggle for justice in the American coalfields," Tutu wrote in an August 1st letter to Trumka. "I believe your desire to sustain a strong trade union in the coal mines is a basic human right and denounce any effort by your employers which would deny you this elemental right."

By mid-August, Hanson had to admit that the strike had already cost the company almost $200 million, much more than officials had predicted just a few months earlier. The *Financial Times* concluded that "the Peabody strike is now inflicting real pain" on the company.[24] *The Guardian* asked, "How long is Hanson prepared to pay such a price?"[25] The strike's ongoing impact on the company's profits, its impact on the Appalachian and midwestern regional economies, and the UMWA's campaign to expose U.S. anti-union labor laws to international scrutiny compelled the Clinton Administration to get involved. In September Secretary Reich appointed William Usery, a former Secretary of Labor, as a "super mediator" to help resolve the dispute.

Conclusion

On December 7, 1993, the UMWA and the BCOA reached a tentative agreement that was subsequently ratified by the union's rank and file. The five-year agreement guaranteed better wages and pensions, protected health care and working conditions, and drew the line against double-breasting in the coal industry with the strongest job security and job opportunity guarantees of any National Bituminous Coal Wage Agreement. Included in the contract was an unprecedented memorandum of understanding signed by the BCOA's members' parent companies guaranteeing job transfer rights for UMWA members at all their bituminous coal subsidiaries. Also included in the agreement was the first-ever labor-management cooperation program in the industry.

In addition to the eighteen thousand members who went on strike, tens of thousands more were covered by the agreement, including many miners working for companies that had reached separate interim agreements earlier in the year. The seven-month strike had begun back in May with the coal companies' attempt to marginalize the union. Their attempt failed miserably because of the UMWA's energetic strike and corporate campaign. The battle had been long and tough, fought bitterly against some of the world's most powerful corporations. Mediator Usery noted, "This was without question the toughest set of contract negotiations I've ever been involved with, but the result is an agreement UMWA families can be proud of."[26]

The UMWA's campaign held many lessons. The union had defied the company's expectations of what a strike would entail. Management's cost-benefit analysis had to be revised substantially. For most of the dispute, the union chose the field of battle, not the company, which never knew when or where it would be struck next. This was important in keeping the company on the defensive throughout the strike. Also, the union successfully defined the issues and its adversary. Thus it was able to maintain the moral high ground and could keep the public's attention focused on its own compelling story rather than on the company's message.

Contrary to the media's conventional wisdom that strikes in the United States are no longer effective, the UMWA showed that a strike can be very costly to a company when the union is well-prepared and has a disciplined rank-and-file membership and when the strike affects a large amount of the company's production. Through its long tradition of solidarity, its experienced leadership team, and its well-organized union structures, the UMWA crippled the largest privately-owned coal company in the world. When all was said and done, the UMWA dispute cost Hanson $307 million in lost profits.

The campaign also drove a wedge between Hanson's management team and its owners. Lord Hanson's blunder in proposing disenfranchising amendments to the shareholders in the midst of the strike, combined with his underestimation to the shareholders of the strike's financial impact, caused institutional investors to take a much more jaundiced view of the chairman's operating methods. Because of the union's campaign, a man once esteemed by investors during the Thatcher era for his buccaneer ways was quite suddenly publicly humiliated in the eyes of those same investors.

Also critically important was the UMWA's willingness to ask for assistance and solidarity both from its labor allies and from community, religious, political, and other leaders in the United States and abroad. The UMWA's outreach was built on years of painstaking effort to forge bonds with allies. From the United States to the United Kingdom, from Australia to South Africa, the UMWA built a strong coalition that cost Hanson profits, turned the spotlight of public scrutiny on the company's abuses, and boosted the morale of the strikers during the long dispute.

The Hanson corporate campaign highlighted the fact that the dominant companies in the coal industry had created global problems for workers and their unions that required international solutions. For this reason, national unions are building more effective international trade union federations, such as the International Federation of Chemical, Energy, Mine and General Workers' Unions (ICEM) representing more than twenty million workers in 115 countries, to facilitate the solidarity necessary to confront multinational employers. The global character of the coal industry also prompted miners' unions to press for the Convention on Safety in Mines, adopted in 1995 by the International Labor Organization, to ensure that the highest possible standards are applied in every coal-producing country.

Last, the UMWA leadership engaged its rank-and-file members, the union's primary resource, in both the strike and the corporate campaign through seven long months. In doing so, the union not only won this particular contract dispute but strengthened itself for the long road ahead.

12

Local and Transnational Campaigns to End Sweatshop Practices

MARK ANNER

One day during the summer of 1997, employees of a relatively small garment factory in Guatemala went to work wearing white T-shirts with "*Queremos un pacto*" (we want a contract) written across the front. The sight of the shirts made the local managers uneasy, but work appeared to proceed as normal. The workers, the majority of them young women, went to their sewing machines and began working at the established pace. Despite the T-shirts, there was no sign of a slow-down or work stoppage.

A few hours later, however, all the workers began shouting in unison: "Queremos un pacto!" Managers ran out to the shop floor prepared to fire one or more workers, or at least to cut pay should production stop, but it did not. The chanting finally ceased and managers breathed a sigh of relief, believing that they had seen the end of the protest.

Then word arrived from New York. The clothing made at the factory was produced for Phillips-Van Heusen (PVH), and labor activists in New York City were leafleting stores that sold the company's products. Their flyers highlighted the abusive conditions that existed in the Guatemalan factory where the shirts were made and demanded that PVH ensure respect for labor rights, including the right to organize. There was one more detail: all the activists in New York were wearing white T-shirts with the slogan "we want a contract" written in bold letters across the front.

These events were highlights of what became a highly coordinated transnational campaign to improve conditions in a Guatemalan garment factory by ensuring workers' right to organize a union and negotiate a contract. The campaign entailed more than local and international protests; it also exploited PHV's fear of having its reputation tarnished in the eyes of consumers. By August 1997, for one of the very first times in the history of the country's export-oriented manufacturing sector, local managers and a le-

238

gally established union negotiated a collective bargaining agreement that significantly improved workers' conditions.

The story took a turn for the worse in late 1998, when management closed the factory—highlighting the extremely mobile nature of the industry and the difficulties of improving conditions in just one factory in a globalized economy. Yet the Phillips-Van Heusen case highlights many important lessons for future campaigns. It shows how U.S. activists and workers in less developed countries can join forces to improve conditions and empower workers in this age of internationally segmented production. Distinct from labor campaigns in the past that developed around international ties among production workers in a particular industry, the PVH campaign suggests the importance of simultaneously targeting the point of production in one country (Guatemala) and the point of consumption in another (the United States).

Although examples of union actions such as the PVH campaign are becoming more numerous, many unanswered questions about cross-border cooperation among unions remain. How and why did such a coordinated campaign come into being? Why did workers in one country pursue their demands through alliances with sympathetic groups in another country? Does such a transnational strategy supplant local collective endeavors for change, or do the two somehow complement and energize each other? How might workers target local government authorities and institutions as part of their campaigns? And if they have become involved, what roles have the authorities played? Finally, how successful have these cross-border campaigns been? What are some of the unforeseen obstacles that still need to be overcome?

This chapter seeks to provide at least a partial answer to these questions by looking at three case studies, two from Guatemala and one from Haiti. All three involve attempts to improve conditions for workers in export-oriented garment manufacturing plants.[1] I argue that labor in globalized production regimes is beginning to pursue its demands in innovative ways by developing ties to new allies both within and across countries. Concomitantly, I argue that studying labor relations in a globalized economy requires new models. While traditional industrial relations theory sheds light on many components of these cases, social movement theory can complement our understanding of the dynamics of transnational labor contention. This is especially true when labor activism involves countries where industrial relations practices have been less institutionalized.

These three case studies entail diverse attempts by workers in the Caribbean Basin to develop transnational alliances with labor and human rights groups in the United States. The multinational corporations (MNCs) that contract production to the Caribbean Basin are U.S.-based and export the vast majority of clothing produced back to the United States for sale. Alliances with U.S. activists enabled local workers to exploit corporate concerns about the reputations of their brand names among American consumers. These cases suggest, however, that transnational activism can never supplant local organizing but only complement it. Indeed, my argument is that successful campaigns have been those that adequately integrated transnational and local activism.

These three campaigns are just a few of several important efforts to improve conditions in garment factories in Central America and the Caribbean (see Chapter 9). Because more than 95 percent of the garment workforce in the region is unorganized, sustained attempts at cross-border organizing between the United States and the Caribbean Basin will continue to influence the evolution of labor-management relations in the region. The cases highlight different forms of labor activism in maquila factories and offer lessons about the dynamics of successful cross-border activism. At the same time, they suggest the need to evaluate more critically the applicability of traditional industrial relations approaches to the study of transnational labor activism in the garment sector.

The Industrial Relations Framework and Its Limitations

John Dunlop, whose writings in the 1950s had a profound impact on the field of industrial relations, developed a systems approach to the study of labor relations. For Dunlop, industrial relations (IR) occur within a subsystem that exists within each country. "The rules and practices of the work place are developed by the interaction of managers, workers and their organizations, and government agencies in an environment of technology, labor, and product markets, and government regulations" (Dunlop 1958/1993, 8). The study of industrial relations is largely a study of how labor, management, and business interact through established national institutions with commonly agreed upon rules and practices.

Kochan, Katz, and McKersie (1994), while taking issue with some aspects of Dunlop's framework,[2] remain within the institutionalist, systems approach. Like Dunlop, they focus on within-country interactions among labor, management, and government and they develop a three-tier framework for studying labor dynamics. The tiers include long-term strategy and policy-making at the top level, collective bargaining and personnel policy at the second level, and workplace relationships at the bottom level.

In sum, Dunlop and Kochan, Katz, and McKersie limit the study of labor relations (and thus labor conflict) to clearly defined institutionalized rules and practices that exist within each country. The actors in their systems are largely limited to management, workers and labor unions, and government. Their approaches do not envision the possibility that labor may pursue its demands outside highly institutionalized settings, through interactions with other actors (consumers and nongovernmental organizations, for example) and beyond national borders. In their frameworks, factors emerging from the *international* arena, such as competition resulting from economic globalization, are conceived of as external influences to which *national* IR system actors respond. Thus the international arena is not envisioned as a space in which significant actor interaction occurs.

Richard Locke laments that much of prevailing industrial relations theory rests on the assumption that the scope of the market is somehow limited by national borders. "Just as the creation of national markets and the rise of the national union were central to the development of national industrial relations systems theory, now the demise of these conditions creates the need for new explanations" (1992, 230). Further, "markets have become simultaneously globalized and segmented" (1992, 229). Thus Locke—who explores divergent IR patterns within Italy—encourages labor researchers to follow political and market activity and the corresponding IR dynamics that occur both below and above the national level.

Richard Hyman also questions the traditional levels of analysis explicit in most IR frameworks by noting, "Today it is evident that the issues of industrial relations are embedded in national—and more crucially, transnational—structural dynamics" (1995, 42). The failure of many scholars to recognize the larger global dynamics reflects the fact that the IR field has been obsessed with creating a theoretical niche for itself, thus becoming "another means of fragmenting understanding of the totality of social relations within which work and employment are located" (1995, 35).

In sum, Locke directs our attention to the structures created by globalized markets, while Hyman emphasizes the broader social relations in which traditional IR interactions are embedded. Yet to be explained, however, is how these two insights might alter the way we study labor in a globalized economy.

The Contribution of Social Movement Theory

John Kelly (1998) notes that much industrial relations theorizing does not adequately account for the role of power in the dynamics of labor conflict. He suggests that social movement theory might fill the void. Kelly is mostly interested in long-term patterns of labor activism. He develops those aspects of social movement theory that focus on historic trends of periods of worker mobilization, alternating with government and management counter-mobilization, as linked to shifts in the economy.

Social movement theory can assist understanding the dynamics of labor conflict. Unlike Kelly, I am more interested in the short-term dynamics of specific cross-border campaigns. In this vein, I find that social movement theorists such as Sidney Tarrow can more adequately explain why and how Caribbean Basin garment workers pursue their demands. Tarrow defines social movements as "collective challenges by people with common purposes and solidarity in sustained interaction with elites, opponents and authorities" (1994, 3–4). Given the right circumstances and opportunities, structurally weak sectors of society may resort to contentious collective action to pursue their demands. "Contentious collective action is the basis of social movements; not because movements are always violent or extreme, but because it is the main, and often the only recourse that most people possess against better-equipped opponents" (1994, 2).

Once movements are established, Tarrow explains, "they exploit political opportunities, create collective identities, bring people together in organizations and mobilize them against more powerful opponents" (1994, 3). Favorable cultural values, powerful allies, and access to networks through which to pursue demands are circumstances that may provide crucial support for societies' weaker sectors.

How do these insights explain the dynamics of transnational labor unrest in the global garment industry? Social movement theory directs our attention not only to the problems faced by workers but also to the opportunities available for mobilization and pursuit of workers' demands. Labor's opportunities often lie outside the standard national industrial relations framework (such as workplace committees, collective bargaining mechanisms, government agencies), especially in precarious economic sectors intricately tied to the global economy.

Moreover, the cultural contexts of both the country in which problems occur and the country in which campaigns are developed influence the nature of the demands that are pursued and the forms of protest. For example, while in Central America workers may feel that their most urgent need is acquiring greater respect for the right to organize, U.S. solidarity activists may find that their campaigns receive more sympathy from the U.S. public when they focus on the fact that Central Americas garment factories often employ women who are fourteen and fifteen years old. Child labor, and not the right to organize, may become the focus of the campaign because of the limits and opportunities presented by the transnational cultural context.

Movement resources also help to explain movement outcomes. Resources entail not only the material endowments of organization (i.e., staff and budget) but also the existence and strength of local and international allies, as well as the capacity to protest. In sum, opportunities, cultural frames, and resource mobilization all shape workers' ability to improve their conditions.

Labor Power, Social Movement Theory, and Caribbean Basin Garment Workers

Power relations are crucial in determining the outcome of labor conflicts. Early accounts of power in labor relations focused exclusively on structural factors. British economist Alfred Marshall (1920) argued that the power of unions is related to the elasticity of the demand for labor. Workers will have a greater chance of improving their conditions to the extent that demand for labor is inelastic (i.e., significant wage increases will not result in large reductions in employment). Typically, labor demand is more inelastic when unemployment levels are low, skill requirements are high, and the ratio of labor costs to overall costs is small. Conversely, when unemployment levels are high, skill requirements are low, and the production technology is labor-intensive, the demand for labor is highly elastic. These are precisely the labor market conditions associated with the Export Processing Zones (EPZs) throughout the Caribbean Basin. Conditions for labor are worsened by decades of economic stagnation, debt crises, and, in the case of Guatemala, war. Marshall's economic analysis would suggest that, should workers manage to form unions under these circumstances, they would most likely be weak. Consistent with this prediction, the unions that emerged during the 1980s in the Caribbean Basin invariably were weak and often divided.

High unemployment rates in the 1990s further weakened labor's bargaining power. Garment manufacturing has low skill requirements and labor costs represent a high percentage of overall costs since contractors are not responsible for the cost of the material used in the production process. (This is provided by the MNC.) As a result, labor costs are often the contractor's greatest expense, causing even greater pressure to keep wages low. The small-scale and decentralized nature of production further weakens labor's power, as do the low levels of value added by the sector and the high competitiveness generated by the low cost of entry. In sum, using Marshall's criteria, we can conclude that structurally, labor in EPZs is extremely weak vis-a-vis employers.

But Marshall's analysis has limits. His structural account goes a long way toward explaining why the vast majority of workers in EPZs are not organized into unions.[3] But structural accounts do not help us understand how workers may pursue their goals, on occasion successfully, in situations where structurally they are at a tremendous disadvantage. Here social movement theorists remind us that one response of structurally weak actors, given the right opportunities, is to protest, since protest is a form of power. Clearly, workers' collective capacity to disrupt production is a source of power. Yet contentious activity has other consequences. As Sidney Tarrow writes, "Organizers use contention to exploit political opportunities, create collective identities, bring people together in organizations, and mobilize them against more powerful opponents" (Tarrow 1998, 3).

Protest will often *start* at the level of the local factory since workers identify the factory as the most immediate source of their problems. However, because Central American and Caribbean labor laws make legal strikes next to impossible, and because high unemployment levels and low skill requirements ensure an abundance of replacement workers, this traditional form of protest most often leads to limited success at best (at least if not accompanied by other activities). Indeed, although workers may act creatively and heroically while attempting to take advantage of very limited opportunities for protest at the plant level, they frequently experience dramatic failure. In the early 1990s, the vast majority of organizing drives failed outright, and most ended with the workers involved being fired (Arévalo and Arriola 1996). In Honduras, Guatemala, and Nicaragua, massive firings and blacklisting became the standard response to organizing drives. Often plants were closed and moved elsewhere to avoid collective bargaining.

Typically, workers were frightened by these experiences. Many simply resigned themselves to poor working conditions or, if necessary, exercised their "right" to exit.[4] However, some workers did not give up and decided instead to pursue their struggle politically. Given the regional history of economic inequality and political polarization, Latin American unionists almost invariably have been politically active. If opportunities to produce change at the plant level were too limited, many believed that the government would prove to be more effective in helping to improve working conditions.

Labor unions have lobbied politicians, petitioned labor ministries, and proposed, and in some cases achieved, the enactment of new labor laws. The result of these combined efforts has been less than satisfactory. Labor law reform has changed little at the workplace because few resources were appropriated for enforcement. For example, in El Salvador only sixty-four people were employed in the department of workplace inspection in

1995, of whom thirty were inspectors with a weekly salary of $80, making them extremely vulnerable to bribes by factory owners (Arévalo and Arriola 1996).

Even well intentioned inspectors often find themselves unable to enforce the law. In one instance in Honduras, unionists angered over the illegal firing of their members took their case to the Ministry of Labor. The Ministry sent an inspector to the factory with a copy of the labor code. When she informed the factory owner that firing workers for forming a union was a violation of Honduran law, the Korean owner took the labor code from her, ripped it in two, and threw it down at the inspector's feet, telling her never to return to his factory. To date, neither she nor anyone else from the Ministry of Labor has been back to the plant.[5]

Theorizing Transnational Contention

Jackie Smith (1997) suggests that transnational activism is more likely when local activists, unable to find points of access or vulnerabilities in the national political system, find favorable opportunities on an international level. Garment workers in EPZs clearly have been unable to find or exploit local and national opportunities. Their ability to improve working conditions therefore has become dependent in many ways upon exploiting international opportunities.

In the Caribbean Basin, EPZ workers came to realize that something was fundamentally different about the structure of production in these factories compared to traditional ones. For example, in EPZs the name of the factory was not the same as the name on the clothing labels. Factories were more often foreign-owned and moved with greater frequency. These observations gave workers a sense that they were part of a production network, or what Gereffi, Korzeniewicz, and Korzeniewicz (1994) refer to as a global commodity chain.

Workers would also discover that this global production chain had one link that was particularly vulnerable: the importance of brand identity and the good image of the retailer's label. This vulnerability becomes particularly acute when the low wages of those who produce the garments are compared to the high profit margins of the retailers, about whom Andrew Ross wrote:

> The high-reward strategy, spurred by 400 and 500 percent retail markups, also carries some risks. . . . None are greater than the potentially embarrassing exposure of human rights violations in the factories of companies

that cannot afford to have the names of their designers, endorsers, or merchandising labels publicly sullied. . . . [Clothing retailers'] chief point of vulnerability is their good name, susceptible to bad publicity and to consumer boycotts. (1997, 25)

Corporate executives have publicly acknowledged such vulnerability. In the words of Peter Jacobi, president of global sourcing for Levi Strauss, "The corporate reputations behind the brands have become increasingly important to people when they decide what products to buy. . . . If your company owns a popular brand, protect this asset at all costs" (cited in Nichols 1993, 15–16).

Thus what Smith posits as a precondition for transnational activism—international opportunities—did exist in the form of MNCs' brand name vulnerability. The fact that the MNCs that produced garments in the Caribbean Basin sold their products in the United Statets and were based in the United States is significant. Thomas Risse-Kappen (1995) argues that the cultural context is an important influence on the effectiveness of transnational campaigns. Concern in the United States about sweatshop conditions grew when a New York-based labor rights group, the National Labor Committee (NLC), exposed the fact that television personality Kathie Lee Gifford had her name on a line of clothing produced in Honduran sweatshops by child labor. At first Gifford denied the charges. As the media barrage against her intensified, however, she decided to publicly join forces with then-U.S. Secretary of Labor Robert Reich in his crusade against sweatshops. This brought attention in the United States to the sweatshop issue and created possibilities that future campaigns could exploit.

The Presence of Allies

Social movement theory suggests that structurally and institutionally weak social actors can pursue their campaigns more effectively if they develop strong ties with more powerful allies. The first and most logical place to look for allies is locally. Indeed, in many cases unionists did develop contacts with local religious, women's, and human right organizations. These groups became involved in the sweatshop issue because of the nature of the problem. Women's groups were motivated by the fact that the vast majority of workers in these factories were female. Religious and human rights groups noticed how the nature of the violations taking place—lack of adequate drinking water, denial of permission to use the bathrooms, and physically inhumane conditions—went beyond standard labor rights violations to entail fundamental human rights violations.

In El Salvador, unions and local nongovernmental organizations (NGOs) formed a coordinating body to address the sweatshop issue. While these alliances were extremely important, these groups found that the international structure of the garment industry was such that, even with relatively strong local coalitions, resolving the sweatshop problem would require international alliances, most importantly with groups in consumer countries.

The most obvious potential allies for Caribbean Basin unionists are U.S. unionists. The AFL-CIO leadership acknowledged as much when then-President Lane Kirkland noted, "You can't be a trade unionist unless you are an internationalist."[6] In this vein the U.S. clothing and textile workers' union, the Union of Needletrades, Industrial and Textile Employees (UNITE), has supported the efforts of garment workers overseas. In a speech to Central American and Caribbean unionists, Alan Howard, assistant to the president of UNITE, stated the union's position: " It is very difficult for us to organize in the U.S. apparel industry if you are unable to organize your workers. We need a new strategy on a global scale. Each day we in UNITE see how our destiny is linked to your destiny. Transnational corporations cannot be organized only within one nation."[7]

Of course, union-to-union relationships between workers in very poor countries and workers in highly developed countries are not without their problems. Fear that U.S. unionists may still be motivated by protectionist tendencies has led some Caribbean Basin workers to pursue the relationship with caution. Nonetheless, what Howard's statement suggests is that even if we assume that self-interest is the prime motivating factor for U.S. unions to pursue these ties, that does not preclude the ability to establish effective cross-border campaigns. Intertwining self-interests can lead to very strong and sustainable relationships. Indeed, despite occasional problems and misunderstandings, UNITE has worked effectively with unions in the Dominican Republic, Honduras, and Guatemala, and has actively supported campaigns in El Salvador, Nicaragua, and Haiti for the better part of the 1990s.

But union-to-union relationships are not the only component of international campaigns. Because the United States is the point of consumption and not only the point of production, cross-border alliances involving Caribbean Basin labor activists have not relied exclusively on U.S. unions. International NGOs are often more clearly motivated than unions are by a commitment to certain values and norms, assuaging fears that they might be driven by a protectionist agenda.

Perhaps the most active U.S. organization involved in transnational labor activism with Central American and Caribbean garment workers is the NLC, an NGO with a five-person staff and an annual operating budget of $250,000. In the early 1990s the NLC grew increasingly concerned with reports of labor rights abuses in Central America's mushrooming EPZs. The NLC quickly learned that to pursue its concerns in the United States, it had to frame the issues so as to resonate with the U.S. public. In the words of NLC executive director Charles Kernaghan, "You can have the greatest issue in the world, but if you don't know how to move it, that issue doesn't exist. . . . We do thorough research. But then we translate it into a human story. We use anecdotal examples and language that's accessible to people."[8]

Kernaghan found that speaking tours of young female garment workers were a powerful mechanism for building support for NLC campaigns. He explains: "We wanted the most authentic, direct, virtually naive workers we could find. We had faith that these kids would simply tell the truth, and that would be more damaging than anything an academic could say."[9]

The damage, of course, was directed at carefully selected U.S. clothing retailers who had production contracts with the targeted factories. The NLC's campaigns combined these speaking tours, letter writing, protest activities and a very effective use of the media.

Another important transnational actor in the anti-sweatshop movement is the Guatemalan Labor Education Project (GLEP), a Chicago-based NGO. The organization was founded in 1987 by a handful of activists in the Chicago area who had participated in an international solidarity campaign with Guatemalan Coca-Cola workers in the mid-1980s. In the 1990s, GLEP activities in the United States involved publicizing violations of labor rights in Guatemala and mobilizing grassroots activism to pressure multinationals doing business in the country to respect labor rights. GLEP was actively involved in the successful campaign against Phillips-Van Heusen.

The Dynamics of Anti-Sweatshop Activism: Three Case Studies

International opportunities, issue framing, and strategic alliances all played a role in the three cases explored below. These cases suggest that campaigns with a weak or nonexistent international component will fail or meet with limited success. However, these cases also suggest that international support can never replace sustained organizing efforts by local actors at the point of production. It is the combination of these two components that best account for successful efforts to improve workers' rights in EPZs in the Caribbean Basin.

Daimi Atlántica in Guatemala

Daimi Atlántica, a Korean-owned factory, first began operations in Guatemala in 1992.[10] Attempts to organize a union resulted in the firings of all the activists involved. In the spring of 1997, the Confederation of Guatemalan Trade Union Unity decided upon a more systematic approach. A team was formed to make initial contacts with workers who were interested in joining a union. Potential members were contacted clandestinely. They began participating in small-group training seminars offered by the union. The small groups made education easier and gave a sense of common commitment that facilitated collective action.

When the union began to organize more openly, the company responded almost immediately by firing some of the most supportive members. The unionists continued their efforts to consolidate the organization, and more workers were fired. The Guatemalan unionists knew that they were producing for a U.S. clothing manufacturer named Rifle, and they asked UNITE to pressure the company. According to UNITE, it was able to effectively pressure Rifle in the United States, and Rifle responded by strongly pressuring the owner of Daimi Atlántica to respect the union. But the local factory owner in Guatemala was indifferent to Rifle's pressure and fired more workers.

One of the Guatemalan organizers, Veronica Rosales, complained about what she perceived to be an inability of the international campaign to produce the needed results. Rosales was in charge of dealing with all the fired workers, who frequently requested information about the international campaign. They wanted to know when their international allies would force the company to rehire them. The workers needed their jobs to support their families. The lack of unemployment insurance or other social benefits in Guatemala make the situation of fired workers particularly acute. Rosales, of working-class origins herself, empathized with the hardship of the workers. But the international campaign could do very little if the local company was indifferent to pressure, and the workers never got their jobs back. Still bitter about the failure of the campaign, Rosales said, "We are not working with things, tables or chairs. We are working with people. This hurts me."[11]

This case highlights that even the best local organizing endeavors in the maquila will have a difficult time succeeding if the international campaigns are unable to produce the desired results. Not all local producers respond the same way to international pressure. The international component of a campaign can fail for a variety of reasons, many of which are outside the control of the international allies. International campaigns also entail a lot of work and resources. They require prolonged, systematic, and concentrated efforts. International allies will not always be able to meet the needs of all the local organizing campaigns that may be occurring at any given time. Literally thousands of small garment factories exist in the region, but international labor organizations are often able to target only a few MNCs at a time.

Walt Disney in Haiti

Soon after its success in publicizing the child labor and sweatshop abuses involving Kathie Lee Gifford in the summer of 1996 the NLC decided to confront another industry giant, the Walt Disney Company. Haitian garment workers were producing Mickey Mouse T-shirts and Pocahontas pajamas for 28 cents an hour. In an open letter to Disney CEO Michael Eisner, the NLC documented the horrendous conditions of the workers who produced Disney garments. It demanded improved working conditions in the factory and a "living wage" which, the NLC argued, would mean raising salaries to 58 cents an hour. Haitian labor activists were interested in international campaigns. Yannick Etienne of the Batay Ouvriye Workers' Center said, "We know the Haitian private sector is well connected with American companies and the American government. So we have to put pressure on them as well as the Haitian factory owners. That is why international solidarity work is important to our work in Haiti."[12]

The campaign included letter writing, leafleting of stores, and use of the media, and it generated an awareness in the United States of the plight of Haitian workers. According to the National Labor Committee, "as a result of the pressure from the campaign, most companies in Haiti pay at least the minimum wage." And companies in Haiti appear somewhat more cautious about blatantly destroying newly formed unions.[13] Yet the campaign did not succeed in raising wages to 58 cents an hour or establishing a union and collective contract in factories producing for Disney. Indeed, one major local producer of Disney clothing, H.H. Cutler, which had subcontracts with ten assembly plants employing twenty-three hundred workers, closed its operations in Haiti.

Why did the campaign fail? The NLC put as much energy into the Haiti campaign as into all its other campaigns and it used all the same tactics. The reason, it appears, lies in the fact that there were no relatively solid Haitian labor unions able to systematically organize the EPZ. For Yannick Etienne, "[Haitian union] organizations are too bureaucratic and opportunistic, and they have sold out to the factory owners. Some of them even support structural adjustment programs and different anti-worker government policies."[14]

Batay Ouvriye, which was formed in the early 1990s, is a self-defined workers' center that has attempted to fill the void left by traditional unions. But it is fighting an uphill battle, especially in the export processing zones. In many ways, after the brutal coup in 1991, and given massive poverty and a horrific economic situation, Haitian labor is only beginning the long and arduous process of rebuilding representative organizations. In the meantime, without an established labor movement, it is very difficult to pursue local protest activities in coordination with an international campaign. In such a situation, the tendency can easily become for the international component of the campaign to proceed more rapidly than local activists can assimilate.

In the near future, U.S. unions appear inclined to focus their efforts on countries with relatively stronger local unions, such as the Dominican Republic. International NGOs and solidarity groups, however, continue to press to improve working conditions in Haiti. For the last several years a coalition of U.S. religious groups representing Disney stockholders has presented the company with stockholder proposals calling for improved wages and respect for labor rights. At the same time, local groups like Batay Ouvriye are continuing the difficult task of rebuilding the Haitian labor movement.

Phillips-Van Heusen in Guatemala[15]

Workers at the Camisas Modernas garment factory in Guatemala organized their union largely on their own in the late 1980s. However, the union could not muster the strength to force the company to negotiate a collective contract. According to Guatemalan law, 25 percent of the workforce must belong to the union in order to oblige the company to negotiate. Union representatives said they had enough members; the company said they did not. The matter went to the Ministry of Labor which, according to NGO activists involved in the case, "abdicat[ed] its responsibility and invit[ed] the union . . . to take [its] concern to the labor courts" (DeSimone 1998, 146). With well over a thousand cases backlogged in Guatemalan labor courts at any given time, waiting for a judicial verdict might easily take two or more years.

The factory was owned by Phillips-Van Heusen (PVH), the U.S. shirt maker that sold many of its products at J.C. Penney retail stores. U.S. solidarity activists in GLEP learned of the situation and thought it presented all the components of a good international campaign. There was a functioning local union to work with, PVH provided a good target, and the Guatemalan unionists were receptive to the idea of working with GLEP.

After gathering information from the union, GLEP began leafleting PVH outlets and J.C. Penney stores in the United States and began a letter-writing campaign directed at PVH management. One campaign highlight was the day that U.S. activists and Guatemalan unionists, wearing similar T-shirts, participated in the simultaneous protest activity described at the beginning of this chapter.

The stalemate between workers and management continued until U.S. activists discovered that the CEO of PVH, Bruce J. Klatsky, was also a member of the board of a well recognized U.S.-based human rights group, Human Rights Watch (HRW).[16] GLEP decided to put PVH in a bind by asking management to accept an HRW fact-finding trip to Guatemala. HRW would be asked to investigate whether the union had the needed 25 percent support of the workforce. Klatsky was caught. How could he reject the findings of a group of which he was a board member? He thus found himself having to accept the fact-finding trip and, a priori, the HRW findings.

HRW investigators traveled to Guatemala in January 1997 and concluded that the union did meet the representation requirements under Guatemalan law. Two months later, PVH agreed to recognize the union and negotiate a collective contract. Through bargaining the workers achieved an 11 percent wage increase the first year and a commitment to a 12.5 percent increase the second year. They also won job stability, subsidized transportation to work, and mechanisms that would facilitate union communication with the workforce. The combination of effective transnational activism and sustained local organizing made success possible, at least in the short term.

A year and a half after negotiation of the contract, on December 11, 1998, PVH closed the Camisas Modernas plant. PVH justified the plant closure as an appropriate response to the loss of a major client. An equally plausible explanation is a desire to destroy the only active union in Guatemala's garment export sector. Assuming the latter, we must be careful not to draw the wrong conclusions by suggesting that the campaign was somehow fundamentally flawed. What the closing of the PVH factory does highlight is the extreme difficulty of sustaining improvements in one garment factory while all others in the region are not unionized.

Conclusion

The three case studies suggest the importance of two factors in accounting for successful campaigns to improve conditions in Caribbean Basin maquilas: local organizing and transnational activism. The PVH case in Guatemala best combined these components and, at least in the short term, was the most successful. The Walt Disney case in Haiti and the Daimi Atlántica case in Guatemala essentially failed because one of the components was either very weak or nonexistent.

To understand the dynamics of these campaigns, we have drawn upon social movement theory. The traditional industrial relations framework for studying labor relations may be good at explaining the dynamics of labor activism in highly institutionalized and relatively stable settings, but it is less effective in explaining how structurally weak garment workers in countries with underdeveloped systems of industrial relations might pursue their demands in a globalized economy. Social movement theory has helped us explain how garment workers were able to pursue their demands by participating in contentious activity, developing ties with more powerful allies, framing their concerns to address societal norms and values, and exploiting key vulnerabilities of their opponents.

The cases were not chosen to empirically test any hypotheses in a rigorous way. (Hypothesis testing would require a far greater number of case studies that could be analyzed systematically over time.) Rather, the cases were selected to illustrate and bolster my thesis, and to suggest ways that labor responses to globalization could be studied more effectively. It is my hope that these cases offer lessons for labor activists who are exploring ways to respond to the challenges presented by globalization.

This chapter focuses on the short-term dynamics of these campaigns, and consequently leaves many issues unexplored. For example, cross-border alliances between organizations with such vastly differing resources can create long-term difficulties. Often the organization with greater resources is able to exert greater control over the strategy of the campaign. This can create tensions and inhibit local activism, when objectively it appears to be in everyone's interest to work together. How this tension might be resolved is an issue worth exploring.

Second, although NGOs can provide crucial support to labor-oriented campaigns, the NGO-union alliance may experience tension as well. On the one hand, NGOs such as religious and human rights groups add greater legitimacy to the demands made by labor activists. Further, small NGOs often are able to respond much more quickly than large labor unions to requests for assistance coming from garment workers. On the other hand, unions may feel that NGOs are less understanding of what it takes to organize workers to achieve sustainable change. A good media blitz can occur in a matter of days, but solid local organizing can take months to build. Thus the potential for the international campaign, especially the media component, to proceed much more quickly than the organizing may result in disjuncture between the two components. It would appear useful for strategists to contemplate how these differences might be resolved to ensure that the goodwill, legitimacy, and resources of NGOs can be appropriately incorporated into these campaigns.

Finally, while at least short-term success seems to entail a combination of international campaigning and local organization, the subsequent closing of the PVH factory in Guatemala raises the question of the sustainability of dramatic changes in one factory. The anti-sweatshop movement, for long-term success, needs an industry-wide strategy. One proposal was to establish an industry-wide code of conduct and allow for independent monitoring of the factories to ensure compliance. This proposal is still under debate. MNCs favor a system in which they can use international auditing firms to monitor factory conditions, whereas unions, NGOs and an increasingly active student movement prefer corporate compliance with a strict code verified by local non-governmental organizations. The most important goal is to ensure that all garment manufacturers are forced to operate by the same set of labor rights standards to prevent a race-to-the-bottom dynamic.

The changing nature of production, specifically its segmentation and dispersion on an international scale, makes the need for transnational labor solidarity all the more urgent. UNITE and other organizations are exploring the possibility of improving and expanding their work abroad. This activity is not limited to the Caribbean Basin and the garment sector. The United Electrical Workers (UE) have been involved in cross-border activism in Mexico for quite some time. The United Auto Workers, prompted by NAFTA and the dramatic growth of jobs in Mexican auto parts plants, are beginning to explore ways to develop better ties with unions in the region. And the AFL-CIO is dramatically altering and restructuring its work abroad. The AFL-CIO's international work in the region is now organized by the American Center for International Labor Solidarity, which is supporting organizing projects to a much greater degree than its predecessor, the American Institute for Free Labor Development.

International labor solidarity in the Americas is still in its infancy. The three case studies explored in this chapter do not tell an overwhelmingly positive tale. Two campaigns failed outright, and the third achieved only limited success. But workers and campaign activists did achieve something. Even the "failed" campaigns left their legacies on the maquila managers, who now think twice before blatantly violating labor rights. But perhaps more importantly, these campaigns provide crucial lessons for future cross-border activism. These cases suggest that even in some of the world's poorest countries, and within one of the more precarious sectors in those countries, workers can organize and achieve important improvements in their living and working conditions. Certainly that is no small accomplishment.

13

Making Transnational Collaboration Work

MICHAEL E. GORDON AND LOWELL TURNER

The need for transnational collaboration among unions across the world is great and growing in the global economy. Case studies presented in this book demonstrate the active fermentation in cross-border relations and a variety of different approaches, goals, and targets. Yet the barriers to successful collaboration among unions in different countries remain immense: from differences in union structure, ideology, and culture to conflicting interests and differing levels of economic development. What unions have accomplished by operating internationally is important, indeed much more substantial today than ever before. Yet these efforts remain a drop in the bucket compared to the need for coordinated action created by the relentlessly globalizing economy. Unions need closer relations among networks of activists in different countries, between comparable national and local unions, and within multinational corporations. They also need closer relations among key union leaders who, when necessary, can shift resources into transnational cooperation so as to coordinate actions that may lead, ultimately, to cross-border collective bargaining. Finally, unions need a stronger, more coherent and cohesive voice in regulating the global economy, especially in strengthening its much needed "social dimension." Labor's voice should be included among those of decision-makers at the World Trade Organization (WTO), International Monetary Fund, and World Bank, and unions should be guaranteed a role in tripartite trade decisions at the national level.

Taken together, the papers presented in this volume suggest a number of basic principles about the potential success of international cooperation among unions. Defining such principles is a first step toward empirical tests of the efficacy of different collaborative approaches designed to promote the causes of worker and human rights. The experiences examined here suggest the following conclusions for mounting and sustaining successful transnational collaboration. We present them in order of their level of abstraction rather than of their importance: we begin by discussing the necessary atmospheric qualities for successful collaboration and proceed to more specific tactical details.

(1) Resource dependency theory (Pfeffer and Salancik 1978) suggests that, in general, organizations tend to avoid forming controlling relationships that increase their reliance on other entities, even if this means relinquishing only some decision-making autonomy as opposed to more tangible assets. Historically, the threat of loss of autonomy has been one factor cited as a hindrance to greater cooperation among unions (e.g., Ulman 1975). Martin and Ross demonstrate that this concern persists, in their discussion of the obstacles created by national trade unions in Europe to the formation of a transnational industrial relations policy (Chapter 7). Wilson's discussion of the tortuous creation of an international union association and coherent union strategy in the media sector sheds more light on the entropic effects of differing political and professional ideologies (Chapter 8).

Hence *the perception of interdependence* is an essential precondition for interorganizational cooperation in general and for transnational union collaboration in particular. Such a perception, it seems, must be based upon a commitment to a shared goal the attainment of which is contingent upon the cooperation of individual organizations. In this sense, it appears that international labor associations (e.g., the ITSs and the ICFTU) must attempt to identify superordinate goals that will heighten awareness of trade union interdependence throughout the world. This leads us to our second point.

(2) Despite the advisability of identifying one or more superordinate goals as a means to create labor internationalism, it is clear that *traditional ideologies have not played a substantial role* in promoting and maintaining such cooperation. Rather, cooperation has been geared to win very specific, tangible objectives that expand the rights of workers. If anything, the lesson of current international labor activism is that commitment to narrow, traditional ideologies and national interests must be replaced with an expanded open-mindedness to the testing of new tools, including the formation of alliances with groups that have only marginal interests in labor. As unions acquire greater experience from these new structural arrangements, new ideas may emerge that can provide the push of a superordinate goal, including the notion of a "global solidarity movement" (Waterman 1998, 349) whose strength is derived from allies with strong grassroots interests in ecology, children's and women's issues, and the democratization of global capital.

(3) The collection, analysis, and exchange of information across na-

tional frontiers are not superficial or secondary activities. Regardless of the nature of workers' objectives (for example, organizing a plant or negotiating a labor contract), and despite the impediments introduced by management, *knowledge is a key tool* and systematic intelligence is arguably essential for progress. Indeed, Lee (1996) considers the Internet—replete with e-mail, databases, discussion groups, online chat, and electronic publishing—the communication tool that will serve as the foundation for the revival of labor internationalism. This idea is consistent with McLuhan and Powers' (1989) thesis about a "global village" created by electronic media, which decreases the significance of physical presence in people's experience and thereby has the capacity to unify the human race.

Besides reliance on the Internet, information gathering should include existing business and investor databases. These data must be supplemented, however, with sources of information developed and disseminated by workers with first-hand knowledge of management and MNCs, gathered locally and then collated and analyzed at a central clearinghouse. In this vein, Lee (1996) recommends creation of an international online labor press, an online labor archive, and an early-warning network on union rights. Waterman (1998) points out that these proposals, although novel in the realm of organized labor, are consistent with actions already taken by social movements in other realms, including environmentalism, feminism, and human rights.

(4) Although the world has changed, nothing that we have learned about transnational union collaboration has altered the vital *necessity for workers to be willing and able to mobilize and take risks* to defend and improve their own working conditions. The severest conflict in unions' international activities still takes place at work sites where workers risk their jobs and well-being in order to establish or maintain collective bargaining rights. Many of the cases in this book discuss local unions and their leaders who endured a great deal of hardship (from strikes to beatings and firings) to persevere in what often turned out to be lengthy struggles. The strength of the "troops on the ground" often determines the willingness of other organizations to support their cause. For example, given its limited resources and the number of requests for assistance it receives, the ICFTU assesses the strength of local support before deciding to support an international campaign (Chapter 5). Although the vigor of local union efforts is an essential ingredient in successful organizing campaigns, Anner (Chapter 12) concludes that it is not sufficient in and of itself to win official union recognition, at least in Central American maquilas. Rather, concerted on-site job actions must be supplemented by effective and imaginative international support that pressures MNCs at their headquarters and in their markets.

(5) In order to improve the relationship between companies and their employees, *union collaboration must first alter existing relationships between employers and various external stakeholder groups.* This aspect of transnational collaboration may be understood best in terms of Evan's (1966) concept of the "organization-set," a somewhat stable network of organizations with which a "focal organization" (178) regularly interacts in order to secure inputs or dispose of outputs. In this case the focal organization is the employer. Interactions between the focal organization and each member of its organization-set typically occur for one of the following reasons: exchange (the buying or selling of goods or services); information (the sharing of data of interest to one or both organizations); or normative (the attempted imposition of the values and goals of a member of the organization-set on the focal organization). Transnational union actions invariably are focused on altering these interactions. For example, labor laws define the normative interactions between a government and the corporations operating within its jurisdiction. Transnational union cooperation often entails pressure on governments to strengthen their normative interactions with employers who are ignoring local labor regulations. This scenario was reported by Jessup and Gordon (Chapter 9) and Cohen and Early (Chapter 10) in the Dominican Republic and Mexico, respectively. Transnational pressure also often tries to change the nature of the interactions between a focal organization and its customers. Jessup and Gordon and Anner describe how groups raised the consciousness of customers about the conditions endured by the workers who produced the goods they were about to purchase. At an as yet undefined point, stimulation of the customer's social conscience transforms her/him into a "political consumer—a demanding, ethical, socially-conscious being" (Waterman 1998, 368) who is willing to superimpose normative standards on existing economic exchange relationships.

Reporting on a forum on trade policy held at the American Enterprise Institute, Jessup (personal communication, November 24, 1998) noted that "the discussion . . . was remarkable for the near unanimous and grudging resignation among free trade policy wonks that labor and environmental issues must now be accommodated on the trade agenda." Adoption of the labor-supported notion of a social clause (Chapter 3) was not favored (suspicion still abounds about protectionist motives of Western unions). However, free traders of the stature of Jagdesh Bhagwati, professor of economics and political science at Columbia University, now recognize that the concerns of advocates for a civil society that places greater emphasis on human and environmental values can no longer be ignored.[1] It is therefore incumbent upon supporters of free trade to recommend other mechanisms to deal with working conditions. At this juncture it is not clear what sort of leverage the new proposals will provide for transnational union collaboration in the future. Nonetheless, these conversations among free traders acknowledge the pervasiveness and significance of customer willingness to impose normative standards on the providers of the goods they buy, and this has obvious implications for international unionism.

(6) Internationalization adds a new level of complexity to labor conflicts, and thus requires *a new level of sophistication in union strategy*. For example, cross-border campaigns must walk a fine line when pressuring companies to accept unions, so that employers do not simply close the plants. Securing the cooperation of customers, therefore, does not necessarily mean asking them to cancel contracts with the offending employer. Such cancellations can lead and have led to layoffs and even plant closures. Rather, campaigns strive to exert just enough pressure to improve working conditions without crossing a line that leads to major job loss. It is difficult to know the exact location of this line. Bibong Apparel, as we have seen, was pressured from a number of quarters before capitulating and signing a contract (Chapter 9). Disney, on the other hand, bolted from Haiti at the first real signs of organized activity (Chapter 12). Greater experience with cross-border campaigns may enable organizers to forecast employers' responses more accurately so that jobs are not lost.

(7) In labor conflicts with an international dimension, often involving anti-labor MNC activity in a particular country, *unions in the nation where the offending multinational is headquartered can play a particularly important role*, especially if the firm is significantly unionized at home. Such unions often have leverage with high-level management that can be used to defend worker organizing within overseas subsidiaries operating "union-free" and determined to stay that way. The IG Metall in Germany is one example of a union that has been able to offer support for foreign unions from its strong position of influence inside German MNCs.

(8) Unions' cross-border campaigns have often been successful when they *put a human face on the conflict*. Unions can gain cross-national labor, public, and even shareholder support when they personalize the fight with the anguished expressions of workers who have suffered the loss of their jobs or even physical abuse as a result of their organizing. Other social movements have learned to use this tactic successfully—environmentalists, for example, who involve indigenous groups in public campaigns, from presentations to corporate boards of directors to the building of broad support.[2]

Conclusion

Of the current union strategies for revitalization (including organizing, political action, partnership, mergers, and internal restructuring), international collaboration, although growing, remains the smallest. The current underdeveloped state of transnational cooperation does not make it any less important, however, for the future of modern trade unions—quite the contrary. Government, business, and labor leaders alike appear to be converging on the conclusion that, for better or worse, debates and conflicts on the social dimension of the global economy are growing and will not go away.

The events in Seattle in 1999, and Washington, D.C., in 2000, at meetings of the World Trade Organization (WTO) indicated considerable movement toward increasing normative pressures on employers by linking labor and environmental issues with international trading rights. Dozens of labor, environmental, consumer, human rights, and religious groups demonstrated to open up WTO decision-making, for transparency and to bring in the voice of concerned citizens and interest groups, and to include labor, social, and environmental standards (from collective bargaining rights to protection of rain forests) in global trade agreements. The AFL-CIO played a major role in this broad coalition of protest, contributing to the building of an alternative perspective to footloose globalization, unregulated and massive capital flows (with potentially devastating consequences as evidenced in the Asian economic collapse of 1997–98), and the growing and unchecked economic and political power of MNCs. Although the demonstrations failed to influence the meetings, and although press coverage of the meetings appeared to focus on the militancy of protestors, a few officials, including President Clinton, publicly acknowledged the legitimacy of the demonstrators' claims. These demonstrations are quite possibly a sign of things to come: on the negative side a "mobilization against globalization," on the positive side an opening for activist networking and the spread of international collaboration among unions and others concerned about worker and human rights in the brave new world economy.

Escalating union internationalism is, we believe, essential. If the obstacles are imposing, the possibilities for a prosperous global economy based on strong worker rights, enforceable labor, social, and environmental standards, and diminishing inequality are there to be fought for and claimed.

Notes

Chapter One

1. Helene Cooper and Thomas Kamm. "Much of Europe Eases Its Rigid Labor Laws, and Temps Proliferate," *Wall Street Journal*, June 4, 1998, A1, A6.

2. See Kochan, Katz and McKersie (1994) for a discussion of the situation in the United States.

3. See Beedham (1999) and Woodiwiss (1996) for discussions of differing points of view about the meaning of globalization in economic and geopolitical terms.

4. Percy Barnevik, President and CEO of ABB (Asea Brown Boveri), contended that MNCs do not undermine the sovereignty of nations. Rather, the actions of MNCs simply "speed up" economic adjustment processes among nations that would normally be governed by market forces. As a "lubricant for economic integration," MNCs "make visible the invisible hand of global competition" (Taylor 1991, 105).

5. The concept of a "race to the bottom" was embodied in the writings of early nineteenth century humanitarians such as Robert Owen, who believed that international cooperation among all governments (as opposed to a class struggle uniting workers of the world) was a prerequisite for permanently improving working conditions. "Under conditions of international trade, work standards in all countries tend toward the lowest level existing in any one country" (Peterson 1963, 224, 225).

6. In some cases, public sector workers may have fewer rights to join unions and take collective action. The rights of public sector workers in Africa are severely circumscribed; see Chapter 5.

7. Peter F. Drucker, "The Rise of Production Sharing," *Wall Street Journal*, March 15, 1977.

8. For example, by threatening to close its Louisville, Kentucky, plant and shift the work to Mexico, General Electric won substantial concessions on staffing from its union.

9. Similar concerns in 1925 about foreign intrusion into the hemisphere, along with fears of spreading communism, motivated the AFL's Committee of Resolutions to prepare a labor corollary to the Monroe Doctrine: "Neither the Red Internationale of autocratic Moscow nor any other internationale may in complacency ignore this definition of American labor policy. It will contest to the last every inch of ground whenever and wherever autocracy seeks to invade the hallowed soil of this hemisphere. And we shall accept no pretense of 'world labor unity' as a mask for invading disrupters and destroyers" (Andrews 1991, 4).

263

Chapter Two

An earlier version of this paper was presented at the University of Warwick, May 17–18, 1996. I am grateful to the participants in that session for raising a number of important points. I would also like to thank amongst others Jennifer Bair, Gary Gereffi, Bruce Herman, Paul Marginson, and Chris Smith, all of whose discussions with me around the themes raised here have been a great help. Last, but certainly not least, the editors of this volume have made heroic efforts to render the text intelligible. It remains to add, of course, that try as I might I can find no way to blame any of these contributors for faults that remain entirely of my own making.

1. See Ramsay (1997; forthcoming) for further discussions of these issues.

2. Many summaries of these theories can be found. I have drawn particularly on Hax and Majluf (1996); De Wit and Meyer (1998); and Johnson and Scholes (1993).

3. A more complex analysis would introduce greater variation, and would need to include factors other than labor.

4. In order to deal with criticism that the two dichotomous dimensions of the BCG matrix ignored strategy implications for the average business, subsequent portfolio matrices have at least three categories on each dimension, as in Figure 2.2.

5. In some instances, decreased control from the top of the organization may be accompanied by more severe pressure exerted through narrow accounting-driven targets on local management, forcing these in turn to be visited on employees at the subsidiary.

6. See Ramsay and Haworth (1990) for a more detailed description.

Chapter Three

The opinions expressed by the author do not necessarily reflect the views of the International Labor Organization.

1. For Iraq, s. 27(8) of that country's Trade Union Act of 1987; see in particular International Labour Conference, Eighty-First Session (Geneva, 1994): *Freedom of Association and Collective Bargaining* (ILO: Geneva, 1994), para. 197 and footnote 18. For Zambia, see Panford (1994).

2. For Cameroon, s. 19 of Decree No. 69/DF/7 of 1969 with regard to trade unions or professional associations of civil servants; see International Labour Conference, Eighty-Third Session (Geneva, 1996): Report III (Part 4A), *Report of the Committee of Experts on the Application of Conventions and Recommendations* (ILO: Geneva, 1996), 145. For Kenya, see Panford (1994).

3. International Labour Conference: *Freedom of Association*, para. 197.

4. ILO: *Freedom of Association. Digest of Decisions and Principles of the Freedom of Association Committee of the Governing Body of the ILO* (Geneva, 1996), paras. 622–48.

5. S. 270 of the Labour Code; see International Labour Conference: *Freedom of Association*, para. 197 and footnote 20; see also ILO: *Freedom of Association. Digest of*, paras. 632–633.

6. ILO: *Freedom of Association. Digest of*; and International Labour Conference: *Freedom of Association*, para. 197 and footnote 22.

7. International Labour Conference: *Freedom of Association*, para. 60 and footnote 29; *ibid.*, Eighty-Second Session (Geneva, 1995): Report III (Part 4A), *Report of the Committee of Experts on the Application of Conventions and Recommendations* (ILO: Geneva, 1995), 153, 184–185.

8. See, for example, Freedom of Association Committee: 241st Report, Case No. 1323 (The Philippines); and 249th Report, Case No. 1726 (Pakistan).

9. By December 31, 1995, ILO Conventions Nos. 87 and 98 had been ratified by 114 and

125 states, respectively; see International Labour Conference, Eighty-Third Session (Geneva, 1996): Report III (Part V): *List of Ratifications by Convention and by Country* (ILO: Geneva, 1996).

10. See, for example, the report prepared by the International Confederation of Free Trade Unions (ICFTU) for its Sixteenth World Congress (June 25–29, 1996): *The Global Market—Trade Unionism's Greatest Challenge* (ICFTU: Brussels, 1996).

11. See Ben-Israel (1988), Betten (1993), ICFTU (1996a), Servais (1984).

12. International Labour Conference: *Freedom of Association*, paras. 244–47.

13. Section 13(3) of the Industrial Relations Act of 1967, as amended.

14. Section 17 of the Industrial Relations Act of 1968, as amended.

15. For recent discussion of this controversial issue see Bamber and Lansbury (1993), Frenkel and Harrod (1995), and Locke, Kochan, and Piore (1995).

16. See, for example, Young Ki Choi, "Recent trends and a prospect for joint consultation in Korea," in *The Development of Sound Labour Relations*, Report of the ILO/Japan East Asian Subregional Tripartite Seminar, Hong Kong, March 25–26, 1991 (ILO: Bangkok, 1991), 57.

17. *European Works Councils Bulletin*, Issue 3, May–June 1996, 5–7, 16–17.

18. Workers' Representatives Convention (No. 135) and Recommendation (No. 143), 1971.

19. Rural Workers' Organisations Convention (No. 141) and Recommendation (No. 149), 1975; see also the Right of Association (Agriculture) Convention (No. 11), 1921.

20. Labour Relations (Public Service) Convention (No. 151) and Recommendation (No. 159), 1978.

21. Collective Bargaining Convention (No. 154) and Recommendation (No. 163), 1981; see also the Collective Agreements Recommendation (No. 91), 1951.

22. Examination of Grievances Recommendation (No. 130), 1967.

23. Voluntary Conciliation and Arbitration Recommendation (No. 92), 1951.

24. Cooperation at the Level of the Undertaking Recommendation (No. 94), 1952; Communications within the Undertaking Recommendation (No. 129), 1967.

25. Consultation (Industrial and National Levels) Recommendation (No. 113), 1960.

26 See *Decent Work*, Report of the Director-General to the International Labour Conference, Eighty-Seventh Session, 1999 (ILO: Geneva, 1999).

27. World Summit for Social Development: *Declaration and Program of Action of the World Summit for Social Development. Report of the Main Committee*, Doc. A/Conf. 166/L/Add.1–7 (United Nations: Copenhagen, March 10, 1995).

Chapter Four

1. Continuing a policy of weakening the Party's hold on the economy, the Deng regime was interested in observing how managers reacted when they assumed greater responsibility for profits and losses of the enterprise (Crane 1990). See Shieh (1998) for a detailed description of the reform experiment in Fujian Province.

2. Usually, EPZs in industrialized countries are located in remote and economically undeveloped regions as, for example, Australia's Trade Development Zone in its Northern Territory.

3. The Manaus Free Zone in Brazil is an exception to the rule of not being allowed to produce for domestic consumption. Because more than 90 percent of the goods produced are sold on the domestic market, this EPZ has been described as an "import processing zone" (Romero 1993, 5). However, Brazil's government has threatened many of the subsidies enjoyed by Manaus employers and exerted pressure to convert its production to goods intended for export (Moffett 1998).

4. Perhaps because of their economic importance, research dealing with China's SEZs is more extensive than research on EPZs in other countries.

5. The decentralization and/or outsourcing of production functions is consistent with a more general trend in which clusters of business units coordinated by market mechanisms are replacing multilevel hierarchies of highly integrated firms (Snow, Miles, and Coleman 1995). Companies are urged to search globally for opportunities and resources, perform only those functions for which the company has, or can develop, expert skill, and outsource those activities that can be performed quickly, more effectively, or at lower cost by others. "Instead of advocating resource accumulation and control, this equation linked competitive success to doing fewer things better, with less." (Snow et al., p. 612).

6. "Export Processing Zones" http://www.wepza.org/world/epzs.htm

7. For example, the Jinqiao SEZ near Shanghai boasts the following MNCs among its forty foreign investors: Sharp, Hitachi, Ricoh, and Mitsubishi from Japan; Ford, Hughes, International Business Machines, General Motors, Whirlpool, and Kodak from the United States; Siemens and Leica from Germany; and Royal Philips Electronics from the Netherlands. (http://www.sh.com/zone/other/jinqiao.htm)

8. A few MNCs (e.g., Levi Strauss, Nike, and Danon) have, either of their own volition or as a consequence of public pressure, adopted codes of conduct for their contractors, to assure at least minimum standards for working conditions. Such codes are problematic due to a lack of independent monitoring, although a number of local religious groups and human rights NGOs have offered to serve as impartial monitors.

9. It should be noted that when the Indian economy began to prosper in the mid-1990s, these restrictions made the EPZs less attractive investments ("Islands of Despair" 1996).

10. For example, the natural geographic advantage of Panama's Colon Free Trade Zone is touted to potential investors. "Poised on the cusp of the Pacific and Atlantic oceans, Panama is well positioned as a global transportation and logistics hub that can import and export goods quickly and efficiently," according to a senior commercial specialist for the U.S. Embassy in Panama (Kalman 1999, 16).

11. A "nice life style" has been reported to be an important determinant for investors in the Philippines' Cebu island (ICFTU undated) and in Mauritius (Roberts 1992).

12. For example, sectarian violence in Sri Lanka has worried potential investors in that country's EPZs (Wijesekera 1987).

13. EPZs often were located in undesirable commercial areas because of domestic political considerations or to avoid threatening local industry. The lack of appropriate infrastructure to supply energy, treat waste, and transport workers also presented problems for investors in these early EPZs. Transportation is still a serious problem for workers in a great number of EPZs, especially for women, who often must travel to and from work in darkness.

14. There are other economic costs that stem from incentives offered to EPZ investors. For example, environmental problems in host countries may be exacerbated because MNCs seek to invest where they are least hampered by regulation (Brinkerhoff and Coston 1999).

15. Although a number of problems had to be overcome to reach its present level of prosperity, Mauritius now has a shortage of labor that has forced exporters to establish subsidiaries in Madagascar and to recruit specialists from abroad to work in its EPZs (Cooper 1998; Ryan 1994).

16. "WEPZA Code of Conduct," http://www.sni.net/world/ethics.htm.

17. Lack of union representation in EPZs is also associated with excessive demands for overtime.

18. "Panama's Export Processing Zones," http://www.pty.com/gala/english/z_process. htm. However, outside the zones, the Labor Code "aims to promote further unionization of labor and to encourage workers to join freely any existing unions" (Julio Cesar Contreras III, "A Lawyer's Guide to Panama," http://www.hg.org/guide_panama.html#labor).

19. Mauritius provides another example of different labor standards within and outside of EPZs. In contrast to businesses outside the zones, firms in the EPZs apply the "double cut" system (derived from colonial law) that permits employers to deduct two days' pay whenever a worker is absent on a Monday (Roberts 1992; ILO 1998, 23, 24).

20. For example, only one of sixteen firms in the Kingston, Jamaica, EPZ had union representation. The low rate of unionization has been attributed to the weakness of the Jamaican labor movement and the lack of interest in collective bargaining among the relatively well-paid, high-skilled workers in the zones (van Heerden 1998).

Chapter Five

The author would like to thank Anthony Freeman and Rudy Oswald for their comments about an earlier version of this chapter. Dwight Justice of the ICFTU also deserves thanks for providing a great deal of source material on the Confederation.

1. The concerns of the U.S. government about the WFTU were spawned by lobbying efforts of the outspokenly anti-communist American Federation of Labor. In France, the government closed the Paris headquarters of the WFTU in 1949 following an attempt by the French Communist Party to gain control over the labor movement (Freeman 1985).

2. Establishing the ICFTU meant that the AFL had to reverse its "policy of insisting that any international labor organization must be composed solely of representatives from the 'dominant' labor movement in each country—in other words, their acceptance of a policy of sharing representation with the CIO" (Peterson 1963, 221).

3. Jacobs (1973) found it ironic that the ICFTU could embrace union movements with strong Marxist traditions such as the German DGB while chastising the WCL, a strongly anti-Communist Christian international, for failing to sever its ties to the WFTU.

4. More than one trade union center from any given country may be affiliated with the ICFTU, as is true for Bangladesh, Brazil, Columbia, Denmark, El Salvador, India, Italy, Pakistan, and Sweden.

5. The financial problems of the Confederation are attributable to the "miserable financial commitment" of its affiliates (Waterman 1998). Membership fees at the ICFTU represent approximately one percent of income of those affiliates that are willing to pay.

6. This estimate was provided by human rights activist Harry Wu; see "Human Rights Activist Calls for ILO Action on Forced Labor," 1996.

7. The ICFTU's European Regional Organization was abolished in January 1970. In its place, the fully autonomous European Trade Union Confederation (ETUC) was created by seventeen ICFTU affiliates to focus on the development and employment issues of the European Community. The term "free" (signifying secular non-Communist unionism) was deleted from the new organization's name, which opened its doors to Christian and internationally nonaligned unions.

8. The address of the ICFTU homepage is: http://www2.icftu.org/. Regional organizations can be reached at: AFRO (icftuafro@form-net.com), APRO (http://www.icftu-apro.org), and ORIT (http://www.ciosl-orit.org).

9. A cursory review of the Committee's annual reports reveals frequent reliance on the following standard petition for information, progress reports, and specific behavior from governments: "The Committee hopes that the Government will make every effort to take the necessary action in the very near future."

10. The *Green Globe Yearbook* (Bergesen, Parmann, and Thommessen 1997) lists the ICFTU as one of the most important NGOs worldwide with regard to nature conservation.

11. The UN, ILO, and European Commission have supplied funds for a variety of ICFTU projects. However, extra-budgetary funds typically are foreign aid grants to developing coun-

tries from the treasuries of certain nations (e.g., the Netherlands and the Nordic countries) to fund development programs sponsored by the ICFTU.

12. For example, the Unit investigated charges against Howaldtswerke Deutsche Werft of West Germany for selling blueprints, Aerospatiale of France for the development of military helicopters, and Mecar of Belgium for arms exports and fruit imports.

13. The ICFTU has addressed domestic violence and dowry deaths (the burning to death of young brides because their families have not been able to meet the demands of the husband's family), sexual harassment, child care, the disproportionate representation of women in the poorest sectors of society, the protection of homeworkers, the effects of new technology on the nature and level of female employment, and the obstacles to equal participation in unions.

14. In 1994, the RUGMARK Foundation began operating in New Delhi as a private, voluntary nonprofit institution. Participating carpet exporters have a contractual relationship with the Foundation that permits its inspectors to conduct unannounced audits of their manufacturing facilities to assure that child labor is not used. Carpet importers pay one percent of the export value of the carpets to a child development fund administered by UNICEF to provide schools and vocational programs for children in regions where carpets are manufactured (Leipziger and Sabharwal 1996).

15. Another instance of ICFTU cooperation involved the Amalgamated Clothing and Textile Workers Union (ACTWU), which received substantial and effective assistance during a boycott of the U.S. company Farah Manufacturing (Douglas 1986). The action began in 1972 and ended twenty-one months later, and by most accounts helped to secure recognition of ACTWU as the bargaining representative of Farah workers.

16. For example, considerable tension exists over efforts by the ICFTU to introduce minimum work standards as a condition for internal trade supervised by the WTO between its affiliate from the North (who support the initiative) and the South (who view the initiative as injurious to their members). The AFL-CIO's opposition to President Clinton's trade initiative with China has led to disagreements among its affiliates. Whereas unions led by the United Automobile Workers are vehemently opposed, other affiliates that represent workers in public- and private-sector domestic service industries believe that the AFL-CIO is squandering too much social and financial capital on the controversy.

17. For example, below is the statement of an industry spokesperson about the Sialkot project that is attempting to rid the manufacture of soccer balls of child labor. This passage is representative of the entire article, which focuses exclusively on the actions of employer organizations and ignores the important role of the ICFTU, the ITSs, and other labor organizations in the campaign.

> I am very proud of the soccer industry's program to eliminate child labor in the production of hand stitched soccer balls in Pakistan. The voluntary program, with pledges from 55 international brands, has revised Pakistani production procedures. In fact, the initiative was recognized in early June by the Council on Economic Priorities (CEP) at the 11th annual Corporate Conscience Awards in New York. CEP presented the Pioneer Award in Global Ethics to the Sporting Goods Manufacturers Association (SGMA), SGMA's Soccer Industry Council of America (SICA), and the World Federation of the Sporting Goods Industry (WFSGI). (Riddle 1997, 32)

Chapter Six

1. Relations between the ITSs and the ICFTU have always been free of friction. In the 1950s and for part of the 1960s, the ITSs maintained a joint Liaison Office staffed by a full-time paid official, mainly to coordinate the ITS side in dealings with the ICFTU. But as rela-

tions became more routine, and ITS autonomy more accepted, the need for a collective ITS representation declined.

2. Even before the collapse of Communism and its institutions mooted the question, a decision by the European Trade Union Confederation (ETUC) to accept the CGIL and subsequently the CCOO into its own ranks, and a parallel decision by the Trade Union Advisory Committee to the Organization for Economic Cooperation and Development, led several secretariats to reverse their previously negative positions. That decision did not apply, however, to the French CGT, which was regarded as too closely tied to Stalinist policies and whose affiliates were not eligible for ITS membership.

3. Approval of the membership application of the AFL-CIO's Building and Construction Trades Department was received at the same time as an important election for general secretary of the IFBWW. Debate about the legitimacy of admitting a department of a labor federation ensured the election of a general secretary who did not have the support of North American affiliates. Consequently, the few North American affiliates terminated their memberships in the IFBWW, the Building Trades Department withdrew its contested application, and the IFBWW is the only secretariat without members from the United States.

4. The one exception was the now defunct International Federation of Petroleum and Chemical Workers, which set up its central office in Denver, Colorado.

5. The European Industry Federations are sector-level versions of the ITSs. In 1990, they were awarded seats on the board of the European Trade Union Confederation. They were instrumental in establishing Workers Councils in European MNCs, and have cross-border collective bargaining as their primary goal (see Chapter 7).

Chapter Seven

This chapter is based on the authors' chapter, "In the Line of Fire: The Europeanization of Labor Representation," in Martin and Ross, with others (1999).

1. The EMU members are: Austria, Belgium, Finland, France, Germany, Ireland, Italy, Luxembourg, Netherlands, Portugal, and Spain. In addition to these, the EU includes Denmark, Greece, Sweden, and the United Kingdom.

2. Although the EMU went into effect in January 1999, the national currencies of the EMU member countries will remain in circulation until July 2001. However, their exchange rates relative to each other and to the Euro were "irrevocably fixed" and all the transactions by companies or governments across the borders of the member countries have been denominated in Euros since the start of EMU.

3. The 1951 Treaty of Paris set up a precursor, the European Coal and Steel Community (ECSC). What is now the EU was established by the 1957 Treaty of Rome which set up the European Economic Community (EEC), or "Common Market." This treaty is in effect the EU's constitution, setting up and defining the jurisdiction of the political institutions for decision making and implementation. A companion treaty was set up by the European Atomic Energy Community. The three Communities came to be referred to simply as the European Community (EC). The EC began with only six countries: France, Germany, Italy, Belgium, Netherlands, and Luxembourg. Seven others chose to stay out and form a more limited European Free Trade Area (EFTA): Austria, Denmark, Norway, Portugal, Sweden, Switzerland, and the U.K. All but Switzerland eventually joined the EU.

The 1986 Single European Act (SEA) revised the Rome Treaty, modifying the policy decision-making procedure and expanding its scope in order to bring about a "Single Market" by the end of 1992.

The 1991 Treaty on the European Union (TEU)—"Maastricht Treaty" continued the process of political and economic integration, symbolized by renaming the Community as Union. It provided for an Economic and Monetary Union (EMU), set a timetable for establishing it, and defined requirements for membership in it. It made further changes in decision making, increased financial support for poorer regions, and took steps toward common foreign and military policy, common policies in the areas of public order and immigration, and unified communications and transportation infrastructure.

The 1997 Amsterdam Treaty established rules for enforcing budgetary discipline (Stability Pact) on member states who join the EMU, added a chapter on employment, further expanded the Parliament's legislative role, and provided for the future admission of some former Soviet bloc countries to membership.

4. The Council, which meets formally approximately monthly, is composed of different ministers, depending on the subject of proposed legislation. Thus, it consists of finance ministers when the subject is economic, environment ministers when the subject is environmental, etc. There is also a European Council, consisting of the heads of government, which meets semi-annually or more to adopt broad guidelines which shape the policy agenda, but it does not vote on proposed legislation. The Presidency of the EU and its various Councils rotates among the member states for six-month periods.

5. Delors, with a background in both the French central bank and the progressive Catholic labor movement (the CFTC which became the secularized CFDT) was Finance Minister under the French Socialist President, François Mitterand, between 1981 and 1984. Delors became President of the European Commission in 1985 and was reappointed for a second five-year term in 1990.

6. Perhaps the most significant proposal involved establishment of "European Works Councils" in transnational firms. But this and a proposed directive applying legal and collectively bargained rules in force in a member state to workers "posted" by their employers to work in that state temporarily, along with a later proposal prescribing parental leave, were not enacted until the Maastricht Social Protocol could be used.

7. The scope for legislation under this procedure is expanded to include social security and social protection of workers; protection of workers whose employment contract is terminated; and representation and collective defense of the interests of workers and employers, including co-determination, but only after unanimity. Moreover, legislation is limited even in these areas by a clause explicitly excluding any EU legislation dealing with pay or the rights to organize, strike, or impose lockouts.

8. Dølvik (1997) and Gobin (1997) were our main sources for the ETUC's history.

9. The Commission set up a "Social Partners" unit plus various sectoral tripartite bodies, the most important being the tripartite Advisory Committee on Safety and Health in 1974, providing a forum for union input into proposals for workplace health and safety directives. Although the ETUC was not formally represented on the Committee, it came to play an information and coordination role for the national trade union representatives in it.

10. The Commission underwrote ETUC meetings in Brussels and elsewhere (travel, translation) to the equivalent of several million dollars per year. It was also quite generous to the European Trade Union Institute (ETUI), the ETUC research arm, and funded a body called AFETT (established in 1986) to train unionists about new technologies. It then provided subsidies enabling the ETUC to set up two new units. One was the Trade Union Technical Bureau (TUTB), to deal with workplace health and safety policy. The other was the European Trade Union College (ETUCO), to prepare national trade union officials for European-level activity.

11. A new budget line for these meetings set up by the European Parliament in 1992 amounted to more than four times the total of all existing EIF budgets combined and quickly became a major factor in EIF growth. Although most of the money covered meeting costs, it also covered related EIF expenses, enabling them to hire additional staff, while adding very substantially to the very meager resources at their disposal for serving their constituents.

They were thus able to gain a higher profile and legitimacy within ETUC as well as with their own member unions and, importantly, with the workplace-level activists who attended the meetings.

12. Concrete proposals in this direction were limited, however. The EIFs were to be given voting rights on the Executive Committee except on constitutional and financial issues (on the ground that the EIFs did not pay dues, inasmuch as their affiliates paid dues to the national confederations), and they were allotted three seats, rotated among them, on the new Steering Committee.

13. While the Italian and Belgian confederations pushed especially vigorously in a transformative direction, the Nordic confederations and the British TUC opposed significant departures from the ETUC's established practices. The DGB, having brokered the changes aimed at re-energizing the ETUC, was itself barred from supporting genuine supranationalization by its own member unions, notably IG Metall.

14. Social dialogue has, nevertheless, been established in some sectors, typically with Commission support, and typically where there are special EU programs, as in vulnerable sectors such as agriculture, coal and steel, and textiles. However, business participants usually have followed UNICE's line opposing anything like negotiations.

15. Employer unity behind UNICE's opposition to sectoral social dialogue has not been complete and durable. Some employers, like those in construction and commerce, have stated that UNICE does not represent them and have readily entered into sectoral dialogue with EIFs. Even within UNICE, there has been some retreat and consideration of organizational changes to avert the defection of employers with an interest in sectoral level discussions. EIF strategy for bringing employers to the table has focused on making the most of this possibility. EIFs thus have begun to seek circumstances under which employers can be drawn into discussions over an issue where there is some potential for a precedent-setting agreement. Such circumstances typically arise when there is some Commission action employers want to influence, and they have reason to believe that they will be more successful if they approach the Commission or other bodies jointly with unions.

16. Transnational linkages on the local level are also being constructed through Interregional Trade Union Committees (ITUCs) set up by the ETUC in regions where there are crossborder labor markets. Twenty-eight ITUCs existed by the end of 1995, but there was significant activity in only a few of them (Prince 1995).

17. The EU money enabled the EIFs to organize over 490 preliminary meetings, usually at union request, in 290 multinationals between 1991 and summer 1994, resulting in a modest growth in agreements prior to the directive's enactment. The EMF alone, which concentrated on this activity, held 155 meetings in over one hundred different companies during this period, followed in many by meetings that went on to further stages. As of August 1994, the EMF meetings had culminated in agreements in eighteen companies, plus unwritten understandings with seven others. Once the directive had been adopted, many companies that had refused to set up works councils unless legally obliged to rushed to make voluntary agreements before September 1996, when the directive went into effect.

18. ETUC, "Jobs and solidarity at the heart of Europe," Resolution adopted at the Eighth Statutory Congress, Brussels, May 1995, 27, 29.

19. Works councils are plant or company level committees composed of representatives elected by the workers in those units, whether they are union members or not, which exist in various forms in most continental European countries. The councils have various rights to be consulted and informed about management plans, particularly as they affect employment and work organization, and in many cases to negotiate over changes. Their negotiating rights more rarely extend to wages and other terms of employment. While they may compete with local union representatives, and sometimes enable employers to enter into "microcorporatist"

deals which deviate from agreements negotiated by unions, works councils are often dominated by local union representatives and give unions a presence where their actual membership is low. For more detail, see Rogers and Streeck (1995). The new European Works Councils are much weaker bodies than most works councils.

20. Opportunities for excluding unions in setting up EWCs, though varied, are substantial. A few companies tried it with mixed success before the directive came into force, but union avoidance has not become harder since then, for nothing in the directive requires union involvement. Even if unions are not entirely bypassed, there is plenty of scope for limiting their influence in the negotiation, composition, and operation of EWCs. The effect EWCs may have on employee relations in multinational corporations and suppliers could run in quite different directions, either diffusing higher standards of information and other practices to suppliers or preserving stratification between a privileged core of workers in the multinationals and the supplier workforces with inferior standards.

21. The exceptions may not prove the rule, but they throw it into sharp relief. As far as we know, the Volkswagen and Thomson Consumer Electronics agreements are the only ones in which consultation is more meaningful, at least on paper, than an "exchange of views" after the fact. In VW, the Council or its executive committee has a right to comment on major planned changes—in this instance cross-border transfers of production—and get a reply from management before the decision is made. Thomson has similar provisions. In only one case, Danone (formerly BSN), has an EWC gone beyond consultation to negotiation. There several "joint texts," including one on "trade union rights," were agreed upon, causing some to believe that the first steps to a European collective bargaining system had been taken (Hall et al. 1995).

22. Tensions between EWCs and national unions analogous to those historically observed between intra-firm employee participation structures and cross-firm union structures could well result, intensified to the extent that cross-border company loyalty is fostered by EWCs.

23. The 1977 McDougall Report recommended a budget of 5 to 7 percent of community GDP and the ETUC has been urging an initial increase to at least 3 percent (Pochet and Turloot 1996, 24).

24. Germany's powerful IG Metall has an interesting approach to averting such whipsawing. The union is trying to get metals sector unions in neighboring countries to commit themselves to base wage claims on a common standard of productivity growth plus targeted inflation. These efforts are being supported by the European Metalworkers Federation (Schulten and Bispinck 1999).

25. "Creating the European Social Dimension in the Internal Market: European Social Program." Adopted by the Executive Committee, December 1988.

26. "European Social Program," and "Community Charter of Fundamental Social Rights," adopted by the Executive Committee, December 1988.

27. For a survey and analysis of social pacts, see Fajertag and Pochet (2000). See also Rhodes (2000) and Dølvik (1997).

Chapter Eight

1. The International Graphical Federation (IGF) and the Postal, Telegraph, and Telephone International (PTTI) were established long before this period. However, it is only in recent years that these ITSs began to consider themselves part of the media. They will not be considered in much detail here.

2. ISETU was founded directly by the ICFTU, and its first secretary was a paid staffer of the ICFTU. ISETU was immediately recognized as an ITS, although no other ITS had emerged in such a way and none accepted such organic links with the ICFTU.

3. In 1998, the Inter-American Regional Coordinator for Entertainment Workers (CREA) was formed in a joint regional meeting of PANARTES, FIM, and FIA held in Mexico.

Chapter Nine

1. For example, beginning in 1984, the Central Bank took steps to unify the exchange rates on imports and exports as part of an International Monetary Fund adjustment program (Willmore 1995).

2. Differences among EPZs reflect a change in the type of investment. For example, pharmaceutical and electronics companies are the primary employers in the Itabo EPZ, whereas textile and garment plants employ all the workers in the Cotui EPZ.

3. See Medina (1998) for a brief description of the various categories of Dominican EPZs.

4. A twenty-year exemption is available to investors in EPZs located along the border between the D.R. and Haiti.

5. In order to put them on a more equal footing with materials that zone operators could import directly, a Dominican enterprise supplying a zone investor may import products for processing without paying import duties.

6. U.S. trade provisions limit much manufacturing in the D.R. to assembly operations. For example, under the Caribbean Basin Initiative, garments will be guaranteed access to the U.S. market at reduced tariff levels provided they are produced from cloth woven and cut in the United States.

7. The average wage of workers in the zones is approximately one-third of the wage required to stay above the poverty line and is lower than the indigence level, the wages required to pay for a family's food requirements (Medina 1998).

8. The GSP allows certain countries to export a list of products to the United States duty-free as long as they abide by certain conditions. The AFL-CIO lobbied for inclusion of a provision in the trade law that requires countries that enjoy the special trading privileges to be "taking steps" to afford their workers internationally recognized worker rights (e.g., freedom to join a union and bargain collectively, freedom from compulsory labor, and minimum age levels for employment). The U.S. Trade Representative may be petitioned to review charges against a country which, in turn, is entitled to present its version of events. Termination of GSP trade benefits is one potential consequence of the review.

9. Employers in the La Vega EPZ prevailed in both court decisions. In the case of Importación y Exportación, the judge inexplicably dismissed the case despite the fact that a blacklist used to fire union members was introduced as evidence. In the case of the FAB Company, the judge not only failed to rule against the employer; he instead acted to dissolve the union for technical mistakes in its registration papers.

10. *Listin Diario*, May 4, 1993.

11. *Listin Diario*, May 19, 1993.

12. The ITGLWF is an international trade secretariat headquartered in Brussels. It represents the interests of garment, textile, and leather workers.

13. "Dominican Labor and the GSP," *Journal of Commerce*, September 9, 1993.

14. Translation of Statement of the Federation of Free Zone Workers of the Dominican Republic, March 2, 1994, Washington, D.C.

15. Law 8–90, Art. 41 states that "Free Zone Operators and Enterprises must comply with all laws and regulations governing labor matters. They must also comply with the Social Security Act, the Law governing the Workers' Bank, Law No. 116 which creates the National Institute of Technical and Professional Training (INFOTEP), the international treaties and conventions signed and ratified by the Dominican government; and the public health laws relative to industrial facilities." Art. 45 states: "Free Zone enterprises which violate the provi-

sions of this law and its regulations are subject to cancellation by the National Council of Free Zones of their licenses to operate in the Free zones and/or to export therefrom."

16. AFL-CIO submission to the Subcommittee of the Generalized System of Preferences, March 20, 1994.

17. Translation of Statement.

18. Negotiations were under way for a third contract as this chapter was being written.

19. Translation of Statement.

Chapter Ten

1. Even before AT&T's later restructuring in 1996 (which spun off the manufacturing subsidiary now known as Lucent), the company's long distance operation was downsizing its "unionized core" and reducing the percentage of its union-represented workforce from 67 to 42 percent. By 2000, the growth of AT&T's largely non-union wireless subsidiary and its acquisition of two almost entirely unorganized cable TV companies (TCI and Media One) had reduced union membership within the company to 25 percent or less.

2. MCI WorldCom, as well as Vodaphone, Quest, and Global Crossing, have built huge market capitalizations with relatively few employees and are now the models for and acquirers of older telecom and cable TV firms. In late 1999, MCI WorldCom launched the largest corporate takeover bid in U.S. history. Its $140 billion merger with Sprint was still awaiting regulatory approval at this writing. If approved, the deal will create a long distance carrier with market capitalization of $200 million, annual revenues of $47 billion, and 141,000 employees.

3. In just one week in September 1999, AT&T and BT proposed to link their wireless services worldwide, followed days later by an agreement between Bell Atlantic and Britain's Vodaphone Airtouch to combine their U.S. cellular subsidiaries into a single national network— America's largest called Verizon Wireless.

4. Michael Rosansky, "Merger Will Create More Jobs, Bell Atlantic Chief Asserts," *Philadelphia Inquirer*, April 27, 1996.

5. Meanwhile, BT has eliminated more than a hundred thousand jobs at home in response to the lower-labor-cost competition from these new cable television and telecommunications rivals. Union influence has been eroded as a result.

6. See Early (1998). For a detailed explanation of this program, see "Mobilizing For the '90s," a 1993 manual available from the CWA Education Department, 501 Third St., N.W., Washington, DC 20001. See also a 1994 CWA booklet (available from the same source) titled, "Changing Information Services: Strategies for Workers and Consumers."

7. See "Holding the Line in '89: Lessons of the NYNEX strike," a fifty-page analysis of the strike prepared by Steve Early in 1990 and available from CWA District One, 100 Tower Office Park (Suite C), Woburn, MA 01801. A key factor in the CWA's ability to win the NYNEX strike was international labor support of the most material sort. When the union's national defense fund was on the verge of insolvency late in the strike, the Japanese telephone workers' federation, Zendentsu, made a $15 million low-interest loan that enabled CWA to continue paying regular strike benefits for the duration of the job action.

8. At the time of the campaigns described in this chapter, the PTTI was an international trade secretariat (ITS) of 254 unions from 120 countries representing 4.6 million workers in telecommunications, cable and broadcasting, and public postal services. In 1998, it was renamed the Communications International and then merged with three other ITSs to form Union Network International. UNI combines unions representing media, information technology, graphic arts, office, professional, and other white collar workers with postal employee unions and telecom unions like CWA. UNI affiliates number eight hundred, claiming a total membership of fifteen million.

9. For more on the Nortel story, see Cohen (1991) and Early (1992).

10. This coalition was somewhat unusual because the three unions involved disagreed about the advisability of the North American Free Trade Agreement (NAFTA). The Mexican union leadership supported NAFTA, while the U.S. and Canadian unions opposed it. See Moody (1998).

11. See the NLRB's December 17, 1996, decision and order in *LCF, Inc. d/b/a La Conexion Familiar and Sprint Corporation and Communications Workers of America, District Nine and Local 9410, AFL-CIO.* Case 20-CA-26203. The ALJ's acceptance of Sprint's argument that there were economic reasons for the closing was reminiscent of the position taken ten years earlier by the NLRB's regional director in Michigan, in an office closing case involving MCI. That situation involved the high point of CWA organizing to date at MCI just as the LCF campaign was the closest the union has ever gotten to a representation election at Sprint's long distance division. MCI laid off an entire group of four hundred customer service representatives near Detroit—shifting their work to a contractor in Iowa—after a CWA organizing committee developed strong majority support and the union petitioned for an election.

12. For more on the suppression of Bronfenbrenner's findings in the final version of this report, see Thomas Goetz, "The NAFTA Effect," *Village Voice*, February 15, 1997, 32–33; Laura McClure, "NAFTA Unsuppressed!" *Labor Party Press*, July 1997, 8–9; and Bill Mesler, "Sprintgate," *The Nation*, June 30, 1997, 20–23.

13. See "CWA Joins Mexican Workers In Organizing Battle With Maxi-Switch," October 1996, *CWA News*, and a follow-up article in November 1996.

14. See "New NAFTA Challenge Over Labor Rights," *Working Together: Labor Report on the Americas*, July–August 1996, a newsletter published by the Resource Center of the Americas, Washington, D.C.

Chapter Eleven

1. For example, safety standards were sometimes disregarded where the companies could get away with it, and that spelled tragedy for miners and their families. In 1995, the International Labor Organization estimated there were 10,800 coal mining deaths annually.

2. "Miners in Australia Walk Out to Support UMW Strikers in U.S.," *The Wall Street Journal*, June 4, 1993; Philip Nussel and Pat Sanders, "Coal Strike Expands, Spreads to Australia," *Charleston Daily Mail*, June 3, 1993.

3. Anne Marie Obiala, "World Solidarity, Talks in Washington Boost UMW," *The Southern Illinoisan*, October 15, 1993.

4. Tempus, "Trust Hanson," June 14, 1993.

5. "Hanson Changing Rules But Not Playing the Game," June 11, 1993.

6. Norma Cohen, "Hanson Softens on Voting Rights," June 14, 1993.

7. Michael Walters, "Hanson Wants to Lord It," June 12, 1993.

8. "Scots Reel at Hanson Power Play," June 16, 1993.

9. Michael Tate, *The Daily Telegraph*; Neil Bennett, *The Times*; Ben Laurance, *The Guardian*; Norma Cohen, *Financial Times*; all June 18, 1993.

10. Tempus, "Hanson," June 18, 1993.

11. "Hanson PLC Drops Proposals Following Holders' Objections," June 18, 1993.

12. Clare Sambrook, "Hanson Act of Apology Over Script," June 26, 1993.

13. Jon Ashworth, "'I Apologize,' Lord Hanson Tells His Shareholders," June 26, 1993.

14. David Porter, "Hanson Beats a Tidy Retreat," June 26, 1993.

15. Roger Cowe, "Miners Exotic Paradox," *The Guardian*, June 26, 1993; Maggie Urry, "Hanson Shares Dip on US Strike Warning," *Financial Times*, June 30, 1993.

16. Seumas Milne, "Labour Warns of Hanson 'Pillage,'" *The Guardian*, July 21, 1993.

17. For example, Fred Brown, "Church Leaders Push for No Coal Strike," *Knoxville News*

Sentinel, May 1, 1993; Kathryn Rogers, "Striking Miners Gain Support from Churches," *St. Louis Post-Dispatch*, July 19, 1993; Associated Press, "Church Leaders Want to Bring Two Sides Together," *Charleston Gazette*, September 4, 1993.

18. Maurice Weaver, "Archbishop Caught in Row Over Support for Striking US Miners," *The Daily Telegraph*, November 6, 1993; Ben Laurance, " 'Courteous' Carey Courts Controversy with Message to Striking US Miners," *The Guardian*, November 6, 1993.

19. Shellee Nunley, "Pickets Target Businessman's Home," *Deseret Sun*, February 3, 1993; "Show of Solidarity for Mine Workers," *California AFL-CIO News*.

20. "Mayor Offers Support to Mine Workers Union," *St. Louis Post-Dispatch*, April 25, 1993.

21. Randolph Heaster, "Local Activist Group Shows Support for Coal Miners," *Kansas City Star*, April 20, 1993; Randolph Heaster, "Union Leader Urges Price to Intervene in Coal Talks," *The Kansas City Star*, May 18, 1993; Jim Gallagher, "Miners Take Dispute to Mercantile Lobby," *St. Louis Post-Dispatch*, September 1, 1993; Randolph Heaster, "Kansas City Feels Coal Strike," *The Kansas City Star*, November 3, 1993; "Solidarity!: Kansas City Labor Backs Coal Miners on Strike for Five Months," *The Labor Times*, November 1993.

22. Bob Niedbala, "Miners Dig In at Waynesburg Rally," *Observer-Reporter*, July 15, 1993; "Calls for Hanson Union Council," *Financial Times*, July 15, 1993; C.M. Mortimer, "Trumka Rips Mine Owners," *Herald-Standard*, July 15, 1993; Frank Fisher, Associated Press, "Leaders Rev Up Strikers: International Unionists Tell of Global Walkouts," *St. Louis Post-Dispatch*, July 16, 1993; John H. Croessman, "World's Top Labor Leaders in Pinckneyville to Show Support for Striking Coal Miners," *The Daily American*, July 16, 1993; Frank Fisher, Associated Press, "World Labor Leaders Back Striking Miners," *The Benton Evening News*, July 16, 1993; James B. Parks, "World Labor Digs in to Help Mine Workers," *AFL-CIO News*, July 26, 1993.

23. United Press International, "South African Union Strikes to Back U.S. Miners," August 6, 1993.

24. Roland Rudd, "US Miners Contribute to 16% Fall at Hanson," August 18, 1993.

25. Roger Cowe, "Hanson Admits Higher Strike Cost," September 2, 1993.

26. Cassandra Burrell, "Tentative Agreement Reached on Contract to End Coal Strike," Associated Press, December 7, 1993.

Chapter Twelve

The author wishes to thank Matthew Evangelista, Carolina Quinteros, and Sidney Tarrow for their many helpful comments on earlier versions of this paper.

1. In Central America, this sector is commonly referred to as the maquila sector. Maquila production entails only a part of the production process, normally assembly. U.S. activists commonly refer to maquila factories as sweatshops. In this chapter I will use interchangeably the terms export-oriented garment manufacturing, maquila factories, and sweatshops.

2. Most notably, they disagree with the assumption that industrial relations actors "share an underlying consensus that defines and legitimizes their roles" (Kochan, Katz, and McKersie 1994, 7). Looking specifically at the late 1970s and early 1980s, they emphasize strategic initiatives taken by management that have transformed industrial relations practices in the United States.

3. It is not coincidental that unions are much weaker in Haiti, where the economy is very weak, than in the Dominican Republic, where conditions are somewhat better.

4. According to Freeman and Medoff (1984), workers who are unable to achieve their desired results through collective action in a free-market system will exit (quit) their jobs in search of something better, thus, in theory, penalizing bad employers.

5. Author's interviews with union leaders conducted in Puerto Cortes, Honduras, March 1996.

6. Cited in French, Cowie, and Littlehale (1994).

7. Comments of Alan Howard, international meeting of garment workers, Dominican Republic, March 1998.

8. Cited in Krupat (1997, 73–74).

9. Ibid., 74.

10. At the time, it was called Prenda Estrella. It closed and reopened in 1996 as Daimi Atlántica.

11. Author's interview, Santo Domingo, March 1998.

12. "Working for Justice in Haiti: An Interview with Yannick Etienne," *Multinational Monitor*, October 1997, 18.

13. National Labor Committee, "Are Human Rights Campaigns Necessary?" July 28, 1997.

14. "Working for Justice in Haiti."

15. This section is based largely on interviews with union leaders from the factory in Guatemala, conducted in the Dominican Republic in March 1998, and DeSimone (1998).

16. See Wendy Bounds, "Critics Confront a CEO Dedicated to Human Rights," *The Wall Street Journal*, February 24, 1997, B1.

Chapter Thirteen

1. According to David Jessup, Bhagwati announced that ideas that would link trade to concerns about how people are treated must be considered legitimate. See "Bhagwati, Free Traders, Concede," New Economy Information Service, November 24, 1998: djessup@newecon.org.

2. Peter Waldman, "A Rain-Forest Tribe Brings Its Eco-Battle to Corporate America," *Wall Street Journal*, June 7, 1999, A1, A6.

References

Abreu, Teófilo (1994). "Reportan Entre Obreras Trastornos 4 Mas Abortos," *Hoy*, March 19.

Aldrich, Howard, and David A. Whetten (1981). "Organization Sets, Action Sets and Networks: Making the Most of Simplicity." In *Handbook of Organizational Design*, Vol. 1, edited by P.C. Nystrom and W.H. Starbuck, 385–408. Oxford: Oxford University Press.

Alexander, Ernest R. (1995). *How Organizations Act Together*. Luxembourg: Gordon and Breach Publishers.

Althaus, Rickert R., and Dean L. Yarwood (1993). "Organizational Domain Overlap with Cooperative Outcomes: The Department of Agriculture and State and International Agricultural Policy During the Carter Administration," *Public Administration Review* 53, 357–67.

American Embassy (1995). *Country Commercial Guide for the Dominican Republic*. Santo Domingo, July (http://www.tradecompass.com/lib . . . s/com_guide/DOMREPUBLICTOC.html).

Andrews, Gregg (1991). *Shoulder to Shoulder? The American Federation of Labor, the United States, and the Mexican Revolution*. Berkeley: University of California Press.

Apec Foundation of Educational Credit (1992). *National Labor Force Survey*. Santo Domingo, D.R., December.

Arévalo, Rolando, and Joaquin Arriola (1996). "El Caso de El Salvador." In *La Situación Sociolaboral en las Zonas Francas y Empresas Maquiladoras del Istmo Centroamericano y República Dominicana*, edited by Oficina de Actividades para los Trabajadores, 109–58. Costa Rica: Organización Internacional del Trabajo.

Bamber, Greg J., and Russell D. Lansbury (1993). "Studying International and Comparative Industrial Relations." In *International and Comparative Industrial Relations* (2d ed.), edited by G.J. Bamber and R.D. Lansbury, 1-26. Sydney: Allen and Unwin.

Barney, Jay B. (1995). "Looking Inside for Competitive Advantage," *Academy of Management Executive*, 9(4), 49–61.

Basile, Antoine, and Dimitri Germidis (1984). *Investing in Free Export Processing Zones*. Paris: Development Center, Organization for Economic Cooperation and Development.

Baum, Joel A.C., and Christine Oliver (1991). "Institutional Linkages and Organizational Mortality," *Administrative Science Quarterly* 36, 187–218.

Beard, Mary (1920; Reprint, 1968). *A Short History of the American Labor Movement*. New York: Greenwood Press.

Beedham, Brian (1999). "The New Geopolitics: False Heaven," *Economist* 352 (July 31), S4–S7.

Ben-Israel, Ruth (1988). *International Labour Standards: The Case of Freedom to Strike*. Deventer: Kluwer.

Bergesen, Helge O., Georg Parmann, and Oystein B. Thommessen (1997). *Green Globe Yearbook*. Oxford: Oxford University Press.

Betten, Lammy (1993). *International Labour Law: Selected Issues*. Deventer: Kluwer.

Brinkerhoff, Derick W., and Jenifer M. Coston (1999). "International Development Management in a Globalized World," *Public Administration Review* 59, 346–61.

Bronfenbrenner, Kate (1997). "The Effect of NAFTA on Union Organizing," *New Labor Forum*.

Bronstein, Arturo (1985). "La Aplicación de la Ley Nacional y la Ley Laboral Extranjera en el Derecho Individual del Trabajo: El Caso de los Empleados de Empresas Multinacionales," *Legislación del Trabajo* 33, 663–77.

Brummer, Alex, and Roger Cowe (1994). *Hanson, A Biography*. London: Fourth Estate.

Busch, G.K. (1980). *Political Currents in the International Trade Union Movement*, Vol. 1. London: The Economist Intelligence Unit.

Busch, Klaus (1994). *Europaische Integration und Tarifpolitik*. Cologne: Bund-Verlag GmbH.

Cantrell, Carl D. (1999). "Sensing the Speed Picking Up." In *CyberUnion: Empowering Labor Through Computer Technology*, edited by A.B. Shostak, 50–54. Armonk, N.Y.: M.E. Sharpe.

Cappelli, Peter, Laurie Bassi, Harry Katz, David Knoke, Paul Osterman, and Michael Useem (1997). *Change at Work*. New York: Oxford Press.

Chandler, Alfred D. (1962). *Strategy and Structure*. Cambridge: MIT Press.

Chen, Xiangming (1994). "The Changing Roles of Free Economic Zones in Development: A Comparative Analysis of Capitalist and Socialist Cases in East Asia," *Studies in Comparative International Development* 29 (3), 3–25.

CIECA (1993). "El Compartamiento del Salario," *Nota de Coyuntura* 23 (May 18).

Cohen, Larry (1991). "Mobilizing Internationally," *Labor Research Review* Issue 21.

Commons, John R. (1946). *History of Labor in the United States*. New York: Macmillan.

Connors, Jane (1996). "NGOs and the Human Rights of Women at the United Nations." In *"The Conscience of the World": The Influence of Non-Governmental Organizations in the UN System*, edited by P. Willetts, 147–80. Washington, D.C.: Brookings Institution.

Cooper, Helene (1998). "Mauritius, a Tiny Fish in a Big Ocean, Makes an Example of Itself," *Wall Street Journal*, July 14, A1, A11.

Coursier, Philippe (1993). *Le Conflit de Lois en Matière de Contrat de Travail. Etude en Droit International Privé Français*. Paris: LGDJ.

Craft, James A., and Marian M. Extejt (1983). "New Strategies in Union Organizing," *Journal of Labor Research* 4 (1), 19–32.

Crane, George T. (1990). *The Political Economy of China's Special Economic Zones*. London: M.E. Sharpe.

De Wit, B., and R. Meyer (1998) *Strategy: Process, Content, Context*. London: Thomson.

DeSimone, Peter (1998). "Guatemala." In *The Sweatshop Quandary: Corporate Responsibility on the Global Frontier*, edited by P. Varley. Washington, D.C.: Investor Responsibility Research Center.

Deyo, Frederic C. (1989). *Beneath the Miracle: Labor Subordination in the New Asian Industrialism*. Berkeley: University of California Press.

—— (1997). "Labor and Post-Fordist Industrial Restructuring in East and Southeast Asia," *Work and Occupations* 24, 97–118.

Din, Musleh-ud (1994). "Export Processing Zones and Backward Linkages," *Journal of Development Economics* 43, 369–85.

Dølvik, Jon Erik (1997). *Redrawing Boundaries of Solidarity? ETUC, Social Dialogue and the Europeanisation of Trade Unions in the 1990s*. Oslo: ARENA/ FAFO.

Douglas, Sara U. (1986). *Labor's New Voice: Unions and the Mass Media*. Norwood, N.J.: Ablex Publishing.

Doz, Y. (1986). *Strategic Management in Multinational Companies*. Oxford: Pergamon Press.

Drucker, Peter F. (1977). "The Rise of Production Sharing," *Wall Street Journal*, March 15, 22.

Dunlop, John T. (1958/1993). *Industrial Relations Systems*, rev. ed. Boston: Harvard Business School.

Dunn, Leith (1994). "Education for Women Workers in Caribbean Export Processing Zones: Challenges and Opportunities," *Labour Education* 96 (3), 21–34.

Early, Steve (1992). "Telephone Workers' Campaign Promotes Labor Internationalism," *Labor Notes*, January, 6–7.

—— (1998). "Membership-Based Organizing." In *A New Labor Movement for the New Century*, edited by G. Mantsios, 82–103. New York: Monthly Review Press.

Evan, William M. (1966). "The Organization-Set: Toward a Theory of Interorganizational Relations." In *Approaches to Organizational Design*, edited by J.D. Thompson, 173–91. Pittsburgh: University of Pittsburgh Press.

Fajertag, Giuseppe, and Philippe Pochet (eds., 2000). *Social Pacts in Europe*. Brussels: European Trade Union Institute and Observatoire Social Européen.

Freeman, Anthony G. (1985). *Primer on the International Trade Union Movement.* Washington, D.C.: U.S. Department of State.

Freeman, Richard B., and James L. Medoff (1984). *What Do Unions Do?* New York: Basic Books.

French, John D., Jefferson Cowie, and Scott Littlehale (1994). *Labor and NAFTA: A Briefing Book.* Prepared for the Conference on "Labor, Free Trade, and Economic Integration in the Americas: National Labor Union Responses to a Transnational World," Duke University, August 25–27, 1994.

Frenkel, Stephen, and Jeffrey Harrod (1995). "Labor, Management, and Industrial Relations: Themes and Issues in International Perspective." In *Industrialization and Labor Relations: Contemporary Research in Seven Countries*, edited by Stephen Frenkel and Jeffrey Harrod, 3–14. Ithaca, N.Y.: ILR Press.

Galaskiewicz, Joseph (1985). "Interorganizational Relations," *American Review of Sociology* 11, 281–304.

Galenson, Walter (1994). "Trade Unionism and Tripartism: In Search of New Strength," *World Labor Report*, 8, 30–32.

Gereffi, Gary (1994). "The Organization of Buyer-Driven Global Commodity Chains: How U.S. Retailers Shape Overseas Production Networks." In *Commodity Chains and Global Capitalism*, edited by G. Gereffi and M. Korzeniewicz, 95–122. Westport: Praeger.

Gereffi, Gary, Miguel Korzeniewicz, and Roberto P. Korzeniewicz (1994). "Introduction: Global Commodity Chains." In *Commodity Chains and Global Capitalism*, edited by Gary Gereffi and Miguel Korzeniewicz, 1–14. Westport, Conn.: Praeger.

Ghoshal, Sumantra, and S.K. Kim (1986). "Building Effective Intelligence Systems for Competitive Advantage," *Sloan Management Review* 28(1), Fall.

Gobin, Corinne (1997). *L'Europe Syndical.* Brussels: Presses de l'ULB.

Godson, Roy (1976). *American Labor and European Politics: The AFL as a Transnational Force.* New York: Crane, Russak & Co.

Goold, M., and A. Campbell (1987). *Strategies and Styles: The Role of the Center in Managing Diversified Corporations.* Oxford: Blackwell.

Haas, Peter M. (1992). "Introduction: Epistemic Communities and International Policy Coordination." *International Organization* 46(1), 1–35.

Hall, Mark, Mark Carley, Michael Gold, Paul Marginson, and Keith Sisson (1995). *European Works Councils: Planning for the Directive.* London: Eclipse Group Ltd and Industrial Relations Research Unit.

Hall, Richard H. (1972). *Organizations: Structure and Processes.* Englewood Cliffs, N.J.: Prentice-Hall.

Hallam, Andrew (1999). "Poland's Tiger Economy," *European Business Journal* 11(2), 72–79.

Hamill, James (1993). "Employment Effects of the Changing Strategies of Multinational Enterprises." In *Multinationals and Employment: The Global Economy of the 1990s*, edited by P. Bailey, A. Parisotto, and G. Renshaw, 69–94. Geneva: International Labor Organization.

Harvey, Rowland H. (1935). *Samuel Gompers: Champion of the Toiling Masses.* Palo Alto: Stanford University Press.

Hax, A.C., and N.S. Majluf (1996). *The Strategy Concept and Process: A Pragmatic Approach*, 2d ed. Englewood Cliffs, N.J.: Prentice Hall.

Helfgott, Roy B. (1983). "American Unions and Multinational Companies: A Case of Misplaced Emphasis," *Columbia Journal of World Business* 18(2), 81–86.

Hill, C., and R. Hoskisson (1987). "Strategy and Structure in the Multiproduct Form," *Academy of Management Review* 12(2).

——, and J. Pickering (1986). "Divisionalisation, Decentralisation and Performance of Large United Kingdom Companies," *Journal of Management Studies* 23(1).

Hopkins, T.K., and I. Wallerstein (1986). "Commodity Chains in the World-Economy Prior to 1800," *Review* 10(1).

Huff, A.S. (ed., 1990). *Mapping Strategic Thought*. Chichester: Wiley.

"Human Rights Activist Calls for ILO Action on Forced Labor" (1996). *ILO Focus* 9(1), 1,6.

Hurd, Richard W., and Joseph Uehlein (1994). *The Employer Assault on the Legal Right to Organize: Case Studies Collected by the Industrial Union Department*. Washington, D.C.: AFL-CIO, May 1.

Hyman, Richard (1995). "Industrial Relations in Europe: Theory and Practice," *European Journal of Industrial Relations* 1(1), 17–46.

ICEM Update (1997). "British and German Unions Agree to Joint Membership Rights." *ICEM@GEO2.poptel.or*, March 3.

—— (1998). "Rio Tinto: World's Unions Launch Action Network," ICEM @GEO2.poptel.or, February 9.

International Confederation of Free Trade Unions (1988). *The Challenge of Change: Report of the 14th ICFTU World Congress on the Tasks Ahead for the International Free Trade Union Movement*. Brussels.

—— (1992a). *Report on Activities: Financial Reports, 1987–1990*. Brussels.

—— (1992b). *Report of the Fifteenth World Congress*. Caracas, March 17–24.

—— (1994a). *Trade Union Rights Under Threat*. Brussels.

—— (1994b) *Child Labour: The World's Best Kept Secret*. Brussels.

—— (1994c). *Twenty-eighth Meeting of the ICFTU/ITS Working Party on Multinational Companies*. 28 MNC-WP/7, Brussels, September 14–15.

—— (1994d). *Recommendations of the 6th World Women's Conference of the ICFTU*. Brussels.

—— (1994e). *Trade Union Rights Under Threat*. Brussels.

—— (1995a, 1997). *Annual Survey of Violations of Trade Union Rights*. Brussels.

—— (1995b). *Manual for Trade Union Development Projects*. Brussels.

—— (1996a). *Behind the Wire: Anti-Union Repression in the Export Processing Zones*. Brussels.

—— (1996b). *Decisions of the 16th World Congress of the ICFTU*. Brussels.

—— (1996c). *Report on Activities of the Confederation and Financial Reports, 1991–1994*. Brussels.

—— (1996d). *The Global Market—Trade Unionism's Greatest Challenge*. Brussels.

—— (undated). *EPZs in Asia: Who Profits?* Brussels.

International Confederation of Free Trade Unions—African Regional Organization

(1995). *Conclusions and Recommendations of the Conference on the Democratization Process in Africa*. Kampala, Uganda.

International Labor Organization (1977). *Tripartite Declaration of Principles concerning Multinational Enterprises and Social Policy*. Geneva.

—— (1996). *World Labor Report, 1995*. Geneva.

—— (1996). *World Employment, 1996/97*. Geneva.

—— (1997). *World Labor Report, 1997–98*. Geneva.

—— (1998). *Note on the Proceedings—Tripartite Meeting on Export Processing Zones-Operating Countries*, September 28–October 2. Geneva.

International Labor Organization and United Nations Center on Transnational Corporations (ILO/UNCTC) (1988). *Economic and Social Effects of Multinational Enterprises in Export Processing Zones*. Geneva: ILO.

Islam, Shada (1994/95). "Pressure on Beijing," *Far Eastern Economic Review* 158(1), 16.

—— (1997). "Carrots, Not Sticks," *Far Eastern Economic Review* 160(13), 61.

"Islands of Despair" (1996). *Business Asia* 28 (18), 7–8.

Jacobs, Eric (1973). *European Trade Unionism*. New York: Homes and Meier.

Jessup, David (1994). "Worker Rights and Trade: Democracy's Next Frontier." Paper presented at the Conference on "U.S.-Latin American Trade and Women: Breaking Trade and Gender Barriers," University of Texas at San Antonio, October 24.

Johansson, Helena (1994). "The Economics of Export Processing Zones Revisited," *Development Policy Review* 12, 387–402.

——, and Lars Nilsson (1997). "Export Processing Zones as Catalysts," *World Development* 25, 2115–28.

Johnson, G., and K. Scholes (1993). *Exploring Corporate Strategy*, 3d ed. New York: Prentice Hall.

Kahn-Freund, Otto, and Bob Hepple (1972). *Laws against Strikes*. London: Fabian Society.

Kalman, Jordan (1999). "Panama Opens Doors to Economic Growth," *Bobbin* 40(11), 16.

Kaplinsky, Raphael (1993). "Export-Processing Zones in the Dominican Republic: Transforming Manufactures into Commodities," *World Development* 21, 1851–65.

—— (1995). "A Reply to Willmore," *World Development* 23, 537–40.

Keller, Berndt (1995). "Towards a European System of Collective Bargaining?" In *German Industrial Relations Under the Impact of Structural Change, Unification and European Integration*, edited by R. Hoffman, O. Jacobi, and B. Keller. Dusseldorf: Hans Bockler Stiftung.

Kelly, G.M. (1995). "Structural Change in New Zealand: Some Implications for the Labour Market Regime," *International Labor Review* 134(3), 333–59.

Kelly, John (1998). *Rethinking Industrial Relations: Moblization, Collectivism and Long Waves*. New York: Routledge.

Kochan, Thomas A., and Harry C. Katz (1988). *Collective Bargaining and Industrial Relations*, 2d ed. Homewood, Ill.: Irwin.

Kochan, Thomas, Harry Katz, and Robert McKersie (1994). *The Transformation of American Industrial Relations*. Ithaca, N.Y.: Cornell University ILR Press.

Kohl, George (1993). "Information Technology and Labor: A Case Study of Telephone Operators," *Workplace Topics* 3(1), 101–11.

Krupat, Kitty (1997). "From War Zone to Free Trade Zone: A History of the National Labor Committee." In *No Sweat: Fashion, Free Trade, and the Rights of Garment Workers*, edited by A. Ross, 51–77. New York: Verso.

Langille, Brian A. (1996). "General Reflections on the Relationship of Trade and Labor (Or: Fair Trade Is Free Trade's Destiny)." In *Fair Trade and Harmonization: Prerequisites for Free Trade?*, Vol. 2, edited by J.N. Bhagwati and R.E. Hudec, 231–266. Cambridge, Mass.: MIT Press.

Lansbury, Russell D., and Greg J. Bamber (1998). "The End of Institutionalized Industrial Relations in Australia?" *Perspectives on Work* 2(1), 26–30.

Larson, Simeon (1975). *Labor and Foreign Policy*. London: Associated University Presses.

Laskonis, Charles H. (1999). "How a Personal Computer Can Enhance Union Political Action." In *CyberUnion: Empowering Labor Through Computer Technology*, edited by A.B. Shostak, 34–39. Armonk, N.Y.: M.E. Sharpe.

Latta, Geoffrey W., and Janice R. Bellace (1983). "Making the Corporation Transparent: Prelude to Multinational Bargaining," *Columbia Journal of World Business* 18(2), 73–80.

Lee, Eddy (1996). "Globalization and Employment: Is Anxiety Justified?," *International Labor Review* 135, 485–97.

Lee, Eric (1996). *Labor and the Internet: The New Internationalism*. London: Pluto Press.

Leipziger, Deborah, and Pia Sabharwal (1996). "Companies That Play Hide and Seek With Child Labor," *Business and Society Review* 95, 11–13.

Levinson, Charles (1972). *International Trade Unionism*. London: Allen and Unwin.

Lindsey, Almont (1942; Reprint, 1972). *The Pullman Strike*. Chicago: University of Chicago Press.

Litvak, I.A., and C.J. Maule (1972). "The Union Response to International Corporations," *Industrial Relations* 11, 62–71.

Locke, Richard (1992). "The Demise of the National Union in Italy: Lessons from Comparative Industrial Relations Theory." *Industrial and Labor Relations Review* 45, 229–49.

——, Thomas Kochan, and Michael Piore (eds., 1995). *Employment Relations in a Changing World Economy*. Cambridge, Mass.: MIT Press.

Lorange, Peter, and Johan Roos (1992). *Strategic Alliances: Formation, Implementation, and Evolution*. Cambridge, Mass.: Blackwell.

Lustick, Ian (1980). "Explaining the Variable Utility of Disjointed Incrementalism: Four Propositions," *American Political Science Review* 74, 342–53.

Lyon-Caen, Gerard (1991). *Les Relations de Travail Internationales*. Paris: Ed. Liaisons.

MacFarquhar, Emily, Robert I. Rotberg, and Martha A. Chen (1996). "Introduction." In *Vigilance and Vengeance: NGOs Preventing Ethnic Conflict in Divided Societies*, edited by R.I. Rotberg, 3–22. Washington, D.C.: The Brookings Institution.

Mahnkopf, Birgit, and Elmar Altvater (1995). "Transmission Belts of Transnational Competition? Trade Unions and Collective Bargaining in the Context of European Integration," *European Journal of Industrial Relations* 1, 101–19.

Mahony, Liam, and Luis E. Eguren (1997). *Unarmed Bodyguards: International Accompaniment for the Protection of Human Rights*. West Hartford, Conn.: Kumarian Press.

Mandel, Bernard (1963). *Samuel Gompers: A Biography*. Yellow Springs, Ohio: Antioch Press.

Marginson, Paul (1992). "European Integration and Transnational Management-Union Relations in the Enterprise," *British Journal of Industrial Relations* 30(4), 529–45.

Marshall, Alfred (1920). *Principles of Economics*, 8th ed. New York: Macmillan.

Martin, Andrew, and George Ross, with others (1999). *The Brave New World of European Labor: European Trade Unions at the Millennium*. New York and Oxford: Berghahn Books.

Martinez Lucio, Miguel, and Syd Weston (1994). "New Management Practices in a Multinational Corporation: The Restructuring of Worker Representation and Rights?" *Industrial Relations Journal* 25, 110–21.

—— (1995). "Trade Unions and Networking in the Context of Change: Evaluating the Outcomes of Decentralization in Industrial Relations," *Economic and Industrial Democracy* 16, 233–51.

Marx, Karl, and Friedrich Engels (1848, 1998 edition). *The Communist Manifesto*. Oxford: Oxford University Press.

McLuhan, Marshall, and Bruce R. Powers (1989). *The Global Village*. Oxford: Oxford University Press.

Medina, Esther Hernandez (1998). "A Brief Profile of Free Trade Zones in the Dominican Republic," http://www.oneworld.org/textver/oxfam/campaign/clothes/ftz.htm.

Millen, Bruce H. (1963). *The Political Role of Labor in Developing Countries*. Washington, D.C.: Brookings Institution.

Miyake, Maiko, and Stephen Thomsen (1999). "Recent Trends in Foreign Direct Investment," *Financial Market Trends* 73, 111–28.

Moffett, Matt (1998). "Deep in the Amazon, an Industrial Enclave Fights for Survival," *Wall Street Journal*, July 9, A1, A8.

Moody, Kim (1998). *Workers in a Lean World: Unions in the International Economy*. New York: Verso.

Morgenstern, Felice (1984). *International Conflicts of Labour Law*. Geneva: ILO.

Mortimore, Michael, Henk Duthoo, and Jose A. Guerrero (1995). *Information About the International Competitiveness of Free Trade Zones in the Dominican Republic*. United Nations Economic Commission for Latin America and the Caribbean, Report No. 22.

Nichols, Martha (1993). "Third-World Families at Work: Child Labor or Child Care?" *Harvard Business Review* 71(1), 12–23.

Oborne, Michael (1986). *China's Special Economic Zones*. Paris: Organization for Economic Cooperation and Development.

Oliver, Christine (1991). "Network Relations and Loss of Organizational Autonomy," *Human Relations* 44, 943–61.

Organization for Economic Cooperation and Development (1995). *Restructuring in Public Telecommunications Operator Employment*. Paris.

Panford, Kwamina (1994). *African Labour Relations and Workers' Rights: Assessing the Role of the International Labour Organization*. Westport, Conn.: Greenwood Press.

Park, Seung Ho, and Michael V. Russo (1996). "When Competition Eclipses Cooperation: An Event History Analysis of Joint Venture Failure," *Management Science* 42, 875–90.

Payne, Phyllis (1977). "The Consultants Who Coach the Violators," *AFL-CIO American Federationist* 84(9), 22–29.

Peterson, Florence (1963). *American Labor Unions*. New York: Harper & Row.

Pfeffer, Jeffrey (1972). "Merger as a Response to Organizational Interdependence," *Administrative Science Quarterly* 17, 383–94.

——, and Gerald R. Salancik (1978). *The External Control of Organizations: A Resource Dependence Perspective*. New York: Harper & Row.

Pochet, Philippe, and Liliane Turloot (1996). "Une Construction Inachevée." In *Union Économique et Monétaire et Négociations Collectives*, edited by O. Jacobi and P. Pochet. Brussels: Observatoire Social Européen.

Porter, Michael E. (1985). *Competitive Advantage*. New York: Free Press.

Prahalad, C.K., and Gary Hamel (1990). "The Core Competence of the Corporation," *Harvard Business Review* 68(3), 79–91.

Prince, Jean-Claude (1995). *Les Conseils Syndicaux Interrégionaux en Europe*. European Trade Union Institute Discussion and Working Papers.

Ramsay, Harvie E. (1995). "Le Défi Européen: Multinational Restructuring, Labor and EU Policy." In *Behind the Myth of European Union: Prospects for Cohesion*, edited by A. Amin and J. Tomaney. London: Routledge.

—— (1997). "Solidarity at Last? International Trade Unionism Approaching the Millennium," *Economic and Industrial Democracy* 18, 503–37.

—— (1999). "In Search of International Trade Union Theory." In *Globalization and Patterns of Labor Resistance*, edited by J. Waddington, Los Altos, Calif.: Mansell.

——, and Nigel Haworth (1990). "Managing the Multinationals: The Emerging Theory of the Multinational Enterprise and Its Implications for Labor Resistance." In *Organization Theory and Class Analysis*, edited by S.R. Clegg, 275–97. New York: Walter de Gruyter.

Rayback, Joseph G. (1971). *A History of American Labor*. New York: Macmillan.

Reed, Louis S. (1966). *The Labor Philosophy of Samuel Gompers*. Port Washington, N.Y.: Kennikat Press.

Rhodes, Anne K. (1999). "Iran Pressing Fiscal Incentives, Assurances to Attract Investors to its Petrochemical Sector," *Oil and Gas Journal* 97(33), 20–24.

Rhodes, Martin (2000). "The Political Economy of Social Pacts: 'Competitive Corporatism' and European Welfare Reform." In *The New Politics of the Welfare State*, edited by Paul Pierson. Oxford: Oxford University Press.

Riddle, John (1997). "Touring Pakistan," *Sporting Goods Business* 30(11), 32.

Risse-Kappen, Thomas (1995). "Bringing Transnational Relations Back In: Introduction." In *Bringing Transnational Relations Back In: Non-State Actors, Domestic Structures and International Institutions*, edited by T. Risse-Kappen, 3–33. New York: Cambridge University Press.

Roberts, Matthew W. (1992). *Export Processing Zones in Jamaica and Mauritius: Evolution of an Export-Oriented Development Model*. San Francisco: Mellen Research University Press.

Rodiére, Pierre (1987). *La Convention Collective de Travail en Droit International*, Contribution à l'Etude des Normes Juridiques de Source Professionnelle. Paris: Litec.

Rogers, David L., and David A. Whetten and Associates (1982). *Interorganizational Coordination: Theory, Research and Implementation*. Ames, Iowa: Iowa State University Press.

Rogers, Joel, and Wolfgang Streeck (1995). *Works Councils: Consultation, Representation, and Cooperation in Industrial Relations*. Chicago: Chicago University Press.

Romero, Ana T. (1993). "Export Processing Zones: Insights from a Recent ILO Survey," *Labour Education* 91(2), 4–15.

—— (1995). "Labor Standards and Export Processing Zones: Situation and Pressures for Change," *Development Policy Review* 13, 247–76.

Rondinelli, Dennis A. (1987). "Export Processing Zones and Economic Development in Asia: A Review and Reassessment of a Means of Promoting Growth and Jobs," *American Journal of Economics and Sociology* 46, 89–105.

Ross, Andrew (ed., 1997). *No Sweat: Fashion, Free Trade, and the Rights of Garment Workers*. New York: Verso.

Ross, George (1995). *Jacques Delors and European Integration*. Cambridge, U.K.: Polity.

Rotberg, Robert I. (1996). "Conclusions: NGOs, Early Warning, Early Action, and Preventive Diplomacy." In *Vigilance and Vengeance: NGOs Preventing Ethnic Conflict in Divided Societies*, edited by R.I. Rotberg, 263–268. Washington, D.C.: Brookings Institution Press.

Ryan, Peter (1994). "African Boom Pends," *Corporate Location* (World Economic Supplement) 11.

Schulten, Thorsten, and Reinhard Bispinck (eds., 1999). *Tarifpolitik Unter Dem EURO*. Hamburg: VSA Vertag.

Senge, P. (1990). *The Fifth Discipline: The Art and Practice of the Learning Organization*. New York: Doubleday.

Seringhaus, F.H. Rolf, and Philip J. Rosson (1990). *Government Export Promotion: A Global Perspective*. New York: Routledge.

Serrin, William (1993). *Homestead: The Glory and Tragedy of an American Steel Town*. New York: Vintage Books.

Servais, Jean-Michel (1984). "ILO Standards on Freedom of Association and Their Implementation," *International Labour Review* 123, 765–81.

—— (1986). "Flexibility and Rigidity in International Labour Standards," *International Labour Review* 125, 193–208.

—— (1996). "The International Labour Organization." In *Encyclopaedia of Law. International Organizations*, edited by M. Eyskens and R. Blanpain. Deventer: Kluwer.

Shieh, Shawn (1998). "Provincial Leadership and the Implementation of Foreign Economic Reforms in Fujian Province." In *Provincial Strategies of Economic Reform in Post-Mao China*, edited by P.T.Y. Cheung, J.H. Chung, and Z. Lin, 302–341. London: M.E. Sharpe.

Shorrock, Tim (1999). "Creating a New Internationalism for Labor," *Dollars and Sense*, 225 (Sept./Oct.), 36–40.

Shostak, Arthur B. (1991). *Robust Unionism: Innovations in the Labor Movement.* Ithaca, N.Y.: ILR Press.

—— (1999). *CyberUnion: Empowering Labor Through Computer Technology.* Armonk, N.Y.: M.E. Sharpe.

Shum, K.K., and L.T. Sigel (1986). "Managerial Reform and Enterprise Performance: Assessing the Experiment in Shenzhen and Zhuhai." In *China's Special Economic Zones: Policies, Problems, and Prospects*, edited by Y.C. Jao and C.K. Leung, 201–225. Oxford: Oxford University Press.

Sit, Victor F.S. (1986). "Industries in Shenzhen: An Attempt at Open-Door Industrialization." In *China's Special Economic Zones*, edited by Y.C. Jao and C.K. Leung, 226–246. Oxford: Oxford University Press.

Smith, Jackie (1997). "Characteristics of the Modern Transnational Social Movement Sector." In *Transnational Social Movements and Global Politics: Solidarity Beyond the State*, edited by J. Smith, C. Chatfield, and R. Pagnucco, 42–58. New York: Syracuse University Press.

Snow, Charles C., Raymond E. Miles, and Henry J. Coleman, Jr. (1995). "Managing 21st Century Network Organizations." In *The Organizational Behavior Reader*, 6th ed., edited by D.A. Kolb, J.S. Osland, and I.M Rubin, 611–624. Englewood Cliffs, N.J.: Prentice-Hall.

Southall, Roger (1988). "Introduction." In *Trade Unions and the New Industrialization of the Third World*, edited by R. Southall, 1–34. Pittsburgh: University of Pittsburgh Press.

—— (1995). *Imperialism or Solidarity? International Labour and South African Trade Unions.* Cape Town: University of Cape Town Press.

Stewart, Frances (1994). "The New International Division of Labor," *World Labor Report* 8, 28–29.

Strauss, George (1998). "Regional Studies of Comparative International Industrial Relations: Symposium Introduction," *Industrial Relations* 37, 273–81.

Streeck, Wolfgang (1991). "More Uncertainties: German Unions Facing 1992," *Industrial Relations* 30, 317–47.

Sugeno, Kazuo (1994). "Unions as Social Institutions in Democratic Market Economies," *International Labour Review* 133, 511–22.

Tarrow, Sidney (1994). *Power in Movement: Social Movements, Collective Action and Politics*. Cambridge: Cambridge University Press.

Taylor, Robert (1998). "New Unionism in the Age of Globalization," *Perspectives on Work* 1(3), 24–27.

Taylor, William (1991). "The Logic of Global Business: An Interview with ABB's Percy Barnevik," *Harvard Business Review* 69(2), 91–105.

Tergeist, Peter, et al. (1994). "The Organization for Economic Cooperation and Development," in *International Encyclopaedia for Law and Industrial Relations*, edited by R. Blanpain, 1–67. Deventer: Kluwer.

Thomson Bankwatch (1997). "Thomson Bankwatch Assigns a Sovereign Risk Rating of B to the Dominican Republic," http://www.bankwatch.com/docs/domin.htm, October 7.

"Too Little, Too Late" (1994). *Business Africa* 3 (17), 16–30.

Turner, Lowell (1996). "The Europeanization of Labor: Structure Before Action," *European Journal of Industrial Relations* 2, 325–44.

Ulman, Lloyd (1975). "Multinational Unionism: Incentives, Barriers, and Alternatives," *Industrial Relations* 14(1), 1–31.

United Nations Economic and Social Council (1994). *Report on the 20th Session of the Commission on Transnational Corporations*, May 2–11.

United States Department of State (1996). *Sri Lanka Country Report on Human Rights Practices*. Washington, D.C.

Valticos, Nicolas, and Geraldo von Potobsky (1995). "International Labour Law." In *International Encyclopaedia for Law and Industrial Relations*, edited by R. Blanpain, 1–222. Deventer: Kluwer.

Van Heerden, Auret (1998). *Labor and Social Issues Relating to Export Processing Zones*. Geneva: International Labor Office.

Waterman, Peter (1998). "The Second Coming of Proletarian Internationalism? A Review of Recent Resources," *European Journal of Industrial Relations* 4, 349–77.

Wedderburn, Lord Kenneth W. (1995). *Labour Law and Freedom: Further Essays in Labour Law*. London: Laurence and Wishart.

Whetten, David A., and Thomas K. Leung (1979). "The Instrumental Value of Interorganizational Relations: Antecedents and Consequences of Linkage Formation," *Academy of Management Journal* 22, 325–44.

Whitley, R. (1994) "The Internationalization of Firms and Markets: Its Significance and Institutional Structuring," *Organization* 1(1), July.

Wiarda, Howard J., and Michael J. Kryzanek (1992). *The Dominican Republic: A Caribbean Crucible*, 2d ed. San Francisco: Westview Press.

Wijesekera, Nalin (1987). "Sri Lanka: Selling Safe Havens Amid Violence," *Asian Business* 23(8), 18–29.

Wilkinson, Barry (1994). *Labor and Industry in the Asia-Pacific: Lessons from the Newly-Industrialized Countries*. New York: Walter de Gruyter.

Willetts, Peter (1996). "Consultative Status for NGOs at the United Nations." In *"The Conscience of the World": The Influence of Non-Governmental Organizations in the UN System*, edited by P. Willetts, 31–62. Washington, D.C.: Brookings Institution.

Williamson, Hugh (1994) "Mixed Feelings," *Far Eastern Economic Review* 157(30), 20.

Willmore, Larry (1995). "Export Processing Zones in the Dominican Republic: A Comment on Kaplinsky," *World Development* 23, 529–35.

Windmuller, John P. (1967). "International Trade Union Organizations: Structure, Functions, Limitations." In *International Labor*, edited by S. Barkin et al., 81–105. New York: Harper & Row.

—— and Steven K. Pursey (1993). "The International Trade Union Movement." In *Comparative Labor Law and Industrial Relations in Industrialized Market Economies*, 5th ed., edited by R. Blanpain and C. Engels, 57–92. Boston: Kluwer Law & Taxation Publishers.

Woodiwiss, Anthony (1996). "Searching for Signs of Globalization," *Sociology* 30, 799–810.

World Bank (1992). *Export Processing Zones*. Washington, D.C.: Policy and Research Series, No. 20, Industry Development Division.

Zhu, Ying (1995). "Major Changes Under Way in China's Industrial Relations," *International Labour Review* 134(1), 37–49.

Contributors

Mark Anner spent ten years living and working in Central America and the Caribbean, much of which time he was employed as a consultant for the Norwegian Confederation of Trade Unions (LO-Norway) and the International Union of Food Workers (IUF). He also conducted research and training sessions focused on El Salvador's growing sweatshop problem for the Salvadoran Center for Labor Studies. Anner earned a bachelor's degree in political science from Tufts University and a master's degree in Latin American Studies from Stanford University. He is presently pursuing a Ph.D. in government at Cornell University.

Larry Cohen has been organizing for the Communications Workers of America (CWA) since 1976. He was a founder and member of the national steering committee of Jobs With Justice, a national workers' rights coalition of labor and community organizations. In 1998, Cohen was elected Executive Vice President of the CWA, after serving as an Assistant to the President and Director of Organization. He has written frequently about organizing, coalition building, and international issues.

Steve Early has worked as an organizer or international representative for the CWA since 1980. He helped coordinate the union's 1989 strike against NYNEX in New England and also assisted CWA's transnational organizing in support of striking Northern Telecom workers. He serves on the editorial board of *New Labor Forum* and the policy committee of *Labor Notes*. He has written about labor issues for *The Nation, The Progressive, The Boston Globe, The New York Times, The Wall Street Journal*, and other major newspapers and labor publications.

Michael E. Gordon is a Professor of Organization Management at Rutgers, The State University of New Jersey. He has published behavioral research on the relationship between unions and their memberships. Gordon has served on the editorial boards of the *Employee Responsibilities and Rights Journal*, the *Journal of Applied Behavioral Science*, the *Journal of Applied Psychology*, and the *Industrial and Labor Relations Review*. He was a co-editor of *Workplace Topics*, a journal published by the Economic Research Department of the AFL-CIO. He received his Ph.D. in psychology from the University of California, Berkeley.

David Jessup is a consultant for the New Economy Information Service, a network for information sharing, analysis, and discussion among trade unionists and other civil society leaders concerned about the effects of globalization and technological change. Prior to September 1998, he was Assistant Coordinator of Global Programs at the AFL-CIO's American Institute for Free Labor Development. In this capacity he worked to expand international organizing by encouraging union cooperation across borders and using international worker rights mechanisms to enforce labor laws. Before 1985, Jessup was an Assistant to the Director of the AFL-CIO's Committee on Political Education. He has also been National Director of Frontlash (a youth voter project) and a Peace Corps volunteer in Peru.

Andrew Martin is a Research Affiliate of the Center for European Studies at Harvard University. He received his Ph.D. in political science from Columbia University. He taught there as well as at the University of Massachusetts, Boston University, Harvard University, and, most recently, the Institute of Political Economy at Carleton University in Ottawa. As a German Marshall Fund Fellow during 1999 and as co-chair, with George Ross, of a Council for European Studies Research Planning Group, he is conducting research on the implications of monetary union for European welfare states and industrial relations. Martin is a member of the Canadian International Labour Network, and he has done research on changing work organization in the U.S. automobile industry at the Industrial Relations section of the M.I.T. Sloan School. Martin has published extensively on the Swedish political economy as well as on comparative and international political economy and industrial relations. Among his most recent publications is *Brave New World of European Labor* (with George Ross and others).

Harvie Ramsay[†] was a Professor of International Human Resource Management and Director of the Center for European Employment Research at the University of Strathclyde. He studied the political economy of employment relationships since the early 1970s, and wrote extensively on industrial democracy, management fashions, the global restructuring of capital and its implications for labor, unions, and gender issues related to work. He was an advisor to unions who was moved by the belief that the understanding of management forms is a crucial element of any serious, long-term labor strategy. Quite unexpectedly and suddenly, Professor Ramsay died on the 24th of April, 2000.

George Ross is Executive Director of the European Union Center and Senior Faculty Associate of the Minda de Gunzburg Center for European Studies at Harvard University, and Morris Hillquit Professor in Labor and Social Thought (in the sociology and politics departments) at Brandeis University. He is co-editor of *French Politics and Society*, Chair of the West European Politics and Society Section of the American Political Science Association, Executive Secretary of the Conference Group on French Politics and Society, and a member of the European Union's "Team Europe" in the United States. Ross served as Chair of the Council for European Studies from 1990-1997. The recipient of numerous international awards, Ross has produced nine books, including the 1999 *Brave New World of European Labor* (with Andrew Martin and others), and published more than 150 articles. He and Andrew Martin are co-chairs of the Council for European Studies Research Planning Group on the European Monetary Union and the European Model of Society.

Jean-Michel Servais is Research Coordinator of the International Institute for Labour Studies of the International Labor Office in Geneva. Previously he served as Chief of the Task Force on Industrial Relations at the ILO. Servais received his Ph.D. from the University of Liege, Belgium, in 1968, and was awarded an honorary doctorate from the University Attila Jozsef, Szeged, Hungary, in 1997. He was elected Deputy Secretary General (1987), then Secretary General of the International Society for Labor Law and Social Security (1988). Servais is a member of the Swiss Society of Labor Law and Social Security and of the International Industrial Relations Association. A visiting professor at the Faculty of Law of the University of Liege since 1993, Servais has authored numerous publications in the field of international and comparative labor law and industrial relations.

Lowell Turner is a Professor at Cornell University in the School of Industrial and Labor Relations. He has a Ph.D. in Political Science from the University of California at Berkeley. Turner is the author of *Democracy at*

Work: Changing World Markets and the Future of Labor Unions (1991) and *Fighting for Partnership: Labor and Politics in Unified Germany* (1998) and is the editor of *Negotiating the New Germany: Can Social Partnership Survive?* (1997). His current research is on comparative labor movement revitalization, in the United States, United Kingdom, and Germany, with a focus on the relations between institutions and social movements.

Jim Wilson is Director of UNI-MEI, the sector for Media and Entertainment of Union Network International (UNI). He was General Secretary of Media and Entertainment International (MEI or its predecessor organization) from 1992 until MEI became part of UNI, January 2000. Prior to this, he did media work for the International Federation of Commercial, Clerical, Professional and Technical Employees (FIET), and the International Union of Food, Agricultural, Hotel, Restaurant, Catering, Tobacco and Allied Workers Associations (IUF). Wilson was the executive producer of a documentary film ("The Real Thing") about the effectiveness of international organizing in the struggle for union recognition by workers at a Guatemalan Coca Cola bottling plant. He served in the Peace Corps in Colombia and worked as a business agent for the National Association of Broadcasting Employees and Technicians. In 1979, Wilson completed his doctorate at the ILR School at Cornell University. The author of a number of articles published in academic and trade union journals, he participated directly in most of the MEI campaigns described in Chapter 8.

John Windmuller is the Martin P. Catherwood Professor (emeritus) at Cornell University, in the School of Industrial and Labor Relations. He has done research in the areas of international and comparative labor relations, including Western European labor relations, employers associations, the international trade union movement, and the foreign policies of American labor. He has held Fulbright and Ford Foundation fellowships and was a senior staff member of the International Labor Office in Geneva. In 1987, Windmuller represented the ILO Director General on a mission to the Netherlands to help resolve a labor dispute involving the government, employers, and trade unions. His many publications include *Labor Relations in the Netherlands* (1970), *The International Trade Union Movement* (1987), *Employers Associations and Industrial Relations* (1985), and *Collective Bargaining in Industrialized Market Economies: A Reappraisal* (1987).

Kenneth S. Zinn is the North American Regional Coordinator of the International Federation of Chemical, Energy, Mine and General Workers'

Unions (ICEM). Before taking this position, he was Special Projects Coordinator of the United Mine Workers of America (UMWA), where he served more than eleven years in several capacities, including director of the union's international affairs and corporate campaign programs and Assistant to the President. As director of the international affairs program, Zinn provided assistance to unions in other countries, was actively involved in the successful struggle to end apartheid in South Africa, and built support for the UMWA overseas. He directed the corporate campaigns against the Pittston Company during the 1989 strike and the Bituminous Coal Operators Association during the 1993 strike, among other campaigns. Prior to his union career, Zinn served as Associate Director for the Washington Office on Africa and as Southern Africa Coordinator for the Coalition for a New Foreign and Military Policy. His writings have been published in the *Washington Post*, the *Manchester Guardian Weekly*, and *Labor Research Review*.

Index